OUR COMMON COUNTRY

MIDWESTERN HISTORY AND CULTURE
General Editors
James H. Madison and Andrew R. L. Cayton

OUR

FAMILY FARMING, CULTURE,

COMMON

AND COMMUNITY IN THE

COUNTRY

NINETEENTH-CENTURY MIDWEST

SUSAN SESSIONS RUGH

INDIANA UNIVERSITY PRESS
Bloomington & Indianapolis

This book is a publication of

Indiana University Press
601 North Morton Street
Bloomington, IN 47404-3797 USA

http://www.indiana.edu/~iupress

Telephone orders   800-842-6796
Fax orders   812-855-7931
Orders by e-mail   iuporder@indiana.edu

The paper used in this publication meets the minimum requirements of
American National Standard for Information Sciences—Permanence of
Paper for Printed Library Materials, ANSI Z39.48-1984.

Manufactured in the United States of America

Library of Congress Cataloging-in-Publication Data

Rugh, Susan Sessions.
   Our common country : family farming, culture, and community in
the nineteenth-century Midwest / Susan Sessions Rugh.
      p.   cm. — (Midwestern history and culture)
   Includes bibliographical references and index.
   ISBN 0-253-33910-3 (cl : alk. paper)
   1. Middle West—Rural conditions. 2. Farm life—Middle West—
History—19th century. 3. Community life—Middle West—History—
19th century. 4. Fountain Green (Ill. : Township)—Social conditions—
19th century. 5. Fountain Green (Ill.: Township)—Economic
conditions—19th century.   I. Title.   II. Series.

HN79.A14 R84 2001
307.72'0977—dc21
                                                    00-046097

   1 2 3 4 5   06 05 04 03 02 01

FOR
TOM

CONTENTS

ILLUSTRATIONS

PREFACE AND ACKNOWLEDGMENTS

It would not be entirely fair to blame Laura Ingalls Wilder for my fascination with the countryside, but childhood memories of my mother reading me *Little House in the Big Woods* remain powerfully imprinted on my mind. My heritage, a blend of town and country, also helps explain my historical curiosity. My mother grew up on a farm and told me stories of my grandmother killing snakes in the cellar, baking bread, and saving the milk money for the children's shoes. My father was reared in a small town; his father owned a furniture store that brought cosmopolitan style to the homes of Utah Valley. My attachment to place can be chalked up to my parents' habit of episodically moving to advance my father's academic career. The abrupt transfer from Utah to Perú when I was a teenager accounts for my interest in comparative cultures. Ultimately, it was not until I recently returned to my roots that I was able to piece together my vision of America's rural past. It means more than I can say to wake every morning to the sight of the Wasatch Mountains, where my ancestors settled so long ago after leaving the rolling prairies of Illinois.

It is my pleasure to acknowledge the many debts I have acquired in the process of writing this book. First, I owe the people of Fountain Green appreciation for assisting me in finding local history sources and in literally showing me the lay of the land. I am particularly grateful to Jean Geddes Lynn and Randall Little for making available precious family letters and photographs. The staff of the Hancock County Clerk's office made me feel at home and guided me to much-needed public records.

I am indebted to staffs at the following institutions, without whom this project would not have been possible: Regenstein Library at the University of Chicago, Chicago Historical Society, Newberry Library, Illinois State Historical Society, Hancock County Historical Society, Illinois Regional Archives Depository at Western Illinois University, the National Archives and Records Administration, the Archives of the Church of Jesus Christ of Latter-day Saints, and the Church's Family History Library in Salt Lake City, Utah, and its branch in Chicago Heights, Illinois. I am grateful to Steven Schmitt of the Cartographic Services Unit at the University of Chicago for his expert preparation of the maps.

This book originated as a dissertation at the University of Chicago under the careful guidance of Kathleen Neils Conzen, to whom I remain grateful for wisdom and insight into the cultures of the Midwest. Fortunately for me, when my scholarly interests turned from the frontier West to the countryside, she continued to lead the way with her probing questions and endless curiosity. I also appreciate the guidance of committee members Edward M. Cook and Leora Auslander. To his family, I gratefully acknowledge the assistance of the Harry Barnard Dissertation Year Fellowship in American History. I am grateful to graduate school colleagues Maureen Harp, Franklin Yoder, and Christopher Thale for their stimulating criticisms and support.

I wish to acknowledge the generosity of my former colleagues in the History Department of St. Cloud State University for their donation of travel funds, especially Paul Vaughter, Edward Gambill, and the late David Overy. I am also grateful to SCSU for summer Faculty Research Fellowships. At Brigham Young University I have been substantially aided by the Camilla Eyring Kimball Endowment Award for Faculty Research granted by the College of Family, Home, and Social Sciences. I thank the BYU Department of History for reducing my course load and in other ways accommodating my scholarly needs. I am grateful to my colleagues in the Department Writing Group, who read parts of the manuscript and provided encouragement at critical junctures, especially Ignacio García, Brian Q. Cannon, Thomas G. Alexander, and Jenny Hale Pulsipher. Richard I. Kimball graciously read the final draft of the entire manuscript and made valuable suggestions and editorial corrections. The students in my seminar on Agrarian America deserve credit for the cogency of the book's introduction. I appreciate the diligence of my student research assistants, Hillary Pothier and Heather Budge.

I thank my fellow historians for their comments and suggestions in presentations of my research at various professional meetings and public forums, particularly Deborah Fink, Jon Gjerde, Joan Jensen, Timothy Mahoney, Mary Neth, Walter T. K. Nugent, and Jane Pederson. I appreciate those who read the manuscript in whole or in part: Barbara Welke, Richard and Claudia Bushman, James Oberly, Marvin Hill, Hal Barron, and Susan Gray. Despite this help, any errors remain mine alone. I owe a special thanks to Susan, who introduced me to Joan Catapano at Indiana University Press, with whom it has been my pleasure to work. For their encouragement and suggestions, I am grateful to the anonymous reader and to the editors of the series in Midwestern History and Culture, James H. Madison and Andrew R. L. Cayton.

Last, I pay tribute to those closest to me. My dear friends Gail Radford and Barbara Welke have nurtured me; to Barbara I am especially grateful for cheering me on down the home stretch. My family has stood by me in the years it took to write the dissertation and the seven additional years required to make it a book. My parents, Barbara Bickmore and Sterling David Sessions, have shown me how to balance motherhood and scholarship; my six brothers and sisters have provided loving support. I am grateful to my sister, Elizabeth Sessions Eastmond, for a thorough stylistic reading of the entire manuscript. I appreciate the assistance of my aunt, Jean Bickmore White, who has mentored my scholarly career over the years while excelling in her own field.

In the years since I first visited Fountain Green my three boys have become exemplary men; to Jeffrey, Jacob, and Peter I owe any sensitivity I possess toward the complicated issues of masculinity. Tom's faith in my abilities has been a sustaining force; in honor of his love and devotion I dedicate this book to him.

Susan Sessions Rugh
Provo, Utah
May 2000

INTRODUCTION

In late summer, rows of cornstalks obscure the approach to Fountain Green, Illinois. After ascending the timbered banks of Crooked Creek, the blacktop curves eastward to reveal the white steeple of the Presbyterian church on the prairie expanse. Beyond the church one notices the small frame houses with overgrown lilac bushes in front and swingsets out back, a modern brick fire station, and an auto parts salvage yard that spreads like a cancer through the town. Down the road is the cemetery, the resting place of Fountain Green's founders, who envisioned a glorious future for a place they hoped would be home to their children and their children's children.

If the founding families were to rise from their graves, they would be saddened to see that their splendid farmhouses have long since burned down and that C. C. Tyler's country store, where they gathered, is merely a proud memory. But they would recognize the church and the tall stalks of corn that still provide a livelihood for Fountain Green's families on the fertile prairie along Crooked Creek. Successful farming has wrought changes in Fountain Green that the founding families could not have foreseen.

Our notions of the traditional family, of small-town community, and of grassroots democracy are rooted in America's agrarian past. We can trace these time-honored values to places such as Fountain Green in America's heartland, a region that has come to represent America itself. Rooted in Jeffersonian ideals, agrarian ideology flourished in the nineteenth-century Midwest, where countless settler families carved homesteads out of the prairie wilderness in order to farm as a way of life.

That way of life gave rise to an agrarian myth that endures even when much of rural America is dying a slow but inexorable death. One quarter of America's population lives in rural areas (defined as less than 2,500 population), but farm residents account for just 2 percent of the total U.S. population and just 7 percent of the rural population.[1] We can easily see our attachment to our agrarian roots in the commercialization of country living. A raft of magazines with "country" in their title espouse hometown values, family togetherness, and traditional roles, a surrogate for authentic country which is fast disappearing. Country music, country decorating, and countrified chains of motels and restaurants capitalize on a hunger for a mythic past, for all that is good and memorable about home, family, and community.[2]

We cannot appreciate the continuing power of the agrarian myth in our national psyche without understanding the sources from which it sprang. This book is about the making of the family farm culture out of diverse groups in the nineteenth-century Midwest, the relationship of that culture to the expanding market, and the ways that the changing values of the broader national culture threatened rural society. Family farming was more than an economic enterprise; it was a way of life that took place in the context of a distinctive local farm culture. The family farm culture became a means to resolve the contradictions between the family and the market, community and individualism, tradition and transformation.

Family farm culture supported the growth of agrarian capitalism which helped power the emergence of the industrial Midwest. The commercial possibilities of the Midwest were so important that in his 1862 plea to Congress to end the Civil War, President Abraham Lincoln called the region "our common country," the geographic and commercial center of the nation.[3] Scholars have long considered the Midwest as the most American of all regions and argue that its agrarian values have come to symbolize American values.[4] By focusing on its rural peoples, this book traces the historical trajectory of the predominantly agrarian Midwest. We cannot understand the making of the Midwest and the nation without coming to terms with our agrarian past at its apogee in the nineteenth century.

Lincoln's description of the Midwest as "our common country" captures the agrarian nature of the region as countryside, a patchwork of family farms dotted with small farm villages which produced the foodstuffs for an expanding national and global market. The first wave of settlers in the Midwest were heirs to an agrarian ideology promulgated by Thomas Jefferson. He argued that the nation should develop its agrarian interests because independent land ownership allowed the farmer to possess the virtue unavailable to those who owed their livelihood to others.[5] The belief in an independent farm, a place to raise one's family and earn one's daily bread, powered government policies that opened the national domain for sale to individual freeholders, built roads and canals to move settlers westward, and opened domestic and international markets for American produce. Agrarian ideology was central to the expansion of the core of the United States population onto freehold farms in its newly acquired territories and to the simultaneous displacement of Native American populations.

These farm families were part of a massive migration of American population from the eastern regions of the United States to the vast inner territories of the Midwest during the nineteenth century. Hundreds of thousands of families packed their household belongings into wagons or onto boats, bid their relatives farewell, and settled on the cheap land their government sold them beyond the Appalachian Mountains. Within fifty years, farming families had transformed the prairies and river valleys of the Midwest into a phenomenally productive agricultural sector of the economy that fed people in the nation's burgeoning cities and in turn bought the goods urban people manufactured. By 1880, over 100 million acres of land had been put under the plow in the Midwest, over one-third of the cultivated land in the entire United States.[6] The family farm culture created in the small towns and farm villages of the Midwest nurtured values that would define a national ethic of self-reliance, hard work, community, piety, and patriotism.

By the end of the nineteenth century Jefferson's ideal had been supplanted by a vision of industrial capitalism.[7] The economic opportunity available in cities made the urban way of life paramount, luring farm children to labor in city shops and factories rather than on the land. Farm boys and country girls carried the values and habits of American farm family culture to the cities as the urban age took hold. By looking at the family farm culture in the Midwest from its inception in the age of Jefferson until the industrial era, we can understand both how it succeeded and its role in the making of the Midwest and the nation.

Lincoln was himself a product of "our common country," a mixing ground for cultural groups who settled the region and created a new western society. Born in the upland South, Lincoln came to represent the Republican Party, an amalgam of Yankee ideals and western practicality opposed to the expansion of slavery in the West. His major opponent in 1860, Illinois senator Stephen A. Douglas, was born in New England, but as the leader of the Democratic Party voiced the beliefs of those who sympathized with the South and tolerated its system of slavery. The Midwest was created by this convergence of cultures from New England, the upland South, and, less noticeably, migrants from the mid-Atlantic states. As the sectional conflict over slavery worsened, migrants to the Midwest who had shed their regional identities to become westerners again clothed themselves in sectional garb through partisan loyalties.[8]

Without knowing what happened in the countryside, we cannot understand how the Midwest became Republican and middle class, nor can we appreciate the extent of resistance to the transformation. Underneath the layers of regional and political identities were fundamental ideological differences between those who feared government power would curtail liberty and opportunists who pursued government support to advance the spread of the market.[9] Midwestern Yankees successfully promoted an aggressively entrepreneurial economy and linked it to a cultural agenda characterized by self-discipline and moral uplift. Upland southerners, who accepted the market but rejected the Yankee cultural reforms as a threat to hallowed republican ideals of independence, were subordinated in the midwestern middle-class culture which emerged. Republican support of big business marked the capitulation of the countryside, as farmers vainly protested the hegemony of industrial capitalism which rendered them rural curiosities, backward targets of social reform. What remained was a strain of rural producerism which defended traditional agrarian ideals, a discontent which occasionally erupted in rural vigilantism.[10]

Rural history, the study of social changes associated with the expansion of market agriculture, offers a framework for analyzing the formation of the family farm culture. Historians of agriculture in the Midwest have ably outlined the contours of changes in agricultural technology and farming practices, but only recently have social historians attempted to explain how the spread of the market altered rural social relations and how farmers resolved the tensions between the market imperative and their commitment to family land and labor.[11] What began as a polarized debate over the nature of capitalist change in the countryside has evolved into consensus that capitalist development in the countryside was complex and ambiguous. Communal values and market behavior were not mutually exclusive, and interactions with the market were shaped by cultural constructs.[12]

Historians have recognized the important role of cultural attitudes in approaches to the market economy. Immigrants tenaciously clung to cultural habits in the trans-Atlantic migration and adapted them to a new environment. For example, although immigrants usually adopted the isolated homestead and cropping patterns of native-born farmers, they were more likely than the native-born to rely on family labor and to retain land in the family line. When their numbers were large enough, they clustered in enduring church-centered communities, where they dominated local government and the land market. The isolated rural environment in the Midwest where one cultural group could become dominant allowed cultural constructs to determine the direction of agrarian capitalism.[13]

Native-born migrants carried elements of their own distinctive regional cultures to the frontier to structure the development of farm family culture. Regional histories of the Midwest have recognized that the initial sources of native-born migration streams shaped the development of midwestern culture. Historians have moved beyond contemporary stereotypes of southern "Sucker" and northern "Yankee" to explore the changing meanings of such labels and their roots in the upland South and New England. However, the importance of migrants from the middle states has largely been overlooked, in part because their identity became absorbed into the Yankee label. Lodged in the center between two distinct cultural groups, those from the middle states were particularly well-adapted to take advantage of the opportunities agrarian capitalism offered. Neither Yankee townsmen nor southern yeomen, they operated as cultural brokers between the two, providing a middle ground which accommodated differences in local politics and rural society. The result was midwestern family farm culture, a hybrid of traditional agrarian values and the ideals of progress.[14]

Once we begin to understand farm family culture we can better explain how family farming helped fuel the massive economic and social changes of the nineteenth century in both the Midwest and the nation. By tracing our habits of civil society to their small-town beginnings in rural America, we can understand how family farm culture molded the meaning of community. We will also come to understand the values that rural people brought to political culture and

how they relied on political parties to express fundamentally different understandings of democracy. Finally, we can trace the influence of family farm
culture in reshaping and resisting notions of class and gender identity, which
culminated in the ascendance of the more egalitarian family of the twentieth
century. Only then can we appreciate the persistent power of the agrarian
tradition in our national consciousness.

Understanding family farm culture in the Midwest can help us make sense
of the many paradoxes of the agrarian myth. Once we call into question the icon
of the white yeoman farmer, we begin to understand the homogenizing process
by which diverse groups were amalgamated into a gendered and racialized
agrarian ideal. By exposing the conflicts that convulsed the countryside, we see
the darker side of rural culture—how violence was used to exclude undesir-
ables, to enforce patriarchy, and to sustain a culture of resistance. We also
understand how the agrarian ideal came to permeate American culture as farm
children carried values and habits westward and to cities where they became
embedded in our national consciousness. The making of family farm culture in
the Midwest is about the making of the American tradition, the myths we
believe about ourselves as a nation.

To explain the making of family farm culture in the Midwest, I focus on the
first half-century of rural Fountain Green township in western Illinois, roughly
1830–1880. In its establishment and maintenance of a family farm culture,
Fountain Green Township was the Midwest in microcosm. Fountain Green
typifies the Midwest's diversified grain and livestock agricultural economy, its
cooperative, frugal, church-centered rural culture, and the mixing process of
settlement streams. In the Illinois countryside, we see the local ramifications of
the nineteenth century's important transformations: geographic and social
mobility, the spread of the market, sectional struggles, and the construction of
gender and class identities.

Fountain Green is a peculiar place as well, primarily because of its role in the
Mormon conflict in Illinois in the mid-1840s. While few communities experienced the violence that took place there, what happened there could have
happened anywhere in the Midwest. The conflict throws into sharp relief the
process by which a diverse group of people were amalgamated into a homogeneous farm culture. The appeal of Mormonism to the local people allows us
to see the familial and cultural tensions which grew out of ambivalence toward
the market and the determination of the settlers to exclude at any cost those
who challenged their ideals. What is typical and peculiar about Fountain Green
recommends the place as a window to view the forces originating in the
countryside transforming the Midwest and the nation.

A community study allows us to see the closely textured patterns of change
which can be obscured by bolder threads in the fabric of history. By tracing

changing cultural identities of groups in the local farm culture we understand the variety of ways rural people responded to the market. In Fountain Green, settlers from the middle states were instrumental in the rapid expansion of agrarian capitalism and in brokering the conflicts between the ambitious Yankees and the tradition-bound southerners. Their importance to the local farm culture warns us of the folly of dividing the native-born population into simplistic dichotomies of Yankee and southerner, or in posing the Yankee as a mere foil to the immigrant. Similarly, the history of Fountain Green emphasizes the importance of looking beyond the ideal of the white male farmer to study his wife and children. Changing ideologies of gender transformed farm production practices, family structure, and community relations. Finally, contrary to the pastoral nature of much rural history, the violence in rural Illinois helps us understand how various groups were excluded to produce a more homogeneous agrarian culture.

To understand family farm culture, I explore three intertwining aspects of the transformation of the Midwest: changing cultural identities, the expansion of the market, and the weakening of agrarian patriarchy. The book unfolds chronologically in three parts keyed to stages of market development in the Midwest, from a frontier subsistence economy to a selective engagement with the regional economy to market-driven capitalism beyond local control. Each part features a major community conflict that highlights the transformations taking place in the economy and society. The story alternates between changes in family farming and the larger community: Chapters 1, 3, and 6 focus on changes in the family farm, and Chapters 2, 4, 5, and 7 analyze the transformation of community.

By following several generations of settlers, we follow a saga of families who were faced with choices shaped by the limits of their circumstances and their culture. These human vignettes are embedded strongly in the story, a social history narrative of a people in one place. To underscore the importance of gender, three women's voices tell us the story of rural community in the Midwest: Martha McConnell Walker, a frontier farm wife; Susan Walker Geddes, wife of a prosperous Republican farmer and mother to Civil War soldiers; and journalist Jennie Hopkins, who fled Fountain Green for the city but longed for the country life she left behind. Sources include federal and state censuses, land deeds, tax records, court cases, and wills. These public records are supplemented by church records, newspapers, letters, and diaries. A complete run of general store ledgers and account books affords an analysis of material culture, including the social patterns of consumption and production.

In Fountain Green, as in the Midwest, by tracing regional identities we can examine the interplay between the expanding market and changes in the farm household. In Part 1, we see how regional identities initially structured settlement patterns, market orientation, and community institutions but were subordinated in the frontier campaign to remove the Mormons. The development of market agriculture in Fountain Green was inextricably intertwined with changes in family farm culture which weakened agrarian patriarchy. In the settlement period, farmers were ambivalent about the market and participated in exchange to achieve family goals such as the retention of the farmstead. Families relied on their own land and labor to produce a marketable surplus, including the products of women's labor. By comparing regional groups within the emergent farm culture, we can see that they pursued distinctive paths to market engagement.

In Part 2, I explain that the growth of the regional market at mid-century increased demand for farm products, so farmers mechanized production and families relied on kin to supply land and labor. A sense of community emerged as small towns sprang up to serve as commercial hubs and social centers for the expanding rural population. By the time of the Civil War, the Pennsylvania Scots-Irish contingent of the township formed a core group which dominated local government and religion, pushing Catholics and the southern-born to the margins. The sectional conflict over slavery transposed regional identities into political identities—Yankee and southerner, Republican and Democrat, victor and vanquished—which split the community. The North's victory set the stage for Yankees to impose their bourgeois ideals.

Part 3 argues that after the Civil War the family farm adopted capitalistic practices such as hiring laborers and renting farm land. In the process the local community lost control over the terms of exchange. Instead, corporations and regional market structures dictated the terms of the rural economy's interaction with the market. Farm people adopted new middle-class ideals which elevated individualism and reorganized notions of gender, thus weakening rural patriarchy. The transformation did not go unchallenged; farmers protested their loss of power and a rowdy male subculture resisted attempts to impose bourgeois ideals. In the end, we are left with the ironies of towns disappearing, young people leaving home, and German immigrants taking over the farms of the native-born. Farming as a way of life was transformed, and its transformation reflected broader developments in the history of the Midwest and the nation. To understand that transformation, what we claim as our American tradition, we must go back to hidden places such as Fountain Green.

OUR COMMON COUNTRY

PART I

1

Collected Springs
Founding a Farm Community

There was a spot, many years ago, amid the
rank prairie grass which usually grew as high
as a horse, where there was a smooth turf, such
as [is] found in an English park. The sod
quaked under the weight of man: it was, in
fact, the covering of a spring or succession of
springs, and through openings on the turf the
water could be seen, and reached, while from
the collected springs the water flowed the year
round in a strong stream.[1]

—FOOTE'S *FOUNTAIN GREEN ALMANAC*

By the time Ute Perkins got to Crooked Creek in 1826, he was an old man. His fair-skinned face was lined with the wrinkles of a man nearing 70 years of age, and he leaned slightly from the musket ball in his shoulder, a souvenir of the Revolutionary War. Ute's wife, Sarah, dark-eyed with a strong nose, no longer stood six feet tall in her seventy-first year. It may have been Ute's idea to move from Tennessee to Illinois, but it is more likely that he and Sarah were following their children and grandchildren to the western frontier. Three generations of the Perkins family settled along Crooked Creek in 1826, a clan of relatives who had come for the cheap government land of the Illinois Military Tract.[2]

The Perkins family was the first of three migration streams which collected in Fountain Green Township to found a new farm community on the frontier. Because Fountain Green Township was located midway between North and South, diverse regional cultures converged in western Illinois. While some mixing of migrant streams is typical of the Midwest, Fountain Green is unusual because the settlers of the township could trace their roots back to three recognized population hearths: Virginia's coastal and Piedmont regions, New England, and the mid-Atlantic region. The upland southerners were a mixture of migrants from the mid-Atlantic and Virginia regions, the northerners were transplanted from New England, and the Pennsylvania Scots-Irish migrated from the mid-Atlantic region.[3] Each group carried cultural baggage which influenced patterns of settlement, agricultural production, and community interaction in the Midwest. Those values would influence decisions of everyday life: what to plant, who should do the work, what to name the town, where to build the roads, where to put the church. The splicing together of diverse traditions made the early Midwest and the rural culture which was its foundation.

What the settlers shared was a commitment to farming as a way of life for themselves, their children, and their grandchildren. Their overriding goal was independent family farming, an agrarian ideal praised by Thomas Jefferson as the key to independence and virtue. Agrarian ideology had its roots in the revolutionary republican ideal of putting the public good before private gain. Both were threatened by the market revolution, an explosion of commerce following the Panic of 1819. Private capital and state governments built canals and railroads which moved people West and farm produce East to feed the burgeoning city population at work in multiplying factories.[4] The market revolution unleashed a fiercely competitive individualism which posed a threat to the republican legacy and, some felt, to the republic itself. An adherence to agrarian ideology and commitment to republican ideals propelled farmers and their families toward the frontier, where they settled on land the government acquired and prepared for them under the terms of the Northwest Ordinance.[5]

Fueled by the press of a rapidly expanding population against a limited supply of farmland, the farm families who moved west sought to carry on farming as a way of life. Rather than send their daughters to work in the factories, or their sons to learn a trade in the cities, farmers in the North packed up and moved west. Southern yeomen, who either could not or would not rely on slave labor, migrated west to preserve their independent way of life. Pennsylvania farmers who tired of the long overland trips to market, the rocky soil, and the encroaching iron furnaces headed for fertile prairies to raise wheat and rear children. Committed to Jeffersonian ideals of independent farm ownership, all made a conservative choice; rather than adapt to local circumstances they decided to do what they were doing somewhere else. It was not that they rejected the market; rather, they wanted to participate in the market on their own terms. They chose to preserve their way of life with their own hands on family land so the next generation could inherit the homestead. The differences between them determined the shape of the community they created.

Opening the West

The availability of cheap land for all three generations drew the Perkins family to the Illinois frontier. In 1826, when Ute Perkins and his family settled along a wooded stream at the headwaters of Crooked Creek, they squatted on land owned by the U.S. government. Under the terms of the Northwest Ordinance, in 1815 surveyors from the General Land Office began marking out the 87,000-square-mile wedge of land between the Illinois and Mississippi Rivers (see Fig. 1.1). The Fourth Principal Meridian lay due north from the mouth of the Illinois River; the Base Line extended seventy-two miles due west and east.

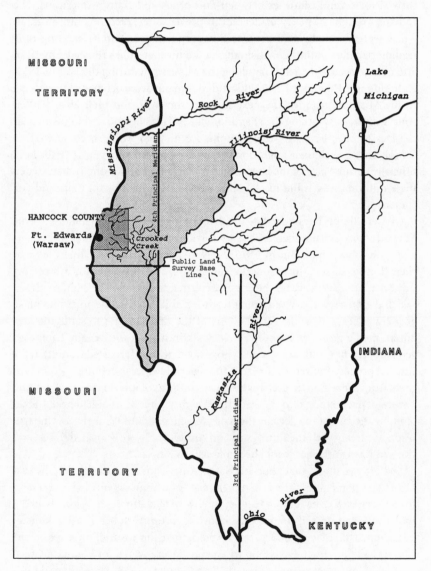

FIGURE 1.1. The Illinois Military Tract. From Joseph Yeager, *Geographical, Statistical and Historical Map of Illinois* (Philadelphia: Carey & Lea, 1822).

From these axes the surveyors spun a web of invisible lines, which intersected at one-mile intervals marked by a gash in a tree trunk or a rude pile of stones. As contractors of the federal government, the surveyors laid a grid of geographical boundaries on the land, securing it for the nation's white citizens.[6]

Preparation of the land for white citizens required the removal of the indigenous inhabitants, the Sauk and Mesquakie. An amicable fur trade had thrived for several centuries between Europeans and Native Americans. The Indians brought in peltry of deer, bear, beaver, otter, raccoon, and muskrat, which were shipped via St. Louis to Pittsburgh on the Ohio River. Long-time trading partners with the British, the Sauk and their allies resisted American attempts to secure the territory along the Mississippi during the War of 1812. Although in 1813 about 1,500 Sauk and Mesquakie were persuaded to relocate to the Missouri frontier, the next summer the Sauk and their allies battled American troops, forcing the abandonment of Forts Mason and Johnson near the Des Moines River. Yet their dominance of what would become western Illinois ended with their migration southward into Missouri. In 1816 the land officially became part of the United States, when the Potawatomi Indians ceded the 6 million acres in Illinois Territory previously ceded by the Sauk and Fox Indians.[7]

When Illinois became a state in 1818, the seventy white inhabitants at Fort Edwards were outnumbered by a total tribal membership of 6,500 persons along the Mississippi. But by 1830 the Native Americans had largely vacated their Illinois villages, including the village of Quashquame just north of Fort Edwards. For several years the tribes were free to hunt in the Military Tract, which they regarded as within their territory, and they would sometimes make acquaintances with white settlers. One of the first families to settle the area entertained a group of friendly Black Hawk Indians at their cabin. Later they remembered how difficult it was to choke down the birds roasted whole that the Indians prepared in return. In 1832, the Black Hawk War definitively removed them from the region. In exchange for a few months of idle service, the Fountain Green men who fought in the war earned eighty acres of what had been Indian land. By the end of the decade, the Sauk, Mesquakie, and Winnebago, who had traded so freely with the Europeans and Americans, were relocated to reservations in Iowa and what would become eastern Kansas.[8]

The government that removed Native Americans from the land in the War of 1812 prepared it for the war's soldiers, each of whom was entitled to 160 acres for his service. Of the Illinois Military Tract's 5,360,000 acres, two-thirds, or 3.5 million, were reserved for soldiers' bounties. From October 1817 to January 1819 approximately 17,000 patents were issued for 1.8 million acres in the Illinois Military Tract. Forty bounty warrants were issued for Fountain Green Township, most between October 1817 and January 1818. The military bounty of 160 acres was a full quarter-section of township land, a generous surplus in an era when hand-tool farming limited feasible cultivation to about forty acres, with another forty acres reserved for pasturage and woodlot.[9]

The military bounty provided the veteran with a large tract of western land, but most soldiers were not inclined to settle on the western frontier. They sold bounty warrants to land agents, who in turn sold them to speculators who were eager to buy up land in the Military Tracts.[10] During the 1830s, disappointed in the returns on land for which they were being taxed, speculators gradually sold their land to resident owners. Settlers who could not afford to pay the high prices speculators charged could either buy a tax lien on lands in delinquent status or squat on government land until it was ready for sale.[11]

The opening of the Quincy land office in February 1831 set off a wave of migration which became a land boom in 1835, when the entire Military Tract was subject to entry at the low government price of $1.25 an acre. Sales increased to a peak of 5,838 tracts in 1836, then collapsed in the Panic of 1837. Squatters quickly purchased the land in Fountain Green Township; of the 239 parcels sold in the township, 199 of them were purchased by the close of 1836.[12] The burst of purchases suggests that settlers had long squatted on the land, waiting for the land office to open to legally secure their claims.

Marketing the Military Tract

The settlers rushing to buy land were drawn to the Illinois Military Tract by guidebooks which promoted its attractions: cheap land, fertile soil, and nearby connections to markets. One popular 1837 emigrant's guide to Illinois tendered a near-guarantee: "Any laboring man with reasonable industry and economy with a family, may arrive here without any capital, and in half a dozen years be the owner of a good farm, with stock in abundance." It promised that "in no part of the United States can uncultivated land be made into farms with less labor than in Illinois." In just a short time an immigrant could buy a quarter section of timber and prairie for $200 and have it under cultivation. If families were short of cash, they could squat "unmolested" on public lands, although one or two thousand dollars afforded "peculiar advantages."[13]

The guidebooks assured their readers that the soils in the West were exceedingly fertile: "Everything that grows *well* in New England, grows *better* in the West." Moreover, the prairie offered ample free range for livestock. An 1818 guide predicted yields of sixty bushels of corn or thirty bushels of wheat per acre, while it boasted that cattle raised on prairies brought five to seven dollars per hundredweight. And all this was attainable by family farmers: "A small farm, well cultivated, and in the vicinity of the prairies, which afford an inexhaustible range for cattle, horses, and hogs, insures the most speedy and the most certain sources of wealth."[14] While some predictions were clearly promotional rather than factual, they were enough to convince thousands of immigrants to choose Illinois.

The fertile land of the Military Tract provided ample incentive to prospective settlers. Except for the bottomlands along the river, nearly all the Military Tract was uplands. The southern part of the tract was originally forested, and the northern was predominantly prairie. The soils were glaciated and fertile, gently rolling or level in the north and cut by wooded streams into hilly or broken land in the south. By avoiding the prairies and sloughs, farmers lost an opportunity to acquire land that would later prove to be superior to the hilly bottomlands where they settled. But until the steel plow became available, it was easier to girdle and fell trees on wooded land than clear away the densely rooted grasses of the open prairie.[15]

The stream valleys were unsuitable for cultivation, but timbers of burr oak, hickory, butternut, or black oak offered wood and water.[16] Timber was needed for buildings, fuel, and rail fences to keep hogs out of the corn. Timber also provided free range for the hogs that rooted for mast on the forest floor. The forest supplied game (turkeys, deer, quail, and rabbits) to supplement the frontier diet of corn dodger and pork. A nearby water source was vital, because digging a well with a pick and shovel through prairie grasses was a daunting task. A fast-flowing stream could provide power for a small flour or lumber mill, and smaller ones supplied water for the household and feeding the stock.[17]

Fountain Green Township, where the Perkins families settled, was situated in the wooded area along Crooked Creek, with openings of prairie meadow and a share of marshy land. The forest-prairie ecology lent itself to a mixed farm economy of grain cultivation and livestock raising, either hogs or cattle.[18] Tributaries of Crooked Creek wound through Section 32 of the township, making it one of the best-watered sections of the township. The land was hilly near the stream gullies but leveled out into broad prairie spaces beyond the waterways. Guidebooks characterized Section 32 as "good farming land," timbered with oak, hickory, and elm.[19]

According to the guidebooks, not only was fertile land and free range available, but markets were said to be within easy reach. One guidebook recommended the Military Tract because of its "great rivers . . . and the thousand other navigable streams which flow through this charming country."[20] In the early decades of settlement, the rivers were the highways to market, where a farmer could increase his wealth by selling his produce.

Farm families such as the Perkinses bought land not only because of its low price but also because of its accessibility to the river market. On the west, the Mississippi River provided a major transportation route for migration and trade downriver to St. Louis and New Orleans. To the east, the Illinois River and its tributaries offered only limited opportunities for transportation. Because no point in the Military Tract was more than forty-five miles from either major

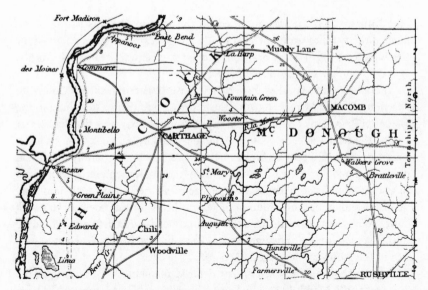

FIGURE 1.2. Hancock County, Illinois, 1839. From David H. Burr, *Map of Illinois and Missouri: Exhibiting the Post Offices, Post Roads, Canals, Rail Roads &c.* (London: J. Arrowsmith, 1839).

river, every farmer had some access to these waterways. The poor condition of the roads and the seasonal rains made overland travel slow and difficult, but the location of the Military Tract was superior to the inland prairies.[21]

Cheap land, fertile soil, and river markets would allow a farmer to achieve a competency, a "comfortable independence" which included providing land for his children to settle around him.[22] Early guidebooks directed at speculators emphasized wealth, but guidebooks aimed at westward migrating farmers promised the farmer a competency.[23] In an appeal to paternal feelings, one guidebook author warned his readers that if they were unable to provide land for their sons, they would either be a burden upon the household or "they must then be turned out upon the world, and trust to the winds and waves of fortune, which may waft them on to competency and virtue, and which may bear them away to utter and hopeless poverty and irreclaimable vice."[24] The compelling appeal to the farmer made the choice clear: stay and children would be lost to worldly vice or poverty, or go west where children could be nearby. By focusing on the ideal of competency rather than wealth, the guidebooks persuaded many farmers to move to the Illinois frontier.

The cheap land and river access in Military Tract first drew farm families from the upland South—Kentucky, Tennessee, Virginia, and the Carolinas. Hancock County, where Fountain Green Township was located, was one of nine new counties created in the Military Tract in 1825. Named for John Hancock, signer of the Declaration of Independence, the county took in 780 square miles of the Military Tract. It was bounded on the west by the Mississippi River, stretched thirty miles from north to south, and was an average of twenty-four miles wide (see Fig. 1.2). A prairie occupied the central area of the county, watered by branches of Crooked Creek.[25]

When the Perkins families arrived in the eastern part of Hancock County to settle along Crooked Creek, most of the county's population still clung to the Mississippi River bank on the western edge of the county, where they had better access to the river trade. By 1830, 463 persons lived in Hancock County, just a fraction of the 13,000 in the Military Tract as a whole. The family migration pattern of the Perkinses was typical of early county settlement. Eighty-seven households were listed with an average size of six persons in each, and only seven households had no children. The families who migrated to Hancock County were young; two-thirds of household heads were between 20 and 40 years of age. There were only slightly more men than women, but men predominated in the group of those aged 21 to 40.[26]

The slow pace of early settlement delayed the choice of Carthage as the county seat until March 1833.[27] By September a log cabin courthouse had been constructed on the main square, but since Carthage was not large enough to have a lawyer, court cases were argued by itinerant lawyers who rode the circuit. Carthage became the center point for county roads and business transactions. In a short time the town square was bordered by three stores, one grocery, and the shops of three carpenters, a blacksmith, two cabinetmakers, a wheelwright, a brickmaker, and a physician. A tavern provided a convenient place to discuss the political issues of the day.[28]

When Hancock County's officials chose the rising sun as the image to be engraved on the circuit court seal, they displayed their faith in the county's future.[29] The plow and the steamboat pictured on the seal of the county commissioner's court symbolized the promise of prosperity in an agrarian market economy.[30] In 1837 a sheaf of wheat replaced the plow and steamboat on the seal, symbolizing the profitable frontier crop that launched the county's farming future.[31] To fulfill the promise of prosperity, families continued to flock to the region to clear land and establish farms.

Migration Streams to Fountain Green

Whether from the upland South, New England, or the midlands, all streams of migrants who settled on the land in the township of Fountain Green brought patterns of culture from their former homes as they established farms in Illinois. The family migration pattern meant they created regional neighborhoods with unique ways of arranging farmsteads on the land. While they shared a commitment to earning a competency by farming, they grew different crops and varied in their approaches to the market. The differences due to regional identity also shaped the nature of community, where they mingled in churches and stores and carried out their civic duties. (Table 1.1 in Appendix 1 lists the early settlers and their region of origin.)

Ute Perkins was patriarch of a clan that spread out over the Military Tract in a staged migration from Tennessee to Jacksonville, Illinois, to Fountain Green. The families of two of his children settled on Crooked Creek, while two other children and their families settled twenty miles east in McDonough County. By choosing to settle away from the Mississippi River, the main conduit of trade, they displayed an orientation toward distant markets typical of the upland South. Accustomed to a sparsely settled backwoods community, the river market was near enough for the few items they could not supply themselves.[32]

In migrating westward to Illinois, Ute Perkins was repeating a familial pattern of continual westward migration in search of better land. His father was born in Baltimore, Maryland, in 1736, and migrated to North Carolina's Piedmont, where he settled on a grant of land west of the Catawba River, where Ute was born in 1761. After Ute married Sarah Gant of Granville, North Carolina, in 1783, they moved to Abbeyville in the South Carolina uplands, then to White County, Tennessee, west of the Appalachians. The moves to newly opened frontiers in South Carolina, Tennessee, and Illinois were efforts to find cheaper land for their large family of eleven children.[33]

The Perkins were quick to buy land when the government opened the land office in Quincy. In 1835 and 1836, Ute's son, William G., bought four parcels of land totaling 200 acres in Sections 31 and 32 of Fountain Green Township and ninety-six acres of land in nearby townships. His brother Absalom bought 120 acres, and a nephew, Andrew H. Perkins, purchased 140 acres near William's land. The purchases were made to secure clear title to land on which they had been squatting more than a decade. The improvements they made—clearing the land for farming and building cabins and fences—solidified their claims to the land.[34]

More southern families followed on the heels of the Perkins vanguard. The Brewers, Days, and Wrights belonged to a larger migration of upland southerners who moved westward to Illinois and Missouri in the early part of the nineteenth century. Rising land values in the South made it more profitable for farmers to buy western land at low government prices than stay and settle for smaller parcels. The Panic of 1819 struck the southwest particularly hard, and about one-third of those purchasing land in new districts lost their claims. Antipathy toward slavery was also a factor in the decision of many to move out of the southern upcountry to Illinois.[35]

Part of the southern stream of migrants were the Lincoln and Mudd families, a sprawling network of relations whose blood connections tied them together on the land. Mordecai Lincoln, born in 1771 in Augusta County, Virginia, was the patriarch of this clan of southern Catholics. His parents had migrated to the Kentucky frontier in 1782, and after his marriage to Mary Mudd in 1792, he migrated farther westward, settling along a fork of the Green River in the Knobs beyond the fertile bluegrass region of the state.[36] Mordecai achieved prosperity in Kentucky and by 1810 owned over 400 acres of land. Settlers in that region practiced semi-subsistence farming, raising corn on the rough-cleared ground, distilling it into whisky, and floating it downriver on flatboats to New Orleans or Natchez. Families grew their own vegetables and tobacco, and women wove linen to trade for store-bought calico and other necessaries.[37]

The Lincolns left Grayson County, Kentucky, in spring 1828 with four of their six grown children, part of a larger migration of Catholic families that began in Maryland in the 1780s. In 1795, Mary Lincoln's forebears established the Catholic settlement of Bardstown, thirty-seven miles south of Louisville in Washington County, Kentucky. Migrating in groups so the church would follow them, the numbers increased in 1795 when the Treaty of Grenville opened Indian lands to settlers. By 1811 there were over 1,000 families in thirty Catholic congregations in Kentucky. The scenario repeated itself in the 1820s, when rising land values sent Catholic families north and west to Indiana, Missouri, and Illinois.[38]

Marriage linked the large southern families into clans that extended three generations to form the basis of community on the Illinois frontier. Headed by aged patriarchs, the settlers secured themselves in a web of relationships. Ute Perkins, Jr., admired the sewing skills of Anna Warren, whom he asked to stitch a vest for him. Her domestic skills passed this test, and they married in February 1835. Deaths also reconfigured families on the frontier. Mordecai Lincoln was caught in the Big Snow of 1830, a storm which lasted three days and nights, windblown into twenty-foot drifts. When his horse returned without him, his family suspected the worst, but his body was not found until the snow melted in April. Years later a grandson recalled: "We cut down a tree, hewed out puncheons and made a coffin and buried him where we found him." Others succumbed to the hardships of living on the frontier. One man was killed by a falling tree limb, and another was poisoned by herbs taken to cure the ague.[39] Southern families depended on ties of kin and neighbor to survive.

Typical of southern back-country settlement, the first settlers scattered their farmsteads on the timbered land, out of sight of their nearest neighbor. The few Indians who straggled through the area were friendly enough to invite to dinner, so settlers had no reason to cluster together for safety. They built log cabins, cleared land for corn, and kept herds of swine, which foraged in the timber. Armed with shotguns, farmers hunted for game such as deer and turkey to supplement the family diet. They hauled some of their agricultural surplus overland to Mississippi River towns, but a commercial network that reached inland had not yet been established. The southern families transplanted a pattern of safety-first farming (producing primarily for family needs), supplemented by trade to distant markets, to the Illinois frontier.[40]

The southern settlers were joined by families from New England and New York in the early 1830s. Jabez Beebe, son of a Baptist preacher from Connecticut, was the first New Englander to buy land in Fountain Green Township. Before moving to Illinois, Beebe had operated a tavern and kept an inn in Hinsdale, New York. Hindsdale's poor soil and hilly and broken upland did not offer a farmer much prospect of prosperity. The harvest in Hinsdale was trees, and logs were rafted down Olean Creek and the Allegheny River to Pittsburgh and Cincinnati. We do not know whether it was Hinsdale's population boom, the rapid deforestation, or the scarcity of good land that dislodged Beebe, but we do know he looked west for a new start.[41]

Beebe wintered near Fort Edwards during the Big Snow of 1830, then moved north of Perkins Settlement to Horse Lick Grove, named for its underground springs that watered livestock.[42] Beebe, his wife Martha, and their seven children settled on the east half of section 28, by virtue of a bounty patent he had purchased in New York.[43] Beebe's sister, Eunice, and her husband, Stephen Ferris, followed them with their six children, setting out for Illinois from Chenango County, New York, in the spring of 1832. Low water levels on the river delayed the Ferris voyage to Illinois, so it was autumn before they were able to journey down the Allegheny and Ohio Rivers to Pittsburgh. They floated with the current on a flatboat with two other families to Cincinnati, then took a steamboat to St. Louis, where they arrived December 1st. A small steamboat took them farther upriver to Trader's Point, Iowa, where Ferris paid $16 to have his family and belongings ferried across the river to Fort Edwards, Illinois. After their arrival on December 13th, Ferris and son John walked the twenty-two miles to Horse Lick Grove, where they hired a wagon and ox team to haul the family and goods across the county. The Ferris family stayed with the Beebe family in a double log house until spring, when Ferris broke land for a farm and constructed a small tannery on 110 acres he bought from Beebe.[44]

Ambitious Yankees Beebe and Ferris, caught up in the speculative town-building boom of the mid-1830s, renamed the humble Horse Lick Grove the patrician-sounding Fountain Green, after the springs which bubbled out of the prairie sod. They laid out the town in the southeast quarter of Section 28, dividing it into sixteen blocks of four lots each. Two blocks were reserved for a town square and public park which fronted on a public road named Commerce Street running east and west.[45] Just as the southerners distributed themselves on the land in patterns learned from the past, the New Yorkers perpetuated the ideal of the New England town as the center of community.[46]

By 1837, Fountain Green was advertised in guidebooks as a "flourishing settlement" ten miles northeast of Carthage. Founder Jabez Beebe held the title of postmaster. The town's commercial establishments included a blacksmith, wheelwright, farrier, tinsmith, and general store. The store would become a center point for the community, drawing local settlers into its commercial and social network.[47] The Yankees depended on the town to provide the social and economic links that family relationships supplied to the southern clans.

Upland southerners and Yankees were already on the land when the third migration stream flowed to the township. In 1837, Thomas and Susan Walker Geddes and two small sons made the forty-day journey from Path Valley in Franklin County, Pennsylvania, to Fountain Green. They settled on land in the east half of Section 20 that he had purchased for $650 from land agents the previous October. After boasting to the folks at home that his Illinois land was free of rocks, relatives joined the Geddes family in Illinois.[48]

The Geddes, Walker, and McConnell families were prominent among the Scots-Irish who settled Path Valley before the Revolutionary War, contending with the Native Americans for the western lands.[49] Franklin County's farmers grew abundant yields of wheat, enough to send upward of 150,000 barrels of flour a year to Baltimore, but the shale soils in the Path Valley were much less productive. Isolated by steep mountains from easy routes to transport grain to markets, and farming less productive land than their neighbors in the county, many of Path Valley's farmers were ready to move west for more fertile soil and cheaper land.

The families from Pennsylvania left friends and relatives behind. The sundering of family ties is poignantly conveyed by young Martha McConnell in 1840, who begins a letter to her "very Dear Aunt Martha" with a tone of regret: "Two years and five months have gone round since we parted and yet none of you have come to see us; and I thought certainly I would be home again in two or three years at the most, but oh how vain have been my expectations."[50] Moving to the frontier, she came to realize, severed family ties. Martha asked her aunt to "give my love to all our friends and remember us kindly to all our relatives . . . and all the rest of our neighbors."[51]

The family migration pattern created regional neighborhoods of southern and northern settlements along the banks of Crooked Creek (see Fig. 1.3). Southerners settled the southern parts of the township near Perkins Settlement, New Englanders clustered around the town of Fountain Green and throughout the upper two-thirds of the township, while the Pennsylvanians surrounded Section 20.[52] Naturally, families and friends who traveled to Illinois together settled near each other once in Fountain Green. The clustering reflects not only familial strategies of land settlement but also a deliberate distancing from strangers of a different regional culture.

Settlers relied on family cooperation to buy land, pool resources, and squat on parcels to be kept in the family. Ute Perkins's sons Absalom and Andrew and

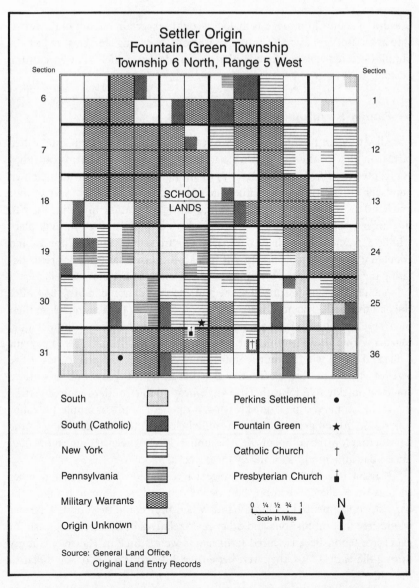

FIGURE 1.3. Settler Origin, Fountain Green Township. From Illinois, Secretary of State, Public Domain Sales Land Tract Record Listing, Record Group 103.227, Illinois State Archives, Springfield, Illinois.

grandson William bought thirteen parcels within a year that spread a checkerboard of Perkins dominance over Sections 31 and 32 in the southwest corner of the township and extended into adjacent townships.[53] In many cases these purchases were formal recognitions of title by occupancy (squatting), but the breadth of acquisition suggests that all recognized certain regions of the township as territory set aside for future expansion. By buying land close to kin, the families created neighborhoods of regional identity which allowed cultural customs to persist.

Family Farming on the Frontier

All settlers in Fountain Green, from whatever regional group, established farms on the frontier. Once they had acquired land for a farmstead, they confronted the difficult task of clearing, planting, and harvesting with their own hands. Frontier farming was limited not only by the constraints of scarce labor and hand tools, but also by a primitive marketing apparatus connecting them to the larger Mississippi Valley River trade. Agricultural production took place within a framework of habits transplanted from their former homes and adapted to the new environment. Attitudes toward the market also varied, dictating the contours of the community taking shape in Fountain Green.[54]

A letter Martha McConnell wrote home to Pennsylvania in July 1844, after she had married Alexander Walker, aptly conveys how families relied on their own land and labor to farm on the frontier. With the harvest fast approaching, Martha wrote: "If we get our wheat safe in I think it will enable us to pay our debts and then I will feel more comfortable." Alexander had planted forty-five acres of wheat, a marketable frontier crop that grew readily in the virgin soil and could be quickly sold for cash. Growing wheat on the frontier required getting it "safe in," or harvesting it quickly when it ripened. Land was ample, but labor was scarce. Alexander worked so steadily helping other farmers bring in the harvest that Martha complained, "A[lexander] has not been at home more than once a day and Sundays for nearly three weeks."[55]

Martha noted that "A. has gone to get harvest hands."[56] Young farm families such as the Walkers relied on the labor of kin and neighbor to bring in the harvest, supplemented by hired hands when they could be found. A farmer would rely first on his sons and other male relatives before spending cash for expensive labor. Because hired farm hands were scarce in Hancock County during the early 1840s, they were expensive, fifty cents a day or ten dollars a month.[57]

As the farmer's wife, Martha played a crucial role in farm production. Although women did not work in the fields, their labor was vital in bearing children who were future laborers and providing food for a hungry farmer and his hands. At harvest time those were competing demands. Once she had a baby, Martha was concerned about being able to feed the threshers: "I expect I will have a pretty strong time of it as I have no [hired] girl. My babe with ten or twelve men will keep me moving, but if my strength holds out and my babe keeps well I think I can get along someway."

Martha's duties included managing the farm household, which required frugality and reliance upon barter: "I try to be very economical. I have bought nothing but the bare necessities of life and sometimes not that hardly." She used coffee sparingly, only for guests and as a medicine; the rest of the time she roasted wheat to make a strong hot drink. When she wanted something, she paid for it with the products of her own hands: "I have knit stockings to get what things I needed before I was sick and I have only bought fifty cents worth in the store since that. I paid with butter and meat and some crocks I got Saturday for butter."[58] Martha was willing to work hard, go without, and barter to pay off the debts incurred in establishing a family farm.

As Martha's letter makes plain, family land (acquired from the government) and family labor were the twin pillars on which the frontier family farm system rested. But families were far from self-sufficient in production and consumption habits. Farmers ameliorated labor shortages by drawing upon the pool of neighbors and relatives, and farm wives bartered with family and friends to provide necessaries for the household. Furthermore, farmers such as Alexander Walker planted and harvested wheat to sell it for cash or trade, not merely to sustain the family diet.

Martha's letter also takes us inside the farm family to see a gendered system of household production. The family farm system of the Midwest was an agrarian patriarchy based on male landownership. Farm women were subordinate to male farmers in part because women had only limited access to land (primarily as widows holding land for sons). Just as he controlled the land, the farmer similarly controlled decisions about farm production and labor assignments. He supervised the family labor force for the entire farm enterprise, but the farm wife presided over work in the house and yard. In the patriarchal farm family, one's gender and age determined the assignment and value of work on the farm.[59]

Because hired labor was scarce, the labor of farm children was vital to frontier farming. Farm families counted on the vested interest of their children in the future farm enterprise to motivate them to work. Farm children were expected to labor on the farm as they matured, and their tasks followed that of their parent of the same sex. Sons followed their fathers into the fields, while daughters aided their mothers in the house and garden. A farmer with mature sons was less in need of hired or traded labor, as in this humorous anecdote in a frontier newspaper: "A short time since, a man was heard lamenting the death of two of his sons. 'Two, stout, hearty boys,' said he, and 'died just before hayin' time—it almost undid me!'"[60] Because agricultural production was limited by the use of hand tools, only a grown boy could swing a scythe or successfully guide a plow through the prairie sod.

The abundance of land and scarcity of labor determined cropping patterns on the frontier. Like Alexander Walker, in the first years of settlement farmers raised wheat because it was less bulky than corn and brought a higher price at market. Wheat culture required only a plow and a scythe and, once harvested, wheat kept well and could be held for a higher price or ground into flour for domestic use. An early settler reminisced about the high yields and fine crops of the virgin soil along Crooked Creek: "We raised as fine wheat then as I have ever seen. The ground was new and produced fine crops."[61] Estimates in Hancock County place average yields at thirty bushels of wheat per acre in 1842. Winter wheat was initially preferred over spring wheat because its hardness made it easier to mill.[62] By the 1840s wheat surpluses in the Military Tract were so far above local needs that large quantities were shipped to market.[63] This initial production of wheat is evidence of a market mentality, a willingness to take the risk of concentrating production in hopes of the most profitable returns.

The scarcity of labor limited farm production because farmers relied on hand tools such as scythes to harvest the wheat. Once the wheat had been harvested, it was trampled by horses to loosen the heads from the chaff, which was shaken out by standing on a raised scaffold and gently turning the grain onto a sheet below. The wind blew away the chaff and the grain was collected into bushels, ready to carry to market. The lists of tools in the estates of deceased farmers confirm that hand tools limited the pace of harvesting and winnowing the grain on the frontier. John Roberts, who died in 1842, owned only one plow, two scythes, and a cradle, with a total value of $11.25. Six years later, when David Alton died, he was still harvesting with a scythe, but he had invested in a shovel plow and a wheat fan to boost efficiency.[64]

Corn production remained important to frontier farmers, especially those from the upland South, where the corn-and-hog economy was first established. Corn was easier to plant and harvest, and it restored soil depleted from continuous wheat cultivation. Two men and a boy could take care of 100 acres of corn but only twenty-five to fifty acres of wheat. Corn was planted in rows about four feet apart, and once the initial six-week weeding period had passed, corn outstripped weeds and required little care. Corn could stay on the stalks until spring (although most was harvested in October and November), but wheat had to be harvested within days of when the grain ripened.[65] Rain threatened the wheat crop, and dry spells afflicted the corn crop.[66] Most farmers reduced risk by planting both.

Cultural Patterns of Production

The three streams of population that founded the community of Fountain Green Township varied in their approaches to agricultural production. Production patterns reflected different strategies of market involvement, perhaps even varying degrees of comfort with the demands of the competitive marketplace.

These variances in Fountain Green confirm that farming took place within a cultural framework that was rooted in habits transplanted to Illinois.

The families who first settled in Fountain Green Township had farmed in areas with distinctive cropping patterns. The migrants transplanted these patterns to a new environment and initially differed in their approaches to the market. White yeoman farmers from the upland South, reliant more on family than slave labor, raised tobacco, grains, and cattle and distilled whiskey for transport to distant markets. Farmers from New England relied on family labor to produce diversified crops on small farms clustered around villages and market towns. Mid-Atlantic farmers, who are portrayed by historians as eager capitalists, produced wheat for distant markets and their wives produced butter for local sale.[67] While-native born and immigrants alike tended to eventually adopt the prevailing patterns of agricultural production, some initial variance in farming practices did exist in Fountain Green Township.[68]

Upland southerners, the first to settle the Fountain Green region, tended to stick with their traditional pattern of production of corn and hogs. They grew almost six times more corn than wheat (a ratio of 5.6 to 1) in 1850, the highest of all the settler groups (see Table 1.2). They did not lead in total corn production, but of all the groups they did produce more corn in comparison with wheat. The average southern-born farmer owned thirty hogs, well above the average of twenty for northern-born farmers. In 1850, the average value of their farms ranked second among all groups, but they ranked first in the value of stock and cattle, largely because a few farmers owned large numbers of horses.[69]

Settlers from New England and New York depended on a mixed farming strategy, bolstered by small crafts carried on in town. They ranked third in 1850 in factors of production such as improved acres, farm value, and implement value. They also came in third in production of both grains and livestock. They grew five times more corn than wheat and devoted proportionally more land to wheat than did the upland southerners. Their farms were the smallest of the three groups, perhaps because they combined farming with a trade, making them less committed to farming as their sole source of income. For example, New Yorkers Horace Aldrich and John White were both carpenters and farmers. Their dual strategy of craft and farm was focused on the local market in the town of Fountain Green.[70]

Pennsylvanians continued to cultivate wheat, achieving greater yields on the Illinois soil than they had in Path Valley. This preference for wheat production is evidence of a cultural continuity transplanted from the high wheat-producing states of the middle Atlantic region. In 1850 they produced about four times more corn than wheat, the highest proportion of wheat production of any group (Table 1.2). Perhaps because of their dedication to wheat as a cash crop, by 1850 farmers born in the mid-Atlantic states dominated in production.

They were the largest group and the most wealthy, with over $250 more than the average in property and farm value. They surpassed the other groups in average output of wheat, corn, and swine. Because they concentrated on producing the cash crop of wheat, theirs was an aggressive approach to the market.

Farm Women's Productive Work

The production of wheat, corn, and hogs was only part of the gendered household economy. Although women rarely worked in the fields, they made a significant contribution to the farm family enterprise by producing commodities for use or sale and were directly involved in the marketing of those commodities. In a letter written before her marriage, Martha McConnell detailed the arduous work involved in weaving cloth, raising chickens, collecting eggs, and churning cream into butter.

Textile production provided an important commodity to trade for "necessaries" they could not produce themselves. Martha's family grew flax for linen and raised sheep for wool. She boasted to her aunt, "We have a great deal of flax which is very good." With flax hatchels made by her father she separated the fine threads of flax from the shorter, coarser fibers of tow. Both fibers were put to good use: "We have one web of linen twenty five yards spun and spooled, and what coarse tow spun will make a piece of bagging." She spoke of future plans to make "a piece of check next and then a piece of linen with cotton chain." The linen was a valuable barter item; one yard could be traded for three yards of lighter-weight muslin.

Farm families raised sheep so women could spin their wool into yarn. Martha informed her aunt that "we will have the wool of fifteen sheep if nothing kills them." Only after many hours of work were fibers transformed into marketable commodities. Martha reported that she knit socks from the wool of their sheep and made jeans from the tow.[71] The jeans she traded at the river port were the first that Martha had made, completed in less than a week under the instruction of her mother: "I was very afraid to attack it but mother basted it and showed me how to go on."[72]

In addition to producing textiles, women made butter and raised poultry to help sustain the household economy. Martha reported, "We have seven cows to milch and feed and their offspring to attend to which is not a little work in wet weather, and we expect four to five more this summer and that with our flax and wool I think will keep us cutting around right smart."[73] Butter production was women's work, as was milking, during the frontier period of family farming. However, by mid-century men may have been taking over that chore. In a letter to his intended bride in 1848, Thomas Brewer of Fountain Green chided her for thinking that he had "come to the conclusion to milch the cows." Refusing to assume that duty, he wrote, "I must talk with you about that hereafter."[74] At least in this case, it was a task the woman wanted the man to take over.

Just as farmers relied on their sons to plant corn or help harvest the wheat, farm wives depended upon the labor of their daughters to sustain domestic production. By relying upon their daughters' help, farm wives also taught them skills they would need after they had their own households. By working for her mother, Martha learned how to fill the shoes of a farmer's wife with its demands for household production of marketable commodities.

Going to Market

Despite the limitations scarce labor imposed on production in the frontier stage, families produced a surplus which they sold in the Mississippi River Valley market system. It was a multi-tiered system, with produce collected at successively larger market towns before it was shipped down the Mississippi to St. Louis or New Orleans. This frontier stage of production and sale was constrained by unreliable transportation and outdated information about prices. After loading the sacks of grain in the farm wagon, farmers in Fountain Green had to plan on a three- to four-day trip to a river port, where they might find out that prices had fallen or the river was too low to ship produce to New Orleans.[75] That farmers and entrepreneurs participated in it at all is evidence of a commitment to the profits of the market.

Warsaw, about twenty miles west of Fountain Green on the Mississippi River, was the major link between Fountain Green and distant markets. Built in 1834 upon the site of abandoned Fort Edwards, Warsaw was situated just below the lower rapids, about nineteen hours above St. Louis. The river port of Warsaw was served by steamboats that made weekly circuits among the riverbank market towns such as Quincy, Illinois, and Keokuk, Iowa. Steamboats sped produce to market much faster·than did a fully loaded wagon pulled by oxen, which may have covered only three miles an hour. The difference between overland and river travel explains the rivercentric transportation system of the Mississippi River Valley, where the most logical route to market was via the closest river town.[76]

Once at Warsaw, a farmer could take his grain to one of several general commission and forwarding agents. For example, in July 1843, agent T. J. Perkins advertised for wheat but would also take corn, pork, hides, or flax seed in exchange for dry goods or sugar. Twice a week a regular packet picked up the produce and took it to Quincy, St. Louis, and New Orleans and from there on to Baltimore, Philadelphia, New York, and Boston. Quincy, which collected about half the wheat destined for St. Louis in the 1840s, shipped $8,000 worth of wheat in 1837 and $275,000 in 1841. Like Quincy and the other river towns, Warsaw was built on the trade with farmers.[77]

Farmers read the newspaper for information about prices downriver, trying to gauge the best time to sell their wheat. Farmers who held out for higher prices later in the season took the risk of barely passable roadways. As one newspaper remarked: "We will remind the farmers—especially those residing at a distance—that 62 or 63 cents now, and *good* roads, may be better than 75 hereafter, and *bad* roads."[78] The price constantly fluctuated, although in the 1840s it was usually between forty-five and fifty cents a bushel.[79]

Marketing corn required a more complicated approach but reduced risk by offering farmers a choice. Because farmers were paid less for a bushel of corn than a bushel of wheat, at times corn was not worth the cost of shipping. On those occasions, farmers marketed their corn by feeding it to hogs. Whether to market corn as grain or on the hoof was a decision made after a careful comparison of prices. Many farmers knew how much corn it took to produce 100 pounds of weight gain, and if they could buy that amount of corn for less than the price of 100 pounds of live pork, they fed it to the hogs. If the necessary quantity of corn cost more than the 100 pounds of pork, the farmer would be better off selling his corn as grain.[80]

During the 1840s, corn was usually marketed on the hoof. Farmers could choose to have their hogs slaughtered and packed locally or drive them to river towns, where they were shipped downriver to packing houses at Alton and St. Louis. Across the river from Hancock County, Keokuk and Ft. Madison, Iowa, were home to smaller hog-packing factories. The expansion of the hog-packing business in Quincy (which paralleled the expansion of the grain trade) shows how committed western Illinois farmers were to raising hogs. Only 500 hogs were packed in Quincy in 1837, but by 1841 over 10,000 hogs were funneled through the river port. That amount had doubled by the mid-1840s, and it reached 40,000 by 1854. Farmers began to pay attention to better breeding, which transformed the frontier hog of sinewy flesh into a plump beast with succulent meat for table consumption.[81]

Fountain Green farmers could choose to drive their hogs to market at Warsaw or sell them to a local middleman. Stephen Tyler of Fountain Green opened a pork house in 1836, where hogs were butchered, dry salted, and cured. Much of the hog was wasted, since only the hams, bacon, and shoulders were marketable. The pork was then hauled in wagons to Warsaw for shipment to St. Louis. Middlemen assumed considerable risks, as Daniel Prentiss of Fountain Green discovered in 1839. He loaded a steamboat full of Tyler's pork and sailed downriver to New Orleans, only to find a complete lack of demand for pork. He dumped the entire cargo into the river, then returned home.[82]

Families from Fountain Green regularly made the three-day wagon trip to Warsaw to market their produce and to choose their rewards. Martha McConnell's 1840 letter makes it clear that women also participated in the Mississippi River Valley market system. She wrote that "we have a tolerable market at Warsaw for anything we have to sell and get most of the necessaries of life there in exchange for our truck, as the Suckers [southern settlers] call anything for sale." When her father took wheat to Warsaw, Martha and her mother went along, carrying 100 dozen eggs, the fruit of several months' labor. They earned twelve and a half cents for each dozen eggs and sixteen cents for each pound of butter, which was spent on factory-made cloth for her mother and sister at thirty-seven cents a yard. The crowning purchase was cloth for a new cloak: "It is figured purple and cost $1.72 per yard for it. I must tell you I gave stockings at 50c and jeans at 87c for it, and altogether I did not think it cost me so much more than it would at home. It is very handsome and the only piece that I have seen since I came here that was good for anything."[83] Her satisfaction with the yard goods was ample compensation for months spent collecting eggs in the henhouse, churning butter, and weaving tow.

Some historians have argued that women were sequestered in the household and did not participate in the public arena of buying and selling.[84] However, evidence from Fountain Green suggests women were aware of and even participated in the exchange of farm produce and domestic commodities in the market. In her letter, Martha not only informs us of the products she purchased, but she also displays a keen grasp of the Mississippi River Valley economy. She wrote that it was hard to buy "finery" in Warsaw because of the shortage of cash in the depression following the Panic of 1837: "The times are so hard the merchants find it difficult to get enough money to carry them to St. Louis with their produce which they exchange for goods." She explained that while some of the Warsaw merchants brought back goods from New Orleans, they were more expensive than commodities bought in St. Louis. The scarcity of cash made women's products all the more valuable as a medium of exchange, allowing them to obtain goods that created an improved standard of living.

Transplanting Cultures

As migrant streams from various origins collected in Fountain Green, they also wove strands of regional culture into the fabric of community. The Yankee towns became the centerpiece of community, a place to trade and to socialize. The settlers from the upland South dominated local government, which regulated commerce and settled disputes. The Kentucky Catholics and the Pennsylvania Scots-Irish established churches, transplanting familiar patterns of worship to create a sense of belonging in a new place. Transplanted habits of commerce, government, and religion coalesced to form a distinctive local farm culture on the Illinois frontier.

Towns were first and foremost trading centers. If families did not care to go to market in Warsaw, they could trade their produce locally at Fountain Green's general store established by Connecticut Yankees Martin Hopkins and Stephen Tyler. Like a magnet, the store drew farm families to the town of Fountain Green. While they shopped, customers traded gossip, remarked about the weather, and argued about politics around the store's pot-bellied coal stove. Hopkins & Tyler was a place to visit as well as a place to trade.

Customers could purchase a wide range of consumer goods at Hopkins & Tyler: yardage and sewing supplies, clothing and shoes, household items (from tableware to chamber pots), and staples such as coffee, sugar, and baking powder. The farmer could buy farm tools such as scythes, rifles, bridles, and plows, and could keep up the premises with paint and nails. The store supplied settlers with comforts such as brandy, whiskey, tobacco (chewing and smoking), tea, and snuff.[85]

The store records echo the seasonal cycles of farming. After a slow period in early winter, the volume of purchases peaked in late spring and early summer with the returns of the winter wheat harvest. Men bought scythes and whiskey, and women stocked up on dry goods to sew clothes for the family. In the fall, farmers brought in tallow to credit their accounts and purchased wicking so their wives could make candles from the fat left from slaughtering. Parents purchased primers, spelling books, and shoes for children who had run barefoot in the summer heat.

Women traded what they had made with their own hands for factory yard goods, ribbon, and coffee. For example, in May 1838 the account of William Gough was credited with $7.50 for twenty yards of flax linen, which was offset immediately by the purchase of eight yards of calico and a pair of combs. We cannot be completely certain women made these transactions in person, but the choice of items suggests they did trade at the store.[86]

The scarcity of cash and the face-to-face social relations among those in the township made the familiar system of barter and book debt workable in Fountain Green. Occasionally cash would be applied toward an account, but more often families would bring in commodities which would be assigned a value and credited to their account. For example, in January 1838, Arius Beebe brought in an axe handle to credit his account fifty cents. Mordecai Lincoln's son, Abraham, promptly purchased the handle and an axe for $1.75, creating a debit on his account. A few days later John Day paid $4.96 on his account by bringing in nineteen bushels of corn. In what may have been a prearranged transaction, Stephen Ferris bought the corn on the spot. In addition to corn, farmers brought in produce such as pork, timothy seed, and wheat. Some farmers paid for the purchase with their labor by chopping wood or hauling pork or grain to the river port of Warsaw.[87]

Commerce in Fountain Green rested not only on social relations between farm families and storekeepers but also among farmers who used the store as a place to exchange what they produced for what another could supply. Hopkins & Tyler provided store goods for the neighborhood at a convenient location not far from the farms and homes just being established on the frontier. Because the exchange was sustained by an extensive web of credit between people who dealt with each other day by day, it relied as much on cooperation as commerce.

Local Government

Settlers were also required to cooperate in local government, which was the primary means of keeping order in the frontier community. In the early years, local government had three main functions: to carry out elections, guide the development of commerce, and settle disputes. By virtue of their early arrival, settlers from the upland South filled most local governmental offices in the first years of settlement. They brought with them an affection for republican ideals which stressed local control and minimal governmental interference. First on the scene, they imprinted the local political structure with their brand of politics.[88]

While settlers were founding the farm community, the Era of Good Feelings dissolved and the second party system coalesced on the national political scene. Philosophies about the role of the government in economic development sharply divided voters into two parties: Democratic and Whig. Democrats were heirs to Jeffersonian republicanism, fearful of monied elites, and worried that government power might endanger their liberties. While party loyalties were not as sharply sectional as they would later become, the southern-born settlers in Hancock County tended to espouse the republican philosophy that privileged local control. Hancock County's sympathy for the Democratic Party can be traced to the origin of its settlers, yeomen smallholders committed to independent self-reliance. As such, they preferred that government not interfere in their lives and interpreted tariffs and taxes as tantamount to tyranny.[89] Indeed, the major Democratic newspaper in the county was aptly named the *Carthage Republican* (which became a misnomer in 1856 with the founding of the Republican Party).

Although some settlers from the northeast were Democrats, especially the town craftsmen, generally speaking the arrival of the northern element in the county strengthened the local Whig Party. Whigs were strongest in the northern part of Illinois near Chicago, where ambitious Yankees planned large-scale internal improvements such as the Illinois and Michigan Canal.[90] While upland southern settlers wanted more access to markets, they protested proposals for railroads which would primarily benefit Chicago and demanded their fair share of state largesse. The early years of Illinois state politics were marked by struggles to build political coalitions to deal with the vexing questions of banking and how to retire the massive debts of internal improvements.[91]

However, local offices were more a matter of community duty than party affiliation. Fountain Green Township's highest authority was the justice of the peace, cabinetmaker James Lincoln from Kentucky, elected in 1832. Local men were also appointed to supervise elections and serve on juries. By June 1830 there were enough settlers to create the Crooked Creek election district in newly independent Hancock County. Rural voters in the two townships were invited to cast ballots at the home of Ute Perkins. Men from the upland South dominated local government: Kentuckians John Brewer, his father Thomas, and Henry Donaho were appointed judges of election. The southerners were named to county juries the same month, along with Kentucky Catholic James Lincoln, upholding republican ideals through their service to the county.[92] In order to fulfill their duties, they had to travel to Carthage, ten miles southwest of Perkins Settlement.

Local government officials not only arranged elections, they also regulated commerce. The brisk trade in wheat required mills to grind the grain into flour and ferries to cross streams on the way to market. Local government bodies raised money and regulated commerce by taxing taverns and stores and awarded permits for the operation of ferries and mills. Three mill owners received such permits to build dams on Crooked Creek in the 1830–1836 period, based on the recommendations of a committee of twelve men who inspected the mill site and set a height limit for the dam (usually nine to ten feet). In one committee report to the county commissioners, the men stated that they did not "consider it [the mill dam] will be injurious to any land or animals."[93] The process of granting mill permits suggests broad local participation in allocation of shared resources. The lack of contention over mill permits in these early records also implies community support for mill construction.

Local government also promoted commerce by dedicating tax revenues to construction and maintenance of roads and bridges.[94] The county was divided into successively smaller road districts as increases in the population demanded the construction and maintenance of new roads to market. The proliferation of roads served the needs of farmers who traveled overland to trade their produce in the river towns, millers who ground the grain, and storekeepers who took in eggs for calico. Seven road districts in March 1831 doubled to fourteen within two years.[95] Soon roads were laid out to connect the settlement neighborhoods along Crooked Creek and to link them to other frontier settlements. Each man was expected to donate three days' labor on the roads each year. The road district supervisor kept an account of the labor performed and collected fines from those who were delinquent in their duty.[96] Thomas Brewer was the first supervisor of road district Number 7, which encompassed Perkins Settlement; he was succeeded by his son John, who began his term in March 1832.[97]

Before a road was built, an appointed committee of men carried out the process of "viewing" the road, surveying it by blazing trees in forests, and setting out stakes on prairies. Viewers were charged to lay out roads "on good and suitable ground" so they would be "of general utility and convenience."[98] Local men were also appointed to change the location of roads. When New Yorker Jabez Beebe complained in March 1833 that he was "aggrieved by the present location of a road" that ran across his land, southerners William G. Perkins and Benjamin E. Mudd were appointed to alter the road course.[99] Laying out roads, changing roadways, and overseeing maintenance were crucial functions of the county commissioner's court. The administration of roads had a major and immediate impact on the everyday lives of the settlers, and it was important that the decisions of the commissioners be equitable to all parties.

Settlers relied on the institutions of local government to settle disputes, such as moving the road from Jabez Beebe's land or keeping track of stray animals in a landscape where fencing was rare. A brand or mark identified the stock in the cornfield; one then applied to the stray's owner for damages. For example, James Lincoln marked his own animals with a split in the right ear and a smooth, square crop in the left ear.[100] This time-honored system of tracing lost animals operated on a basis of trust among the settlers and was enforced by the authority of the justice of the peace.

Other disputes proved more difficult to resolve. In a community that was home to groups of people from diverse regional origins, there was bound to be some clash of cultures. One guidebook explained that the population in Illinois was made up of immigrants from Kentucky, Virginia, and the Carolinas and warned his reader that "they have brought all their high-souled feelings with them."[101] He suggested to New Englanders that they handle the situation by rehabilitating them to the right way of behaving. He advised a hypothetical educated young man from the East to "mingle freely and unsuspiciously with his neighbors and while he sinks his manners to their level, strive to bring up their habits, by a successful example, to the New England standard."[102] Such arrogance could hardly have escaped notice.

Ebenezer Welch, a young man who left Maine to settle just north of Hancock County, fits the description of the arrogant New England settler. In a letter to his brother in 1841, Welch noted the strangeness of the southern culture that surrounded him. He gave his brother a sample "Western sentence," then translated words such as "slew" (stream), "glut" (wedge), "reckon" (guess), and complained that the word "heap" was overused as a degree of comparison. He disparaged the marriage customs of southern settlers as abrupt and raucous, made fun of women who rode on horseback with men, and considered their diet of bacon, cornbread, and mush beneath the manners of the Yankees. He could not understand how they could be content to live in a one-room log house. Welch even criticized their work habits: "Their greatest desire seems to be to live easy. In their work they are slovenish, & care but little about improvements."[103] There were fundamental differences of understanding between northerners and southerners regarding the use of land and how to live.

These differences led to conflict in Fountain Green Township. In the spring of 1835, Jabez Beebe made a formal complaint against a group of a dozen men, all farmers who were southern settlers in the township. Beebe charged that "they had made threats to use violence against his person & property." The men were required to post a bond of security totaling $700 and to appear before the September term of the court. We do not know the precise cause of the attack, but the offenders may well have been jumping Beebe's claim to land in the southern region of the township. The outcome of the judgment is also unknown, but Beebe's charge carried enough weight to result in the order to post bail.

Jabez Beebe continually experienced difficulties with others in the community, which was attributed to Yankee arrogance. Unlike the southerners, Beebe was a latecomer to Crooked Creek; but in his five years' residence there, feelings of animosity had developed. The blame may have rested with Beebe, since his eulogy remembers him as "a man of very decided convictions, firm and unyielding in his opinions, and outspoken in his intercourse with his neighbors." The incident in 1835 was not the only one in his long tenure in the county, and some chalked it up to his origins: "Being a Yankee withal, he became obnoxious to a portion of the settlers composing the Southern element around him—a circumstance which led to some difficulties and violence." The southern settlers were not only irritated by Beebe's cantankerous personality but were perhaps protesting the invasion of the johnny-come-lately settlers who were attempting to control local affairs.[104] Conflicts such as this one demonstrate the importance of regional identity in the settlement period, with its tensions that occasionally flared into incidents like this one.

Pioneer Churches

If disputes over land claims and clashes of regional identity divided rural community, building churches brought them together. The township's two prominent churches, Catholic and Presbyterian, were rooted in regional cultures brought from the South and East. The brief interval between settlement and church construction testifies to the importance of a church to the community of farm families. The establishment of both churches required the settlers to sacrifice money, goods, and time to procure clergy and construct a meeting place; their sacrifice strengthened communal bonds.

The first church in the community was founded in 1832 by the Catholic settlers from Kentucky. When they built St. Simon the Apostle Church on Section 34, they upheld a frontier church-building tradition. Constructing the church took the better part of the decade, slowed by lack of finished wood.[105] In the meantime, an itinerant priest celebrated mass in the Hardy family home. Father St. Cyr, the founder of St. Simon the Apostle, ministered to the communicants at Fountain Green in 1837 and 1838 before he transferred to Kaskaskia, Illinois.[106] Near the church a cemetery provided the final resting place for the clans of southern settlers.

The church of St. Simon the Apostle demonstrated the success of the migration of Catholic families from Kentucky to Illinois. Because the Catholic colony numbered some thirty families, the missions attentively served the Fountain Green group. Births, deaths, and marriages demanded the sanctification of priestly ritual, even if the surroundings were primitive. Keenly aware that if they were to pass on their faith to their children, the settlers' churches had to be established on the frontier.

The Scots-Irish Presbyterians from Pennsylvania founded the other major church in the township in November 1840. "It was a most solemn time," wrote Martha McConnell, "Oh, it was both solemn new and interesting to me and a time that will not soon be forgotten."[107] The founding members of the church presented their letters of admission brought from Pennsylvania. The names are common to Path Valley and southwestern New York—Geddes, McConnell, Glass, Leal, Foy, and McClaughry. The establishment of the Fountain Green Presbyterian Church by Pennsylvania emigrants represented a colonization of their religious culture.[108]

Presbyterians and Congregationalists from New York and New England joined in the church-building effort of the Pennsylvanian Scots-Irish. Unlike the exclusive Catholic church, the Presbyterian church attracted members from all community groups, including southern settlers from Tennessee and Kentucky whose ancestors were Pennsylvanian Scots-Irish. Adults either presented letters of admission from their former church, or were "examined on [their] knowledge of religion and experimental piety" to be received as members.[109] Young people were also examined before admission. The itinerant minister baptized babies and small children as they swelled the population of Fountain Green.[110] Like the Catholics along Crooked Creek, the Presbyterians felt it was important to raise their children in the faith of their fathers.

In the space of fifteen years, three groups had come to settle on the timbered prairie of Crooked Creek, where they transplanted cultural habits and ideals to a new environment. Southerners spread their families out on the land, established a corn-and-hog economy, and took up the duties of local government. The settlers from New York and New England founded the town of Fountain Green, where they established stores and opened shops to create a commercial and social center for the rural community. The Scots-Irish from Pennsylvania cultivated wheat together, traded in the river market, and founded a church that fused regional cultures. They began to intertwine distinctive strands of regional identities, creating a new local farm culture in western Illinois.

This process was typical of the mosaic of settlement in the early nineteenth-century Midwest. Not only New Englanders and southerners but also settlers from the mid-Atlantic region helped determine the shape of the community, the terms of market engagement, and the relations between settlement groups. Those settlers eagerly participated in the market, yet maintained their commitment to an independent family farm operation. They were agrarian capitalists, ready to take advantage of the market to earn profits to invest in more land for their children. Unlike the southern yeomen, many of whom were less aggressive in their approach to the market, and unlike the profit-minded New England craftsmen for whom farming was a sideline to trade, the mid-Atlantic farmers looked to the market with their hands firmly on the plow.

But just as the first phase of frontier settlement ended, the community-building process was interrupted by the introduction of a new religion into the neighborhood of Crooked Creek. It came neither by migration nor by birth, but by conversion to the preaching of missionaries migrating from Ohio to Missouri. The area's founding settler, Ute Perkins, was the first to be baptized. Within a decade, the turmoil that resulted would cleave the Crooked Creek community in two.

2

Conflict in the Countryside
Removing the Mormons

Sometime in the spring of 1839, Ute Perkins was baptized a member of what was called the Mormon church. The old man's immersion in the chilly waters of Crooked Creek set in motion a chain of events that irrevocably altered the shape of community in Fountain Green. Perkins's baptism was a harbinger of the immigration of Mormons, who numbered nearly 600 in the township before they were expelled in 1846. The presence of Mormons brought the rural farming community into the maelstrom of the Mormon conflict in Hancock County, which ended only after vigilante attacks removed the Mormons.[1]

What happened in Fountain Green is important not only because it highlights the rural dimension of a puzzling conflict of the Jacksonian age but also for what it reveals about the rural commitment to Jeffersonian republicanism. Despite differences of regional identity, the farming community was united by fundamental agrarian values: the right to own private property, to trade in a free market, to participate in local self-government, and to exercise patriarchal control over the family. Private property ownership allowed a man to be independent—to vote for whom he pleased, to keep trespassers off his land, and to freely trade his produce at market. Local government upheld and enforced the observation of these communal values by maintaining courts to adjudicate disputes, punish thieves, and build roads and bridges.[2]

On every front the Mormons trespassed the values which were the bedrock of the Fountain Green community. Mormons voted the way their leaders told them to, held property in common, created a separate economy, and practiced polygamy, a clear affront to agrarian patriarchy.[3] Like many others drawn to utopian alternatives in the capitalist chaos of the market revolution, Mormons felt threatened by the tides of change and saw Mormonism as safe harbor in a storm. As the Mormons moved from Ohio to Missouri to Illinois in an attempt to establish an earthly kingdom of God, the search for security extended beyond doctrine to political and economic monopoly.[4]

To the farm families of Fountain Green, the behavior of the Mormons pushed the boundaries of religious toleration beyond the limit. It was not religious intolerance per se, but the way Mormons fused religious persuasion and political behavior that offended the established settlers. Ultimately, the common bonds with the Mormons—of family, friendship, and commerce—snapped when faced with the heightening hostilities. The competition between the Mormons and the self-proclaimed "old citizens" (early settlers) of Hancock County for political power, property, and trade ended in a tragic conflict that cast a long, dark shadow over the rural community.

While few midwestern frontier communities became embroiled in as violent a conflict as this one, this episode is a mirror in which we can see the reflections of midwestern culture in the making. The settlement process—migration, taking land, making farms, building towns—allowed all comers unrestricted access to the region, but the Mormon conflict illustrates the limits to diversity in the early Midwest. The frontier period culminated in a winnowing of those who did not fit into the larger community. Those who did not share agrarian values and its way of life moved on or, in the case of the Mormons, were forcibly removed. Initially divided by diverse regional identities, the community came together to enforce the communal will. When their efforts to regain the upper hand in the political arena proved fruitless, they resorted to vigilantism to remove the Mormons.

Because the winnowing process in Hancock County occurred at a crucial moment in America's market revolution, we can see the conflict as a "growing pain" in an increasingly individualistic, competitive, industrializing era. The Mormon conflict illuminates the way in which older republican ideals were superseded by a society characterized by liberal individualism, religious pluralism, and market capitalism. The resolution of the struggle for power would prove critical to the transformation of Fountain Green at mid-century, spurred by its engagement into an expanding national market system.

A New Church along Crooked Creek

Fountain Green's involvement in the Mormon conflict began with Perkins's baptism by Joel Hills Johnson. Johnson was typical of Mormonism's early converts, most of whom were farmers or artisans of modest means from New England or New York, where the church had its beginnings.[5] Born in Grafton, Massachusetts, in 1802, Johnson was the first of sixteen children. His parents, Julia Hills and Ezekiel Johnson, migrated from Royalton, Massachusetts, to Hardin County, Vermont, in 1806, and then to Pomfret, Chatauqua County, New York in 1814.[6] Like so many New England families who migrated to New York's western frontier, they were seeking land for their children. Ezekiel turned to drink; his son later blamed his intemperance on the exhausting labor of carving a farm out of the wilderness.[7]

Julia Johnson, Joel's mother, was religious and made sure her children attended weekly Sunday School. The children learned to read from the Bible and were inculcated with the Calvinist ideas of salvation and damnation prevalent in that day.[8] As he grew to manhood, Joel became distraught over the subject of his own religious condition. By the time he was 16 years old, he would "sit up late at night to read religious tracts and papers by fire light, for my father, being poor, could spare me no time to read by daylight." He found solace in reading the Bible, and felt convinced that he would some day possess "the faith that was once delivered to the Saints."[9] In 1826, Joel married Anna Johnson and continued to work at his trade of shingle cutter. They moved to Lorain County, Ohio, where two Mormon elders preached the gospel and baptized him and his brother Benjamin in June 1831. The following October he met the charismatic Joseph Smith, and "heard the words of life from his mouth which filled my heart with joy and thanks to God."[10]

Like Joel Johnson, Joseph Smith had experienced an adolescent religious awakening. The Smith family lived on a farm near Palmyra, New York, but even with several grown sons, it was difficult for the family to make payments on their farm. Like Joel, Joseph had grown up reading the Bible at the knee of his mother, Lucy Mack Smith. She attended the Methodist church, but Joseph, confronted by the religious revivals in his neighborhood, was confused about which church to join. He was a boy of 14 in 1820 when he retired to the woods near the farm to ask God which church he should join. As told in his later accounts, his prayerful supplication was rewarded by the appearance of God the Father and Jesus Christ in a vision, who told him to join no church. Indeed, the heavenly being informed Joseph that "all their creeds were an abomination in His sight."[11]

By 1830, Smith claimed to have translated engravings on metal plates delivered to him by an angel, records of a record of a lost civilization in ancient America. The translated record was called the *Book of Mormon,* after the ancient prophet who abridged the writings. Smith founded his own church on April 6, 1830, at a meeting of a small group of about thirty converts in a member's home in Fayette, New York.[12] The Latter-day Saints, as they eventually called themselves, moved to Kirtland, Ohio, in February 1831, where early convert Sidney Rigdon had converted a group of 100 Campbellites to the new faith. Missionaries spread into nearby Pennsylvania and as far away as Maine to bear witness to a church restored by God in the latter days.[13] Joel Johnson made a missionary journey to New York in 1832, and his mother and several siblings, including his brother Benjamin Franklin Johnson, joined the new church.[14]

By the summer of 1835 the Mormon community in Kirtland numbered over 1,500 people who constructed homes and built a temple for worship and instruction in ancient languages and new rituals.[15] Joel and Anna Johnson moved to Kirtland, where he built a sawmill to cut lumber for the temple. Joel's father had not converted, and hearing of opportunity in Chicago, he headed west. The rest of the Johnsons joined Joel in Kirtland.[16]

In 1833, a small group of Mormons journeyed overland to Jackson County, Missouri, which Smith had designated as the site of Christ's millennial return. They were driven out of the county by violent means, and settlers in nearby Clay County helped Mormon leaders find an unsettled area northward where they could live.[17] The difficulties of sharing property communally and the failure of a church bank led Joseph Smith to abandon Kirtland in March 1838 for Missouri. In an act of privation and panic, 5,000 of his adherents followed him west that summer.[18] The Mormons' stay in Missouri would be brief. It was marked by acrimonious relations with local settlers, who were angered by Mormon bloc voting and disputes over property. Relations were complicated by Mormon looters called Danites who justified their actions by the claim that they were God's chosen people, entitled to the earth and its fruits. It was in Missouri that the Danites were organized, a secret fraternity that executed acts of revenge upon those who destroyed Mormon property.[19]

Johnson had not gone on to Missouri from Ohio with the main body of the church because he was entrusted with the care of those too ill to make the journey. He spent the winter of 1838–1839 in Springfield, Illinois, along the route west, presiding over a detachment of the sick. As he recalled in his memoirs, in early January 1840 "the Lord showed me by revelation that I must immediately go to Carthage in Hancock County."[20] Johnson commenced preaching in the area and "rooted out much of the prejudice existing in the minds of the people in reference to the difficulties at Far West [Missouri] and gained many warm friends to the Saints in and about the vicinity of Carthage."[21] The old citizens of Hancock were well aware of the troubles the church had experienced in Missouri, and Johnson had to work to convince them the Mormons had not deserved such harsh treatment.

Among those he convinced were the Perkins family. Ute and his wife Sarah were in their seventies when they joined the church, along with their sons Absalom and William G. Perkins, their married daughters Elizabeth Welch and Nancy Vance, and grandsons Ute, Jr., and Andrew. Andrew was the son of Ute's son Reuben, who had been converted in Missouri but who stayed in Missouri because he owned slaves.[22] Johnson organized the embryonic group of Mormons into the Crooked Creek Branch on April 17, 1839.[23] In late June, Joseph Smith visited the Perkins home, and the next day he spoke "with considerable liberty to a large congregation."[24]

In February 1840, missionary Joel Johnson moved his family from Carthage to the west branch of Crooked Creek, where he had purchased a sawmill on a piece of land. He immediately started preaching and within a month baptized about twenty persons with the help of two other men, bringing the size of the Crooked Creek Branch of the church to fifty persons.[25] The Perkins and Johnson families were the backbone of the branch.[26]

In July 1840, Ute Perkins, two of his sons, and a local farmer sold 285 acres of land to the church to establish the town of Ramus (Latin for branch).[27] Old citizen William Donoho and Mormon William Perkins surveyed the town into twenty-four blocks of four lots each.[28] Johnson promoted the expanding town in a letter to the Nauvoo *Times and Seasons* in November 1840, declaring that it was "in the midst of a beautiful and fertile country" and that the soil was "rich and productive." Lots in town could be purchased on "very reasonable terms." Johnson noted that already "quite a number of buildings, mechanical shops &c., have been erected, and many more in progress." Saw and grist mills were situated nearby, and more sites were available on the many streams. The location was also handy for Mormons migrating to Illinois from the east, because it was just fifty miles west of Beardstown on the road from Springfield to Nauvoo. Johnson's letter must have drawn a positive response, because the following February nine more blocks were added to Ramus.[29]

The old citizens must have been astounded at the sudden influx of Mormons into Fountain Green Township. By the summer of 1840, fifty-two Mormon households, or about 300 persons, roughly doubled the population of the township. By the spring of 1842, between 500 and 600 Mormons, about eighty families, had settled just a few miles away from Fountain Green.[30] The fifty inhabitants of Fountain Green were vastly outnumbered by the large number of new residents in the township.[31]

In March 1843 the state issued a charter that renamed Ramus as Macedonia.[32] A seven-member board of trustees assumed responsibility for keeping the streets clean, licensing taverns, and keeping the peace. The town was large enough to be divided into four wards, and the trustees appointed officers such as constable, assessor, collector, and treasurer.[33] Plans were made to build a grandiose Macedonian Religious and Literary Seminary. It was to have been a two-story brick edifice located on the south side of the public square, paid for with $1,000 of Mormon church funds.[34] A visitor to Macedonia in the summer of 1843 spoke with glowing praise of the small agricultural town.

> The buildings, yards, barns, etc. seemed well constructed and tastefully arranged. Macedonia is surrounded by numerous mills and good farming lands. . . . The place seemed much unlike any in my knowledge. Mechanics of most kinds seemed plenty and busily employed. Every house seemed occupied. A beautiful square lay near the centre of town, on which we were informed a house for literary and religious purposes was to be erected.[35]

In many ways the two towns, Fountain Green and Macedonia, were more alike than different. Macedonia was predominantly an agricultural community, with its town businesses servicing the local farm economy. Many of the Mormons practiced trades, and Macedonia had its share of millers, blacksmiths, tailors, and shopkeepers.[36] Presumably, many Mormons settled there on farms, but because land titles were held through the church corporation there is scant record of land ownership in county records.[37] The differences between the Mormons and their neighbors lay not so much in how they farmed, but in how they organized their society. The Macedonians had set up a typical agrarian economic structure of a village surrounded by farms locked in a network of mutual obligations.

Economic ties flourished between the two towns, and the Mormon trade was initially welcomed in Fountain Green. The Mormons of Macedonia made frequent purchases at the general store of Hopkins & Tyler, from whiskey and salt by the men to yard goods and buttons by the women. Like the people of Fountain Green, they occasionally paid off their accounts with cash or brought in domestic products such as woven cloth. Ute Perkins visited four or five times a month, maybe to pass the time with old friends. Ute's grandson, Andrew H. Perkins, stopped by occasionally for some tobacco, along with Mormon lawyer Almon W. Babbitt, missionary Mathias Cowley, and Scotsman James Fife.[38]

The extent of these accounts with Mormons shows that many Mormons shopped regularly in Fountain Green and that the proprietors were willing to trust them with long-term credit. They were good customers and made a significant contribution to the prosperity of the firm. Beyond the obviously healthy relationship with the proprietors, one can only speculate about encounters between the Mormons and the store's other customers. We cannot know if the commercial relationships went beyond mere pleasantries, but clearly a measure of cordiality existed that allowed Mormons to mingle with the residents of Fountain Green at the country store.

Similarly, whether they were Mormon or not, farmers went about their work in much the same way. The inventory of Francis Beckstead, who died in the spring of 1842, portrays what may have been a typical Mormon farm household. Beckstead owned a modest amount of livestock, with two steers, three heifers, a bull, and several head of sheep. He left behind a horse and mare, complete with saddle and bridle. Typical of the corn-hog agricultural economy, he owned about a dozen hogs. The quantity of corn, oats, potatoes, and wool show a productive year. His wife, Catherine, probably cared for the half-dozen geese, eighteen chickens, and five cows with their new calves. Catherine spun wool into yarn, and Francis hunted wild game to supplement the family diet. Household furniture and farm equipment, including a wagon, harrow, and plow, brought the estate's value to $322. The value of the estate was offset by debts, probably incurred to set up the farm. Beckstead owed $34.50 worth of notes to fellow church members and $40 to storekeepers in Warsaw. Beckstead's farm household reflects how most Mormon farmers made a living, which was probably not much different from how their non-Mormon neighbors farmed nearby.[39]

Perhaps most important, kin ties connected the old settlers to the Mormons. Although most of the Macedonia Mormons joined the church in Ohio and migrated from Missouri, a few local settlers were converted when the Mormons came. One would expect that the southern neighborhood would have initially accepted the church because of the influence of Ute Perkins in that community. But it is somewhat surprising to note also the conversion of several of the Catholic families who made their homes in this neighborhood.[40] The conversion of the Perkinses and the location of Macedonia suggests that the southern-born were more attracted to the Mormon church than the northern-born in the township. However, those who joined the Mormons came from all three migrant groups to the area, southerners, New Yorkers, and Pennsylvanians.[41] So many of the Crooked Creek settlers, Mormons and non-Mormons alike, were from western New York that it is not surprising that some family relationships existed.[42]

Despite the economic and kin ties, religious differences made the old settlers suspicious of the Mormons. Martha McConnell, who wrote a letter to her aunt in Pennsylvania in 1840, recounted her recent visit to Macedonia to help sew burial clothing for the young child of her Mormon uncle. Although the family did not mention their religion to her, she wrote "how strange I felt to be surrounded by such people."[43] She felt threatened:

> Not one could I speak my mind to at such a time. I never was more rejoiced than when I saw Alex [her brother] coming for me as I was really afraid of them beginning their Mormon ceremony. I could not have seen them laying hands on the little boy, praying for him when he was at rest, and kept quiet.[44]

She remarked that Mormons believed in baptism for the dead, and misunderstanding the doctrine, she seemed afraid that they would perform "their Mormon ceremony" on the helpless dead child whose body she would have felt compelled to protect.[45] McConnell's letter displays a fear of Mormons, even of her Mormon kin. She was suspicious of their doctrine and disapproved of it. For McConnell, kin ties could not bridge the gap opened by religion. While there was cooperation among family members and aid in time of need, fear blocked understanding or respect.

As the Mormons rapidly settled Fountain Green Township, broke land for farms, and founded a town, they were motivated by a shared religious commitment. While the Fountain Green community was built on rural trade, local self-government, and religious pluralism, in Macedonia the Mormon church emphatically dominated all aspects of settlement and commerce. This dominance was patterned after the unity of local government, land distribution, and church organization in Nauvoo, where the headquarters of the church was located on the Mississippi River north of Warsaw.

Nauvoo

In spring 1839, the same time that Joel Johnson was baptizing the Perkinses, Mormons fleeing the persecutions in Missouri established Nauvoo at a landing at the head of the lower rapids of the Mississippi River.[46] Under the leadership of church president and prophet Joseph Smith, the Mormons swelled the population of the county from a little over 3,200 in 1835 to 9,600 in 1840.[47] By 1845 the population had more than doubled to 22,559 to become the most thickly populated county in the Military Tract.[48] Nauvoo's population alone was said to be close to 11,000 in 1845, dwarfing Warsaw's mere 472.[49] With the Mormons in outlying rural settlements, they made up more than half the population of the county. As the hub of a wheel of settlements that radiated outward into the countryside, Nauvoo was a religious, economic, and legal center for the Mormons in Hancock County.[50]

As a religious center, the city of Nauvoo was extremely successful. It became a central gathering place for converts who missionaries baptized in the eastern United States, in the South, and in England. But historian Robert Flanders has argued that Nauvoo failed to achieve its founders' visions of commercial development. First, it was handicapped by its location just above the lower rapids of the Mississippi, cut off from effective trade with the lower Mississippi Valley. Warsaw, just below the rapids, continued to be the major river port for the county. Second, there was not enough farmland to support more than a subsistence for the huge number of converts who streamed into the city. They situated on small plots of land in town where they could grow a small garden and maybe keep a cow, and some people cultivated farm land outside the city.

Finally, many of the converts, especially those from England, were not suited to farming but were accustomed to working in the mills and factories of Manchester or Liverpool. While church leaders launched several schemes for the industrial development of Nauvoo (including a joint stock company and an ambitious plan to divert river water to a canal running through town for power), they lacked sufficient capital. Partly in order to supply employment to the desperate, church leaders funneled resources into a public works project of building a temple for worship. Thus the Nauvoo economy remained largely preindustrial, a collection of small shops and trades that could not employ all of the city's population.[51]

The old settlers' misgivings about Mormon communal approaches to the economy were exacerbated by the church's central control of land. While in most midwestern frontier towns the immigration of new settlers was enough to propel robust economic growth, immigrants to Nauvoo were frequently so destitute that they brought few assets to the developing city. Church leaders had to resort to mortgaging church land to borrow cash for development. Because the church members donated land to the church which held it in trust, the church enjoyed a monopoly on land sales. Outsiders criticized the church for charging poor converts inflated prices for land when they arrived. Some were persuaded to trade title to their land in the East directly for land in Nauvoo, a practice which the old citizens considered a "swindle."[52] The centralized nature of the church's transactions in land directly contradicted the old citizens' strong commitment to independent land ownership.

Nauvoo's role as a legal center for the Mormons clearly challenged the agrarian value upholding the power of local government in Hancock County. Criticisms of Nauvoo mounted after the state legislature granted the city a charter in December 1840 with unusually broad powers.[53] Like other charters, Nauvoo was granted the right to organize its own militia, but few cities had a militia as large as the one in Nauvoo. The Nauvoo Legion numbered several thousand men, its officers resplendent in colorful uniforms and shining scabbards. The charter allowed the city government (which consisted of a mayor, city council, and aldermen) to enact laws that were not "repugnant" to the state or federal constitutions. However, because Smith and other church leaders filled the major city offices (Smith was mayor and chief justice), outsiders objected to the failure to separate church and state in Nauvoo.[54]

The sharpest criticism was aimed at the charter's provision allowing it to operate its own court system, specifically the provision granting the city power to issue writs of habeas corpus. In practical terms, the provision allowed Mormons to try offenders captured outside the city in Nauvoo's courts. It also protected Mormons from outside prosecution, thereby creating an island of legal safety in Nauvoo. The county's long-time citizens accused Mormons of putting themselves above the law through frequent resort to the habeas corpus privilege.[55]

Political Resistance to Mormon Control

Only a few years after the Mormons arrived, the old citizens of the county organized to defend their republican ideals of local self-government against what they viewed as Mormon tyranny. Resistance to the Mormon political and economic power in Hancock County was centered in Warsaw, the Mississippi River port and home to the county's only non-Mormon newspaper, the *Warsaw Signal*. Its editor, Democrat Thomas C. Sharp, led the charge against the Mormons in the pages of the paper, wielding it as a powerful tool not only to express views against the Mormons but also to issue calls to action to counter their dominance. His rhetoric echoed his party's fear of political power's threat to liberty and drew upon a heritage of republican ideals calculated to strike a chord within the primarily agrarian county.

Sharp's first target was the Mormon habit of bloc voting, which, because of their greater numbers, allowed them to take control of the county government. The Mormons gained their reputation for bloc voting in the 1840 election, when they switched their traditionally Democratic loyalties to the minority Whigs. At a time of fierce party loyalty in America, the Mormons thus helped the Whigs maintain their control of Hancock County. At the same time, Democrats sponsored legislation for the Nauvoo charter, and new congressman Stephen A. Douglas courted the Mormon vote. They returned to Democratic allegiance in 1842, when they voted for Democrat Thomas Ford for governor in response to accusations of polygamy in Whig papers.[56] And in 1843, despite the Whigs' assistance in defying an order extraditing Joseph Smith to appear on charges of the murder of Missouri governor Liliburn W. Boggs, the Mormons voted overwhelmingly for the Democrats.[57]

The polygamy scandal intensified anti-Mormon feelings in the county. Confidence man John C. Bennett had been one of Joseph Smith's inner circle, but as he defected from the Mormon camp, he accused Smith of having multiple wives. The leaders in Nauvoo denied the charges, but historical evidence now confirms that church leaders were indeed secretly practicing polygamy, including prominent men in Macedonia.[58] Almera Johnson, Joel Johnson's sister, became a plural wife of Joseph Smith in spring 1843 at the urging of her brother Benjamin, a close friend of Smith's. The *Warsaw Signal* reported the accusations and used them as evidence for its portrayal of Smith as a debauched drunk who had duped his followers.[59] Because polygamy was so well concealed, we do not know how seriously the old citizens took the charges, but they added to the suspicion of the Mormons.[60] The practice of polygamy was a strong affront to the patriarchal values of the farming community, which subscribed to notions of virtue and fidelity in the domestic sphere.

In an attempt to counter the Mormon majority, in 1841 local Democrats and Whigs set aside party differences to form what they called the Anti-Mormon Party. Despite their unlikely political coalition, they still lacked the numbers to defeat the Mormon bloc vote.[61] Citizens of the county were outraged by Smith's manipulation of the Mormon vote and saw it as an attack on white male suffrage, newly expanded in the age of Andrew Jackson's common man. In 1842 Thomas Sharp of the *Warsaw Signal* editorialized that Hancock County's old citizens were "totally deprived of one of the dearest rights of Freemen—the Elective Franchise." He argued that the Mormons had made them essentially "political slaves."[62] Protestant missionary Milton Kimball agreed that because of bloc voting, Mormons were a threat to political liberties: "Nauvoo is a city of slaves, exiled in the most despotic manner by their *apostolical* chiefs. . . . They acknowledge no law but the revelations of their prophets."[63] He saw Mormon men as having lost their manhood, arguing that "under Mormon government a *manly independence* is an *unpardonable crime.*"[64] Because Mormons held the majority of the votes, political power eluded the grasp of the original settlers. Although they still possessed the right to vote, as a minority the old settlers were effectively shut out of the county's political structure.

The old citizens recognized that the Mormon majority would allow them to control the county business. Presbyterian missionary William King reported that Mormons were "rallying from every point to this county for the purpose of carrying the elections, and then getting all the publick business of the county into their hands."[65] As King predicted, the Mormons did control county business, in particular spending public funds to build more roads to serve the expanding Mormon population. The number of road districts more than doubled from sixteen in 1833 to thirty-nine in 1844.[66] The county authorized new roads and road improvements from Nauvoo to Warsaw and Carthage and between Nauvoo and other Mormon settlements such as Macedonia. Because of Mormon control, they decided where the roads should be built, and farmers who did not live near Mormon settlements were out of luck in bringing roads to their part of the county. Hampered in carrying their produce to market, farmers were angered by the diversion of road-building to Mormon areas.

Furthermore, the county commissioners awarded the lucrative road-building contracts to Mormons, not the old settlers. In September 1844, the county awarded a contract worth $898 to Macedonia Mormon J. M. Benson to build a bridge over Crooked Creek between Carthage and Macomb. Most other contracts for bridges were for $100 or $150, and large contracts were awarded for improving the river road extending southward and northward out of Nauvoo.[67] It is difficult to know whether or not Mormons were actually being awarded more road contracts than others, but the large disbursements to Mormons and Mormon sympathizers were galling to the old settlers. Mormon control of the road construction and the patronage associated with it was seen as pork barrel politics at its worst.[68]

The old citizens claimed that Mormon control amounted to tyranny which robbed them of their own liberties. Missionary Kimball complained that "since they [the Mormons] have seised upon all the county offices we are exposed to every species of misrule and oppression."[69] Kimball spoke for many when he voiced his feelings that he was being oppressed and tyrannized. Frustrated by fruitless attempts to counter the Mormons' legitimate political control, the old citizens went outside the law to reclaim what they saw as rightfully theirs.

Rural Vigilantism

The murder of Mormon leader Joseph Smith in June 1844 was to have been the blow that ousted the Mormons, but instead it set off a chain of violent events that shook the entire countryside surrounding Warsaw and Nauvoo. In the end, it was not the murder of Smith but rural vigilantism which forced the Mormons out. While historians have concluded that the mob of men who murdered Smith represented only the most aggressive of the Anti-Mormons, by the time the Mormons agreed to leave in October 1845, the entire countryside had been aroused to action. The general populace joined in the efforts to remove the Mormons out of a fear for the safety of their property, fears which were fed by a carefully orchestrated campaign of anti-Mormon publicity in the pages of the *Warsaw Signal*. Because of the Mormons at Macedonia, Fountain Green was integrally involved in conflict.

To fully understand how events escalated into armed attack, we must return to the days leading up to the murder of Joseph Smith and his brother in June 1844. On June 7, dissenters in Nauvoo from the Mormon church published a newspaper, the *Expositor*, which charged that Smith was practicing polygamy. Under the direction of Mayor Joseph Smith and ordered by the city council, the printing press was completely destroyed. The county's old citizens immediately met in Carthage on June 13 to draft resolutions in response to the destruction of the press. Three men from Fountain Green were active in carrying out the purposes of the meeting, among them storekeeper Stephen H. Tyler, who helped staff the Central Corresponding Committee. Expecting violence, the men at the meeting designated places of encampment in the countryside "to arm and equip ourselves."[70]

In an attempt to forestall violence, Mormon leaders appointed delegates to travel to each precinct, "to lay a true statement of facts" before the public.[71] Meanwhile, the Macedonia companies of the Nauvoo Legion were called in to defend Nauvoo. Benjamin Johnson remembered that "to avoid attack [the men] traveled all night across the prairie through mud, rain and darkness, terrible to those who were there." Because of the heavy rains, they had to make their way across twenty miles of prairie "half a leg deep in water."[72]

Once the men of Macedonia reached Nauvoo at daybreak, they told a harrowing tale of being attacked by a mob on their way out of Macedonia. As Joseph Smith later retold it: "The company from Macedonia opened fire about ten feet apart and marched past them within rifle shot, while the mob fired several guns at them, the balls whizzing past their heads." Smith laid out his military strategy to the rural Mormons; retreat to Nauvoo if attacked by a superior force, "but never give up your arms, but die first." The men from

Macedonia rested a few days before they were sent back to Macedonia to keep up a home guard.[73]

In nearby Fountain Green, Martha McConnell Walker described in a letter written on June 18 how the local populace wanted the governor to give orders to arrest Smith:

> And if he don't give them leave they are determined to take the law into their own hands and bring them justice or clear them out which would be better. And now the drums are beating on every side, guns firing and Alan and brother A. have just left this day with provisions ammunition and all for Carthage. They are to try which, them or the Mormons are the strongest.[74]

Martha was left alone, "sitting here with my babe in my lap, and not a creature only a Mormon family nearer than a mile." She was leaving soon for her parents' home in town, where some men were on guard. "I think we are not safe as the Mormons in Ramus [Macedonia] have refused to go and may do some mischief."[75] Martha felt vulnerable with the Mormon enemies nearby.

Anti-Mormon agitators had long wanted to take Smith into custody; the destruction of the *Expositor* press provided them with that opportunity. On June 24, Joseph and his brother Hyrum Smith were arrested on charges of riot and incarcerated in the county jail at Carthage.[76] Illinois governor Thomas Ford called in the militia to maintain order in Hancock County. Seventeen hundred men from the militias of Hancock and neighboring counties encamped around the county seat at Carthage.[77] The men from Fountain Green were commanded by Thomas Geddes, who later claimed that Ford said he would stand aside to let forces in the county drive out the Mormons. When Ford disbanded the militia at about five o'clock in the afternoon on Saturday, June 27, Geddes led his men home to Fountain Green. The governor left for Nauvoo with a small guard company, ostensibly to persuade the Mormons to surrender their arms.[78]

Late that afternoon a mob of men with blackened faces surrounded the county jail where the Smiths were being held. The Carthage Grays were left to guard the jail, but it was understood that "they were guards that did not guard."[79] The guards quickly gave way to the onrushing crowd of men from the Warsaw Militia, who stormed upstairs to the chamber where the Smiths and two companions attempted to defend themselves with a pistol Smith had smuggled into the jail. A warning shot pierced the door, which the mob forced open just as Joseph Smith leaped out the window. Shots from below instantly killed him, and his body fell to the ground, where it was propped up against a well. His brother Hyrum was also murdered in the attack, but their companions escaped death by hiding under the bed.[80] Because they feared Mormon retaliation for the murders, the residents of Carthage hastily left town.[81]

When the Mormons in Macedonia learned of the assassination of the

Smiths, Scottish immigrant Robert Crookston remembered: "The people wept aloud. One could hear their sobs and crying from every quarter. They felt as though the hosts of hell were let loose to do their murderers work of extermination."[82] While the Mormons in Macedonia mourned, the residents of Fountain Green prepared to defend themselves from expected Mormon revenge. Martha Walker's interrupted letter picks up again on July 1 with her reaction to the deaths of the Mormon leaders.

> You will hear of the death of the prophet and his brother before this reaches you. Much as I thought before that he ought to be killed, when it was done I felt that it was wrong, at least, the time and manner it was done appeared barbarous. Our men were discharged that evening but were not home till they were killed. They were shot at five o'clock. . . . The word come to the Green. None went to bed that night. There they lay on the floor on their guns. Our men loaded theirs and set them in reach. You may guess there was two eyes unclosed that night.[83]

Martha assured her aunt they were prepared to defend themselves with "a cannon in the Green and ammunition plenty."[84] Her words convey the suspense and terror of the situation, the sleepless nights, the hazards of living so close to the Mormons at Macedonia. In the letter Martha also reveals her support of mob action to murder the Smiths, despite her misgivings that it "appeared barbarous." Such moral equivocation led the forces opposing the Mormons outside the law to retaliate. Once held politically hostage, residents now feared that their lives were in danger from their Mormon neighbors two miles away in Macedonia.

Because of intervention by state authorities and Mormon church leaders, such hostilities were avoided. In the aftermath of the murders Martha felt "calm and resigned to the will of an all-wise Providence. He will order all for the best."[85] Several weeks after the assassination, Gov. Thomas Ford cautioned county residents that although Mormons in Macedonia and another rural settlement had been warned to leave, they had "a right to remain and enjoy their property."[86]

The trial of the accused murderers of Joseph Smith in May 1845 is further proof of the alienation of the old citizens from the Mormons. By refusing to convict the accused murderers of the Smiths, the old citizens of Hancock County expressed their approval of the murders.[87] The foreman of the jury was Jabez Beebe, early settler who had founded the town of Fountain Green.[88] In the space of just fifteen years, from the time Beebe and Ute Perkins settled the township, the turn of events had caused a fissure between the two communities along Crooked Creek. When old Ute Perkins died in April, social ties between the two towns snapped.[89] Now Ute's sons and grandsons were in the Mormon camp, opposing Beebe and the others from Fountain Green.[90]

Removal

Having failed to dislodge the Mormons by killing Smith, the leaders of the anti-Mormon movement began to depict Mormons as a threat to property. Their campaign publicized crimes of property allegedly committed by Mormons, featured against the backdrop of a decline in property values because investors avoided the area in the wake of the Mormon troubles. Carthage minister Benjamin Gallop lamented, "All our business is in trade. Money is verry scarce since the troubles with the Mormans property has falen two thirds below par and we fear may remain so for some time."[91] It was also a time of financial difficulty throughout the state, which was suffering from a statewide depression and laboring under the burden of the debt from expansive internal improvement schemes.[92] Both the crime wave and the decline in property values threatened private property, the foundation of a man's political independence and the means of earning a livelihood from farming.

The final campaign against the Mormons focused attention on economic problems at Nauvoo. Indeed, with the continuing stream of indigent immigrants, conditions at Nauvoo were worsening. Missionary Kimball wrote that it was common knowledge in the county that "Nauvoo is now a place of much suffering an improvident multitude collected into a place of very little business. Their little money soon spent, they already find it very difficult to find the necessaries of life."[93] Kimball thought many of the Mormons were ready to leave "that wretched place where they have found neither the freedom of speech, of the press, nor a plenty of bread."[94] The problem was acute in the spring of 1845, worsened by the poor fall harvest in 1844 because of the rainy weather and flooding.[95] In February there were reports of destitution:

> The great mass of the population of the city is in a state bordering on starvation. There is no business going on, and no means of obtaining subsistence only by charitable donations from the richer classes. Subscriptions are passing thro' the city for the relief of the poor, & every day baskets are carried around to collect provisions for the starving."[96]

In order to keep the city's economy afloat, church leaders focused their energies on building the massive Nauvoo temple. Thomas Sharp, editor of the *Warsaw Signal,* alleged in September 1844 that the construction of the Nauvoo temple provided the only source of support to the citizens of Nauvoo. The death of Joseph Smith had scared off new investors, who were waiting to see how the city would recover from the death of its leader. Rumor had it that property had fallen to about one-third of its value in the city—sellers hoping to leave outnumbered buyers.[97]

By soliciting donations and constructing the temple, church leaders in

Nauvoo attempted to relieve the distress of the poor and revitalize the local economy, but the size of the problem led them to seek assistance from the county. In 1844 the Mormon majority elected two Mormons, George Coulson of LaHarpe and Andrew H. Perkins, and a Mormon sympathizer, John T. Barnett of Nauvoo.[98] The Mormon county commissioners freely reimbursed the Mormon bishops who brought expense claims to the court. In March 1845, Mormons were paid $141.25 by the commissioners, while three other poor districts asked for a total of only $46.23. In May the Carthage poor relief amounted to $62.38, but those in Nauvoo collected $205.28 from the Mormon commissioners. In June another $72.50 was disbursed to relieve the poor in Nauvoo.[99] While on a per capita basis the demands for Nauvoo's large number of poor may not have been disproportionate, outcries against the Mormons intensified in response to the expense of poor relief for the growing numbers of destitute Mormons.

It was in this context of a struggling local economy that the *Warsaw Signal* alleged that Mormons had turned to thievery to support themselves. It is impossible to know if the "crime wave" was as extensive as editor Thomas Sharp said or even if the thieves were indeed Mormon. However, we can be certain that a widespread perception of Mormons as criminals did exist, and that the allegations of crime convinced heretofore reluctant bystanders to join in the efforts to remove the Mormons from the county. Nauvoo's separate court system came under attack as providing cover for Mormon thieves to escape the rightful punishment of the county courts.

The *Warsaw Signal* urged county precincts to collect the facts on thieving for transmission to a central committee. By late January 1845, the newspaper was running lists several columns wide listing Mormon thefts, precinct by precinct. Farmers reported that Mormons were stealing fine horses, corn, and even beehives and carrying stolen property into the safety of Nauvoo, where they were impossible to prosecute in the separate Nauvoo court system.[100] Most of the alleged thieving activity took place around the cities of Nauvoo and Warsaw on the western side of the county, but at least one Fountain Green farmer claimed to have livestock stolen by Mormons.[101]

Because the lists of items allegedly stolen by Mormons dated back to 1839, the claims show that Mormons and old citizens at one time had trusted each other enough to allow each other into their homes, but that trust had evaporated. One farmer reported that he had a new axe stolen from his wagon while he was warming at a Mormon's house in 1840. Another killed a deer near a Mormon's house. He went home for his wagon and the deer was taken in his absence. A Mormon lodger reportedly stole a vest in 1844, valued at $4. An inflated claim accused a Mormon of robbing a cupboard of bread, pies, and butter worth $4 at a time when land was going for $5 an acre.[102]

In addition to the criminal assault on property, the *Warsaw Signal* charged that Mormons were passing counterfeit specie. Local farmers who had once profited from selling grain to the Mormons at Nauvoo complained now that they were paid the worthless currency of Nauvoo's deteriorating economy.[103] Warning against trading with the Mormons, the paper reported that "not less than a dozen farmers who have taken their pork to Nauvoo have been paid in spurious coin or counterfeit bills."[104] It is unclear whether the currency was intentionally passed as counterfeit or was simply local scrip worthless to outsiders. But it is obvious that the Mormons in Nauvoo were short of both cash and goods to trade for farm produce. The farmers felt they were stung both by selling produce to Mormons and by being victims of Mormon theft.

Sharp's newspaper campaign exposing Mormon theft was very convincing. In rural St. Mary's, Thomas Holt wrote to his family that "there is such a stir in this section of cuntry that we gentiles as the mormons call us that we can scarce make out to live for they steal all that honest farmers makes."[105] Missionaries and ministers of other religions were most disturbed at the effect of the Mormons on their own proselytizing efforts. Milton Kimball, who had moved to Augusta in Hancock County, wrote that "the frequent outrages, thefts, and robberies committed by the Mormons and the constant exposure to injury from a piratical society who hold all the civil offices of the county at their disposal, keeps up a constant irritation most unfavorable to the interests of religion." He condemned the Mormons in the language of a religious crusade: "Their prophets and apostles are infidels and their following malignant fanatics, thieves, robbers, & assassins."[106] Minister B. A. Gallop of Carthage complained about the Mormons, saying that "stealing horses Chattles Beehives &etc is the common order amongst them."[107]

Given the hostile feelings toward them, we cannot take the accusations against the Mormons at face value.[108] However, the accusations were not a total fabrication, because at least several cases of Mormon theft seem well documented. Under the headline, "Another Mormon Rogue Caught," Zeno wrote a letter to the *Warsaw Signal* about Charles Chrisman, "one of the most influential Mormons of Macedonia," who was caught stealing in Morgan County. The sheriffs there had noticed that iron bars and the spikes that held them to the rails were disappearing, endangering the passengers on the railroad. On a tip authorities pursued Chrisman to his home in Macedonia, where the authorities found the perpetrator at home. They also discovered the iron bars and "about a peck of spikes" on his land in Macedonia. According to the reports, Chrisman, a blacksmith, had been filching the iron to make farm tools to sell in his neighborhood.[109] In 1843, Chrisman and Abraham Lincoln of Fountain Green had together surveyed a road from Macedonia to Nauvoo, and just a year earlier Chrisman and Jabez Beebe had viewed a road from Fountain Green to Macedonia.[110] The trust and cooperation that may have once characterized the relations of Mormons to old citizens had evaporated in accusations of the crime wave.[111]

The Mormons were particularly vulnerable to charges of theft because some Mormons had justified thieving as their God-given right. The bulk of the church had been in Missouri when the militaristic attitude of expropriation developed among many members of the Church, not just the self-proclaimed group called Danites.[112] Despite the official position of the church against stealing, in November 1841 four Mormons in Macedonia were accused of stealing and were jailed in nearby Henderson County. Mormon leaders quickly expelled the accused from the church and issued epistles that condemned stealing and disowned any Mormons who were guilty of such crimes.[113] They also repudiated any notion that the church approved of stealing, although Danite activity suggests that such repudiation may have been only for the sake of public appearance.[114] Because the habeas corpus provisions of the Nauvoo Charter allowed Mormons to escape the prosecution of local justice of the peace and county courts, the church appeared to be harboring the criminals in Nauvoo. Victims of theft felt they had no recourse but to publicize their losses in the *Warsaw Signal*.

Reports of the alleged crimes led many to renew efforts to remove the Mormons, by vigilante force if necessary. By December 1844, the local citizens were organizing vigilante groups in rural precincts to combat the crime. Farmers in Augusta formed a Mutual Protection Society and designated eight riders to pursue thieves when notified.[115] Those who met in Carthage in January 1845 were warned that if they did not act, "We will be driven to the humiliating necessity of quitting our homes and the place of our adoption, and seek a country where we may not have our hard earnings filched from us by the midnight marauder, and ourselves and families left without subsistence, and that too, without the possibility of redress.[116]

While earlier objections to Mormons had been made in the name of defending free trade and the rights of citizenship, only when the old citizens felt their property was at stake did they form a broader coalition to remove the Mormons. In response to charges that the campaign against the Mormons was only of Whig design, leading county Democrats declared that "party considerations have had nothing to do with the actions of the old citizens." Instead, they argued that the widespread opposition to the Mormons was simply "the necessary defence of their own constitutional rights . . . without which opposition and defence, the people of Hancock would be unworthy the name of American citizens."[117] The signers of the statement couched their protest in the language of republicanism, justifying their actions as defending rights of citizenship granted to them by the Constitution. The old citizens feared that the Mormons held entirely too much power, and they felt that such power subjected them to an oppressive tyranny.

By joining together as Whigs and Democrats, the eleven signers from Fountain Green Township also bridged differences in regional identities, north and south. Early resistance to Mormons by Fountain Green Township residents had been led by Democrat Stephen H. Tyler from Connecticut, and Whig Thomas Geddes of Pennsylvania, who represented Fountain Green on the Correspondence Committee.[118] This 1845 declaration was the first public statement by old settlers from Kentucky and Tennessee, many of whom owned farms adjacent to Macedonia. When they felt their property was threatened by the nearby Mormons, they overcame initial reluctance to resist the Mormons.[119]

By 1845, Hancock County citizens were living in a state of fear and suspense. The bonds of trust that allowed rural people to live in peace had dissolved. Old citizens felt the Mormons could not be trusted and set up an apparatus of vigilance and protection. Ultimately, they felt so endangered that they were willing to violate their own ideals, destroying the property of others to defend their own.

Conflict in the Countryside

The Mormons won the August 1845 elections handily; nearly 2,000 Mormons voted in Nauvoo alone. The Anti-Mormons did not even try to oppose the Mormon slate.[120] Shut out of political power and economically threatened by the overwhelming numbers of Mormons, in 1845 Anti-Mormon forces again employed illegal strategies to reclaim the county. Nauvoo, with its size and well-trained militia, was clearly impregnable. So the Anti-Mormons turned on the small isolated Mormon villages that were half a day's ride from Nauvoo.

The attack started near Green Plains, southeast of Warsaw, the Anti-Mormon stronghold. While the local citizens were holding an Anti-Mormon meeting at the schoolhouse on September 9, 1845, they heard shots outside. They presumed the shots to be an attack on them, and in retaliation they set fire to the cabins of Mormons at Morley's Settlement nearby. Before they were finished, the whole village lay in ashes, over 100 houses. Although the inhabitants of the cabins were warned out first, the destruction was still devastating. The Anti-Mormons had come upon a winning strategy, because the rural Mormon towns were vulnerable to attack in a way that Nauvoo was not. They later would come to regret the attack, which cost them the sympathy of the public outside the county.[121]

Frightened by the burning of Morley's Settlement, inhabitants of Macedonia in Fountain Green Township prepared to defend themselves. British immigrant Thomas Callister remembered that first the men met "to consult what was best to be done for the mob was burning houses in the other branches turning sick women and child out to doors in a most shameful manner."[122] They decided to post a guard at night and infiltrate Anti-Mormon meetings nearby.[123] Mormon leader Brigham Young advised them "to give them the cold lead, or obey the sheriffs counsel" if they were disturbed by mobs. He directed them to evacuate if necessary, but planned to "sustain you where you are."[124]

The fatal shooting of Anti-Mormon Franklin Worrell of the Carthage Grays (militia) by Mormon-elected Sheriff Jacob Backenstos on September 16 sparked a renewal of violence against the Mormons.[125] The *Warsaw Signal* announced the murder of Worrell with a blazing headline, "Call to arms!" The story warned, "There is no longer peace for Hancock. Blood will and must flow if necessary to rid the county of the cursed authors of our troubles."[126] Sharp's extremist threats show how far the old citizens would go in defending their values, although their actions violated their own ideals.

The men of Fountain Green rallied to Sharp's call to arms. On September 20, Callister infiltrated a gathering at Fountain Green. "I whent and fount about 50 men Arnold . . . Maclery . . . swerying he would drive the Mormons out with some difficulty I got home unhurt."[127] Two days later, Mormon Bishop William G. Perkins reported to Brigham Young that there was "some little stir about our borders and the mob are training today at Fountain Green . . . and we are informed that this night is set apart and appointed for the burning of this place." Perkins hastily penned a request to Brigham Young for fifty to one hundred troops to arrive by evening. By midnight the next night the posse arrived from Nauvoo, fewer than half the amount requested.[128] Not until Ford appointed Illinois militia general John J. Hardin to take military control of the area did the violence end.[129] Despite some anxious moments and some saber-rattling, no one had attacked Macedonia.

However, damage to Morley's settlement was extensive. Estimates vary, but before the hostilities ended, 150 to 200 cabins had been burned and several men had been killed.[130] Thomas Sharp, editor of the influential *Warsaw Signal*, justified the attacks on the countryside as "opposition to tyranny" in an extra edition quickly printed up as a broadside to be posted around the county. His vituperative language is worth quoting at length:

> We had been robbed of our property times without number; many of our citizens had been grossly abused and insulted; the lives of some of the most estimable men in our community have been threatened, for no crime other than opposition to tyranny; our political rights have been so taken from us; we could get no justice in the courts of our own county.[131]

Drawing upon the language of republicanism, Sharp justified the actions of the cabin-burners as a defense of the property and political rights of the old settlers who were denied justice in their own courts. Depicting the old citizens as robbed, abused, insulted, and threatened, he spoke for those who saw violent action as the only means to preserve their political rights. The Mormons' refusal to evacuate left them no choice but to burn them out: "The little band of men who commenced the work, . . . finding it impossible effectually to drive the Mormons without destroying their dwellings, gave them time to remove their furniture and then committed their worthless cabins to the flames." Sharp's characterization of Mormon homes as "worthless cabins" was a rhetorical ploy calculated to diminish the true scale of the attack.[132]

It became obvious by late September that decisive action was required. Citizens from several nearby counties converged in Carthage on October 1 to demand Mormon removal. Brigham Young, warned by Congressman Stephen A. Douglas and General John J. Hardin that the Mormons could no longer be protected because of the popular feeling against them, pledged to leave. At the same time, state leaders warned the vigilantes that further aggression would mean "the sympathy of the public may be forfeited," and condemned the house-burnings as "criminal" and "disgraceful."[133] Committees were appointed in the outlying settlements to prepare for removal for an unspecified western location; among their members was Andrew H. Perkins, formerly of Macedonia.[134]

Before the year was out, much of the Mormon property in the outlying areas of the county had been sold, including land in Fountain Green Township. The buyers in Fountain Green who bought Mormon land at bargain prices were the same men who had played a part in the drama of the conflict: Jabez Beebe, foreman of the jury that acquitted the accused murderers of the Smiths, Col. Thomas Geddes of the Illinois militia, and southern-born farmers who in May 1845 publicly declared their opposition to the Mormon presence.[135]

The bulk of the membership of the Mormon church began crossing the Mississippi River in early February 1846 on their way to the Rocky Mountains. During the spring most of the Mormons packed up and moved out of the county.[136] In mid-April 1846, Absalom and Nancy Perkins sold their town lots in Macedonia for $234. Mormon converts William and Margaret Miller deeded their land to church trustee Almon W. Babbitt for just one dollar, "in love and consideration for the church."[137] A few days later, in the *Hancock Eagle* printed by Mormon sympathizers in Nauvoo, Macedonia was described as "The Deserted Village":

> It owes its existence to that trait in the Mormon character, which enables them to concentrate their energies and form communities of their own. In a locality of this kind, they mingle but little with the world, and gain an humble subsistence by cultivating small tracts of land. Such were the people of Macedonia.[138]

In a certain sense, the *Hancock Eagle* was right. Although just a few miles from Fountain Green, the small town of Macedonia formed its own culture which was never interleaved with the Fountain Green community. Ties of kin and commerce did not prevent animosity, but they may have forestalled violence. Initially the inhabitants of the two communities in Fountain Green Township fought their battles on political turf, at the ballot box, and in county-wide organizations. When the citizens of Fountain Green began to feel that Mormon political control threatened their ideals and their property, they agitated for removal of the Mormons from the county.

The men from Fountain Green resisted the Mormons in a final act of violence—the Mormon War of October 1846, which removed the last and poorest of the Mormons. Robert McConnell, whose father Francis fought in the War of 1812, was detailed to take supplies to the troops at Nauvoo. Jary White, whose wife's parents were Mormon, fought in the war, and Col. Thomas Geddes was in charge of maintaining the peace after the skirmish ended.[139] Gov. Ford put an end to the disorder with his appearance in November, but he was mocked by the women of the county who presented the governor with a black silk petticoat as a symbol of their displeasure with his pacifism.[140] Further violence was condemned in the press, and the process of healing the wounds began before the year was out.

For the people of Fountain Green Township, the Mormon presence was an affront to their fundamental beliefs in a freely competitive market, local self-government, private property, and the patriarchal family. When they felt these beliefs were threatened, they set aside their differences to remove the Mormons. Town patriarchs from Pennsylvania and New York became leaders in the early partisan struggles in the political arena. Perhaps because they may have valued associations with their neighbors more than their own property interests, it was not until later that the southern-born in the township joined them, turning away from regional loyalties that bound them to Mormons from the South. Bonds of association were forged that transcended sectional tensions, but only time would show if the coalition was an uneasy alliance or a lasting partnership.

As 1847 began, Thomas Sharp, leader of the agitation against the Mormons in the press, suggested that all Mormon place-names be obliterated, thus erasing the painful events of the past. Referring to national condemnation of the old citizens' vigilantism, he acknowledged it would take years "before we expect to wipe out the black stain which they [Mormons] brought upon our fair escutcheon," but "we can at least remove all outward evidences of their career."[141] As was already done by practice if not by law, Macedonia began to be called Webster, presumably after the prominent Whig statesman. Thus purged of all references to Mormons, the empty town of Webster became habitable again, taking on a new identity as a trading center in the southern neighborhood of the township.

In early 1846, Macedonians moved en masse with the general Mormon exodus across Iowa. They retained their local church organization while in

Winter Quarters, Nebraska, then migrations to Utah dispersed the camp of Mormons from Macedonia.[142] In an ironic sequel, George Washington Johnson, who had left Macedonia when a young man of twenty-three, was called by Brigham Young in the summer of 1859 to pioneer on Uintah Springs in Sanpete County, Utah. Perhaps in hopes of recreating the verdant Illinois town of distant memory, he named his new settlement Fountain Green.[143]

PART II

3

"To keep the family together"
Family Farming in an Expanding Market

In mid-August 1844, Jary and Lucina White sat down with their son and put their affairs in order. The indenture they filed with the county clerk was a complicated agreement of filial responsibility. In exchange for 100 acres of land in Section 23 of Fountain Green Township and "all personal goods and chattels and chores in action," John made certain covenants that would ensure the support of his aging parents and their minor children. First, he agreed to pay his father's debts from any profits from the land. Second, he agreed to provide his parents with "a good and convenient dwelling house" and allow his father the use of the coopering shop and tools so he could continue his business. Furthermore, he agreed to "decently lodge and furnish decent food and raiment" for his parents and to supply them with "a good Horse & Buggy and Harness" and "two good milch cows" for their use. John White was additionally obligated to provide for his younger brother until he was twenty-one and his sister until she was eighteen, including a "common English education." When she reached the age of majority, he was to bequeath her "sixteen sheep or other property equal in value," and at her marriage he was to provide her as much property as her older sisters had received from their father. Perhaps the obligations were too weighty for John to assume. When his father died less than a year later, he quit his claims to the property rather than perform the covenants to which he had agreed.[1]

That the Whites made such a detailed agreement for their own welfare, witnessed and signed by local Justice John M. Ferris, did not mean that they did not trust their son to care for them. The agreement was a prudent course to follow to maintain harmonious relations between parents and children. Through written agreements, expectations were clearly defined to keep the land in the family and to strengthen the obligations of family members to each other. That John later chose to release himself from the covenants he had made with his parents is a signal that children were less willing to burden themselves with family responsibilities.

Few agreements such as this can be found in the county deed records. Much more common were agreements between parents and children that transferred assets in terms of dollars and acres, not cows, coopering shops, or furniture. By the end of the century, farmers even bequeathed their children portable assets in the form of stock or bank notes. At the core of the wills that documented the strength of family bonds were family labor and land—a corporate commitment to the farm as first and foremost an economic enterprise.

Historians have held varying views regarding the significance of family bonds in the unfolding of rural capitalism. Were farmers entrepreneurs who competed for profit in an atomistic market, or yeomen, agrarian patriarchs whose main concern was providing land for the lineal family?[2] The two categories of yeoman and entrepreneur are too crude to capture the patterns of landholding in Fountain Green, where the native-born held a range of attitudes toward the land and employed a variety of strategies to carry out their goals.[3] In Fountain Green, family labor and land bolstered the pursuit of wealth in the marketplace, and lineal family values assisted the development of agrarian capitalism. Reliant largely on their own labor, farm families retained traditional family ties to land through various strategies of estate distribution while they oriented production to the demands of the marketplace. Not easily classified as yeomen interested only in family land or as entrepreneurs hungry only for market profits, Fountain Green farmers were a blend of both.

Different approaches to land and labor resulted in part from different cultural values and farming practices carried from eastern origins and handed down through the family. Indeed, certain cultures were better poised than others to take advantage of the market expansion. Farm families who were the most skilled at investing and utilizing their resources stood a better chance at staying in the community beyond one generation. The resources of skill and wealth tended to follow family lines and thus enhanced the prospects of the regional group of which that family was a part. In Fountain Green, the most successful group were those from the mid-Atlantic states, especially the Pennsylvanian Scots-Irish. Their success strengthened their claim to Fountain Green and prepared them to settle subsequent generations on the land. The transformation of frontier farming into commercialized agriculture thus assisted the Scots-Irish in eventually impressing their own identity upon the character of community in Fountain Green.

The Risks and Rewards of Market-Oriented Agriculture

During this second stage of agrarian capitalism in Western Illinois, farm families struggled to maintain a measure of local autonomy within an expanding market system. Increasing engagement with the regional market system decreased local control and exposed farm households to the risks of market participation. Families altered cropping patterns and pursued innovative strategies of supplying labor and land to diminish the effects of that risk. Thus the turn toward the market was given impetus not only by population growth and changes in technology and transportation but also by a commitment to traditional goals of maintaining lineal family commitment to land.

The transition from safety-first production with a marketable surplus to production primarily for market was sudden and dramatic. The number of improved acres in the county nearly tripled from about 80,000 in 1850 to 212,000 a decade later. In the same decade, the total value of farms for the county increased five-fold from $1.4 million to $7.1 million due to rising land values and an increase in improved acreage in the county.[4] Population growth helped fuel the massive increase of agricultural productivity in western Illinois. The county's population, which had reached 25,000 in the mid-1840s with the Mormon influx, stood near 15,000 in 1850; but in the decade of the 1850s the county's population would more than double. A significant portion of that increase was due to the arrival of foreign-born immigrants, almost one-fifth of the county's population in 1860, anchored by the influx of Germans into the river port of Warsaw.[5]

A central factor in market engagement was the availability of rail transportation to Chicago. Until the opening of the Northern Cross Railroad from Quincy to Chicago in January 1856, farm produce from Fountain Green Township was generally hauled overland twenty miles to the Mississippi River port of Warsaw. The route of the Northern Cross Railroad lay nine miles southeast of Fountain Green, so Fountain Green farmers traveled only a short distance to the depots at Tennessee, Colchester, or Colmar (see Fig. 3.1). Whether they shipped their produce on the railroad or hauled it to Warsaw depended on the condition of the roads and the river and the difference in freight rates.[6]

As the land in Fountain Green Township was settled, farmers increased the productivity of their farms by clearing wooded farmland along the creek banks.[7] The average size of a farm did not change much over the decade of the 1850s (151 to 148 acres), but the number of improved acres (cleared land) increased from about 38 percent to 51 percent of the total farm acreage.[8] While some of the increased farm value was caused by the improvement of land through clearing and the construction of buildings, much of the rise in farm value can be attributed to rising land values. The value of farm land in the township (calculated as the farm value divided by the number of improved acres) more than doubled from $18.42 in 1849 to $41.95 in 1859 (Table 3.1).[9] The rise in land value during the 1850s is a sign of a growing population committed to the land in a rapidly expanding market.

Farmers invested in mechanical implements to increase grain production.

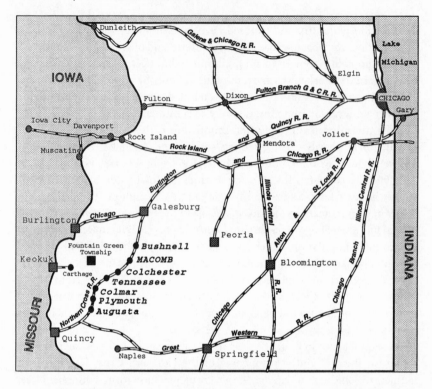

FIGURE 3.1. Railroads of Western Illinois, 1860. From *D. B. Cooke and Co.'s Great Western Railway Guide* (Chicago: D. B. Cooke & Co., 1856) and *Miniature Railway Map of the Great West* (Chicago: D. B. Cooke & Co., 1860).

The average value of implements per farm in Fountain Green rose 17 percent in the 1850s to $105.90 in 1859.[10] Farmers primarily used hand tools in the frontier period but added machines as they could afford them. For example, when James Walker's estate was inventoried in 1866, he owned two plows, two harrows, a double shovel plow, two corn plows, and a shovel plow. He also owned a fan mill worth $15, a corn planter worth $39.50, and a riding plow worth $61. The capstone of his inventory was a McCormick reaper. While Walker was more prosperous and older than other farmers, he was typical of wealthy farmers who relied on mechanized agricultural implements to expand production.[11]

Farmers discovered that volatile prices, vulnerability to bad weather, and disease were risks that made concentration on wheat production an uncertain proposition. European demand elevated prices and lured many farmers to concentrate on wheat production, but winter wheat was almost a total failure in 1857.[12] By fall, county farmers were holding back grain because of low prices caused by the Panic of 1857.[13] Farmers who had lost winter wheat sowed spring wheat to make up the difference, but by the beginning of June, spring wheat had become infested with weeds and farmers were advised to plow it under and plant corn.[14] The failure of the wheat harvest hit Fountain Green hard; farms there produced on average only half (70 bushels) the amount of wheat they had ten years previously.[15]

Farmers reacted in 1859 by pursuing the more cautious practice of diversifying—planting one-third more corn than they had previously.[16] County-wide, the corn output for 1859 was nearly a three-fold increase over 1849 output, from 689,110 to 2,056,177. In that year, Fountain Green's farmers harvested thirteen bushels of corn for every bushel of wheat, in contrast to the five bushels of corn for every bushel of wheat they had harvested in 1849 (see Table 3.2).[17] The increase in corn production in the 1850s was not accompanied by an increase in hog production; indeed the average number of swine per farm was only about 60 percent of totals a decade earlier (see Table 3.2).[18] However, some farmers began to specialize in raising cattle. With the advent of rail transportation, stock raising was transformed from merely a convenient way to market corn to part of a long-term production scheme. Once railroads penetrated the countryside, farmers could be more sensitive to market prices in deciding whether to ship their livestock to market or hold out for higher prices.[19]

Improved breeding and dissemination of scientific knowledge of farming also increased farm productivity. Every issue of the local newspaper carried a column with advice on farming, and many farmers subscribed to the Midwest's agricultural sheet, *The Prairie Farmer*.[20] In September 1855, the Hancock County Agricultural Society held its first fair, an important venue for sharing knowledge of breeds of stock and showing off one's own expertise in farming.[21] Fountain Green's progressive farmers were among those who organized and exhibited at the county agricultural fair. Perhaps the best showing for Fountain Green was at the 1860 fair, when James Curry took a prize for the best unspayed sow, Osee Tollman for the second-best stallion over three years old, William Lenix for the best colt, and Kendrick N. Leach for the best jackass.[22] While the farmers won prizes for their livestock and implements, the women of Fountain Green received accolades for their domestic products. Thomas Geddes's daughter Eveline won one dollar for the best cake and fifty cents for the best mold candles. Besides cakes and candles, women exhibited patchwork quilts (special prizes went to the best white quilt) and woven fabrics such as jeans. The prizes for the women's products, however, were worth a fraction of the prizes men earned, which ranged from two to ten dollars.[23]

All these developments—improved transportation, rising land values, mechanization, and better breeds of livestock—meant that operating a farm was a more expensive proposition at mid-century than in the frontier period. To finance the improvements, farmers went into debt. While they could finance machines through their manufacturers, farmers put up personal property, or chattel, as collateral to obtain loans for other improvements. For example, on October 18, 1859, Robert Glass, the oldest son of Samuel Glass, contracted a mortgage with his father for $375 for two years. Among the property he encumbered were two horses, a wagon and a buggy, four cows, and substantial shares of the forthcoming harvest of wheat, rye, and corn. In Fountain Green Township, thirty-three chattel mortgages were contracted from 1851 to 1865, with a peak in 1858 and 1859, presumably due to the Panic of 1857.[24] Without banks to turn to, relatives or prosperous neighbors were the source of the capital needed to maintain one's independent status as a farmer. However, the actual independence of the farm was threatened by the debt farmers assumed in the rush to market agriculture in the post-frontier period.

Farm families reduced expenses by clinging to subsistence habits, growing fruits, vegetables, and sorghum to supply their own needs. To reduce cash outlays for sugar, families grew sorghum for molasses, tended bees, or collected sap to make maple sugar. In 1860, nearly half the farms grew sorghum.[25] Several farms produced sorghum for the market; David Leach produced 900 gallons of molasses, and James Yager and Basil Wright produced 200 gallons each. Some who made molasses used it as credit on the accounts at the store of McClaughry & Tyler. Only a few farmers grew hops, and a small handful from the South grew a patch of tobacco for home use.[26]

Fruit orchards and a vegetable garden were the mainstay of a self-provisioning farm but could also augment earnings if sold on the local market. Samuel Jacob Wallace of Carthage, who always took first prize in the county fair for his sumptuous display of produce from his garden, recommended a garden of two or three acres. This would be ample for a family, but it could be enlarged by a few acres for market production.[27] By 1880 (the first time such data were collected), 60 percent of the farms in Fountain Green Township had orchards, most large enough to produce a generous marketable surplus.[28]

A small number of farms near towns specialized in growing fruits and vegetables to supply the local market for produce. Potatoes were commonly cultivated on individual farms for domestic use or for trade at the store, but others marketed them more widely.[29] In 1860, Fountain Green farmers Martin Yetter and Daniel Beebe tried to drum up business by bringing "mammoth" potatoes to the editor of the *Carthage Republican*—three of them nearly four pounds each![30] Yetter also brought in apples, proving to the newspaper editor that he was a "thrifty farmer, and among the most successful fruit growers in the county." The samples of produce brought into the newspaper editor were a shrewd way for local farmers to advertise their produce and make profits in the local market.[31]

Regional Cultures and Agricultural Production

While the main trend in agricultural production was a move away from wheat to a corn-and-hog economy, individual family farms took their own approaches to the market in this period of expansion. Culturally influenced patterns of production that had been evident earlier remained important for farmers from the three settlement groups: Yankees from New England and New York, mid-Atlantic farmers such as the Pennsylvanian Scots-Irish, and upland southerners.[32] We can add a fourth group, immigrant farmers from Canada, the British Isles, and Germany, who arrived in the late 1840s and 1850s.[33] Finally, the Illinois-born sons of the settlers constitute a fifth group which displayed distinctive patterns of production.

Farmers born in the mid-Atlantic states such as Pennsylvania continued to dominate agricultural production in the 1850s and remained the largest group in 1860, while the number of farmers born in the South decreased (Table 3.3). Midlands farmers were the richest farmers on average, with a gap of more than $400 between them and the next group in 1860. They displayed a commitment to market agriculture beyond any other group; they had more improved acreage and a greater investment in farm implements. Their larger households and extensive kin ties also provided a pool of labor in a period when hired labor was scarce and expensive.[34]

By 1860 the commitment of the Pennsylvania-born farmers to wheat may also have stemmed from an investment in machinery that they had to justify even as wheat cultivation became more risky because of disease and depleted soil. But the high demand for wheat in the 1850s meant that the farmers who were successful at cultivating wheat reaped higher profits than those who depended on only corn and hogs. Wheat produced the profits that allowed them to invest in implements and buy land for their offspring.

Southern-born farmers came in second in production to the mid-Atlantic group in 1850, but a decade later they had lost considerable ground. Although still second in improved acreage, production of corn and wheat, and stock value, they fell to third in amount of real estate owned, and fourth in value of implements and production of cattle.[35] They remained second in number of swine. During the same period, the number of southern-born farmers also decreased, from thirty-nine in 1859 to twenty-four in 1860, because of decreased immigration from the South and the deaths of the original southern-born settlers. In the 1850s, their strategy was not as successful as that of the wheat-oriented farmers originally from the mid-Atlantic region.[36]

Yankees traded places with the southern-born by 1860, rising to second in farm value, implement value, and value of real estate. But despite this advance in position of wealth, they remained third in production of grains and livestock.

They had all but abandoned wheat cultivation by 1860 in favor of corn.[37] The rapid Yankee switch to a corn-and-hog economy may indicate a greater sensitivity to market forces, unencumbered by a cultural commitment to growing wheat exhibited by farmers from the mid-Atlantic region.

The small size of the immigrant group makes it difficult to generalize about their patterns of agricultural production. Also, the figures are skewed by the wealth of the four Canadian-born sons of Scotsman William Bullock. The immigrants were the oldest of all the groups of farmers, and in 1860 they had the largest households. Fourth in farm value in 1850, they rose to second in 1860, partly by sticking to wheat even more assiduously than farmers from the mid-Atlantic states. They ran neck and neck with groups from the South and the North in per-farm production of corn by 1860, surpassing those born in Illinois.[38]

The Illinois-born, sons of the older farmers from the south, north, and middle states, climbed upward in the 1850s. They were much younger than the other farmers, so were less wealthy. Their households were smaller, so they had fewer children to provide farm labor. Compared to the other three native-born groups, they committed early to mechanization. In 1850 the value of implements was 14 percent of average total farm value for the Illinois-born, compared to 8 or 9 percent for the other groups of farmers. The Illinois-born led in number of cattle and cows in 1860 and were ahead of the northern-born in number of swine, but they would have to wait to displace the older farmers in terms of wealth and production values.

Did the women likewise vary in patterns of domestic production? No clear pattern of cultural influence emerges from an analysis of butter production, typically woman's domain (see Table 3.4). In 1849, farms owned by southern-born male farmers led production with an average of 163 pounds per farm. All groups increased butter production by 1860, led by the foreign-born and followed by farms owned by those from the north and middle states. By 1870, the leaders in butter production were the wives of the younger Illinois-born farmers whose butter-making helped provide the cash needed to buy machinery. Their position suggests that by 1880, age of the farm wife may have been more critical than region of origin in butter production. By 1880, the range of production was small, and the few farms owned by those from the South lagged behind the rest.[39]

While the farmers in Fountain Green followed the main road from subsistence plus surplus to producing mainly for market, cultural factors were critical to charting the path each farm took to market. Farming practices and market strategies, aspects of family behavior that displayed tendencies according to region of origin, may have been as important as technological forces in determining success. Over time, as farm families adopted local practices, these regional differences became less distinct. But in this post-frontier period, the differences in farming practices remained significant because patterns of production could determine market position. The propensity of those born in the middle states to farm wheat, combined with their wealth and the labor provided by their larger families, gave them an early advantage over other farmers in the township who were similarly groping their way toward profitable farm operation in a developing regional economy.

Family Labor: The Work of Women and Children

To compete within the developing capitalist marketplace farm families depended on the labor of all family members, even young children. The labor of the farm family was an investment in their future. For the children, the payoff could be a share of the family land or a bequest based on the capital of the family land. For parents, the labor they invested could mean financial security for old age and a home place on which to spend their waning years. For the farm wife, who did not own property or earn wages, the success of the farm meant maintenance for her lifetime and a legacy for her children. Individual interests were subordinated to the welfare of the farm, even if it meant placing the children in harm's way or making a widow dependent on her children for her support. Although it was unevenly rewarded, the work of all family members was vital to powering the move toward market engagement in the post-frontier phase of agrarian capitalism.

Women's labor was critical to the transformation of agrarian capitalism in rural Hancock County. Historian Jeanne Boydston has demonstrated the economic importance of women's unpaid housework to the process of industrialization in the nineteenth-century city.[40] Likewise, farm women's work was vital to the farm economy. In addition to housework and producing commodities for market, farm women were mothers, bearing and rearing children to carry on the farm.

The three-fold duties of the farm wife were intertwined in her roles of producer, wife, and mother. A farmer could not prosper without the housework a wife performed, nor could he father children without a wife as sexual partner. Rural people understood marriage as an ideal union of sexual attraction and shared commitment to the economic enterprise, as in this humorous anecdote:

> Matrimony is said to consist of hot buck-wheat cakes, warm beds, comfortable slippers, smoking coffee, round arms, red lips, etc., etc; shirts exulting in buttons, boot-jacks, redeemed happiness, etc; while single blessedness is made up of sheet-iron quilts, blue noses, frosty rooms, ice in the pitcher, unregenerated linen, heelless socks, coffee sweetened with icicles, gutta percha biscuits, flabby steaks, dull razors, corns, coughs and colics, gout, rheumatism, misery and unhappiness.[41]

Life without a woman to brew the coffee, wash the linens, and sew the buttons on one's shirts would be misery indeed. Farming would not pay if a man had to hire someone to fix the meals, milk the cows, and draw the chickens before stewing them for dinner. By marrying, the farmer gained not only a work partner but also a sexual partner who provided a warm bed, red lips, and, eventually, children.

Housework included obtaining, preparing, and preserving food for the family and hired help; providing and caring for family clothing; and furnishing and cleaning the house. This included the daily preparation of an early large breakfast, the hearty dinner at midday, and an evening supper. The foundation of these meals was food the farm woman had acquired or preserved. In the farmhouse cellar were bins of potatoes and carrots and rows of fruit preserved in glass canning jars that represented days of weeding, picking, culling, skinning, pitting, slicing, and stewing.[42] She raised the chickens and collected the eggs, then caught and beheaded the chickens for the meal. Cleaning and washing were arduous and time-consuming chores for the farm wife. Monday was laundry day, and the farm wife worked to meet ever more exacting standards of appearance, such as the stiff and shining shirt bosom which required hours of starching and ironing.[43]

The farm wife generally had control over the farmhouse and the activities within its walls. Although the native-born farmer and his wife worked on the same farmstead, their tasks were physically separated. He worked in the fields and in the barn; she worked in the house and in the garden. This practice has been most frequently noted in contrast to the behavior of immigrant women, who worked in the fields and milked the cows long after their native-born counterparts had given up that chore. It was a point of pride, even a badge of class distinction, among American farmers that their wives did not work in the field.[44] (The one time this separation may have been abridged was during deep winter, when men were underfoot in the house once they had fed the stock.[45]) This separation meant that each could work without interference from the other, giving each a measure of independence.

A second aspect of farm women's labor was the production and sale of domestic commodities which augmented household earnings. Once the frontier period had ended and cash became more widely available, farm women discontinued the time-consuming process of converting flax into linen and bought inexpensive yard goods at the country store.[46] In 1853, ten cents would buy either a yard of calico or a quart of whiskey.[47] Women nevertheless continued knitting garments from wool yarn from the farm's sheep herds. Most families kept at least a few sheep for this purpose, and certainly those farms that produced sheep for the marketing of wool also reserved some for home use. Given the climate and the scarcity of knitted items in the stores, it is probable that the women spent part of their time knitting socks and sweaters for the family wardrobe.[48]

Instead of weaving cloth, women found production of poultry and butter to be more remunerative. While small-scale dairying remained the norm, one-quarter of the farms were producing enough for market in 1850; a decade later, 72 percent of farm households produced a marketable surplus of butter.[49] Farm families brought eggs and butter to the store to trade for the items they could not produce themselves or could buy more cheaply. Stores in Carthage took in eggs as part of the "country produce" they accepted from farm families.[50] The local store in Fountain Green was willing to take butter or eggs in exchange for credit on account (Table 3.5). In the spring months of the late 1850s, farm women in Fountain Green were marketing an average of over forty dozen eggs and twenty-three pounds of butter weekly at the store.

Production trends demonstrate women's awareness of strategies for market involvement through specialization in readily salable commodities such as eggs and butter. Indeed, changes in women's production paralleled the farmer's shift to grain and livestock production. Both in the house and in the field, farm families embraced the market by intensifying production, yet through home production and diversification they maintained a measure of control.

Reproduction was a third dimension of women's work, sustaining the family farm system by bearing children to work the land and keep it in the family. Most women in Fountain Green married between the ages of 19 and 21, although over time women tended to marry at a slightly older age (Table 3.6). In 1850, married women produced an average of 3.6 children, a figure which includes only surviving children and not those who had died (Table 3.7). By 1860, younger women were bearing fewer children, as shown in the child/woman ratio, which fell dramatically from 1.6 to 1.3 in the 1850s (Table 3.8). The result was a shrinkage of the farm household, from an average of 5.9 to 5.3 persons by 1860.[51]

Because these figures reflect only living children, they obscure the true measure of reproductive work by farm women. Childbearing was fraught with danger for both mother and infant. Death records were not reliably kept in the county for this early period, so the best source of mortality information is cemetery headstones. Of the 329 burials before 1880 in Fountain Green Township cemeteries, 36 percent were of children under the age of 10. About one-fifth (21 percent) were of children under the age of 2. Wagonmaker Isaac Welch and his wife Achsah buried five children in the Webster cemetery, one of whom died at birth and three who died before their second birthdays.[52]

Fountain Green's Dr. Leonard T. Ferris attended the majority of childbirths in the township. Trained in St. Louis, Ferris opened his office in 1845 and practiced for the next fifty-five years.[53] However, even after he opened his practice, many women continued to prefer midwife-assisted childbirth. Grand-mother Lucy Alton from New York was midwife to her daughter-in-law Phoebe at the birth of her grandchildren Sarah, Ina, and Eva in 1850, 1852, and 1854.[54] Margaret Chamberlin was attended by her mother, Mary Groat, when Charles was born in 1851, but she switched to Dr. Ferris for the births of two children in 1857 and 1859. The shift from midwives to doctors may not have improved the treatment women received because puerperal fever, the leading cause of mater-nal mortality, was not understood by the medical community until the 1880s.[55]

The many childhood deaths prove the fragility of health even if a child sur-vived infancy. Accidents and childhood diseases such as measles and whoop-ing cough took a heavy toll. It was common to read reports in the newspapers of children being scalded or drowned after falling into buckets in the kitchens of their homes, as in this incident: "Mrs. Campbell was using a kettle of hot water in the kitchen for some purpose, and left it sitting on the floor. The little girl, which a moment before was sitting at a table eating, came running across the room and accidentally fell across the kettle, turning it over, scalding her breast and arms dreadfully." She "lingered in agony" for another week before dying on September 7, 1871. Her parents were "almost distracted by the sad calamity."[56] Mrs. Campbell may have blamed herself for her daughter's death, but she probably had no choice but to leave the heavy kettle full of hot water on the floor. Accidents in the home show how difficult it was for farm women to prepare meals, do laundry, and mind the children all at once.

Parents deeply grieved the deaths of their children. Emotional losses aside, each death was a loss of investment in future security for the farm couple. County histories are replete with legends of finding a lost child after days of combing the brush for the young one who did not return home.[57] (The loss of these children also suggests that they were not always carefully watched, but were allowed to roam without supervision or were under the supervision of an older sibling.) When 7-year-old Fred Hamilton died of whooping cough in 1867, the newspaper reported that "he was an unusually promising child and the idol to his parents. His loss leaves a vacant place around the hearthstone which can never be filled."[58]

As has been discussed, after the frontier era, farm wives bore fewer children, leading many families to seek alternatives to family labor. Households in Fountain Green decreased in size from nearly six persons in 1850 to nearly five persons in 1880 (see Table 3.8). While historians do not know the causes of the decrease in fertility, they suggest that as affordable land became scarce, families felt pressure to reduce the number of their offspring.[59] A less satisfactory explanation for the higher fertility among frontier populations is that hired help was difficult to obtain on the frontier, so farm families produced children to help on the farm.[60] Because of the time it took for a child to mature, it is more likely that families hired labor, purchased implements, or took in relatives to meet labor needs. However, only wealthy families could afford to hire help. In 1860, Frank Hadley worked as a hired farmer on the farm of John and Jennette Bullock, parents of seven children. Conrad and Celona Cratsenberg employed Mary Rogers, age 18, as a servant in their farm household.[61]

Most families met labor needs by expanding to include relatives and un-related persons. While about 60 percent of the households in Fountain Green Township were composed solely of persons in the nuclear family of husband, wife, and children, the remaining households included persons who were not members of the nuclear family. In 1850, 10 percent of the homes included other relatives, a figure that doubled to 18 percent in 1860. (The decade also saw a corresponding decrease in the numbers of non-relatives in the household, from 20 percent in 1850 to about 12 percent in 1860.) A ready supply of hard-working relatives provided a boost to farm families in the township.[62] Other relatives were often present because a widow or widower had combined a household with the household of one of their children. For example, in 1860 widow Sarah Andrews listed her occupation in the census as "farming"; she owned the farm, valued at $4,000. But her son, Timothy (age 24 years), was formally listed as "farmer," signifying that he was in charge of production. Timothy's wife also helped with the farm work while she took care of the couple's three small children.

At mid-century, a rising cohort of farmers' sons supplied labor for their family's farms, despite the fact they were not paid for their work.[63] The number of sons who claimed the occupational title of "farmer" increased dramatically from 38 to 64 in the 1850s, while the number of sons who identified themselves as "farm laborer" decreased from 23 to 12 (see Table 3.9). This may have re-flected a distinction between sons whose fathers were farming on rented land and those who owned their own farms. It also signified an intention of future independent farm ownership, evidence of rising expectations among sons of future farm ownership and among fathers who expected to provide land for sons. The number of male laborers who were not farmers' sons rose to meet part of the farm labor needs, from thirteen in 1850 to twenty-six in 1860. Farm laborers who were not sons were usually brothers or close relatives of the head of the household. Less frequently, they were fathers or presumably fathers-in-law who had given up active management of the farm to the next generation.

Farm families exploited the labor of their children to sustain the farm enterprise. The use of sons or boys in the labor force, while it presented a low-cost solution to farmers, could be extremely hazardous. County newspapers reported accidents which warned of the dangers of farming to children. In the harvest season of 1858, 14-year-old Stephen Bilbee of Carthage was mowing a meadow with a scythe in the evening. A friend the same age asked to try the scythe. In his inexperienced hands the scythe passed above the grass, swung around, and struck Bilbee in the abdomen. Bilbee fainted while attempting to walk home. Two doctors were called to replace the intestines in the gaping wound and to sew up the two-inch gash. Bilbee died of inflammation before dawn.[64] Even simple tasks such as plowing could present hazards. A decade later a more fortunate farm boy lost control of his mule team while plowing. The plow lines became tangled around his neck and he was "dragged some distance before he extricated himself." He escaped the incident with only bruises.[65] Unsupervised farm boys who wielded dangerous farm tools were more vulnerable to accidents as they went about their work.

As farm work became more mechanized, children were exposed to even greater dangers. In 1865 a 9-year-old boy had his arm crushed in the cogs of a sorghum mill, and a few years later the hand of an 8-year-old boy was "terribly crushed" as it was drawn into a corn-shelling machine. The local doctor had to amputate three fingers and part of his wrist.[66] Both boys escaped mortal injury but were maimed for the rest of their lives. Their handicaps would prevent them from assuming the roles and responsibilities required of an able-bodied adult farmer.

Even if some chores were not hazardous, farming was hard work. The remoteness of fields and meadows from the barn meant that boys were usually unsupervised when performing simple tasks such as plowing and mowing. Hamlin Garland, who wrote about his boyhood on an Iowa farm in the early 1870s, recalled spending entire days for months at a time alone behind a plow. "It was not a chore, it was a job. It meant moving to and fro hour after hour, day after day, with no one to talk to but the horses. It meant trudging eight or nine miles in the forenoon and as many more in the afternoon, with less than an hour off at noon."[67] The labor was arduous and incessant, and Garland had no choice but to do his father's bidding, because his father was busy with more complex farming enterprises. Boys had to be trusted to work alone at their farm tasks in order for the farm to succeed. And even if he did not have to work alone, the nature of the labor meant that the end of the day was a welcome relief. William Spangler, who in 1873 wrote from California to his boyhood friend in Fountain Green, recalled: "Oh! how it used to tickle my lazy bones when as a boy I used to pull corn and saw the end draw nigh."[68] Plowing the earth, planting grain, pulling corn, and shelling it—all these were arduous farm tasks which required the help of all male hands—boys and men.

Daughters of farmers appear to have enjoyed safer working conditions because their work took place largely within the home, which was not mechanized. When not in school their primary task was care of younger siblings. They also assisted their mothers by gathering eggs, churning butter, and preparing meals. Their acquisition of domestic skills such as cooking and sewing prepared them for a future position as the wife of a farmer.

Land: Buying and Keeping a Home Place

Independent landownership was the backbone of the family farm system, and land-holding practices tended to be patriarchal, with fathers passing land on to sons. However, sons of settlers found the acquisition of land more difficult than it had been for their fathers. In the face of a dwindling supply of cheap government land, families relied even more heavily on family ties to acquire land in this second stage of agricultural expansion. Knowledge of land was passed by word of mouth, and those closest to the seller had the best chance of obtaining the parcel. Few could buy land outright with no assistance from family members. Typical was Isaac Hobart, who bought a 100-acre farm from his father at his marriage in 1840. By the time he reached old age, Hobart held a total of 640 acres of farm land.[69] Hobart's purchase of family land at a critical point in the intergenerational cycle allowed him to set up his own household at marriage.

Most farm families of Fountain Green pursued strategies designed to pass on the homestead to the next generation. Inheritance practices, credit, and cooperative land purchase limited the free play of market forces, enabling many families to remain competitive within an expanding economic system. Insulated somewhat from the market, for many the family safety net enabled them to avoid mistakes that could jeopardize their hold on the land. In Fountain Green Township, family land-holding practices provided the security for long-term investment in farming, improved chances of success, and facilitated engagement in the wider capitalist market. Indeed, contrary to the image of the native-born "Yankee" speculator always on the move, family ties to land were vital to market success in Fountain Green.

Almost two-thirds of the farm families in Fountain Green were able to stay on the land (persist) for more than one generation (Table 3.10). While fewer than half the group of farmers survived from one agricultural census to the next, when sons or widows are classified as persisters, the persistence rates are higher (61 percent). Indeed, so strong was the commitment to a patrimony that aging farmers subdivided their land for heirs. Because of a commitment to the land, farm households were more likely to persist than non-farm households (Table 3.11).[70]

The patriarchal nature of the family farm meant that the father-son tie was crucial to retaining land in the family. Although thirty-three farmers in 1860 did not persist to 1880, those thirty-three men passed their land on to fifty-two heirs.[71] Even more astonishing is the accomplishment of a small group of farmers with multiple male heirs who were able to establish more than one son on the land. Two farmers were able to establish four sons each on the land, four farmers were each replaced by three sons, and at least four more were replaced by two sons each.[72] Those sons were much more likely to acquire land in the township than sons whose father was not already settled in Fountain Green.[73] At mid-century, tenancy rates were low, and most tenants were sons of farmers who earned their way up the agricultural ladder to farm ownership.[74]

Why were some families able to retain their land holdings while others failed? To identify the causes, I studied a sample of transfers of deeds for the farmsteads in the township.[75] The difference between those who persisted and those who were transient is one of degree, not of kind. The category of transients included many who had held land in the township for more than a decade. They can be regarded as transient only in comparison with those who persisted, and their land-holding practices offer abundant evidence to contrast with those who persisted. (Note that patronymic naming practices means that land which might have stayed in the family through a daughter's husband might be invisible using this method.)

The misfortune and mistakes of a transient farmer who failed to pass on land to his children provide a lesson, as with the disastrous case of Osee Tollman. Tollman had to mortgage his first land purchase of 140 acres in the township in 1845. Even then, he had to rely on his son to help him pay the $850 due in nine installments at the low interest rate of 3 percent. In 1853, Tollman mortgaged 100 acres of his land for $500, which enabled him to buy additional acreage adjacent to his farm from a widow in 1854. He may have bought the land for his two older sons in their twenties, or he may have been expanding to meet the needs of providing for his seven children. By 1857, in dire straits, he mortgaged all his parcels to a Chicago land agent for the sum of $3,200. He must have also borrowed money from a local moneylender, because in 1859 he took out an additional mortgage to secure his loan. By 1861, the amount he owed had swollen to $5,200, and his creditors became alarmed at the double liens he had contracted for some of his property. The land agent sued him for non-payment of his mortgage, and after he defaulted the county sold his property at auction. The land agent made the highest bid, $3,809.50, and was awarded the land after fifteen months had passed because Tollman had not redeemed the property by complying with the terms of the court-ordered settlement.

Tollman's land acquisitions were accomplished by taking out mortgages for six of the twelve transactions he completed. His goal may have been to provide land for his seven children, or he may simply offer a case of greed in a time of easy credit. His continued mortgage-taking may also have been a way to obtain land to continue farming. At any rate, his house of cards collapsed, and he lost all his investments in one fell swoop. Certainly the foreclosure proceedings must also have cost him his reputation in the community, since it deprived some of his fellow farmers of their investment. Significantly, not one of Tollman's mortgages was with a relative. All his efforts to acquire land were made without the assistance of family connections. His efforts to stay on the land by speculative investment left him ruined, with nothing to pass on to his children.[76]

In contrast, those who stayed on their land were usually aided by relatives. The transfer of land while the farmer was still alive, as in the case of Jary and Lucina White, allowed families the best chance of persisting. At least one-fifth of the land transactions sampled were among persons who were related, and the wills reveal that lifetime transfers of land were commonplace.[77] This strategy created several family-based syndicates of landholders in the township. By this means, families were able not only to preserve their land but also expand their holdings by acquiring enough for their children.

Alexander Walker, a settler in the 1830s from Pennsylvania, provides a good example of this strategy. In 1842, Walker bought 205 acres of land from his sister's husband, Thomas Geddes. Walker married Martha McConnell shortly afterward and settled on the land in Section 20. In April 1850, he expanded his holdings by purchasing 120 acres jointly with two of Martha's brothers. A year later Walker bought out the share of one brother-in-law, and at the death of the other in 1854, he purchased the remaining share from the estate to acquire clear title to the land. When Walker's father died in 1866, the three couples who were heirs to the 520 acres of land broke it into three large parcels. They then sold these parcels to each other at the appraised value. As eldest son, Alexander purchased the largest and most valuable share. At Alexander's death in 1883, his will provided for the same orderly transmission to his heirs. His youngest son inherited the 220-acre home farm in Section 20 (along with the farming equipment), and his married daughter and oldest son received the land he had inherited in 1866.[78] By keeping the land transactions within the larger family network through cooperative purchase and sale of land, and through the subdivision of that land through inheritance, the family was able to retain its hold upon the land.

Farmers who passed land to their children before death had greater control over the longevity of the enterprise. Retirement was certainly not automatic at a certain age, but it was common for men in their late sixties and early seventies to turn the burden of farming over to another—either a renter or a son.[79] Wealthy Yankee Kendrick Leach passed his farm intact to his son Silas, whose older brother had gone to Kansas to be a cattle drover. Kendrick's brother David lost two sons to the Civil War, and his remaining son, Jesse, took over management of the farm while David was "on the decline of life" in his early sixties.[80] Jesse plowed and planted while his father David tended hedge fences and kept records of the weather.[81]

Less typical in Fountain Green was a stem family arrangement, in which an older and a younger couple shared a farmstead. Kentucky Catholics Ivo and Ann Hardy, who in 1870 owned $14,000 of real estate, shared their farm with married son William, who owned $3,000 worth of land. The stem family arrangement not only supplied the labor of six adults to make the farm productive, it also provided for the orderly transmittal of the farm to the next generation. However, William's loyal labor may not have been rewarded in the anticipated manner. In his will, Ivo Hardy directed his son William to farm the home farm for as long as his mother lived, "to have and to hold for the support of his mother and no longer." At the death of the widow, the farm was to be sold and the proceeds divided equally among the eight children. In 1880, William would find himself renting over 300 acres of land.[82]

Inheritance was the most common tool families used to keep their hold on the land. The death of a farmer who had not provided for the succession of his heirs to his land could result in the family's loss of the land. Many things could go wrong. Failed succession usually resulted from debts being greater than the value of the estate, the inability of the administrators to partition the land, the lack of a clear successor to the land, encumbrances on the land, or a surfeit of heirs. The inheritance process was controlled by the patriarch, the male head of household who held title to the land and who wrote a will to direct its distribution at his death. The obligations created by his will helped perpetuate family bonds after his death.

Farmers who did not stipulate how the property should be distributed after their death ran the risks of the dispersal of the farm they had worked so hard to obtain and improve. The estates of farmers who died intestate, or without a will, were subject to division under the provisions of the law, which favored the devolution of assets to the children. The law required that the widow receive one-third of all real estate before the debts were paid (known as the dower right), which she enjoyed until her death or remarriage, at which point her dower right in the property would cease and the property would revert to the descendants of the will-maker. The other two-thirds of the estate were to be divided equally among the surviving children or their issue.[83] A will could subvert the law and provide a custom solution tailored to the wishes of the farmer and the needs of the farm family.

Without a will, conflict among family members could endanger the longevity of the farm, as in the case of the family of Stephen Yager, who died in 1838. Six years later his son Uriah was sued by the other survivors: the widow, her three minor children, two older children, and two married daughters (and their husbands). The plaintiffs petitioned the court to partition the estate because "the said premises cannot be occupied or enjoyed by the said complainants & defendant in any beneficial manner." Because the many members of the family could not peaceably farm the three large tracts of land (amounting to 340 acres), the court appointed three men from the area to partition the estate. The three reported back to the court that it was impossible to divide the land equitably into eight equal parts "without manifest prejudice" to the land or the parties. The case was resolved by selling the land at auction to two buyers, which netted $960 for the heirs. The widow and three minor children received just $360.[84] Because Stephen Yager died intestate, the family was deprived of a large and valuable parcel of land, and they did not stay in the township.

The primary object of the farmer's will was to balance the need to keep the farm together with the desire to provide a bequest for each child. This tension between what historian Toby Ditz has called "unity and provision" led the will-maker to devise a compromise structure of obligations that bound family members together after his death.[85] The tension between unity and provision mirrored the tension between a lineal family mentality and an ethic of individualism which called for children to be treated equally. A sample of 103 wills of decedents of Fountain Green and farmer decedents from three adjacent townships was studied for patterns of inheritance. The will-makers in rural Hancock County pursued one of three options: preferential, partible, or all to the widow. Habits of will-making did not significantly vary over time (see Table 3.12).

The largest share of will-makers, 42 percent, pursued a preferential strategy by bequeathing the real estate to one or several favored heirs. Under the provisions of a preferential will, the favored heirs (usually sons) were directed to compensate the other heirs with cash payments out of the portion of the estate they received. Preferential treatment of the heirs protected the estate from being split into farms too small to support the families of the next generation, while it worked to equalize the bequests given to all the heirs.[86] By pursuing a preferential strategy, farmers in Fountain Green balanced the need to keep the farmstead in the family with the belief that children should receive equal bequests.

A typical preferential will was the complicated bequest of Martin Yetter, written in 1873. In his will he listed all his parcels of real estate and specified how they were to be distributed to his children. He willed the home farm to his namesake, Martin, Jr., but Martin, Sr., held enough land that he was able to give land to each of his seven children, including his daughters. His farm equipment—reapers, mower, horse-powered grist mill, cane mill, blacksmith tools, and threshing machine—was to be shared by two of his sons.[87]

Will-makers who pursued this strategy, well aware that they would not be able to enforce the provisions of the will, usually wrote precise instructions to the heirs in the will. In his 1853 will, Samuel Spangler carefully instructed his four sons to pay bequests to their three sisters out of the farms he had willed them. In an 1868 codicil he added, "I do not wish any litigation or controversy over said conveyances or over said will or this codicil." His will warned his daughters that if they attempted to defeat or set aside any of his provisions, they would forfeit their bequest and the sons would stand released of their obligations.[88] One will-maker stipulated that liens be put on the property he gave to the favored heirs to force them to pay their obligations to the other heirs.[89] The legacy of obligations created by the patriarch of the family yoked the heirs together in sometimes uneasy combinations after his death.

The desire to equalize the treatment of heirs often resulted in larger bequests to younger children than to their older siblings, who had already received substantial gifts or help in acquiring land. For example, Alonzo Barnes excluded his "equally beloved" older children from the gift of real estate. Barnes gave the real estate only to the two younger children, explaining, "They be now of tender age and I know not that I shall ever be able to afford to them a sufficient opportunity to obtain an Education which will properly qualify them to be useful members of Society I have willed that they shall have all my real estate."[90]

Gender was as important as age in the treatment of heirs in the patriarchal family farm system. Sons tended to receive land and daughters cash bequests, so sons usually received more than daughters. However, in at least one case, the daughters received more because they were younger.[91] Although daughters usually received cash in lieu of land, it is clear that some daughters had received loans to finance previous land purchases.[92]

Most bequests conformed to the transfers that had already been made during the lifetime of the will-maker. Few were as specific as Benjamin Crabill, who listed the amounts of the unpaid loans he had made to his children.[93] Anthony Duffy gave one dollar each to two of his sons because he had already given them what he considered to be "their equal share of my estate." Perhaps to soften the blow, he gave them a five-year grace period on the debts they owed him, but they would have to pay to his executors annually the rate of seven percent interest on the loans.[94]

A second strategy, known as partible inheritance, was to divide the estate equally among the heirs, which eventually became the norm in America.[95] Thirty-six percent of farmers were willing to partition the estate in order to achieve a reasonably equal balance of bequests among the heirs. This strategy was often pursued by older decedents who had already made land transfers to their children. In this case, the practice of partibility was a threat neither to the estate nor to the livelihood of the children. Alternatively, farmers who divided equally had sufficient property or no apparent heirs who wanted to carry on the farm. John Brewer went to great lengths in his 1853 will to divide his property equally between his two grown children. His son Thomas and his married daughter Joanna McConnell were to split the farmstead on a north/south axis, including the house. Thomas was to have ownership of the west half of the house and the west eighty acres, and Joanna the east half of the house and the east eighty acres of the farmstead.[96]

The third option was to leave the entire estate to the widow for her to disburse as she pleased. This was a more generous alternative than the one-third dower right required by law. Farmers followed this practice if the couple was older and the children already married and established on farms or, conversely, if the decedent was young enough to have minor children for whom it was necessary to keep the estate whole until they reached adulthood. The one-fifth of will-makers who did not divide their estate left the entire estate to the surviving spouse.[97]

While we cannot know how much a farmer's wife took part in making the decisions about the distribution of property in a will, we do know that she had little legal claim beyond her dower right to the land. Even after married women's property rights were expanded in 1861 to allow them to retain the property they brought to the marriage, most women did not hold title to family land jointly with their husbands. The farm wife's signature as a grantor of property was required not because she held joint title but because of her dower right in the property the couple held. Her signature thus waived any claims she had to the property in question.[98]

So strong was the lineal family commitment to land that the widow's share in the estate was subjugated to the needs of the children. Women's assets were generally limited to lifetime use of the farm and items of apparel and household furnishings. Few women had land to bestow, because the dower right to property ended at their deaths.[99] Lucinda Hadley, who wrote her will in 1859, left her son Franklin hay and corn to keep his horses through the winter, a wagon and harness, two plows, two hogs, and the provisions. Her married daughters received cows and hogs. Finally, she wrote that her executor could decide what to do with her potatoes, which were still in the ground.[100] The bonds of obligation created by wills made the widow dependent on her children, usually her sons, for support after her husband had died. Widows usually received inheritances commensurate with the provisions of the law and not more.

The wills of widows demonstrate the paucity of property they bequeathed. Of the sample of 103 wills, seventeen were written by widows. Their assets were generally limited to personal property, which they distributed on the basis of who had cared for them. Women passed on household effects, such as the new red quilt and the star quilt that Emmeline Wright bequeathed to her son.[101] Catherine Yetter, who wrote her will in 1879 at the age of 65, left her brooch, shawl, jewelry, and "ornaments" to her granddaughter. She specifically stated that she was leaving nothing to certain heirs "for reasons to me satisfactory besides I consider that they have already had sufficient from me and my deceased husband."[102]

Just as she was dependent on her position as a wife for a claim on the land, a widowed farm woman remained dependent; her status was perpetuated by the will that made her children responsible for her care. The death of Jary White, who contracted the indenture with his son John, left the widow Lucina no choice but to move in with one of her children. The elder Whites no longer needed the coopering shop, the horse and buggy, and the milch cows; instead, Lucina would be absorbed in the household of one of her heirs. Like Lucina's claims, the widow's share varied from full control of the estate to being subject to the will of her son for support.[103] Philip Ebert even specified the amount of grain and corn the son was to provide to the widow after his death.[104] Widows of farmers who were wealthy enough to bestow a cash gift enjoyed more independence from their children. Clearly the farmer's first priority was to provide for the next generation.

Often will-makers attempted to preserve the working farm by setting standards of behavior as a necessary precondition for the receipt of the bequest. Such instructions were more common in earlier wills, which were written during the period when farm labor was scarce. In 1852, John White wrote in his will that his son John could have the northwest forty acres of the 160-acre farm "conditionally that he ... stays at home and tries to support and keep the Family together and is industrious and kind to them."[105] Samuel Fortney, who made his will in 1859, directed his two older sons to care for his widow and the three younger children. They were to "live with my wife on the farm during the following winter and the next summer, and that they live off the supplies now on hand that my said sons see to getting wood for fuel & feed the stock and superintend things generally, and that there be no charge for the same."[106] As if he were a benevolent ghost still presiding over the household he once headed, a patriarch specified a code of familial obligation in the will for those who survived him.

The wills of the farmers in the Fountain Green Township area trod the thin line between unity and provision by favoring certain heirs while requiring them to compensate the other heirs. Families were thus tied together in bonds of financial obligation that perpetuated relationships across generational divides. Widows' needs were subjugated to those of their children to achieve the goal of keeping land in the family. It is striking how farmers aimed to provide equally for all children; they were cognizant of earlier gifts to the children and their future needs, depending on their age and station in life. Families who were tied together through the provisions of a will were more likely to stay on the land.

Farm families varied in their approaches to the mid-century market expansion in Fountain Green. Families retained lineal family values through new strategies of cropping and marketing and attempted to reduce risk in a rapidly changing economy. Farm households relied upon the labor of all family members, including women and children, resulting in the subordination of their needs to the success of the farm enterprise. In an intensifying market, habits of passing down land through the family strengthened an agrarian patriarchy which was vital to maintaining the family farm culture in Fountain Green. The cultural habits they brought to a new environment shaped their approaches to the market, resulting in the success of the settlers originally from the mid-Atlantic region, especially the Scots-Irish from Pennsylvania. Their economic success, heavily reliant on webs of kinship, put them in a position to determine the shape of the larger rural community.

4

"A greater pleasure in living"
Community and Commerce

In 1912, Charles C. Tyler, the proprietor of Tyler's Arcade, Fountain Green's largest store, reminisced about his early days in the little farm village. Uppermost in his mind was his uncle's death from pneumonia in January 1855, which is not surprising since it eventually led to Tyler's rise to great fortune as a storekeeper. Tyler remembered that his uncle died in the midst of a three-day snowstorm: "We had great difficulty in reaching the cemetery, having to dig our way through the snow drifts, the intense cold killed prairie chickens and tame chickens as well as game, they being found late in the spring in the drifts."[1] The mental scene of the tall snowdrifts studded with frozen game set Tyler off on a chain of memories, which tell us about Fountain Green's early landscape and the nature of community there.

Tyler remembered Fountain Green Township as open with roads "straight as the crow flies." In those early days, "the country was all open, few fences were necessary, except on the line of the creeks where stock of all kinds ranged." Without fences and roads, in a storm one could easily become lost. "One might as well have been a navigator at sea without a compass as to have been out in the open country during one of those old time storms, there being no fences all traces of a road would become obliterated and one was liable to get out of his true course, become turned around and arrive at the place of beginning."[2]

"But," as Tyler recalled, "we were then young and rather liked it for it made a more lively winter with plenty of good sleighing." Wintertime in Fountain Green was a respite from farm labors, chores reduced only to feeding stock and repairing fences, when one could find them. The break in the cycle of planting and harvesting left country people with time to socialize, as Tyler remembered it. "The country dances, the singing school and spelling school were an attraction for the younger class; the old time quilting bee congregated the older class of women, the corn husking the men."[3] The various components of society—young people, children, women, and men—all mingled in their respective activities, from country dances to corn huskings.

As an old man remembering the good old days, Tyler's recounting here became a jeremiad: "Taking it altogether, there being fewer people, and not that modern feverish desire for riches, there was more sociability, hospitality and a greater pleasure in living than at the present day."[4] As Tyler saw it, because country people in the old days were not so caught up in the acquisitive marketplace, they were more sociable, more hospitable, than people in the early twentieth century. For him, the early days of Fountain Green were free of the "feverish desire for riches" and thus there was "a greater pleasure in living."

While the mental meanderings of an old man must be cautiously interpreted, the idea that the pursuit of individual gain threatened communal relations has drawn attention to rural places such as Fountain Green. Some historians have argued that the spread of the market, with its competitive individualism, threatened the open-country connections of kin and neighbors.[5] As we have seen, while the spread of the market altered the way people farmed and how they provided for their children, we cannot contradict Tyler—community did flourish in Fountain Green. Like countless small towns blossoming across the Midwest, Fountain Green and Webster (formerly the Mormon town of Macedonia) became the centers of community in the local farm culture— places to shop, to worship, to vote.

Histories of the Midwest have emphasized the phenomenal growth of cities and larger towns in fueling the dynamic growth of the market, but we know little about the response of the rural villages of the hinterland to the economic expansion.[6] Nor do we know much about how farm people responded to the politics of cultural definition, in which Republicans promoted bourgeois values of temperance, education, and self-discipline while Democrats resisted the cultural agenda as intrusive.[7] The history of Fountain Green Township suggests that compared to cities, the countryside reacted more selectively and more slowly to the growth of the market, taking a middle road that allowed country people to reap the fruits of the market while retaining a commitment to household agriculture. Likewise, most rural people clung to older forms of community—local trading, strong churches, grassroots government, and neighborhood schools—which rested on the bedrock of the patriarchal family farm.

By mid-century, a stable power elite in the small towns in Fountain Green Township were instrumental in smoothing the shift to market-driven agriculture. In that regard we must question Tyler's tidy equation of sociability with lack of interest in riches. While self-interest was restrained by a vital religious culture which stressed duty and sacrifice, community and commerce were tightly connected. Indeed, by providing a sense of belonging, the churches strengthened local community, anchoring a people to a place. Through local government, the civic community established an orderly society which protected commercial investments and preserved the patriarchal nature of the family farm. Schools inculcated values of self-improvement that would serve as the foundation of bourgeois society in the small-town Midwest and that would eventually erode traditional agrarian values.

Despite the traits it shared with other midwestern towns, as it matured Fountain Green assumed a distinctive identity as Presbyterian, Scots-Irish, and Republican. The ascendance of the northerners, and particularly the Pennsylvanian Scots-Irish, was due in great part to patterns of migration and mobility. Although the southern-born were the first settlers, by mid-century more families followed relatives to Illinois from the mid-Atlantic and northern states than from southern states. Few southerners followed in the footsteps of the community's founders, so the influx of settlers from the Northeast and mid-Atlantic regions achieved numerical dominance. While about one-third of the household heads were from the North in both 1850 and 1860, the share of household heads from the middle states climbed to almost 40 percent of the entire population (Table 4.1). The southern share dropped steadily, from 25 percent of the household heads in 1850 to 17 percent in 1860. Although the county experienced an influx of foreign immigrants (10 percent of the total population in 1860), only a handful of German and Irish families bought farms in the township.[8]

The northern-born predominated in the stable core of leaders who guided the agrarian community as it navigated the onrushing flow of commerce, but they were less successful in their promotion of bourgeois behavior. Yankee entrepreneurs dominated town life, and Scots-Irish farmers from Pennsylvania dominated local government. The group of elites built the stores and churches and controlled the local government, a qualified democracy which upheld hierarchies of gender, age, and wealth. The southern-born retreated to the lower region of the township, patronizing the small town of Webster and building their own churches. While the party loyalties of the voters in Fountain Green had been fairly evenly divided in the frontier period, by adopting bourgeois cultural ideals the elites subtly shifted toward the Republican agenda in the period leading to the Civil War.

By fortifying forms of community—of commerce, religion, and self-government—rural people forestalled the wrenching social changes they would later experience as the market took control of their lives. The sociability Tyler remembered masked dangerous undercurrents which would within a few decades almost destroy what they had so carefully labored to build.

Communities of Commerce: Fountain Green and Webster

The Fountain Green that Tyler recalled was like many small towns which were approaching their apogee, shaped by the expanding market that reached into the most remote corners of the agrarian Midwest. The population of

Fountain Green and Webster swelled as more families moved onto farms in Fountain Green Township. In 1860, Fountain Green Township was home to just over 1,400 persons, and each town was estimated to be about 200 persons.[9] Local businesses proliferated to sell their rural customers sugar and ribbons, to shoe their horses, and to grind their grain into flour. Town and country were symbiotically connected: the patronage of farm people supported the stores and shops, and by extending credit, merchants supplied farmers with capital for the expansion of agricultural production.

Just as town and country were trading partners, town merchants linked the farm trade to a larger regional network of market towns such as Keokuk and the metropolis of Chicago. The dynamic of exchange was propelled by an intensifying consumer impulse among country people which created a thriving commercial community in the two burgeoning villages. As they had in the frontier period, men from New England dominated the town businesses, owning the stores, shops, and mills that catered to country customers. A comparison of the two towns suggests not only the opportunities available to the entrepreneur but also the limits on town growth imposed by geography, availability of capital, and increased regulation of credit.

Because it was the first town founded in the township, Fountain Green had a running start as a center of rural community. Main Street was anchored by

FIGURE 4.1. Residence and Office of Dr. L. T. Ferris. From Alfred Theodore Andreas, *An Illustrated Historical Atlas of Hancock County, Illinois* (Chicago: A. T. Andreas, 1874), 35.

Tyler's general store, A. W. McConnell's Fountain Green Hotel, and Fred Albright's blacksmith shop. Rounding out the array of shops and establishments were the offices of physician Leonard T. Ferris and his new competitor, Morris Crump from Philadelphia (see Fig. 4.1). A small boom in local manufacturing fueled the growth of Fountain Green. The owners of two shingle machines and Arius Beebe's sash and blinds factory were kept busy supplying building materials for farmers who were replacing their cabins with frame houses. The town had its share of the township's five blacksmiths, four wagoners, two shoemakers, saddle and harness makers, and carpenters.[10]

The businesses on Main Street were part of a expanding regional economy which drew upon reserves of credit whose dispensation was governed by nationwide practices. Through the imposition of what historian Christopher Clark calls the long-distance exchange ethic, credit agencies regulated the local economy.[11] While they had never been completely independent, as the small towns became further embedded into the larger economy the price they paid for credit was continual surveillance. Twice each year, agents from the R. G. Dun & Company visited the stores in Fountain Green and Webster and assessed their creditworthiness, which was made available to their creditors. The agents made a point of talking with Dr. Ferris, who appeared to know everyone's business, private and public. Not only did he know who had done well financially but he also knew who had been drinking, a sign of bad character which could put one's credit in jeopardy. Ferris's opinion could make or break a businessman's fortune; for his trouble the agents rewarded him with glowing reports of his own financial success.

The centerpiece of Fountain Green's merchant community was the general store which had been owned by Tyler's uncle, Stephen H. Tyler, before his death in 1855. After Stephen H. Tyler's partner committed suicide in 1856 and the death of Tyler's widow in 1859, the store was purchased by wealthy New York farmer Matthew McClaughry.[12] McClaughry, well into middle age in 1856, provided the store with the credit it had lacked after Tyler's death. Given an "A. No. 1" rating by R. G. Dun & Company, he was characterized as "fair business man good habits honest upright, does well." He had amassed about $10,000 in personal property and was judged to be capable of carrying credit up to $1,500. The store prospered, and by the end of the decade McClaughry had acquired $15,000 in real estate and $8,000 in cash.[13]

McClaughry took on the younger Tyler as partner in 1860, and with the help of his grandparents, Charles C. Tyler became sole proprietor in 1865. Since Tyler's first arrival in Fountain Green from Connecticut in 1852, he had gained retailing experience by clerking at stores in LaHarpe and Rockford. The energy of the younger partner and the capital of the older man ensured that the firm would, in the words of R. G. Dun & Co., be "safe and responsible."[14] After five years of uncertainty, McClaughry's deep pockets and Tyler's ambition saved the store from an uncertain fate.

Yankee storekeepers, well capitalized and experienced in business, dominated the town's business district. The general store catered to the growing consumerism of the neighborhood's farm families. Just as they had in frontier times, farm people stopped in for the usual sugar, molasses, coffee, tea, and baking soda to supplement homegrown produce. However, farm families were cultivating more refined tastes in their diets and purchased ginger, cinnamon, and small luxuries such as raisins for cakes and tapioca pudding. An improving transportation network brought them fresh fish and other perishables. Whiskey had always been a staple grocery item, but in the 1850s the well-to-do could indulge in brandy for a Christmas treat. Families bought candy as well as shoes, slates, and schoolbooks for children. Women bought kitchen furnishings such as kettles, pans, and buckets, and farmers bought tools such as hoes and scythe stones.[15]

Men purchased powder, lead, and caps to hunt game, partly paid for with the dried skins from animals slaughtered on the farm or shot in the timber along Crooked Creek. A man could also buy a buggy whip at the store, sign of an emerging consumer mentality, for those lighter vehicles more suited to courting and outings than the heavy wooden farm wagons used to haul produce. Plugs of tobacco were a perennial purchase. Men often came together to the store, as in June 1850 when James McConnell, Sr., bought a plug of tobacco and his nephew James McConnell, Jr., purchased a pocket knife. They might have whiled away their time on the porch, the uncle chewing tobacco and the nephew whittling a scrap of wood.[16]

Changes in buying habits signaled a growing consciousness of self-presentation. Women no longer wove cloth but instead bought everyday yard goods at the store—calico, gingham, muslin, and jean. And more often than before women began to purchase expensive fabrics such as alpaca, satinette, and Irish linen. George Conkey's daughter bought a black veil and a pair of shoes in April 1850, the same day Laban Oaks's account was assessed $3.70 for a leghorn bonnet, two yards of ribbon, and silk lining. Women were not the only ones interested in fashion and finery, as shown by purchases of suspenders, gaiters, palm leaf hats, and "California boots" by men. The grooming aids available at the store suggest an increasing concern with personal appearance and care of the body. Hairbrushes and combs were common enough, but one is startled to read of a toothbrush being sold to Joseph White for fifteen cents in May 1851. Bottles of liniment were an everyday purchase, no doubt to soothe muscles that ached from shoveling manure or hanging wet laundry.[17]

While the foregoing description of the country store conjures up pastoral images of rural conviviality, the store's hold on its customers may have stemmed as much from the credit it extended to them as the hand of friendship. Small-town businesses such as Tyler's store gave customers items on credit at a time when many stores in larger towns were converting to a cash-only business.[18] As in frontier times, customers let their debts on account build up over time and settled them at the first of the year. By providing store credit, merchants boosted the local economy by allowing their customers to invest in land, seed, or machinery, thus increasing farm productivity. Because customers also exchanged notes of credit to each other through the store's ledgers, the network of credit tied the store's customers not only to each other but also to the store.[19]

The commercial community depended on prompt payment of debts to sustain the relations of credit that connected a farmer in Fountain Green to a manufacturer in Chicago. Without the prompt payment of country customers, storekeepers could not stay in business. An informal balance sheet prepared in 1860, the year Charles C. Tyler became McClaughry's partner, shows that for the first six months of the year the store had sold $2,399 in goods but had received payment for $1,833. They had bills to pay in the amount of $1,634, leaving them with a net profit of just $199. Their creditors in Chicago or New York expected payment, and failure to do so threatened a merchant's credit rating and thus future purchases. However, the store's proprietors could not so easily exact their due from customers with whom they associated at church and in other social settings.[20] The store's prosperity indicates its owners knew when to press for debts and when to be more lenient to retain customers. Tyler also knew when to sue for debt at the local peace court, if necessary, as we shall see.

Despite the availability of credit at the local store, payment trends shifted away from barter and book debt to cash. In the 1840s, families paid for purchases with farm produce such as corn and wheat. By the 1850s, accounts were credited more often with cash than with produce or hides. Farmers no longer sold their grain and hogs to the store but instead carted them to Warsaw, Chicago, or the local rail depot. Only perishables such as vegetables, butter, and eggs were collected at the local country store. The increasing use of cash instead of credit was a sign of the country store's absorption into the regional trade and its regularized standards of a long-distance exchange ethic.

The town of Webster, vacated by the Mormons in the spring of 1846, served as a commercial center for the families in the southern part of the township. Early settler Solomon Salisbury remembered the deserted Mormon town as empty log houses, but two years after the Mormon departure, Dr. Ferris thought that Webster was "improving some." He reported that the large brick building had been completed and that the town boasted several stores, one of them "a going concern."[21] By 1855, a state business directory listed five blacksmiths, five carriage and wagonmakers, three agricultural implement firms, and three carpenters in Webster. The key to its local manufacturing was Crooked Creek, which powered four mills. The town itself was small, its steady businesses a general store and tailor shop owned by Joel Howd and a drugstore owned by Dr. Oliver C. Ing.[22] The fate of Webster, which lacked the customers and capital of Fountain Green, provides a lesson in the risks of nineteenth-century retailing.

In contrast to the report of Fountain Green's steady growth and promising future at mid-century, the local agent for R. G. Dun & Co. reported in January 1858 that "Webster is the smallest meanest place in the county."[23]

Like Fountain Green, the major general store in Webster was owned by a Yankee, tailor Joel Howd, originally from Oneida County, New York. A crippling childhood disease left him unfit for farming, so he learned the trade of tailoring in Warsaw, then moved to Webster after the Mormons vacated in 1846. In the spring of 1849 he put down roots when he married Hester McElvain, a local farm girl whose family had come from Ohio. Made postmaster in 1851, in 1855 he added the general store to his business. An agent for R. G. Dun & Co. regarded him as an "honest and loyal man" and good for small bills because he paid promptly for what he bought. With his $1,000 worth of real estate to back him up, he was "doing a regular & safe business."[24]

Howd's success can be traced to his location on the major east-west highway between the Mississippi and Macomb, the seat of McDonough County. Howd's large illustrated advertisements in the county paper drew in customers to buy an array of fancy silks, challas, and prints as well as common fabrics such as lawn, muslin, and gingham. The mention of mantillas, collars, ribbons, laces, and embroideries would have attracted the aspiring country shopper, who could buy the latest fashion in bonnets, gloves, hosiery, and parasols at Howd's store. Boots and shoes, ready-made clothing, and tableware such as Queensware, cutlery, and glassware were a few of the wide variety of items for sale in tiny Webster.[25]

Those who depended only on the local trade were less successful than Howd. John Bullard and John Mesick had a small trade in dry goods, but they did not have much real estate as backing and only about $500 worth of capital. Bullard & Mesick were assessed in January 1858 as "good clever men doing a small business," but by August their credit was strained and they had not paid promptly for their purchases. Victims of the financial panic of 1857, they did not have the reserves to ride out the storm. "Clever fellows in their way but we don't call them safe," wrote the R. G. Dun & Co. agent. In September, Mesick was replaced by William Alton, whose family were early settlers from New York. The agent reported that "the concern is rather improved by the change," but by the following July, Alton had quit the trade "in disgust."[26]

The stores and mills in Fountain Green and Webster meant that the people of Fountain Green Township could shop without traveling far from home. Both towns linked the township's farm families to the larger regional marketplace, and as rural trading centers they served as social centers for their customers who visited in the stores and streets. Anchored by the prosperous store of McClaughry & Tyler, Fountain Green flourished in this period, while most of Webster's merchants lacked the capital to even stay in business. In this dynamic period of agrarian capitalism, habits of local exchange based on trust were yielding to the protocol of a long-distance market that regularized local business habits by controlling credit.

Communities of Faith

In September 1855, Thomas M. Walker, pastor of the Fountain Green Presbyterian Church, wrote an assessment of the church's spiritual condition to send to the Presbytery. He was pleased that the church was full on Sunday, that the Sabbath school was "full and interesting," and that attendance was "encouraging" at the weekly prayer meeting and monthly concert. But he was concerned about the community at large, in which he detected some "coldness and indifference in religious matters." While drinking and Sabbath-breaking were not common, he felt there were some "who are governed more by public sentiment and convenience than by any fixed principle."[27] We do not know precisely what he meant by "public sentiment and convenience," but his comments convey a sense that for many, church-going was not worth the trouble, or that his church had somehow become unfashionable. Walker sensed a moral relativism in a people increasingly influenced more by public opinion and less by religious principles.

Walker's concern about the entire community was well placed, because his church was the mainstay of the local religious community. Continuing migration from Pennsylvania supplied a stream of Scots-Irish families who found a religious home in Fountain Green. But despite Walker's concerns, at mid-century an increasing population lent a new vitality to the religious community, as small groups of believers established neighborhood churches along Crooked Creek. Changes outside the township also altered the religious landscape; the local Catholic church closed when an influx of Irish immigrants nearby built a stronger church more deserving of diocesan support. And in a move that foretold heightening tensions over gender, prominent women in Fountain Green split from the Presbyterian church to form a new church that allowed them more influence.

These changes reflect the importance of churches to community in Fountain Green. Even in a time of increasingly commercialized production and thriving consumerism, church-going remained an integral part of community life in the rural Midwest. The white steeples that dotted the prairie represented not only places of worship but places frequented by those with similar moral values. The rituals of life's passages—christenings, baptism, marriage, funerals—all took place in a church, binding people together in celebration and suffering. As Robert Swierenga has argued, churches provided essential social service functions: educating children, caring for the sick, burying the dead, helping in times of disaster. In a place that was too sparsely populated to sustain an array of voluntary associations, churches provided identities for their members. Through shared ritual and everyday experience, churches provided a sense of belonging that could counter the fracturing forces of the market. However, as Susan Gray has noted, and as we shall see in Fountain Green, by competing for members, churches provoked ethnic and gender tensions in rural communities.[28]

The distinctive identity of Fountain Green derived in large part from the Presbyterian church dominated by the Scots-Irish families from Pennsylvania. The size of their congregation attracted newcomers and stamped the community with a particular religious and regional identity. From only twenty-one members in 1846, the church tripled in size in the following fifteen years. The largest increase was before 1855, when there were seventy communicants, twenty of them new that year. By the end of the decade the membership reached a stable plateau of seventy-five members.[29] The growth was fueled in part from continuing immigration from Pennsylvania; by 1860, nearly 40 percent of the township's household heads originated in the middle states.[30]

The rise in numbers allowed the church to erect a new building in 1851, supervised by church elders Thomas Geddes and James McConnell, both from Path Valley, Pennsylvania. Assisted by $150 received in May from the church extension fund and using timber Geddes donated, the meetinghouse was built in New England style, with white clapboard exterior, a steeple, and a central entryway.[31] The new building was impressive enough to attract a permanent minister. In June 1852, the congregation extended a call to Rev. Thomas M. Walker to become the "stated supply" of the church. It was a happy choice; Walker accepted a position he would fill until old age demanded his retirement in the 1880s. Because Walker was born in Kentucky and had family roots in Virginia and Pennsylvania, he could fuse the various regional identities of his parishioners. The elders provided a parsonage for the minister, his wife, and their son on the church lot south of town on the road linking Fountain Green and Webster. Walker would become a beloved figure in the community, frequenting the general store to visit with parishioners while he picked up supplies.[32] Through efforts to increase donations, the church achieved financial autonomy by the mid-1850s, increasing the minister's salary by $25 and releasing the Presbyterian Board of Missions from any obligation for his salary.[33]

The church was strong enough that in March 1853 the elders ambitiously took up the issue of opening a parochial school. They felt "the necessity of religious instruction in the schools in which the children and youth in our midst are educated" and designed the school to conform to the specifications of the state board of education. Before tax-supported public education, parochial school was an attractive alternative for those interested in promoting children's education, both intellectual and religious. They may have felt it was their duty when the national church organization urged each congregation to establish a

Christian school. The Fountain Green Parochial School opened the first Monday in April 1854, under the charge of teacher Miss Louisa R. Montgomery. In August 1855, school was suspended, not for "a want of success or a want of interest," but because state legislation mandated tax-supported public schools.[34] The elders' move to found the school implies their interest in inculcating values of self-improvement consonant with bourgeois values of the marketplace.

Like the New England men who ran Main Street, the Fountain Green Presbyterian Church was governed by elders, community patriarchs who had migrated from the church in Path Valley, Pennsylvania. The elders handled the money, set the content and frequency of the meetings, and maintained order by meting out judgment in church disciplinary actions. When Thomas M. Campbell was summoned for an unspecified charge before the elders in 1867, he pleaded guilty and as punishment was "suspended from the sacrament of the church until he give satisfactory evidence of the genuineness of his repentance." His punishment was not removed until a decade later, when he moved to Iowa.[35]

Although the ruling elders were men, women constituted 64 percent of the congregation.[36] We can account for their majority by speculating that daughters may have been more likely than sons to convert as young people and were probably more likely to stay in the community after adolescence. Widows and unmarried women were more likely than widowers and bachelors to join the church. Women sought the associations a church provided and as mothers and wives fulfilled cultural prescriptions that saw them as naturally more religious than men and as the spiritual guide for their children.[37]

Women may also have been attracted to the church because it provided a vehicle for benevolent activities in a community that lacked voluntary associations. Through their access to funds to support a church, it was common for prominent women to exert influence over a church minister or to choose the objects of their charity. The women of Carthage and LaHarpe formed sewing circles and ladies' societies that held fairs to raise funds to decorate their churches, but there is no evidence of these groups in rural Fountain Green Township.[38] Most farmers' wives in Fountain Green were certainly too busy having children and churning butter to engage in these pursuits, which left such activities to the handful of wealthy women in town.

It may have been dissatisfaction with their subordinate role that led to the defection of three women who were instrumental in founding the new United Presbyterian Church. In September 1859, Eliza McClaughry, Mary Mull, and Jane White all left to join the new church, built on the southwest corner of McClaughry's farm on the town's main thoroughfare. As the third wife of widower Matthew McClaughry, Eliza McClaughry had both the wealth and the status to carry out her wishes to establish a new church. Mary Mull was likewise well situated as the wife of wagonmaker Henry Mull. McClaughry and Mull were relatively new to the church, having recently arrived from New York, where they had attended reformed congregations.[39] They had probably attended the Old School Presbyterian Church in Fountain Green because, of the nearby churches, it was the most similar to their brand of congregational worship.

To be sure, the local blossoming of the offshoot from mainstream Presbyterianism reflected in part the splintering of the Presbyterian church on a national level.[40] However, their departure from the Old School church dominated by the Pennsylvania elders could also be seen as a rejection of the strict ecclesiastical patriarchy that gave women no voice in church affairs. As pillars of local society they founded a church that allowed them more religious autonomy and community influence. With the funds the women provided, a critical mass of like-minded Presbyterians who had moved into the area founded a competitor to the Presbyterian church of pioneer days. Eventually the new church drew away nearly one-third of the members of the original Fountain Green Presbyterian Church.[41]

The departure of the New Yorkers left the Presbyterian church more characteristically Pennsylvanian, more of a daughter church of the Path Valley, Pennsylvania, congregation; migrants from that church had come to Fountain Green to farm.[42] The robust growth of the early 1850s was slowing as some left for other churches in Fountain Green or LaHarpe and others moved out of the state.[43] Nevertheless, as the largest self-supporting congregation with its own minister, the church retained its position of dominance in the rural community.

The dominance of the Fountain Green Presbyterian Church overshadowed the other pioneer church, St. Simon, built by early Kentucky Catholic settlers. Although the burial ground remained, in 1860 the decaying St. Simon fell into disuse when a new church was built in Tennessee, Illinois, to serve the influx of Irish railroad laborers on the Northern Cross railway. Tennessee was just nine miles southeast of Fountain Green in McDonough County, and the new church there became the nucleus for the Catholics in eastern Hancock County. Rather than associate with Irish laborers, some of the original settlers maintained the faith privately, such as Ivo Hardy, who kept the candlesticks from the altar for private services in his home.[44]

The demise of St. Simon was symbolic of the waning presence of native-born Catholic families in the township. Migration brought no new Catholic families to the area, and the death of wealthy Abraham Lincoln in 1852 may have adversely affected the financial standing of the local parish. The rise of Masonry and the nativism of the 1850s further weakened the influence of Catholicism in the area. In light of the removal of the Mormons, the closing of St. Simon suggests a marginalization of the Catholic community in Fountain Green Township, part of a subtle process of rejection that reinforced the homogenized white Protestant identity and its bourgeois values that supported the spread of market relations.[45]

By 1860, other churches were established along with the pioneer Presbyterian church. The Free Will Baptists built a large building in Webster valued at

FIGURE 4.2. Majorville Methodist Church. From the author's collection.

$2,000, supported by old settler Stephen Gano Ferris and Jabez Beebe, son of a Baptist preacher. In 1855 the United Brethren Church moved into the brick seminary the Mormons left behind. The Associate Reformed Presbyterian and the Universalist churches each rented a hall to accommodate their membership.[46]

The introduction of Methodism demonstrates the increasing diversity of the township's population. New immigrants from Europe who wanted to worship in their own language built a German Methodist church on the west edge of Section 13 shortly before the Civil War. Like the Irish laborers who built the Catholic church in nearby Tennessee, immigrants established churches to provide a community and an identity in a new place. Southern-born Methodists held meetings in homes and school buildings until Major John Williams, who had emigrated from Kentucky, donated land in 1863 for what would be known as the Majorville Methodist Church (see Fig. 4.2). It was built in the northwest corner of Section 2 of Hancock Township, adjacent to Fountain

Green Township and convenient for residents in the township's southern sections. Built with donated labor in the midst of the Civil War, the church's construction demonstrates rural people's intense hunger for religious fellowship.[47]

Parallel with the expansion of commercial community, the increased population enabled the founding of more sectarian churches which allowed both new settlers and old to find their niche in rural society. European immigrants such as Irish Catholics and German Methodists founded their own churches, transplanting a faith and an ethnic culture that, ironically, displaced native-born Catholic settler families. In the case of the United Presbyterian Church, the split of the New Yorkers reflected underlying gender tensions that challenged the dominance of the pioneer Presbyterian church. Nevertheless, it remained the centerpiece of the community, reinforcing a regional identity among the Scots-Irish from Path Valley. While Rev. Walker's complaints suggest that not all people took religion seriously, a diverse array of churches provided a sense of belonging for most people in Fountain Green.

Civic Community

The commercial and religious dimensions of community in Fountain Green were complemented by a civic culture dominated by a stable core of elite men. The civic culture of Fountain Green was broadly participatory, a local government where farmers cast their ballots and served on juries at the peace court. However, historians are now questioning the supposed democratic nature of antebellum politics and its egalitarian overtones, and have discovered that the elites wielded disproportionate political power.[48] Kenneth J. Winkle has argued that antebellum politics in Springfield, Illinois, was a "proxy democracy" dominated by a stable core of power elites which excluded newcomers and those on society's margins.[49] Like local governments throughout the antebellum United States, it was also a gendered democracy which subordinated women by denying them the right to vote, hold office, or serve on a jury. In Fountain Green as in other small midwestern towns, governance by a public patriarchy sustained the structures of private patriarchy.

A stable core of elite men dominated the township's political affairs, rallying the voters, holding the major offices, and representing the township at county and state party meetings. This core community was committed to the growth of the market while upholding traditional agrarian ideals of independent farm operation. By straddling the fence, neither capitulating to liberal capitalism entirely nor rejecting it outright, the elites eased the integration of the local community into the larger regional market system. While some of the elite promoted bourgeois notions of character, they failed to disturb the patriarchal bedrock of rural society.

The power elites dominated local politics, which were rooted in the social characteristics of the population. In Fountain Green, the dominance of those from the northern and middle states in the population skewed the agenda toward the expansion of the market. Not only were the migrants from the northern and middle states numerically predominant, they were also overrepresented in the top layer of the elites. Only one-quarter of the elites in 1850 were Yankees, but the proportion swelled to 40 percent by 1860. In 1850, 43 percent of the wealthiest household heads (defined as the top 25 percent) had been born in the middle states, even though they composed only one-third of the total number of household heads. By 1860, only 28 percent of the elites had been born in the middle states, but that group constituted nearly two-thirds of the very elite (the top 5 percent). Elites born in the southern states remained in the core, but they represented no more than their share of the population in 1850, when the southern-born made up about one-fourth of both the elites and the general population. A decade later, they maintained that share even as the number of household heads born in the South declined to 17 percent of the total.[50] Despite the southern presence, northerners dominated the group of the wealthiest persons in Fountain Green.

Most of the wealthy men in Fountain Green were farmers. Storekeeper Stephen Tyler, doctor Leonard T. Ferris, and blacksmith Frederick Albright also ranked in this top group. This core group of elites were mature men in their mid-forties, and the households they headed were larger than those of the less wealthy. In 1860, the elites owned approximately 30 percent of the total wealth of the township's households.[51] These men were not afraid to display their wealth to impress others. The wedding of Leonard Ferris to Helen Gilchrist in May 1850 was by rural standards a lavish affair. The highlight of the party was the lemonade made with lemons brought upriver by steamboat from St. Louis. The guests were so impressed by the drink that they took lemon rinds home as souvenirs.[52]

Persistence also played a role in forming a stable core of elites. The top ranks were occupied by the earliest settlers: Yankees Jabez Beebe and Stephen Tyler; Kentucky Catholic Ivo Hardy; the McConnell, Walker, and Geddes clans from Pennsylvania; and southern squires such as Georgian James M. Renshaw, a justice of the peace. Men such as McClaughry, Ferris, Tyler, and Leach shaped the town's immediate destiny and set patterns that would maintain their political power.

Elites from New England and Pennsylvania cemented their position in the stable core by taking prominent offices in township government. In 1851, the Illinois legislature transformed townships from a geographical unit into a political entity with a full complement of local officers chosen at an annual town meeting each April. The highest locally elected official was the township supervisor, who oversaw local government and the collection of funds for taxes and penalties. He also sat on the county board of supervisors, which made decisions about the disbursal of tax monies. Lesser offices included a clerk, assessor, tax collector, overseer of the poor, three commissioners of highways, two justices of the peace, and the necessary number of overseers of highways and pound masters. Justices of the peace and constables each served a four-year term; other offices were for one-year terms only.[53]

Township voters chose officers who they considered worthy of their trust, men who would represent the township in the political affairs of the county. The township supervisors were wealthy farmers, with an average estate of nearly $9,000 each, and they were seasoned, an average of 49 years old when elected. All but one had settled in the county before 1850, so they were men that voters knew well. Despite the dominance of upland southerners in the settlement period, after mid-century the township supervisors tended to come from the northern and mid-Atlantic regions of the United States. During the three decades from 1850 to 1880, eleven of the fourteen supervisors were men who had been born in the North. Only twice did a man from the South hold the office of supervisor; James Renshaw in the early 1850s and Andrew Simmons from Tennessee in the late 1870s. Canadian John Bullock, who was elected in the 1870s, was the other exception to the rule of the northern-born in the township.[54]

Even more astonishing was the hold of the migrants from Pennsylvania on the township's highest office. Of the fourteen men who held the post of supervisor during those years, six were from Pennsylvania and a seventh had married into a Pennsylvania clan. Voters trusted the Pennsylvania Scots-Irish, perhaps because so many of them were their relatives. The election of those from the middle states may have represented an attempt to bridge the differences between settlers born in the South and those born in New England. The Pennsylvanians acted as cultural brokers, able to work with two groups who saw each other as so different from themselves.

A second striking aspect of the group of supervisors was their affiliation with the Whig and Republican parties. While the local Democratic paper contended in 1864 that "township elections are no criterions by which to judge the strength of parties," the dominance of Republicans in a township which voted Democratic majorities in the 1850s was remarkable. The pattern of Whig-Republican dominance was broken only twice; the first supervisor elected in 1850, Democrat Stephen H. Tyler, served a three-year term, and in 1863 Democrat Robert McConnell served one year before being replaced by leading Republican Thomas Geddes.

Township leaders affiliated with other members of their party at county and state party meetings. They regularly served as county delegates to regional and state conventions, traveling to Quincy and Springfield and acquiring a broader perspective on local affairs. Thomas Geddes frequently attended such meetings and became recognized as a major Whig and Republican leader from Hancock

County. Through these associations outside the local arena they acquired a more cosmopolitan outlook which privileged ideals of progress over the agrarian ideals of independence. In that regard, Whig and Republican township leaders displayed the prevailing tendency to define party politics in cultural terms; they agitated for prohibition and hosted organizational meetings and wrote speeches for the county Maine Law Alliance. Several of them were vocal supporters of a measure for prohibition in 1855, which was decisively rejected by 66 percent of the township's voters.[55]

The dominance of the Whigs and Republicans from the North allowed them to promote a commercializing agenda on the county board of supervisors and in the local township. A prime example was their attempt to bring a railroad to Fountain Green in the late 1850s. Like leaders in towns all over the Midwest, they felt that luring a railroad would ensure the success of their investments in the farms and businesses of the township. Fountain Green's failure to attract a railroad demonstrates the limits of localism against larger political and economic forces beyond their control. A further obstacle was the lack of capital in a rural township dependent on farming for an income, coupled with farmers' reluctance to incur debt in a time of financial insecurity.

Wealthy merchant Matthew McClaughry was the first local resident, appointed in December 1855, to collect private subscriptions for the railroad from the Fountain Green area. Fifteen months later, a bipartisan commission of leading men of Fountain Green made plans to raise funds to bring the railroad near Fountain Green. The men who gathered in March 1857 were the best the township had to offer. All but one of the men were in the top fifth of property holders, and four were in the top decile. On average they owned $4,000 worth of real estate and over $1,000 of personal property. The bulk of them were farmers, mature men, with an average age of 49 years. Politically they were bipartisan but leaned slightly toward the Whigs and their commercializing agenda. Only one man was from the South, James W. Roberts, 55, a farmer from Tennessee.[56] All the men had earned their spot on the committee through wealth or political service. If they could not convince the farmers around Fountain Green to subscribe, no one could. Comprised of merchants and wealthy farmers, the railroad committee represented those who stood to profit most by a local rail outlet.

However, when the commission pressed local farmers to subscribe to bring a railroad to Fountain Green, most farmers balked at the prospects of encumbering their farms with the necessary five-year mortgage. Despite desperate pleas from the railroad organizers, Fountain Green pledged only $25,000, far short of the $100,000 pledged by other towns competing for the road. The Panic of 1857 dashed the hopes of the railroad backers, and the farmers of Fountain Green found it impossible to invest an additional $10,000. By the spring of 1858, they were warned that if they did not come up with the money, "they will lose the road."[57] In June 1859, the railroad directors awarded the road to LaHarpe, not Fountain Green.[58] The relocation of the route through LaHarpe, which had a better chance at supporting the railroad because it was a larger town, decided the destiny of Fountain Green.

Certainly the relative proximity of the Northern Cross depots at Tennessee and Colmar played a role in the decisions of some farmers not to subscribe to the road. Since frontier times, the farmers in Fountain Green had hauled their produce twenty miles to Warsaw to be shipped downriver to St. Louis. A railroad to Carthage could cut that distance in half, and a direct connection to Chicago or St. Louis was only nine miles away in Tennessee. What is more, they may have reasoned, they had not paid a dime to tax themselves for the use of the Northern Cross. Faced with the alternative of investing to bring the road to Fountain Green or hauling produce a few extra miles to the Northern Cross depot, the latter alternative was the logical choice. In their rejection of the road, the farmers of Fountain Green displayed their resistance to the commercializing agenda of the elite, with their deep pockets and investments in the town. Like the anti-prohibition vote, the failure to attract a railroad highlights the resistance township elites faced in promoting a commercial agenda and the bourgeois values associated with it. The leaders of Fountain Green could do no more than ponder the irony of LaHarpe's success and curse their own fate.

Peace Courts: A Public Patriarchy

In addition to serving as township officers and party delegates, the stable core exercised control of local affairs in the peace courts. The peace courts formed a public patriarchy, which maintained order by enforcing the collection of debts and by upholding the private forms of patriarchy which subordinated women and younger men. By providing a mechanism for enforcing financial obligations, the justices sustained the orderly growth of the commercial community. Persons could make credit agreements safe in the knowledge that they would be enforced, if necessary, by the arm of the law. By resolving disputes, peace courts allowed members of the bounded community to settle their differences without recourse to violence, but their judgments reinscribed inequalities of gender and status in the rural community.

The peace courts were the first line of defense in maintaining civic order and defusing the tensions that erupted in the rural community. Most local incidents of unlawful conduct were brought before a justice of the peace, a man elected out of respect for his judgment. James Lincoln of Kentucky was the most prominent justice of the frontier era; he was followed by James M. Renshaw of Georgia and Kendrick N. Leach of New York, who was justice for forty years.[59] The court, which was usually held in the home of the justice, was open for anyone to attend. Farmers would often take a Saturday afternoon off to go to town to watch the proceedings. The peace courts were a highly localized form of justice, administered by friends and neighbors who in most cases knew the accused offenders well.

There were at least two such justices in the township during the 1850s. Leach, justice of the peace court for the northwest portion of the township, heard 186 cases for the period 1850–1865. Because the local court was the venue for actions of debt of less than $100, all but thirteen of those cases were for collection of debt (e.g., strays, store debt, disputed prices of sale). Of the thirteen remaining actions, five were for assault and battery, two were for sexual crimes (one rape, one fornication), one was a trespass charge, one was a counterfeiting charge, and three were charges for minor disturbances of the peace (unlawful assembly, verbal threats).[60]

By allowing store owners and others to collect long-overdue debts, the local courts furthered a commercial agenda. Merchants extended credit to their customers because they expected them to pay off their accounts, usually around the first of the year. Customers also paid before they left the community or when an estate was settled. When customers failed to pay their accounts as demanded, the store owners sued for debt at the local peace court. In 1853 alone, storekeeper Stephen Tyler brought eleven suits for debt to the justice in Fountain Green. The amounts were all under $100, but some amounted to eighty or ninety dollars.[61] The prospect of being embarrassed at a public trial was an incentive for people to keep abreast of their financial obligations.

The second major area in which the justices facilitated commercial expansion was by literally keeping the peace, or settling violent disputes. The countryside may have seemed peaceful and sleepy compared to nineteenth-century cities or cattle towns, but the unrelenting face-to-face contact may have actually increased the likelihood of conflict. In the unfenced open country, where guns were handy for hunting and farm tools had sharp points, an argument over a stray cow could quickly become assault, and occasionally such arguments escalated to murder. The cases brought before the local justice of the peace reveal the tensions between farmers and laborers, husbands and wives, fathers and sons. In their decisions the justices upheld the structures of patriarchy, which privileged wealthy merchants and established farmers over their social subordinates. On the rare occasion when the defeated disagreed with the contingent nature of the justice meted in the peace court, they took matters into their own hands, outside the law.

A significant share of the cases of assault and battery were between farmers and their hired men. In one such case, farmer Josiah Huntley accused 17-year-old farm laborer Elijah R. Williams of assault and battery on May 30, 1853. Williams confessed his guilt, paid a $3 fine on the spot, and covered the court costs.[62] Like Williams, hired men were generally sons of neighboring farmers working to earn money for their own land, not a permanent underclass of transient men who drifted in and out of the township. We see in these cases the use of authority to contain their resentments that surfaced in physical attacks. The outcomes suggest an emerging ideology of manhood which entailed controlling physical strength within certain boundaries. The courts assisted fathers in controlling their sons and farmers their hired hands.

Nowhere is the dominance of the public patriarchy more clear than in the cases which came before the court involving women. Women rarely appeared before the justice as plaintiffs or defendants, although it was not uncommon to find them present as witnesses. The gendered nature of civic affairs is apparent in a case of incest that came before the courts in June 1853. Mary Harris was 18 years old when she came before Justice Renshaw to accuse her father, James Harris, of committing a rape on her person. A warrant was issued for his arrest, and the constable returned with the prisoner in custody on July 23. The justices heard the case, and, in a rare turn of events, discharged the prisoner without rendering an explicit verdict. The judges may have been convinced of his innocence or they may have been unwilling to punish him without evidence. The nature of the crime made witnesses unlikely, so the judges had to match the father's word against his daughter's testimony.[63]

Today's understanding of abuse and incest would place more credibility with the accuser. Mary was the oldest of eight children born in quick succession, and in addition to the burden of caring for the younger children, she may indeed have been the victim of her father's sexual abuse. If we choose to side with the victim, then we are led to ask why the justices did not believe Mary, or why they did not punish the offender. If we side with the accused, we must search for a motive powerful enough to bring Mary to subject her family to public shame. The case may have been publicized enough to result in a community judgment against the entire family. For whatever reason, the Harris family had moved out by 1860.[64]

It would be a mistake to see the public patriarchs as always defending men at the expense of women; rather we should see them as defenders of the patriarchal household, the foundation of rural society. In cases of clear-cut complaints supported by the testimony of reliable witnesses, the justice was not afraid to curb the abuses of patriarchy. By protecting victims from its abuses, the justice ensured the continued maintenance of the patriarchal family household. When Jane Cox, whose husband Elijah was a tenant farmer, complained of wife-beating, the court found Elijah guilty and levied a fine of $5 after hearing the testimony of five witnesses. Jane's success may have resulted in part from the presence of witnesses Daniel and Nancy Prentiss, numbered among the elites of the community. The ties she had with other members of the community allowed her to bring public action to ensure private peace.[65]

In a rural community where the question of guilt often pitted one person's word against another, the verdict may have involved questions of status as much as notions of innocence and guilt. Aware of the prejudices of a certain justice, in 7 of the 186 cases plaintiffs requested a change of venue. Relocating the trial was a way of handling personality conflicts, regional rivalries, and status rivalry in a small rural community. Cases involving change of venue were usually characterized by a large number of witnesses, probably because of conflicting testimony. That parties pressed for a change of venue to a court only a few miles away suggests either that the regional neighborhoods were on a small scale or that judicial reputations were well known. For example, when 65-year-old Caleb Thompson was accused of an unspecified charge by Horace Aldrich in November 1853, the defendant asked for a change of venue from Fountain Green to Justice Jabez Beebe in Webster, because "he believes he could not have a fair and impartial trial."[66]

The justice of the peace courts may have settled the disputes through formal legal action, but that did not prevent a disgruntled citizen from settling the score outside the court. In September 1855, Jabez Beebe's barn was set on fire, a loss totaling nearly $500. The origin of the fire was suspicious, and a neighbor had heard a horse and rider on the street by the barn just before the alarm was sounded. Further evidence was provided the next day when tracks of a horse were found leading to and from the barn. The editor of the *Carthage Republican*, where news of the incident was reported, remarked that "a wretch who would destroy property to gratify a malicious spirit of revenge, is unfit to live in civilized society."[67] Had Justice Beebe made an unpopular ruling in a case brought before his own court? Or was the fire started because of a personal grudge someone held against Beebe? "Old Man Beebe" was well known as a crank who, in Dr. Ferris's judgment, "says what he is a mind to & does as he pleases."[68]

The peace court was a civic space dominated by a stable core of respected men, a public patriarchy who enforced the order necessary to sustain the expansion of the market while upholding the patriarchal farm household. That women were largely absent from the courts attests to the role of the courts in adjudicating matters of commerce, the province of men whose status allowed them to direct public affairs. Men dominated public life by dominating its public spaces: polling places, peace courts, militia musters on the green. While women were certainly citizens, without the vote, they could not influence the course of civic affairs. As Mary Harris discovered, women were often mere observers in the civic rituals of rural community.

Communities of Children

As the countryside was commercialized, the township schools created subcommunities of parents and children and provided a means for inculcating social values in the children of the rural community. The building and maintenance of common schools gave parents an opportunity to cooperate in a grassroots effort to educate the township's children. The schools in Fountain Green were required to comply with the 1855 Illinois state law which mandated tax-supported public schools.[69] The legislation culminated a contest between Yankees and southerners in the state of Illinois over the role of government in people's lives. Yankees were viewed as cultural missionaries, determined to promote values of self-improvement, punctuality, and industry, while many of the southern-born settlers saw such efforts as meddling in their affairs, and at their expense. The governance of the local school districts shows a growing commitment to public education associated with the spread of the market economy.[70]

Until the 1855 legislation, the community had depended on local subscription schools and the briefly functioning Presbyterian church school. Susan Alton from New York established the first tuition school in her two-room cabin in 1837. In 1841, the town built a crude wooden schoolhouse, divided the township into six districts, and hired John M. Ferris to teach the subscription school.[71] Beginning in 1855, local taxes and county aid supplemented state funding, which provided about $2 annually per school-aged child. The major expenses were the building and maintenance of the school building and the salaries of the teachers.[72]

The school districts were created to minimize the distance children had to travel to school. They created artificially bounded neighborhoods, governed by trustees who were elected by the voters of the school district (see Fig. 4.3). When a teaching vacancy occurred, the school trustees posted notices advertising an upcoming election in a common meeting place, such as Tyler's general store.[73] School trustees examined candidates for the position of teacher to test their knowledge and assess their moral character. The amount of their salary varied, depending on whether they boarded around the district in the homes of the students or lived at home. Half the teachers in the county were women, a bargain for a local school board, which consistently paid women about half the salary given to male teachers.[74]

Beyond hiring a teacher, the major effort of the school trustees was to build and maintain a local schoolhouse. Country schools were recognizable by their size (twenty-four by thirty feet, twelve feet high), a center doorway, an outside water pump, a hitching rack in front, and an outhouse at each back corner. Inside, the students sat on benches placed on both sides of a long table, boys on one side of the room and girls on the other. The teacher commanded her charges from the end of the table. The primitive room was warmed by a fireplace or stove, and the children were refreshed by water sipped from a common gourd in a bucket.[75]

Children usually started going to school when they were 5 or 6 years old, and almost all of them went to school by the age of 8. The bulk of schoolchildren were between 10 and 14 years of age. By the time children were 15 years old,

FIGURE 4.3. Schools in Fountain Green Township. From *Section Map of Hancock County, Illinois* (St. Louis: Holmes & Arnold, 1859).

many had stopped going to school to work on the farm or as a domestic servant. School attendance became increasingly important to farm families. The proportion of children between the ages of 6 and 16 who attended school increased steadily from two-thirds in 1860 to five-sixths in 1880.[76] The increase in the proportion of children who did attend school shows not only that farm families valued education but also that families demanded less labor from their children over time.

County histories refer to these schools as "common," meaning that they delivered a free public education. Scarce resources and poorly trained teachers meant the curriculum was generally remedial. Farm children, it was thought, required little more to fulfill their adult roles as responsible farmers and farm wives. Those who could afford to do so sent their children on to academies outside Fountain Green for further training, where some discovered deficiencies in their education. William M. Walker, who wrote to his cousin from Monmouth

College in 1869, found himself behind his fellow students in his geometry class. He and another student from Fountain Green were placed in a remedial class, "trying to catch up with the body of the animal."[77]

Despite the limits of the common schools, several students who were products of Fountain Green schools distinguished themselves in their professional careers. Jennie Hopkins, the adopted daughter of Martin and Fidelia Beebe Hopkins, enjoyed a long career as a journalist in Denver and New York City.[78] Martha Berry's sons became attorneys, and one served as a state legislator. The Ferris brothers were schooled well enough to become leaders of the county bar.[79] But these students from wealthy families were the exceptions that prove the rule. Most of the pupils in Fountain Green's schools probably learned only enough to keep farm account books, write letters, and read the newspapers.

School was more than book learning; the young pupils constituted their own community within the larger community. Compared to college, Walker had fond memories of his school days in Fountain Green: he recalled "the fun . . . we used to have when we went to school in the old brick and fought battles with snowballs or tried to see which could walk closest to Johnson's deadline or had the girls to explain the Grammar lesson to us during intermission."[80] For Walker, school had been a place to battle on the playground, test the authority of the teacher, and chat with classmates.

The efforts exerted in building schools and hiring teachers suggest that most in the rural community held a strong belief in education beyond its merely legal mandate. Children from neighboring farms were brought together to submit to authority and learn their lessons. As they did in other public affairs in the township, Yankees and Pennsylvanians dominated school administration and instruction, inculcating values of cooperation and hard work that would prepare children for adult responsibilities in the farm community. As trustee of schools for the township, Thomas Geddes hired relatives and friends from Pennsylvania to teach in the local schools, who transmitted their values along with the children's lessons in "orthography, Reading in English, penmanship, and arithmetic."[81] Dr. Ferris, son of an early New York settler, was appointed to the Hancock County Teacher's Association, an organization to train teachers and generally promote "the cause of education."[82]

However, like the peace courts, instead of promoting equal opportunity, schools sustained a public patriarchy. Few of the little girls who attended in the 1850s would live long enough to cast a vote in a presidential election. State law made women eligible to become school officers in 1873, but women were not allowed to vote in school elections until 1891.[83] Because of their responsibility to rear children, women did have a voice in the civic community, but only as underpaid teachers hired and supervised by male trustees.

School districts constituted neighborhood communities of parents and children who cooperated to build and staff schools. While there seems to have been no local resistance by the southern-born to supporting the common schools, the school trustees tended to be Yankees or Pennsylvanians. The schools were a training ground for the next generation, where teachers taught the values of self-improvement, punctuality, and civic character associated with a commercializing society. In the coming decades, the agrarian values of the children's parents which privileged hard work and independence would be challenged by the values of the marketplace which stressed a desire for comfort and wealth.

Rather than erode community, the dynamic growth of the market at mid-century engendered a new vitality in the township's stores, churches, local government, and schools. Commercial, religious, and civic communities were woven together to provide a sense of belonging as new migrants assimilated into the rural neighborhoods. Anchored by the villages of Fountain Green and Webster, rural people created a local farm culture hospitable to the expansion of the market, which increasingly imposed external standards of exchange on local affairs. The township's religious and civic leaders formed a public patriarchy which protected the structures of authority in farm households, and which upheld traditional agrarian values.

By the end of the antebellum era, a stable core of elites in Fountain Green had taken control of the local political apparatus and pressed for a enterprising agenda to take advantage of the expanding market. At the forefront in crafting an agrarian response to the commercializing regional economy, some agitated to establish bourgeois standards of behavior such as temperance. Although their efforts met with only limited success, they achieved power to lay the groundwork for the later emergence of the rural middle class. The shift toward Republican township leaders in the later 1850s would make Fountain Green Township an irritating counterpoint to the Democratic party's struggle to control Hancock County in the divisive Civil War era.

In this period of forming a local farm culture, Fountain Green took on a distinctive character. At mid-century, the Scots-Irish were making Fountain Green their place through extensive kin ties, a church that overshadowed all others, and a firm hold on public offices. Regional identities were still recognizable—New Englanders ran the town businesses and farmers from Pennsylvania dominated local government—but regional identities were being translated into political and class identities, however faint. The ascendance of the northerners denied political power to the southern-born, and the expansion of Protestantism marginalized the original Catholic settlers who relinquished their community church. The extent of northern dominance and the distinctiveness of the Scots-Irish identity would determine the course the community would take in the war years that followed.

5

"Awful calamities now upon us"
The Civil War Era

In the halls of the Old State Capitol in Springfield hangs a banner painted with a likeness of Abraham Lincoln. Awarded as a prize to the Wide-Awakes of Fountain Green at an 1860 Republican rally, it is a curious sight: the face looks like Honest Abe, but the body is short, more like that of Lincoln's rival in the presidential race, Stephen A. Douglas. While the banner suggests that Fountain Green wholeheartedly supported Lincoln and the Republican Party, in reality conflicting loyalties split the deeply divided farm community. How the men of Fountain Green, Illinois, came to earn such a prize, and what Lincoln's victory meant to the tiny rural town is a story of the Civil War in microcosm.[1]

Because Fountain Green was settled by people from both the North and the South, the Civil War was waged on two fronts, on the battlefield and at home. While their own soldiers were dying to save the Union, Hancock County citizens battled each other at home. Rather than being united by the war, the fabric of the community was rent by adherence to sectional and party loyalties in a contest of wills between those who supported and those who opposed the war. That battle pitted settlers from the North against those from the South, Republicans against Democrats, rich against poor. The North's ultimate victory on both fronts subordinated the southern-born in Fountain Green, resulting in Republican rule for decades to come.

The war at home was a national struggle writ small. Partisan affiliations reflected divergent ideologies: the limits of the power of the federal government in local affairs, the government's role in capitalist development, and, by the 1850s, whether the new territories of the West would be opened to slavery. The emergence of the Republican Party out of the ashes of the Whig party reconfigured the political constellation, reverberating in small towns and villages as voters shifted from the American (Know-Nothing) Party to the new anti-slavery coalition. The strength of the rural citizenry's commitment to party was rooted in broad political participation of not only the male electorate but also the women who carved a niche for themselves in the political pageantry of electoral campaigns. The politicization of country people calls into question the idea that rural voters were so caught up in their daily lives that they were somewhat removed from the political process.[2] The history of Fountain Green suggests otherwise; its citizens were fully engaged in the political process, and their political engagement heightened the tensions during the war.

Rural resistance to Lincoln's war tested the bonds of community. Although the scale of the local protest against the war was not as massive as the New York City draft riots of 1863, local resistance typified tensions in many small, rural midwestern communities. While historians have paid some attention to conflicts on the home front, few have examined the tensions that wracked the farming areas of the predominantly rural Midwest.[3] Because more than half of the white Union soldiers were farmers and nearly half were from the Midwest, the war experience of rural community in the Midwest demands our attention.[4] Only by observing a small farming community such as Fountain Green at a local level can we fully understand the contested loyalties that divided Illinois in the heart of the predominantly agrarian Midwest.[5]

The conflict in Fountain Green can serve as a window on the war's transformation of the Midwest. Ironically, rather than being divided like their community at home, most of Fountain Green's soldiers were loyal to Lincoln and the Republican Party. Their votes would allow the Republican Party to reshape the political and cultural landscape of the Midwest, establishing a bourgeois culture which came to be seen as not only midwestern but also peculiarly American.[6] The history of Fountain Green can help us understand both the social history of the Civil War and the new order that emerged in its wake.

The Strength of Party

Because it was originally settled by yeoman southerners who were committed to independent farm ownership and suspicious of government, Hancock County had long been a bastion of the Democratic Party. Indeed, the county had voted for the Democratic presidential nominee since the time the second party system became entrenched in Illinois politics. County offices were filled by party stalwarts, and the plurality of Democrats on the county board of supervisors (one elected delegate from each township) enforced their control through party patronage. The leaders of the Democratic Party were the elites of the county seat at Carthage, bankers and attorneys who controlled commerce as well as politics.[7] In 1856, the strong showing of the American Party challenged Democratic control and provided a steppingstone for voters to affiliate with the Republicans. In Hancock County, the Know-Nothings and Republicans garnered 51 percent of the vote (24 and 27 percent, respectively); statewide, Democrats earned only a plurality, not the usual majority.[8]

The erosion of Democratic strength in Hancock County can be traced to emerging pockets of Republican voters. The river port of Warsaw, with its rapidly growing German population, was one such stronghold. Another node of Republican dominance was Fountain Green, where, in 1856, 22 percent voted Republican and 26 percent voted for the American (Know-Nothing) Party, cutting the Democratic share to 53 percent.[9] The people of Fountain Green had reason to be attracted to the new Republican Party. The strong Scots-Irish Presbyterian heritage of the populace made them ripe for Republican anti-slavery sentiment, and the party's homestead plank was attractive to farmers. Although the township was home to few immigrants, we cannot discount anti-Catholicism and nativism as factors in attracting voters.

Perhaps more important, personal connections strengthened the commitment of Fountain Green Republicans to Lincoln in 1860. Abraham Lincoln's Catholic cousins were among the original settlers of the township, and the county Republican Party capitalized on that connection by sponsoring Robert H. Lincoln as a candidate for sheriff in 1860.[10] The local Republican Party caucus was led by Scots-Irish Presbyterian Thomas Geddes, who had migrated from Pennsylvania in the late 1820s and had been a militia colonel in the 1846 Mormon war. Geddes had known Lincoln in the Illinois legislature, and their friendship was recognized when Geddes was selected to be parade marshal and to introduce Lincoln in his 1858 speech at Carthage.[11]

By 1860, with its own senator Stephen A. Douglas and former congressman Abraham Lincoln competing for the office of president, Illinois was at the epicenter of the partisan conflict. Illinois voters took sides, choosing Douglas and the Democrats with their pro-Southern bias, or Lincoln and the new Republicans, a Yankee party of anti-slavery agitation.[12] The 1860 presidential election campaign was intensely partisan and sectional in western Illinois. With battle lines thus drawn, as they were around the nation, the campaign split the citizenry in western Illinois.

The opposing positions were laid out in local party newspapers which preached party doctrine, instilling loyalty to party through adherence to a carefully articulated political orthodoxy. The major Democratic paper in the county was called the *Carthage Republican,* a name which made sense in the Jacksonian age but became a misnomer after the founding of the Republican Party. Republicans founded three short-lived papers meant to do battle in the presidential campaign, the *Carthage Transcript,* the *Daily Warsaw Bulletin,* and the *Hamilton Representative.*[13] These local party organs sustained a lively banter over the issues of the election, taking potshots at each other and conducting a highly charged debate replete with personal attacks on leading members of the opposite party.

The rhetoric of the papers makes it clear that the Democrats distrusted government, which they portrayed as a threat to personal liberty. Party leaders promoted popular sovereignty, which allowed territories to choose whether or not to allow slavery, as a way to preserve states' rights from an overpowering federal government. This Democratic privileging of local over national authority resonated in the rural county, garnering votes of support from those who saw Republican attempts to promote temperance and compulsory education as a government conspiracy to deprive them of their personal liberties. Democrats deplored the nativism of the Republican Party and were deeply suspicious of financial and political privilege of wealthy Republicans.[14] The Democrats waged their struggle by raising the specter of "Black Republican" sympathy for the slaves and accusing the Republicans of "fanaticism, sectionalism, and negroism."[15] The campaign rhetoric on both sides played on race-based fears—fears that slavery threatened a way of life dependent upon the freehold family farm.

For the Republicans, the issue of race also centered on the issue of slavery in the western territories. The Republican paper preached free soil ideology as it urged each Republican voter to act as "a freeman and patriot." At issue was not whether slavery should continue in the South "but whether the vast and beautiful expanse of Western Territory now free, shall be peopled solely by free white men, or by a mixed population of white men and negro slaves."[16] Slave labor in the territories imperiled the individualist ethos of the family farm that was expanding into the West. The future of the West was at stake, and only Republican votes would preserve it "for the free white laboring men of the whole country."[17] Free soil ideology resonated powerfully in the agricultural community only one state away from Kansas. The farmer-voters of Hancock County did not fear slave labor at home; what worried them was the threat of slavery to the West, where future generations might settle.

Historians have argued that ethnocultural factors should be considered along with ideological stance in understanding why voters chose a certain party.[18] In the absence of viva voce voting records, we can rely on published accounts of party activities and county histories to identify party affiliation for a cohort of "visible partisans" in Fountain Green, twenty-five of whom were Republicans and forty-three of whom were Democrats.[19] Republicans were older than Democrats; in 1860, they were an average of 46 years old compared to the average of 38 years for Democrats (see Table 5.1). On average, Republicans were about twice as wealthy as Democrats, because except for a miller and a doctor, all the Republicans were land-owning farmers. In contrast, while over half the Democrats were also farmers, they were the party of townsmen—merchants, craftsmen, day laborers, and professionals. The differences in occupation and age help explain the disparity in wealth between men of the two parties. That Republicans were farmers and Democrats were townsmen suggests a town-country split in the rural electorate that was reflected in party affiliation.

While sectional feeling was increasing, the cohort of visible partisans does not show a clear dichotomy based on nativity. However, there is evidence of the tendency of southerners to affiliate with the Democratic party. While both parties had an equal share of men born in Pennsylvania and Ohio (38 percent), a greater share of Democrats were from New England and New York; ten were from New York alone. Democrats attracted more of the southern-born, who constituted 21 percent of their party; only 12 percent of southern-born members of this group joined the Republican Party. So while neither party was dominated by southerners, and while no direct correlation of party and section existed among the visible partisans, more southern-born voters found a home in the Democratic party than the anti-slavery Republican camp.

The visible partisans organized township clubs that enlisted new members and orchestrated local participation in county party activities. Party leaders were eminently successful in getting out the vote in rural Illinois; 75 percent of the male electorate cast ballots in 1856, and in 1860 the participation rate rose to 95 percent. Local rallies drew thousands of rural citizens to hear speeches and register their loyalty for party principles. The parades, rituals, and rhetoric of the rallies politicized the rural citizenry, lining them up on opposite sides of the slavery question. In October 1860, the Democratic rally took place in the county seat of Carthage, an important enough party stronghold to lure Senator Stephen A. Douglas. The "exultant and joyous" crowd that spilled out of the Carthage courthouse square heard Democratic luminaries speak from four different stands. By all reports, the 1860 crowd was overwhelming, more than 10,000 people, a third of the county's entire population. After darkness fell, the Fountain Green Club, "who made a splendid appearance" on horseback, participated in the march of over 2,200 torch-bearers, and fireworks lit up the sky.[20]

The parades gathered a diverse group of people from townships across the county into a symbolic oneness. In wagon after wagon, accompanied by marching bands and men on horseback, township delegations proceeded past the crowds lining the main thoroughfares leading to the county square. Each township was acknowledged in the newspaper report as an important building block at the foundation of the county party organization. Within each township delegation the parades were organized along lines of gender. Like the nearly 200 Hickories from Fountain Green who came to hear Douglas, Democratic voters organized into clubs of Young Hickories that paraded on horseback in a uniform of striped shirt, leather belt, and red, white, and blue caps. Their female counterparts, dressed in white, joined them in wagons, waving flags and banners.[21]

Town women guaranteed their place in the political scene by publicly presenting hand-sewn flags, as the "Democratic Ladies of Carthage" did to the Young Hickory Club. Speaking on their behalf, the daughter of a prominent businessman warned that the flag should never be "trailed in the black dust of abolitionism." Rising to rhetorical heights, she expressed a hope for union, that none of the stars be plucked from the flag, which was "a covenant of white men."[22] By raising their craft to an art, the women conveyed both the Democratic ideology and gendered ideals of feminine virtue in the silk flag with embroidered gold stars.

Vastly outnumbered by Democrats in Hancock County, in October 1860 the region's Republicans rallied thirty miles away in Keokuk, Iowa. After speech-making, the crowd of 25,000 ate dinner set out on tables in halls around the city. At dusk the torchlight procession marched along Main and the cross streets, which "made the whole city one blaze of light." Over twenty-five companies of 2,500 Wide-Awakes swelled the ranks of the parade, dressed in black oilcloth capes and carrying eagle lanterns.[23] Viewed from the bluffs of Warsaw across the river, the procession was "a grand sight, the glittering of lamps and capes, the booming of the cannons and the waiving of flags, banners and transparencies, and the rolling Republican Ball."[24] The Fountain Green Wide-Awakes, one of just six companies who finished the march, took the prize for the largest company, numbering about 160. Their reward was the large banner that now hangs in the old State Capitol, a likeness of Lincoln on one side and the presentation inscription in bold block letters on the other.[25]

The huge party rallies attracted not only the male electorate but also women, who rode in the parade wagons, provided food for the throngs, and stitched flags for local companies. Not mere bystanders, young women dressed in white represented the states of the Union in the parades. In the Republican display the woman who represented Kansas made a political statement by dressing in black and carrying a banner which read, "Democracy won't let me in."[26] The women's contribution of cooking and serving food also involved them in the political pageantry. The *Gate City* had urged the women of Keokuk: "Bake and roast, and boil and fry, to-day, that you may have wherewith to meet the wants of the multitudes who will be dependent on your hospitality tomorrow."[27] Not only male voters were politicized but also women who participated obliquely in the electoral process. Their domestic skills earned them a place in the public arena.

In November, when the ballots were counted, both parties took comfort in their respective victories. Lincoln won the national election, but in Hancock County, Douglas won by a margin of 389 votes, garnering 52 percent of the total (see Table 5.2).[28] Republicans narrowly carried Fountain Green Township for Lincoln, 170 to 152 votes, one of only three county townships with a Republican majority.[29]

Nationally, the price of Lincoln's victory was quickly made clear as the southern states seceded from the Union and formed the Confederacy on February 4, 1861.[30] At the outbreak of war in April, the Democrats lamented that "none but a Black Republican President, and a Black Republican Congress, which rejected every proposition of compromise, could have destroyed the Union and involved the country . . . in awful calamities now upon us."[31] Locally, the Democrats blamed the Republicans for the war and only reluctantly agreed to support the war effort. In an effort to shake off their underdog status, the outnumbered Republicans forged links with state and national party organizations that would set the stage for a wartime clash of wills within the farm community.

War at Home

The war between the Union and the Confederacy echoed in a war at home because the partisan imperatives that structured political activity also shaped responses to the war. Although the Democratic party had campaigned against the war, after war was declared, Democratic party officials such as Douglas encouraged enlistment to support the Union.[32] However, in Illinois, the support of the Democratic party was somewhat tenuous, and Democrats openly criticized the abridgement of civil rights by Lincoln's administration. For example, party leaders sponsored resolutions in June 1863 proposing an armistice to end the war, and the party was constantly involved in disputes with Republican governor Richard Yates, who threatened to prorogue the legislature.[33] In Hancock County, the Democratic *Carthage Republican* continued to rail against the administration, until local Democrats replaced the editor to minimize the political costs of his anti-Lincoln rhetoric.[34] Furthermore, while publicly Democrats declared loyalty, many resisted the war in clandestine activities. Rural townships such as Fountain Green were divided into political sub-communities that heightened social tensions, threatening to permanently divide them.

By 1863, when the human toll of the war was dreadfully apparent, the draft had become a divisive wedge that split the community. Underground resistance organizations in Fountain Green protested Lincoln's radical extension of governmental power, especially the draft. Democrats saw the draft as an infringement on personal freedom, an abuse of federal power, and as favoritism to the rich, who could more easily pay the commutation fee.[35] In defense of the war, Fountain Green's Republicans reached outside the county for political support, engineering a Yankee ascendance that subordinated the southern-born settlers.

Both Republicans and Democrats operated underground organizations to carry out their wartime aims. The political press in Hancock County was quick to charge men with the label of anti-war Copperhead or militant pro-war Union Leaguer, and local lore bears out charges of the active existence of such groups in Fountain Green. In February 1863, the Democratic newspaper "exposed" the formation of the Spartan Band, or Secret Brotherhood, organization of Republicans in the county, which they said threatened to use force against Copperheads. The paper claimed that the leader of the "most infamous organization" was none other than Fountain Green Republican Thomas Geddes, township draft registrar.[36] The fact that the accusations swirled around Geddes suggests that the Republican stronghold was a vulnerable target for the county's Democratic leadership. During the spring 1863 election campaigns, local Democrats met at the Fountain Green schoolhouse and cheered: "Courage, boys! we shall stay the [Union] leaguers in Fountain Green!"[37]

The Geddes family has handed down stories which corroborate the activities of the underground resistance aimed at draft registrars. One story alleged that a secret meeting of the pro-slavery Knights of the Golden Circle was held in the timber a few miles east of Fountain Green to plan the theft of the draft book from Thomas Geddes.[38] Tennessee-born farmer Solomon Dill was reported to have said that since the Geddes family would fight before surrendering the book, if someone was going to get hurt they might as well shoot them to begin with. Dill was opposed by Geddes's fellow elder in the Presbyterian church, who said he would have nothing to do with it. The family was warned, and despite assurances from their parents, the children became so frightened they rose in the night and sat in the dark, loaded guns across their laps. About 10 P.M. they heard noises in the barn, but then they drifted asleep. In the morning the children realized the noises had been made by neighbors and relatives who had slept in the barn in case of attack.[39]

Geddes's concerns were not unfounded. On June 28, 1863, a group of men from Hancock Township (directly south of Fountain Green) entered the homes of enrollment officers and confiscated the draft books at gunpoint. The authorities had to send a detachment of the Sixteenth Illinois Cavalry to complete the enrollment.[40] The following day, John Ritter, a hot-tempered soldier at home on furlough, insulted local Democrats as Copperhead traitors. After he threatened to kill one of them, the sheriff issued a warrant for his arrest on charges of assault and battery. As the sheriff read the warrant, Ritter fired at him, mortally wounding his deputy. Ritter fled town, setting off a day-long chase through the countryside by a self-appointed posse of men who shot him on sight. Ritter later died, and the Republicans made him a martyr to their cause.[41] The Ritter incident sharpened animosities between local Democrats, who resented the Copperhead label, and Republicans, who saw Democrats as dragging their feet to support the cause.

The Geddes family stories singled out as their adversaries men such as Basil and Hickerson Wright. Southern-born Democrats, the brothers were sons of slave-owning families originally from Tennessee. The sons of the Wrights fled to Missouri to avoid the draft and would return occasionally to ride through town on horseback shooting and yelling slogans such as "Hurrah for Jeff Davis!" They stormed the polling place and reputedly tried to control the election by scaring off Republican voters at gunpoint in November 1862. Other Wright cousins avoided service by heading to California, where they profited handsomely in the gold fields.[42]

Tensions in Fountain Green were at their height in the fall of 1864, when Missouri bushwhackers, perhaps tipped off by the Wrights, invaded the countryside. In the early evening of October 18, 1864, a band of forty to fifty men stole twenty horses and firearms from farms on the east side of the township.[43] When the thieves stopped at the farm of C. D. Simmons (an anti-slavery Kentuckian loyal to the Union), he confronted them on the porch of his large farmhouse. His two sons slipped out through a window in the cellar under the dining room, picked up two bridles from the summer kitchen, and freed all their horses from the barn. They bridled and mounted two horses, and spread the alarm through the neighborhood. The four farms that were robbed were owned by Republicans; two German farmers deflected an attack by convincing the thieves that they were loyal Democrats.[44]

The event was spectacularly headlined in the *Carthage Republican* as "A Guerrilla Raid in Hancock County. Fifty Mounted Men Overrun Fountain Green Township." The raid gave Col. Thomas A. Geddes an excuse to create a local militia, which Democrats saw as a thinly disguised Republican attempt to challenge their control of the local political apparatus. When on October 27 Geddes arrived from Springfield with six boxes of guns, Democratic Sheriff Melgar Couchman confronted him at the Carthage rail depot with about a dozen men. Geddes, who had already sacrificed one son for the cause of the Union, defied Couchman's order to hand over the guns. Geddes argued that the state had issued the arms to "a regular organized military company, and if Couchman interfered with them he did so at his peril." The sheriff backed down, and other townships followed suit in obtaining arms from the state.[45] The men of Fountain Green's home guard converted C. C. Tyler's store into a barracks, playing cards or sleeping on the counter all night while pickets marched around outside the premises keeping watch. Meanwhile the Democrats fumed, charging the Republicans with arming themselves to take the elections by force.[46] Geddes used his connections within the Republican Party to obtain arms from Springfield, thus strengthening the Union League defense of Fountain Green. Local Democratic officials were proven powerless in their efforts to stop him.

Even after the prospects of Northern victory improved later in the war, rural people resisted the war by refusing to pay bounties to meet draft quotas. In September 1864, county authorities drafted 456 men; another 82 were called up in November. Twenty men from Fountain Green Township were among that number, which included several sons from families who had already lost sons to the war. To meet the draft quotas, local governments taxed themselves to pay a $400 bounty to enlistees.[47] By war's end, Hancock County had expended $119,885 to pay bounties, in addition to amounts approved by six county townships, which brought the total bounties paid in the county to $174,309. Fountain Green Township alone authorized $8,044 in bounties to soldiers, but many refused to pay the tax to fund the bounty.[48]

How to raise the large sums necessary to pay bounties was a perplexing problem that worried community leaders in Fountain Green. Fannie Leach, daughter of Fountain Green Justice of the Peace Kendrick Leach, wrote to a friend in March 1865: "The men here are in such a panic about the draft, Uncle Jackson, John Mesick, and some others have not done a days work for a month. Look out what time you will and you will see them on the street."[49]

Paying bounties was a volatile issue because it heightened not only partisan and sectional divisions but also class differences. While there was general reluctance to pay bounties, no matter what one's party affiliation, refusal to pay resulted in being labeled as a Copperhead. One "W" wrote to the Democratic paper that the "rich and highborn, the intensely and superlatively 'loyal' Republicans who had for the last four years shouted for 'the last dollar and the last man' to support the rebellion, refused to pay over." He threatened, "'Dough over' gentlemen, and be either 'men or mice,' support the 'government' or you may find yourselves dubbed 'copperheads.'"[50] Others protested the bounties as an unfair reward to those who delayed enlistment and argued that early enlistees deserved the bonus.[51] To meet his obligations, the Fountain Green tax collector had to borrow $1,500 and seize the property of those who refused to pay.[52]

The bounty controversy highlighted the widening gap between rich and poor in Fountain Green. While poor families struggled to farm without the labor of their sons, wealthy farmers mechanized production to take advantage of rising prices. Deprived of the labor of sons and hired men during the 1860s, farmers invested in agricultural machinery such as reapers and corn planters.[53] Farmers almost doubled production of swine and increased cattle production by one-third.[54] Other farmers profited from supplying wartime industries. Responding to demand for wool for soldier's uniforms, a handful of elite farmers specialized in sheep-raising, tripling township wool production.[55] The demand for wool illustrates the profits available to those who owned the capital to invest in sheep.

The production of wool stimulated local processing industries and expanded the rural marketing apparatus. A steam-powered wool carding shop in Fountain Green carded 8,000 pounds of wool worth $4,000 in 1860. In Carthage, grain dealer Boyd Braden began to buy wool fleeces in addition to wheat and corn.[56] A store in Macomb in the next county advertised in the Carthage paper that it wanted 50,000 pounds of wool for the Hoosier Woolen Factory in

Indianapolis.[57] The chain of wool production—from sheep in Fountain Green's fields to regional entrepôts—illustrates the means by which the township was becoming connected to the agricultural market on the national level.

Farm women may have been as sensitive to rising prices and high demand in domestic production as their husbands were in meeting demands for pork and wool. Over 60 percent of Fountain Green farms produced a surplus of butter, but local shortages occurred because butter exports commanded higher prices. At the height of the Civil War, the *Carthage Republican* querulously demanded, "Why is it that this almost indispensable article is so scarce?"[58] The war also saw an upsurge in home textile production as women returned to their spinning wheels and looms to make up for the shortage of cotton cloth.[59]

To meet the demands of the wartime market, farmers' daughters stepped in for their brothers who were away at war. Because the new farm machinery did not require the physical strength and size demanded by hand-powered tools, women were capable of working to maintain high levels of production. An advertisement in the *Prairie Farmer* pictured a well-dressed young woman driving a hay rake, saying, "My brother has gone to the war."[60] The paper published a plea by state agricultural officials to farmers to let their daughters help on the farm, if it would "not compromise their dignity and sense of propriety." Women were asked to put away their piano music, put on their heavy shoes, bonnet, and worn dress, and mount a cultivator, reaper, or mower to help their fathers.[61] The benefits would be remunerative, both politically and economically. Farm daughters who were educated to help on the farms "could never rear a traitor son."[62]

Women in town also took over the jobs of men, such as the editor's daughter who became the typesetter for the *Carthage Republican*. She declared, "In comparison with machine sewing or almost any other species of 'woman's work,' 'type setting' is perfectly delightful." The editor added: "Woman, brave and stronghearted as she is, need no longer fear that her capacities and her mental strength shall lie dormant."[63] The labor of women during wartime restructured work roles and expectations, at least temporarily, loosening the gender restrictions of the patriarchal society.

Not only farmers but also the merchants in Fountain Green enjoyed the prosperity brought by the Civil War. Storekeepers Campbell and Everett expanded their business hours to take advantage of the increased traffic in town.[64] By 1864, Connecticut Yankee storekeeper Charles C. Tyler had done well enough to build a new store in the neo-classical style of city retailing establishments (see Figure 5.1). He named his store "The Arcade," lettered in a large sign on the store's front. The Arcade's design invited shoppers onto its broad porch, where they could gaze at goods through the large windows or promenade in their new finery.[65] While the prosperous Yankees in Fountain Green enjoyed wartime profits, war widows struggled to feed their families and disabled men

FIGURE 5.1. C. C. Tyler's Arcade. From Alfred Theodore Andreas, *An Illustrated Historical Atlas of Hancock County, Illinois* (Chicago: A. T. Andreas, 1874), 67.

searched for non-farm work. The war's toll made opposition to the war repulsive to those suffering from its losses, but that did not quell the divisiveness between Democrats and Republicans on the home front.

Comrades for a Cause

While the citizens of Fountain Green were quarreling over the draft, their sons, brothers and husbands were enduring the privations of war. If the home front was so divided, what kept the men fighting? Historians have argued that soldiers enlisted and fought out of an ideological commitment to the cause and a commitment to their comrades in arms.[66] Men from Fountain Green who had gone to war under party banners were welded into a brotherhood by the shared experience of combat, hardship, and camp life. Men who risked all, who lost brothers and friends to the war, fought even more fiercely for Lincoln and the anti-slavery cause. Thus the war not only created bonds of brotherhood, it made men susceptible to Republican Party ideals.

From the partisan nature of the recruiting for war, one would not suspect that the war made Republicans of many of the soldiers. Because local party leaders organized the military companies, party divisions determined the patterns of recruitment of soldiers within Hancock County. Eager soldiers, among them the sons of Thomas Geddes, affiliated with the Sixteenth Illinois Regiment organized immediately after the outbreak of war by Republicans in Quincy.[67] In contrast, local Democrats did not organize regiments until July 1862, when Illinois governor Richard Yates endorsed President Lincoln's call for an additional 300,000 volunteers. Eight hundred men enlisted in the various companies of Illinois 118th, which assembled men from the many small towns and farm villages of Hancock County.[68]

Democratic party leadership was also important in organizing recruits in Fountain Green. Thomas J. Campbell, local leader of the Democratic party and veteran of the Mexican War, recruited Company A of the 118th Regiment.[69] Party spirit permeated the county organizations, so Campbell's local leadership of the Democratic group was important in influencing men, both Democrats and Republicans, to join him in the local company. One clue to the patriotic fervor is found in the first page of Daybook B of the store where Campbell clerked, where a sketch of two American flags was inscribed with the significant date of the soldier's enlistment: "August 9th AD 1862." It may have been Campbell himself who displayed his patriotism in this little drawing.[70] The men enlisted out of loyalty to the ideals of the union, liberty, and democracy, threatened by secession. Young men may also have seen the war as an adventure, a way to escape farm work and small-town life.[71] For many, soldiering was their passage to manhood, a time when they assumed the linked identities of man, soldier, and citizen.[72]

The majority of the soldiers from Fountain Green served in Company A of the 118th and Company G of the Second Cavalry, which fought alongside the 118th (see Table 5.3).[73] Most of the 140 men enlisted in August 1862, and constituted about 40 percent of the males in the township between the ages of 15 to 44. By 1863, news of casualties in the military campaigns slowed enlistment; the 1864 draft resulted in another twenty-six men from Fountain Green entering the service.[74]

What kind of men became soldiers? Of the 140 men from Fountain Green, 60 can be located in the 1860 census. The typical soldier from Fountain Green was young, Illinois-born, on the lower end of the property scale, and unmarried. Most soldiers were farmers or sons of farmers, a handful were craftsmen, one was a merchant, another a clergyman. One-third of the sixty soldiers were heads of households. The average value of their real estate holdings was about half of that for all household heads (just $1,004 compared to $1,950), perhaps because eight of the men did not own land. The ages of the enlistees followed national patterns; most men were in their late teens or in their twenties. As younger men, the families they left behind were smaller, just 3.7 persons per household compared to 4.3 for the township as a whole.[75]

The 118th was an extension of the local community, composed largely of companies recruited throughout Hancock County in the summer of 1862. The men enlisted together, served in the same company, and fought the same battles, commanded by leaders who were men of standing at home. Among them was storekeeper Matthew McClaughry's son, Robert, a Democrat now of Carthage, who commanded that town's Company B. He was later promoted to the rank of major. Chosen as regimental commander was fellow Democrat Col. John G. Fonda, a Mexican War veteran married to Mary McConnell of Fountain Green.[76] Rev. Thomas M. Walker of the Fountain Green Presbyterian church was selected as chaplain for the regiment, and other officers hailed from county towns.[77]

The 118th remained tightly connected to the home front through letters and reports about the men's living conditions and behavior. Letters from soldiers and their commanders were printed in the county paper, and what a soldier did while he was away from home was scrutinized by men from his own neighborhood or even his own family. Loyalty to fellow soldiers in the company, to brothers and friends from home, no doubt kept many in the service as the war wore on. The experience of combat meant the men shared the horrors of war, binding them together in suffering and devotion to a patriotic cause which supplanted divisive party loyalties.

The flag of the 118th regiment, preserved for posterity, listed the battles in which the soldiers fought: Arkansas Post, Champion Hill, Black River Bridge, and Chickasaw Bluffs of the Vicksburg Campaign, as well as later battles in Port Gibson, Jackson, and Grand Coteau.[78] The war took a deadly toll on the soldiers from Fountain Green. A Fountain Green soldier who went off to war had a three in four chance of surviving the experience, and about a fifty-fifty chance of becoming seriously ill or disabled. Information available for 123 of the 140 soldiers shows that 27 of the men died, most from disease. Only 3 were killed in battle. Another 9 were discharged due to disability, and 16 were discharged for unspecified reasons, perhaps also due to disability. Of the 140, just 67 (48 percent) served their full terms of service with no record of illness or disability.[79]

Illnesses and combat casualties had the effect of diluting the Democratic leadership and transferring it to Republicans. When Company A Captain Thomas J. Campbell was discharged due to illness in February 1863, he was replaced by a Republican, Walker Geddes, who left the Sixteenth to take Campbell's place, thus joining his brothers Cyrus and Robert Geddes in Company A (See Figure 5.2).[80] On May 16, in "the bloody and decisive battle of Champion Hills," Captain Walker Geddes and Lieutenant Thomas B. White of Fountain Green were killed, "braver men than whom never drew steel in the cause of liberty."[81] After Walker Geddes's successor died of malaria in July, Cyrus Geddes replaced him, completing the transition in the leadership of the Fountain Green company from Democratic to Republican.[82]

Following two years of death and disease and hardship, the 118th concluded the war with a relatively placid final year of light skirmishing and chasing bushwhackers. The regiment camped near the city of Vicksburg until mid-

FIGURE 5.2. Lieutenant Walker Geddes. From the Geddes Family Records.

August, when it was ordered down the Mississippi into the Gulf department. The men finished their war duty in Baton Rouge, Louisiana, keeping the Mississippi open to traffic.[83]

Removed from the war's dangers, the months of camp life increased solidarity in the ranks as the chaplains conducted Christian revivals and temperance campaigns. Chaplain William Underwood, Methodist minister from Carthage, conducted well-attended Sabbath meetings and daily devotionals. He observed that since women were in the majority in church services at home, "It seems a little strange to preach to a congregation composed entirely of men." Through the temperance campaign, the chaplain attempted to inculcate men with bourgeois values heralded by the Republican Party. These ideals of manhood emphasized self-control, especially in drinking.[84] Underwood was pleased to report to the home audience that with the establishment of a Good Templar's lodge, "the regiment is not left entirely without moral influence." By April 1865, the Society of Good Templars numbered 156, making the 118th "the banner temperance regiment."[85]

The men of the 118th who went to war to fight for the Union came to know the former slaves as servants in the army and refugees from the South. When forty "darkeys" joined their company to serve as undercooks, Cyrus Geddes reported that the black soldiers were "glad to belong to Uncle Sam." His acquaintance with the sorry condition of the freed slaves may have added the moral intensity of anti-slavery feeling to their ambitions for fighting. In early November, as the regiment returned from raiding southern Missouri they were accompanied by fleeing slaves.[86] Rev. Underwood read his political creed into his letter to the Republican newspaper:

> Do the slaves want liberty? Every horse and mule not mounted by a soldier on the return to Baton Rouge was mounted by a black man or woman and large numbers followed on foot. The scene passes description. Women with children in their arms waded through the mud keeping pace with cavalry. Men packed heavy bundles on their backs.—Creeks had to be forded and through them men and women waded. One woman was confined on the march, but as soon as the child was born, renewed her journey, and keeping up with the cavalry reached Baton Rouge. They had one desire which they expressed in these words, "We's gowan wid ye'all." Well they know that the starry flag would lead them to liberty.[87]

For the soldiers from Fountain Green, as it had for the nation, the war for the Union had become the war to free the slaves. The soldiers showed their allegiance to the cause by voting wholeheartedly for Lincoln in a straw vote during the 1864 presidential elections. The 41 Fountain Green men in Company A voted 35 to 6 for Lincoln, but the men from Carthage in Company B were not nearly so loyal, splitting their vote 20 to 22 for Lincoln. The regiment gave Lincoln the victory, awarding him 257 votes, compared to 106 for McClellan. While these were straw votes only, since Illinois's Democratic legislature did not allow absentee voting, nevertheless they show a trend toward Lincoln and the Republican Party by men from a predominantly Democratic county.[88] The war made Republicans of many of the soldiers from Fountain Green, who were sacrificing for the cause of the Union in companies led by Republican officers.

The loyalty of the soldiers to Lincoln seems to have had little immediate effect on elections at home. Back in Hancock County, the Democrats held on to local control in the 1864 election, but their margin of victory for presidential candidate McClellan was only 275 votes, compared to a 389-vote margin for Douglas in 1860. The margin was slim in Fountain Green, only 21 votes, but Fountain Green was among the seven townships with a Republican plurality, resulting in a gain of four townships countywide for the Republican Party.[89] Party feeling was alive and well in western Illinois, a contested terrain where Democrats struggled to hold onto local offices.

At war's end in April 1865, the flames of war resistance died down to a smoldering resentment. When word of the fall of Richmond reached the county, celebratory bonfires blazed on the courthouse square in Carthage.[90] Close on the heels of the news of victory came the announcement of the assassination of President Lincoln, which the *Republican* printed in black-edged columns.[91] Laura Geddes, just 21 years old, away at school in Normal, Illinois, wrote home about watching the Lincoln funeral train pass on its way to Springfield. She described how the students woke early to see the train arrive at 5 A.M., preceded by an engine draped in mourning black. Her feelings were somber: "I know the words of the motto [Go to thy rest] was the thought in each heart as all stood silently watching till the cars wound slowly round the hill out of sight."[92]

In Fountain Green, the Independence Day celebration in 1865 provided an opportunity for reconciliation, but the partisan and sectional tensions would not be calmed. Between four and five hundred people assembled in a shady grove about a quarter mile north of the village of Fountain Green. Town officers and the orators sat upon a stand ornamented with wreaths and banners. The local band had mastered several military marches for the occasion.[93] According to one J. W., who wrote to the county Democratic paper, "All met to celebrate this day, laying aside their prejudices and greeting one another with the right hand of fellowship as became Christians, patriots, and American citizens." At the Fountain Green Presbyterian church, Rev. Walker opened the service with an "eloquent, patriotic, and fervent" invocation that was "not one-sided or selfish, nor revengeful."[94]

The conciliatory mood was destroyed by the partisan remarks of the featured speaker, Rev. Harris, whom J. W. called an "abolition secessionist." Harris reportedly asserted that free speech began in New England, which J. W. refuted by mentioning Puritan persecutions of dissenters. In fact, wrote J. W., in 1861 the Puritan "reign of terror was again revived, the press demolished, and unless you spoke favorable of New England views and interests you were called a 'copperhead' and 'traitor,' and threatened with death."[95] According to J. W., the speaker maliciously revived old sectional animosities at a time when the terrible price of the war was painfully evident. Typical of Democratic suspicion of government tyranny, J. W. felt he had paid a high price for wartime

Republican dominance of Fountain Green. His was a bitterness born of repression.

Lingering animosities surfaced again in 1866, when the Fountain Green town moderator, D. J. Beebe, refused to allow known draft dodger John M. Bainter to cast his vote in the township elections. Although Bainter had been denied the vote the previous fall by an election board of three Democrats, he waited to sue until Beebe, a Republican, denied him the vote. When Bainter won his suit for damages, the Republican press in the county was outraged, and urged township boards of elections "to refuse votes offered by rebels, deserters, draft skedaddlers, and rebel sympathisers." In the eyes of the editor of the Republican sheet, deserters should be refused because "the rights of our soldiery, and those who stood by, labored and suffered for, the Union, must be maintained."[96] By refusing Bainter the vote, the party leaders in Fountain Green, both Democrats and Republicans, upheld the Union cause and the memory of those who had died.

That memory helped turn the political tide in favor of the Republicans after the soldiers returned in October 1865.[97] Former Company B commander Robert W. McClaughry, who switched from the Democratic to the Republican Party when he took command of the local army delegation, ran for circuit clerk. In 1864, McClaughry could not overpower the local Democratic establishment and lost by over 300 votes, but in 1865 he was successful in his quest for the office of county clerk.[98] In the immediate aftermath of war, Republicans temporarily dominated Hancock County. That control was tenuous, however, and in the presidential elections of 1868 and 1872 the Democratic candidates took 51 and 55 percent of the vote.[99]

In Fountain Green, where Republicans had held only a narrow edge, an increasing share of voters joined the Republican Party. They remained loyal to it in the war's long aftermath and shut the Democrats out of local offices for a generation. Fountain Green voters elected Republican supervisors over the next several decades and awarded Republican presidential candidate Ulysses S. Grant 55 percent of the vote in 1868 and a resounding 62 percent in 1872.[100] While the Democrats in Hancock County clung to local offices, the Republicans took control of Fountain Green and other small villages throughout the Midwest. Although they could not oust Democrats from local office, their votes for congressional and presidential candidates contributed to the Republican dominance of the Midwest and the nation.

The War's Legacy

Fountain Green's soldiers in the 118th did not return home until October 18, 1865.[101] In florid prose, the editor of the *Republican* described their homecoming at the Carthage depot early in the morning:

Shortly before 8 o'clock the expected train came in sight, and with it the hundreds of brave boys who covered the tops of the cars, swinging their hats and wafting their prolonged cheers upon the morning air. They were greeted at the depot with cheers and shouts of welcome from men, women and children, who crowded upon them in an irresistible tide that nothing could restrain.— Wives with glad streaming eyes clasped great brawny, bearded blue coated fellows in their arms; mothers hugged their brave darlings to fond full hearts; fathers embraced sons, brothers greeted brothers, neighbors welcomed with full hearts their returning neighbors—and altogether it was a hilarious, joyful, tearful, solemn, funny, speechless, talkative, quiet, uproarous time.[102]

Not every soldier stayed to partake of the food prepared by the ladies of Carthage. Some "did not stay a minute at the platform, but charged doublequick for the wives and babes at home. One of them sprang from the cars a mile out of town and took a run through the fields the shortest way to mother and sisters."[103] Sweethearts must have been glad to see them. The number of marriages per year in the county (which had languished at about 250 during the war) shot up to 432 in 1866.[104] They were elated to be home in Old Hancock.

Every family that had bid a soldier goodbye in 1862 or 1863 hoped to welcome him home again. But for many families the veterans' homecoming was a bitter reminder that their soldier slept in the South. Families whose sons were buried on the battlefield or in hospital cemeteries did not even have the comfort of a headstone in the cemetery in Fountain Green. Mourning fathers and mothers cherished the tokens of remembrance of young lives sacrificed to a great cause. David Leach carefully folded and kept in the pages of his journal the last letter he received from his son, Kendrick, named for his uncle. Posted from Atlanta not long before his death, the letter described their battle position, the losses they had suffered, and the steady skirmishing day and night in front of their position. He admitted he was "not very well at present but I think it will not amount to much. I hope not at any rate." He closed his letter by boasting of how his army had burned forty miles of rail between Atlanta and Augusta. Unfortunately, Kendrick was wrong about his illness. The letter would become all the more valuable to his father after his death. His father could take the letter from its secure place in the pages of his journal and read it again and again in the evenings as he set down the events of the day.[105]

Families who wholeheartedly supported the cause were remade by the war. The Geddes family sent three sons to war—Walker, Cyrus, and Robert. Walker was one of two local men killed in the Battle of Champion Hills in mid-May 1863; Cyrus took his place as captain of Company A of the 118th. The small children of Walker Geddes would probably not remember their father.[106] Walker's youngest brother, Thomas, begged to enlist, but his rheumatism kept him home on the farm, where he defended the home turf against draft resisters. Their sister, Laura, wrote to her brothers from school at Normal, Illinois, about listening to "red hot abolition sermons" and reading *Uncle Tom's Cabin:* "If I had read it before the war broke out I don't know but I might have turned out like John Brown."[107] Like her brothers, Laura had been raised as a Republican who was opposed to slavery and loyal to Lincoln. Her older sister, Eveline, bore a daughter out of wedlock in 1863, whose father may have been a soldier who did not return from war.[108]

War widows pursued a variety of strategies to support themselves and their children. Marcus Alton's widow Phebe returned with her children to her home in Monmouth, and James Wilson Campbell's young widow remarried in 1869. Thomas White's widow also remarried in 1869, to a farmer in the next township. Margaret Chamberlin opened a millinery and dressmaking shop, which prospered until her death in 1873. Magdalene Brandon was already a widow, having lost both her husband and a baby daughter to the 1854 cholera epidemic in Iowa, when her seventeen-year-old son, Richard, died of typhoid in March 1863. When bounties were offered as draft incentives in March 1865, son Linn (then twenty-five) volunteered for service in the same regiment in which his brother George was serving. She depended on her older son James to farm the family land she lived on in Fountain Green with two young daughters.[109]

Elderly parents dependent on a son's support had to painfully scrape together resources to maintain a living. When Marion Conkey's parents filed a pension claim, the neighbors rallied with affidavits attesting to their poverty. Storekeeper C. C. Tyler said George Conkey had barely been able to "keep the wolf from the door" for thirty-four years, miller John Frank said George rarely found work at his trade of rough carpentry, and a neighboring farmer said the Conkeys farmed poor and broken brush land. Carter Alton, whose brother Marcus had died in the war, remembered that Marion Conkey had supported his parents, giving his mother two cows and a pair of colts in 1864, and had sent home at least $50 of his army pay.[110]

Other families did not survive the war intact. When he left for the front in February 1862, farmer Cyrus Fuller moved his wife, Clarinda, and their two young children in with her sister's family and charged his brother-in-law, Amasa Thomas, with their care. An intimate relationship formed between Clarinda and Amasa, and in April 1863 they deserted home, each taking with them their youngest child. Ironically, their escape west to Kansas was funded by money Cyrus had sent home from the army. Amasa's parents took over the care of the five remaining grandchildren.[111]

The full impact of Civil War service cannot be appreciated without taking into account the disease and disability that plagued the soldiers after their return home. Only two soldiers were disabled by war wounds; one injured his heel and the other lost two fingers at the first joint. The most frequent complaint when veterans later came to file for pensions was rheumatism, probably caused as much by advancing age and hard farm labor as any war experience. John P.

Day claimed that his rheumatism was caused by duty in November 1861, in which he stood guard over telegraph lines in Paducah, Kentucky, in a "very cold drenching rain." His illness required him to spend the next three months in the hospital. Less believable is James C. Robinson's claim that he had suffered from a cough since taking cold while swimming in a Louisiana bayou. The next most common ground for filing an invalid claim was respiratory illness—a cold, catarrh, or lung disease. Diarrhea and piles afflicted eight men, and three survived the more serious malaria and typhoid. Thomas A. Bullock, who was injured when a horse fell on him, said his ribs were "depressed and sore."[112]

Few families who saw men leave for war remained the same during the war. Widows remarried, moved back with their parents, or made a living with the help of children and the goodwill of the community. Neighbors who were better off helped the aged who were deprived of the support of their sons who had died in the war. Relatives and friends pitched in at threshing time. In a very real sense, the war left the families of Fountain Green more dependent on each other and the larger community.

As it did the Midwest, the conflicts of the Civil War transformed the rural community of Fountain Green Township. Some of those changes could be easily seen: new reapers in the fields, Widow Chamberlin's millinery shop, Tyler's Arcade, a veteran limping through the streets of town. The animosities of the inner civil war were not so easily captured by a look around, but they are now evident to the distant eye of the historian. Instead of coming together in a common cause during the war, emotions seethed below the surface, testing the bonds of community. The inner civil war in Hancock County—the draft-dodging, guerilla raids, and vigilantism—exposed the strength of rural resistance. The war polarized rich and poor, Republicans and Democrats, and families from the North and from the South. Like the ultimately victorious Union forces, in the face of stiff resistance from the dissenters within, the Republican Yankees in Fountain Green gained the upper hand, presaging the Republican dominance of the Midwest and the nation. Republicans such as those in Fountain Green may have reinforced the party's hold on the nation, but Democratic control at the local level made it far from hegemonic.

The war that divided the township of Fountain Green ultimately unified its soldiers, many of whom switched to Lincoln and the Republican Party by war's end. The war was a momentous event in the lives of the soldiers of Fountain Green. For many it occurred on the threshold of manhood, and it taught them how to relate to higher authority, how to cooperate in a common cause, and how to endure hardships and sacrifice. Because the men of Fountain Green served as a locally formed unit, the war solidified bonds of kinship and affection that had their roots in childhood. Many lost brothers and friends to disease and battle; others were plagued by wounds and ailments their whole lives that would compromise their ability to make a living. Their commitment to country came at an enormous cost.

The soldiers' participation in a national event, mingling with other soldiers from the Midwest, opened their eyes to an array of opportunities. Sons who had been welcomed home discovered they could not afford land in the township and headed west to homestead. The veterans who married and settled down with the aid of a patrimony would live in a community far different from the frontier settlement their parents had established a generation before. Farmers had crossed an invisible threshold to enter a nationwide market that was increasingly attuned not to agrarianism, but to industrialism. Like other farming areas in the Midwest, Fountain Green had opened itself to the nation, and there was no turning back. The Civil War marked the transition from an era of making a place to the era of finding a place within a larger whole. As they would find out, it was a mixed blessing.

PART III

6

"A market at his door"
The Family Farm at Risk

As Fountain Green recovered from the disruption of the Civil War, an expanding market of goods and ideas was transforming farm family culture. The transformation can be represented by contrasting farmers from two generations, an old settler and the son of another old settler. When Alexander Walker, that "noble old pioneer," died on Christmas Day 1879, he was 66 years of age. Born in Path Valley, Pennsylvania, in 1814, he emigrated to Fountain Green in 1838. In April 1843, he married Martha McConnell, the woman who wrote letters home to Aunt Martha in Path Valley about frontier farming and the Mormon disturbance. Walker fathered three sons and two daughters while making his reputation as "one of the most industrious and successful farmers of the county." He was not regarded as wealthy, but through his economy and industry he achieved a "comfortable competence" for his family. Walker had accomplished well what his generation set out to do in Illinois—achieve a competence that would enable them to settle their children around them.[1]

In contrast, the sons of men such as Walker, the young men of the rising generation of farmers, aimed not to earn a competency but to farm as a business enterprise. A desire to farm took local son William Spangler to Southern California, where he worked as a teamster to earn money to buy farm land. In 1873, he wrote to school chum Thomas Geddes of his ambitions to be a farmer. "It has got to be the hight of my ambition to be a big farmer and *carry the thing on scientifically.*"[2] To be a scientific or innovative farmer required a good piece of land and enough capital to invest in it properly. Perhaps tongue in cheek, he reminded Geddes that "it is conceit and self-esteem that carries a *feller* through the world successfully."[3] The ethic of the self-made man who rises from farm hand to renter to farm owner represented an ideal for many farmers' sons. Unlike those of his father's generation, who came to Illinois for a competency, for Spangler's generation farming had become less a way of life and more a business which demanded knowledge, money, and ambition.

The transition from farming as a way of life to farming as a business resulted from external pressures that altered the economic workings of the farm family culture. Increasing market participation put reliance on family labor at risk, as farmers more often hired laborers to meet their needs. As land became more expensive, many farmers remained renters, tenants on land they did not own, threatening the ideal of independent land ownership. The insecurities of the new market regime provoked the Grange movement, in which farmers rose in protest against the railroads that represented the widening impact of distant marketing mechanisms on the family farm enterprise.

Gender tensions in family farm culture also threatened the elemental patriarchal structure, built not only on a foundation of family labor and land but also on human relationships of blood and marriage.[4] The family farm was patriarchal, meaning the father controlled the resources of land and supervised labor.[5] Family relationships were predicated on inequality; women and children were subordinate to the male head of the household.[6] Rising divorce rates demonstrate that those pressures were mounting in the era after the Civil War, due in part to the spread of ideologies of gender which raised expectations of farm women. As exposure to the market of goods and ideas eroded the values of the farm family culture, intergenerational and gender roles were contested in a conflicted process. For many farm families, their way of life was coming apart at the seams.

Market-Driven Family Farming

The close of the Civil War initiated a market-driven stage of agrarian capitalism in western Illinois which eroded local control. The processes and structures of long-distance trade—the lengthening reach of the railroad, the rise of middlemen, and the rapid availability of market information—increasingly dictated the customs of local trade. Once the railroad connected Fountain Green with Chicago, Philadelphia, or New York, farmers could track the daily prices of farm commodities in the newspapers and reserve their produce for sale when prices were highest. No longer dependent on muddy roads, except the ones between them and the nearest rail depot, they shrewdly watched, waited, and speculated for the best return on their investment. Corn cribs and grain elevators allowed them to store their grain while waiting for the best price. Thus the market connection favored the wealthiest farmers, those who could afford to wait.

The tightening rail connections between Fountain Green and regional market centers facilitated the switch from solely a corn-and-hog farming strategy to a strategy of corn, hogs, and cattle. Before rail depots dotted the countryside, drovers picked up cattle for eastern destinations.[7] However, by decade's end when the Topeka, Peoria, & Warsaw Railroad cut through the county with depots in LaHarpe and LaCrosse, farmers drove their cattle to the depot for shipment.[8] By 1875 there were 24,500 cattle in the county valued at nearly half a million dollars and nearly double that number of hogs, worth about $170,000.[9] The average number of hogs raised on farms in the township jumped an astounding 40 percent in the decade of the 1870s (see Table 6.1). By 1880, over half the farmers in Fountain Green owned some cattle, and some farmers owned large herds of sixty or seventy head of livestock.[10]

Many farmers were drawn into the cattle business during the Civil War when raising cattle was highly profitable. The wartime prosperity declined into the 1873 depression, but those who survived recovered quickly. In October 1875, a local correspondent reported that "the principal topic of conversation among our farmers, is—not 'currency or tariff'—but corn and cattle.... Almost every farmer is crying for—not more greenbacks—but more stock hogs."[11] By the end of the decade, local agents were shipping hogs and cattle to Chicago on a daily basis.[12]

The local agents were an entrepreneurial group of wealthy farmers who purchased local lots of hogs or quantities of grain for shipment to Chicago or St. Louis. Their money was made on speculation, not the labor of their family on land they owned. The railroad shipping business offered opportunities to entrepreneurs such as those in the tiny depot town of LaCrosse, who left farming to ship carloads of hogs or steer to Chicago. The shipping enterprise was highly risky, and only those who had enough wealth to weather the uncertainty of the cash flow could enter the lucrative trade. For example, in 1875 shipper John M. Bainter of LaCrosse lost $1,200 on "a little speculation in Chicago."[13]

Market-driven agriculture increased the farmer's risk because it was impossible to predict market trends. For example, a boom in the hog market in December 1879 caused some farmers to "smile almost audibly, while those who sold before the rise can hardly see where the laugh comes in."[14] The next year many farmers lost their hogs to a local epidemic of hog cholera.[15] To succeed in the market, a farmer needed foresight, luck, and deep pockets. Those who failed to predict market demand properly could take no solace in another's windfall.

To feed their stock, farmers grew more corn (see Table 6.2). Corn was a time-honored adjunct to hogs and cattle; it could be shipped as a farm commodity itself or be fed to the animals, who could then be sold for profit. It was a strategy calculated to deal with market risk, because the decision to sell one's corn or feed it to the animals depended on the price of farm commodities. Corn's versatility made it increasingly attractive to farmers, who in 1870 grew almost six times as much corn as wheat. A decade later they were growing almost ten times more corn than wheat.

To increase grain production, farmers used reapers, mowers, and threshing machines dependent upon horsepower. They purchased sulky cultivators, corn planters, cornstalk cutters, and a large variety of plows—single, double, steel, sod plows with rolling cutters, and the Canton Clipper Plow.[16] The conversion from hand to machine power decreased the need for farm labor and allowed wealthy farmers to sell early, before the glut of new produce lowered prices. In July 1879, the newspaper reported that in Fountain Green Township, "threshing machines are in demand and crowded to their utmost capacity."[17]

Women's Production

While field production diversified in the years after the Civil War, women specialized by channeling their efforts into production of butter, poultry, and eggs.[18] By 1880, the township possessed an average of forty-seven birds per farm and the average farm produced about 160 dozen eggs a year.[19] The production of poultry and eggs was a woman's task, and the proceeds were to be used at her discretion. The records of Tyler's country store show how women chose to spend the proceeds, whether on yard goods, gifts for others, or items the farmer may have considered to be luxuries. For example, in April 1872, Sarah Dill brought in twelve dozen eggs for a credit of $1.20, then she promptly made purchases totaling $6.25 of ten yards of calico, a glass dish, a glass set, and a pair of gaiters, arguably luxuries.[20]

Women's production for market contributed to the health of the farm enterprise, but in comparison with the early frontier period, women produced less at the end of the century. Store accounts show that by the mid-1880s, farm families shipped their cream to the creamery in Carthage rather than making butter at home.[21] While the centralized collection of cream freed the farmer's wife from making butter, the transfer may have deprived her of a source of discretionary income.[22] Although they still managed dairy and poultry production, women's work in textile production was decreased, if not eliminated altogether.[23]

The tasks of the farmer's wife were eased by a modicum of mechanization, which faintly echoed the mechanization of farm production. Like reapers and other farming implements which boosted production while reducing the expenditure of labor, household aids allowed the farm wife to perform her tasks more efficiently, freeing up her time for child nurturance or community activity. An advertisement for the Common Sense Washing Machine in October 1866 recognized this parallel between farm and household machinery. "Our agricultural friends have, now-a-days, many machines to expedite and lessen their work—and it is no more than fair that they should not look out for the interest of the ladies awhile."[24]

Household aids also allowed her to refine and expand household tasks—cooking a wider variety of food or sewing ruffles on dresses, for example. This may have made housework more enjoyable, interesting, and creative, and at the same time, less a drudgery. The first step toward improving the farm kitchen was usually the purchase of a cast-iron stove, which saved fuel and eased the work of cooking with lighter utensils.[25] In an era when all but men's clothing was made by hand, sewing machines were a boon to the farm wife. The number of sewing machines in Hancock County rose 26 percent in four years, from 2,314 in 1874 to 3,122 in 1878.[26] By the 1870s, patterns for women's dresses could be obtained either by mail for $1.10 per year or in exchange for eggs at the local country store.[27] Knitting machines were also available to replace the grandmother in the corner by the fire, although Susan Geddes continued to knit socks for her family.[28] Household aids such as stoves, washing machines, and sewing machines made the process of work more comfortable and less physically demanding.

While such devices were labor-saving aids to the farm wife, husbands controlled their purchase. An 1872 advertisement for Calkins Champion Washer, a wooden bucket with a wringer affixed, promised men: "Buy this Washer and you insure a Smiling Wife."[29] Supposedly the purchase of a washing machine would make the farmer's wife happier and thus a more pleasant companion. Men's control of purchases is even more striking when one realizes that compared to the price of a reaper ($135), the cost of a washer, only $7.50, was minuscule.[30] Advertisers often referred to the purchase of household aids as "presents" for the farmer's wife, indicating that men possessed the funds and the power to make decisions that affected her productivity and comfort.

Although farm or day laborers were commonly used to help the farmer, few families hired servants to help the farmer's wife. In 1860, only one farm family hired a servant, and by 1870 just seven homes had female servants. In 1880, households hired 27 farm or day laborers but only 14 female laborers (5 servants, 6 housekeepers, and 3 seamstresses), and they worked in only a half-dozen homes.[31] Servants were a luxury few farm families could afford, and one that even prosperous farmers had to sometimes forego. When times were hard in 1870, a local observer noticed "many of our first class ladies actually doing their own housework." But they were ashamed to be seen doing the work. The country reporter to the newspaper noted that one woman disguised herself with an "antediluvian specimen of sunbonnet" when she went out to hang her wash.[32]

The strategies of diversification and mechanization continued a pattern of adjusting to factors of production and transportation that had always characterized agriculture in Fountain Green Township. During the frontier stage of local trade, farming families provided for their own needs and raised portable wheat or hogs to trade in the river market. By the 1850s, farmers became more deeply engaged with the market as they concentrated on wheat production, which brought them high profits in a demanding market. An ample labor supply and the beginnings of mechanization allowed them to increase production in the 1860s, but declining soil fertility and disease made wheat cultivation risky. The Civil War boosted the mechanization of the farms, supplying cash for tools even as manpower was reduced. High demand for pork and beef gave impetus to a nascent stock-raising trend which strengthened in the postwar period. By the 1870s, Fountain Green farmers were raising corn to feed live-stock, while some few continued to specialize in wheat. During the market-driven stage of the rural agricultural economy, external forces such as global demand and extensive transport linkages forced changes in farming as a way of life.

Threats to Family Land and Labor

The outside forces which drove the local farm economy began to weaken its characteristic reliance on family land and labor. Instead, land and labor increas-ingly became commodities to purchase, not donate or bequeath. First, the pressure of population against the finite quantity of land meant that tenancy became more entrenched, not just a temporary condition for farmers climbing the ladder to the status of owner-operator. With rising land prices, many fathers could no longer guarantee an apportionment of land for each of their sons, and sons had to resort to debt to finance their land purchases. Second, farmers increasingly relied on wage laborers, hired hands who replaced family labor. Both trends enabled more rapid responses to the market but jeopardized the self-reliance of the traditional family farm.

More men found it increasingly difficult to rise to the ranks of landowners. By 1880, the rate of tenancy (the number of farmers who rented with cash or on shares) was 39 percent, up from 26 percent in 1870; substantially more than the 11 percent rate of tenancy in 1860.[33] Tenants usually fell into one of three classes: sons of farmers who were renting land while saving for their own land, new settlers (including immigrants) just getting a start in the township, and perma-nent tenants who rented land all their lives.[34] While tenancy had long been a way for younger farmers to accumulate the capital necessary to buy a farm, rising rates of tenancy demonstrate the increasing difficulty of achieving farm owner-ship.

Farm ownership was made more difficult by the spiraling postwar prices of land. After the Civil War the average price paid per acre of land tripled (Table 6.3). Doubtless this reflects not only wartime inflation and scarcity but also improvements made to farms, such as outbuildings, cleared land, and fences. The price paid for land dropped only slightly in the early 1870s, a result of scarce money and tight credit during the Panic of 1873.

The rise in tenancy took place in a climate of declining growth. In the 1860s, the number of farms increased from 119 to 168, but only twenty new farms were created in the following decade (see Table 6.4). The group of retired farmers swelled in the postwar era as early settlers turned the operation, but not the ownership, of their farms to a younger man. The tendency of older settlers to retain title to their land when they could no longer farm it themselves increased the demand for good renters. In late March 1875, the traditional month to move from one place to another, the local reporter noted, "The last piece of ground was rented last week—it being the farm owned by the Lincoln heirs—and several good renters are yet unsupplied."[35]

Renters filled a niche in the local agricultural economy by supplying the wealthier farmers with feed for their cattle and hogs. Most tenants rented on shares, paying from one-third to one-half of their produce to the landowner.[36] Tenants tended to grow proportionately more wheat than corn when compared to owners. They owned fewer horses and fewer than one-third as many cattle (Table 6.5).[37] The wives of renters produced less butter and fewer eggs than wives of owner-operators, because renters owned fewer cows and poultry.[38] The differences in the way tenants farmed, which affected yields, may have resulted from the fact that tenants had fewer cash resources with which to manage their farms. The value of implements was comparable for all classes of farmer, but those who rented on shares spent considerably less on hired help, indicating a greater reliance on family labor.

The reluctance of the old settlers to sell their land or pass it to their sons meant that the typical tenant was older than he had been in 1860, when half of the farmers without farms were under 30 years of age and only one-fourth were over 40 years of age. By 1880, only 42 percent of the seventy-six tenants were under 30 years of age, and 25 percent were over the age of 40.[39] Instead of a young son waiting to marry until he could claim his land, by 1870 the typical renter was a married man in his thirties with several children. Typical was Bryson Latherow, born in 1855, who started farm work at the age of 10, which he continued until his marriage in 1880. He and his wife rented a farm for ten years before moving to her family's homestead of 120 acres, which Latherow improved by constructing a home and sturdy outbuildings.[40] By 1880, the proportion of renters who were sons or close relatives of owners rose to 58 percent of the renters, a sign that patriarchs were unwilling to part with their land.[41]

Hardy old farmers held on to family lands long after their sons wanted to operate as independent farmers. For example, Thomas Miller from Pennsylvania, who reported his occupation as a retired farmer to the census taker in 1869, still owned real estate worth $2,500. The operation of the farm probably depended greatly on the labor of his two sons at home, James (age 25) and John (age 21). James may have been a partner in the farm, since in 1870 he is listed as holding real estate worth $2,500. The work of growing 300 bushels of wheat and 400 bushels of corn while raising 30 hogs required more than the capacity of an aged man. However, the elder Miller owned double the real estate of his son and virtually all the personal estate on the farm.[42]

Not until late in life did the Millers bequeath family land to their sons. In 1878, Thomas and Margaret Miller deeded eighty acres each of the farm to James and an older brother, William, for one dollar "and natural love and affection." William was married and already situated on land worth $3,000 he had purchased from another farmer, a purchase that may have been aided by his father. Robert, a third son, was married and the owner of $2,500 in real estate in 1870. The youngest son, John, had to take out a bank loan in 1877 to finance a $500 purchase of 60 acres of land from another Pennsylvania farm family, the McConnells. While the part Thomas Miller played in financing the purchase of land for all his sons is not entirely clear, the elder Millers did bestow land on two sons that gave them a head start in the tight land market of the late 1870s.[43]

Instead of receiving land from their fathers, farmers' sons increasingly resorted to debt to finance their purchase of land. In a township-wide sample of 915 land transactions, 147 involved mortgages, a ratio of one mortgage for every seven transactions. In the period before 1831–1850, only sixteen mortgages were recorded in the deeds records. The number of mortgages tripled to forty-eight in the 1850s, dropped to twenty-eight in the 1860s, and climbed again to fifty-five in the 1870s.[44] Family members were an important source of mortgage funds. About ten percent of the mortgages were between family members (including those from out of state). About the same amount were taken from local merchants or wealthy farmers. The small percentage of mortgages between family members probably means that many mortgages were contracted off the books.

In addition to the rise in the rate of mortgage-taking over time, chattel mortgages began to be replaced by more sophisticated financial instruments that allowed a farmer to put a lien on his land. The terms of the mortgage were commonly six or ten percent for a period of two to five years. Biannual payments and lengthier periods became more common. Although banks were established in the county in the 1850s, they did not commonly become holders of mortgages until the 1870s (when one-fifth of the mortgages in this sample were arranged through banks).

As financial instruments became more sophisticated over time, so did the bequests that farmers gave in their wills. Cash appeared more often as a bequest, and several well-to-do farmers gave their children shares of bank stock or securities or stipulated that their bequests earn interest before being dispersed.[45] The increasing liquidity of the assets that farmers bestowed upon their families allowed their progeny to escape the obligations of support that tied families together. These portable inheritances allowed the children to invest their legacy in something other than farm land. Cash also reduced the intergenerational obligations that tied families to the land and to each other, freeing the children to move away from the homestead in Fountain Green Township.

The shift from family labor toward wage labor further threatened the underpinnings of the family farm system. Like rising rates of tenancy, the use of wage labor diminished the traditional reliance on family land and labor, challenging the agrarian ethic of independent farm operation that had been integral to farming as a way of life. The cohort of wage laborers expanded in size, from thirty in 1870 to forty-seven by 1880, forming a class of laborers in the township that differed from the labor force of previous years. While a portion of the young men in the township had always worked as farm laborers, either for their fathers or for other farmers, by 1880 much of the farm labor force was supplied by men who were not native to the township.[46] Sons were more likely to stay in school and earn their way into farming through renting land.[47] Instead of taking on a temporary role while living at home, farm laborers increasingly came to the township without ties to the community, creating a permanent rural working class.[48]

About two-thirds of the farms in Fountain Green hired wage labor, while one-third relied exclusively on family labor. Forty percent of farmers paid less than $50 in wages during the year, but one-fifth of farmers paid more than $100. Four farmers paid more than $200 in wages to hired help. Of those who did employ farm labor, one-third did so only for the month-long harvest season, and half that many hired labor just for the summer months. The average amount of time a farmer hired labor was two weeks out of the year, although a few farmers paid for labor year round.[49]

Wealthy farmers or farmers without sufficient family labor were the most likely to hire wage labor year round. Older farmers whose children had left, farmers with too many daughters and not enough sons, and young renters were reliant on waged farm laborers. Young farmer A. R. Simmons, who had two small children, paid a full-time hand to supply labor for his corn-and-cattle farm worth $4,500. Wealthy Alexander McConnell also hired a full-time laborer, 23-year-old Cass Wide from Michigan, to help him produce wheat and to breed and raise cattle. Although McConnell had three sons, two of them were still in school and too young to be much help on the 300-acre farm.[50]

Farmers who ran a prosperous business trading in cattle and hogs could afford to pay wages to a farmhand. The hired help was crucial to production in a demanding market. Specialized farm production meant that farmers had to commit to intense labor in a short amount of time instead of dovetailing tasks with a variety of crops. Farmers had to be able to respond quickly to the shifting prices, and could not wait for a young son to grow up to help on the farm.

The Granger Protest

At the Hancock County Old Settlers Reunion in August 1872, speaker William A. Booz remarked that now "every man in the county has a market at his door, and but few live where the sound of the locomotive whistle cannot be heard." Not only had the railroad made marketing produce more convenient, it had also noticeably increased the prosperity of the county. Booz compared the privations of the past to the comforts of the present: "Now the log cabins are gone, and comfortable, spacious and sometimes elegant residences have taken their places; the music of the tin grater, preparing meal for the food of the family, has given place to the more agreeable music of the organ or piano."[51] According to Booz, because the railroad enabled farmers to send produce to market, it brought both the prosperity and the middle-class comforts they enjoyed.

Within months of Booz's paean to the railroad, the farmers in the county flocked to grassroots organizations in a groundswell of agrarian protest. Farmers donated their time, effort, and money to mounting a full-scale battle against the owners of railroads and grain elevators and the manufacturers of farm implements who had supposedly brought them such prosperity. Farmers were not alone in the fight; their families displayed the sheer strength of the mass movement at rallies, meetings, and picnics around the county. The uproar even led to the formation of an independent political party that threatened to upset old equilibriums of power.

The extent of the protest leads one to question the commitment of rural people to market agriculture. Rather than a rejection of agrarian capitalism, the protest movement was an expression of disillusionment with the terms of their participation in the market. The mass movement drew its strength from the conviction that monopoly power, in the form of railroads and other large corporations, was circumventing the free play of market forces. The solution the farmers proposed was to regulate the corporations, using the power of the state to curb abusive practices. Their protest proved to be short-lived, defeated not only by the return to prosperity but also by class-based opposition at the local level.[52] The Grange movement in Illinois was brief and relatively weak in comparison to that in other states, but when examined on the local level, it shows how farmers felt about their position in the market and the damaging effect of commercial agriculture on rural social relations.[53]

The organization of the Grange in Hancock County was part of a national movement to unite farmers and rural people. Like the Populists who would follow them, the Grangers were not anti-capitalists, but they wanted to control what they saw as the abuses of capitalism. Their efforts were threefold: legislation to regulate railroads and grain elevators, cooperative buying and selling to avoid the middleman, and a social program that created a movement culture through the use of ritual and education.[54] The Illinois Grange, first organized in 1870, was reorganized in 1872 to take advantage of the agrarian outcry about the railroads. Over 500 farmers attended a convention in Bloomington in January 1873, and the group passed resolutions urging the legislative control of railroads. In that year alone, 121 Granges and 125 Farmers Clubs were formed in what had been the Military Tract.[55]

The fundamental issue was the rates railroads charged to farmers to ship produce. By 1871, the many local railroads capitalized by the counties in the Military Tract, including those in Hancock County and the Northern Cross Railroad, had merged to form the Chicago, Burlington, and Quincy Railroad. The monopoly meant higher prices, since there was no local competition for rail freight. Because railroads charged more for short hauls (where there was a monopoly) than long-distance business (where railroads faced competition), western Illinois lost its natural advantage of proximity to the market centers. The monopoly meant that railroads, elevators, and warehouses charged farmers more at times of peak demand and lowered freight charges after the harvest season was over.[56] Caught in the upward movement of shipping prices as railroads combined to form regional monopolies, farmers began to feel as if they had been tricked into furnishing profits for the railway owners. Farmers were understandably frustrated by what they saw as abuse of what was to have brought them such prosperity. Due in large part to the groundswell of agitation by farmers early in the decade, Illinois enacted regulatory legislation, which calmed the protest. However, railroads refused to comply with the regulations and mounted a court challenge that was not resolved for an additional seven years.[57]

In February 1872, Grange organizers in Hancock County announced that "the time has come when those engaged in rural pursuits should have an organization devoted entirely to their interests." Obviously an analogue to industrial unionism, the Patrons of Husbandry, like other vocations and classes in the country, would combine in cooperative action "for individual improvement and common benefit." Avowedly apolitical and nonsectarian, the Grange was formed not only to improve methods of husbandry but also "to increase the general happiness, wealth, and prosperity of the country" through its social events which welcomed women. Women were even allowed to participate in the symbolic and secret Grange ritual, an important innovation which garnered their support for the movement.[58]

Hancock County farmers were rapidly organized into Granges under the skillful guidance of local deputies. A flurry of organizing in the first months of 1873 brought the total number of granges to twenty-four by the June meeting in Carthage. Their initial enthusiasm was expressed in a morally charged discourse of revolt against railroads and banks who stole from the honest farmer and laborer. They resolved that "this organization is opposed to railroad steals, salary grab steals, bank steals, and every other form of thievery by which the farming and laboring classes are robbed of the honest fruits of their labor."[59] They further resolved only to patronize implement manufacturers that would deal with them directly and pledged that they would not affiliate with either political party.

Among the Granges organized in the spring of 1873 was the Fountain

Grange of Fountain Green, under the leadership of Civil War veteran, surveyor, and gentleman farmer John G. Fonda.[60] Other officers were likewise drawn from the top ranks of farmer entrepreneurs, such as Samuel Walker and Justice of the Peace Kendrick Leach.[61] All three men were heavily involved in the market and were stock raisers dependent on hired labor and mechanical implements. In 1870, Walker owned nearly 500 acres of land worth $19,000, raised cattle, and paid $800 in wages for hired help.[62] Although it is possible that their early support of the efforts to buy and sell cooperatively may have stemmed from concern to extend benefits to the less wealthy farmers in the township, they also stood to gain the most from lowering the cost of the mechanical implements they needed to maintain production.

By the fall of 1872, the number of county Granges had expanded to forty-one, enough to consider cooperative buying.[63] Plans were made to involve local businessmen to establish a Granger warehouse for agricultural implements in Carthage.[64] The Republican newspaper argued that the cooperative buying system "will enable many a poor man to lift the mortgage from his farm, and save a home for his little ones. By it, many a father will be enabled to send his bright-eyed son or daughter to the college or academy, and the new cottage will take the place of the cabin or the hovel."[65] This list of the benefits that would accrue to farmers is a clue to the changing values in the agricultural community. Farmers wanted to be free of the onerous mortgages they had taken on in the capital-intensive commercialization of farming. The country schools were not enough; farmers aspired to have their children attend college. And farm families were no longer content to live in rude cabins; they wanted to build nice frame houses with the middle-class comforts they read about in the newspapers. It was clear that farmers wanted the Granger movement to bring them enough profits to satisfy their changing needs.

The growing number of Granges and their plans for cooperative buying alarmed the commercial community in the county. "Mechanic" from Hamilton protested that their action would hurt local manufacturers by supporting the "moneyed monopoly." "Mechanic" warned that they endangered local businesses:

> We would ask you farmers, who builds your towns and buys your produce? It is the mechanic, the merchant, and the industrious men of small capital. You send your money away from home: how do you expect to get it back? . . . Farmers, you want us to buy your hay, your corn, your butter, your chickens, your pork, your eggs, and that is not all, you want us to pay for all these things. . . . Gentlemen, your rule works only for yourselves and not for the good of all.[66]

The farmers did not realize, or did not care, that by refusing to buy at retail, they deprived local businesses of their margin of profit. Local retailers, after all, were also at the mercy of the railroads and large corporations that had no stake in the small communities of rural Illinois.

The business and professional classes of Hancock County hurriedly infiltrated the farmer's organization. They found allies in the elite farmers who led the Granges, men whose capital investments, involvement in the market, and standard of living meant they had more in common with town merchants and professionals than with ordinary farmers.[67] Before long the Grange resolutions favored the local business interests by resolving to trade with those already in business (where there were no Grange stores) and to support the cash system.[68] Local businessmen even became involved in plans to set up a Granger warehouse for agricultural implements at the county seat, thus co-opting the Granger agenda for their own benefit.[69]

The strength of the Granger movement was in full evidence at a massive picnic in September 1873 attended by somewhere between two and four thousand persons—"honest grangers in the country with their wives, daughters, sons and their sweethearts."[70] Clad in the sashes and medals of Grange regalia, members of local Granges carried banners bearing mottos: "In Union there is strength," "We are opposed to monopolies and official corruptions," and "Free trade and farmers rights." The stand was decorated with "the emblems of husbandry"—corn, wheat, rye, oats, fruits, and vegetables. The St. Mary's Glee Club opened with music, followed by a prayer and then the reading of the Farmer's Declaration of Independence. The crowd then sang the theme song "Plow Deep," before Republican and Methodist minister John L. Shinn exhorted them to use the ballot to further Granger aims. "Plow, Spade and Hoe" was sung before speeches by Democratic leaders, who argued for the nonpolitical approach to the Grange. Although the proceedings were reminiscent of a Fourth of July picnic—reading a Declaration of Independence, praying, singing, and listening to the rhetoric of patriotic duty—they merely disguised an election rally for farmers' votes.[71]

Bolstered by the coalition of elite farmers and townspeople in the county, both political parties worked to capitalize on the strength of the Granger movement in the 1873 elections. The Democrats, usually victorious in local elections, staved off the formation of an independent People's Party. But the Republicans, always the underdog in local politics, transformed their county convention into a People's Party meeting and slated a farmer's ticket for the fall elections.[72] Although the election was held in the wake of the Panic of 1873, the fusion party was defeated because the Grangers did not vote in a bloc but adhered to traditional partisan loyalties.[73] The flimsy Republican-People's slate could not overturn the local political structure, but the Granger movement suffused the political process with an urgency not felt for a decade. Just as they had in the Mormon era and in the divisive struggle of the Civil War, farm people turned to the apparatus of local government for a solution to their problems. In November 1873, political defeat signaled the inability of the Granger movement to transcend party divisions. By the middle of the next year, county Granges had begun to dissolve, one by one.

Why did the bubble of protest explode so quickly? The swift downhill slide of the county Grange movement resulted partly from the prosperity some farmers enjoyed as the market began to recover from the 1873 Panic. An observer noted, "We never saw the grangers in a better mood—57 cents for corn has made them full of wealth. They can now lift all those old mortgages, pay off all those 20 percent loans and have plenty of currency besides."[74] The elite farmers who led the local Granges would have been among the first to benefit from the resurgence of the market. They apparently abandoned their support of the common goals that would have helped less prosperous farmers who were still trying to pay off their mortgages.

The Grange movement failed in Hancock County not only because of prosperity's return but also because in its attempt to unify farmers, it threatened the bonds of town and country. Among the reasons given by the officers of the first Grange to disband in July 1874 was that the "spirit of class legislation and mutual distrust between the agricultural and commercial intercourse of the land" was "demoralizing and debasing the standard of relations the community bears to each other."[75] The attempt to remedy that split by combining forces drew the ire of the movement's foot soldiers, who argued that farmers neglected the Grange because it had not delivered what it had promised—economic relief. In a letter to the county paper in November 1875, Miss Mollie Mathews said Granges had become corrupted by allowing too many "editors, lawyers, doctors, and preachers" to join who were "too high minded" and "not in sympathy with our hard-working farmers." Mathews argued that the professionals joined only to get the patronage of the farmers and used the social functions of the grange to distract farmers from the economic goals they sought: "They prate about the social and literary qualities of the grange and these become stumbling blocks to retard our progress toward the end for which it was intended."[76] She was tired of picking up the paper and seeing the farmer portrayed as uneducated and stupid. And their wives, "why they don't know anything only to scrub and wash and cook, and wear stoga shoes and sunbonnets all their lives." According to Mathews, farmers had left because they could see that the Grange had been co-opted by the county elite who had sold out in favor of keeping close ties with business. The rural coalitions that took control of the Grange transformed what could have been a radical attack on commercial capitalism into an affirmation of the status quo, abandoning traditional agrarian ideals of republican independence.

The Granger movement was an explosion of discontent by farmers and their families that took place just as they were experiencing the full effects of integration into a national market. It was not simply a revolt of the agrarian classes against capitalism; it was a more complex fragile coalition of rural people who cannot be schematically categorized as capitalists or proletarians. Furthermore, farmers themselves were increasingly fragmented by diverse political and economic agendas related to their economic standing. Farmers depended on the goodwill of local businessmen, and merchants could not live without the patronage of the farmers. The symbiosis of town and country interests was so threatened by the Grange that farmers abandoned the Grange movement altogether. By so doing, they were acceding to a system of market-driven agriculture largely beyond their own control.

"A new order of domestic economy"

As the Civil War ended, the residents of Fountain Green Township were being drawn into a national set of middle-class cultural expectations that were rapidly changing to meet the demands of an industrializing society. At the heart of the construction and dissemination of a bourgeois identity was the reorganization of gender which elevated domesticity and broadened women's legal rights. While the center of the redefinition of class was in the cities, such ideas were also seeping into the corners of the countryside. The idea that a farm wife

FIGURE 6.1. Residence of K. N. Leach. From Alfred Theodore Andreas, *An Illustrated Historical Atlas of Hancock County, Illinois* (Chicago: A. T. Andreas, 1874), 35.

should produce for market gave way at mid-century to the image of the farm wife whose role was to serve the family through cooking, sewing, cleaning, and nurturing of children.[77] As bourgeois ideals were absorbed in rural Illinois, farm women began to pay more attention to the home as a family living space instead of merely a work place. They laid carpets in the parlor, hung lace curtains at the windows, and cultivated flower gardens in the yard (see Fig. 6.1). Families limited the number of children and invested in their children's education as they prolonged their adolescence. When urban middle-class ideals of domesticity penetrated the countryside, women expected more than they ever had before. Rising rates of divorce attest to this disjuncture between shifting gender ideologies and the reality of agrarian patriarchy in rural Illinois.

The idea of women's equality was boosted with the coming of the Civil War. During the war, women moved into many occupations formerly held only by men. In 1872, the state legislature enacted a law which stipulated that women could not be excluded from any occupation on account of their sex.[78] By 1870, women in Illinois could be elected to serve as justices of the peace; in 1873, they were granted the right to be elected to school offices.[79] Readers of the local newspaper could follow the expansion of women's rights in other states, such as the proposal in the new constitution in Wisconsin to give women the right to vote. The editor of the *Carthage Republican* supported women's right to vote, arguing that "should the people of Wisconsin choose to extend the right of suffrage to the female Wisconsians, it would unsex nobody."[80] For many, what was at stake in expanding women's rights was the unsexing of women, which would topple the structures of gender that bound women to a tightly circumscribed social space.

At the same time, married women's property laws broadened women's claims to the joint property of the married couple. Women did not escape *femme covert* status under Illinois law until the passage of the married women's property law in 1861, which granted her full rights to any personal or real property she brought to the marriage as well as any property acquired by her after the marriage. For instance, her husband could not dispose of her property to pay his own debts.[81] In 1869, her rights to property were expanded to include her earnings, which was not to imply that she should be remunerated for services to her husband or children.[82] In 1874, the law confirmed the rights of married women to property by granting her the right to sue and be sued, to convey property, and to make contracts.[83]

Widows benefited from an 1873 state law that exempted $1,000 of the homestead land from debts.[84] Farmers became increasingly more liberal in their provision for widows in their wills. For example, in 1865, Basil Wright specifically directed his wife to take responsibility for the dispersal of the estate, which must have included deciding how to split the real estate between his two sons. He stated that he wished his "wife to controle all my business, dispose of any property that she may think is to her advantage to do so."[85] While over time there was a greater tendency to allow the farmer's widow to manage the affairs of the estate as executor, she was usually paired with an older son or male friend of the decedent.

However, legal sanction of married women's right to own real estate did not materially change property-holding practices among the women of Fountain Green Township. Of a sample of 544 property transactions from 1830 to 1890, only thirteen women purchased property (most were widows), and an additional twenty-nine sold property.[86] One exception was Laura Geddes Brandon, who in February 1873 paid $2,000 for sixty acres of farmland in sections 30 and 33. However, the plat map drawn one year later shows that land as belonging to her husband, George, with an orchard and farmhouse on the land in Section 33. Although Laura held title to the land, it was publicly recognized as her husband's.[87] Of the twenty-nine pieces of property sold by women, most were widows. Not until 1867 did married women sell property. Eight women did so (with husbands listed as joint owners) between 1867 and 1884. Most of the women who owned property were not married or were widows who rented the land or had it farmed by their sons.[88] The increase in the number of female landowners may have resulted from the deaths of the generation of men who settled the township, not to any liberalization of attitudes about married women's right to own property.[89]

Despite the liberalization of women's rights to property, few farm wives chose to claim legal title to the family's land holdings; patriarchal custom to title continued. Certainly it can be argued that the perpetuation of the male land-holding custom is prima facie proof of patriarchal oppression. Conversely, it can be argued that even when ownership was within their grasp, farm women did not seek legal title to land, perhaps because they assumed it self-evident that their position as wives implied a partnership in the land.

Legal advances in the status of women were powered by changing ideologies of gender. The patriarchal model that placed primary importance on relations between parents and children was being replaced by an ideal of companionate marriage that prized romantic love. From reading newspaper stories that romanticized womanhood and love stories in novels and magazines, farm women expected more from the marital relationship. The changing notions of gender brought comment from a country correspondent, who took aim at opponents of women's rights in a letter to the *Carthage Republican* in 1870:

> I perceive that owing to the power of women's rights to be established ere long beyond all male expectation, a new order of domestic economy must be invented. In the unprogressive days of old fogy patriarchs, when a bride was taken to her husband's house, she was presented with a pair of slippers to indicate that there was no need for her to gad abroad, also, a needle, a distaff, a spinning wheel and a cradle were given to her as a hint how she might pass

time profitably at home. Female strongmindedness now prevails and things are
changed. A few days ago, down here near Huntsville, when the groom took his
bride home, among the wedding gifts to her were a pair of high-heeled boots,
a pair of breeches, a razor, a raw-hide, a revolver, a cigarcase, and a jack knife for
whittling purposes!! Hurrah! for women's sphere![90]

This anecdote facetiously predicted the implications for private life if the
changes sought in public came about. Its author teased readers by claiming
ironically that if women's rights were granted, women would become unsexed,
essentially like men. They would wear boots instead of slippers, would pass the
time whittling instead of spinning, and would even grow a beard and smoke
cigars! The letter alludes to fears that women's rights would mean the reversal
of sex roles in the intimate domestic sphere. We cannot be certain the author
celebrated the fact that women were loosening the bonds of "old fogy patriarchs" of the past, but the satire does suggest a sympathy with the women's
cause.

Changing notions of gender were evident in advice given about courtship
and marriage. In the frontier period, the marital partnership was first and foremost an economic one, as men and women joined efforts to support themselves and their children on the farm. In 1841, the newspaper reported that
when asked by a suitor if he could speak to one of his six daughters about marriage, the farmer said, "Take one . . . but mind you no picking and choosing, take
them as they came into the world."[91] When love was not a prime consideration,
one daughter would do as well as another. By the 1870s, the necessity of a union
motivated by love had gained the upper hand. Writing to the *Country Gentleman,* the ladies correspondent warned: "Don't marry just for the sake of getting
a housekeeper. Do you not see that it is the worst kind of cheating to tell a young
woman that you love her when you are really intending to make of her an
unpaid upper servant?" Times had changed, and now, she said, "a true marriage
is not a mere business transaction. It is a love affair."[92]

Small-town newspapers spread the new romantic ideals which criticized
the status of the farm wife. As one anecdote proclaimed, the modern wife was
"more a companion than a drudge." While in the old days husband and wife
"worked together behind the counter and on the farm, each understanding the
labor of the other, and joining as a true yoke fellow in drawing the mutual load,"
now they spend time apart, and he "does not wear his wife out in butter-making
or child bearing."[93] Farm wives with a house full of children and cream to churn
may have wished for the more modern arrangement of marriage they read
about in the papers.

Farm wives began to feel they deserved some financial autonomy. In
February 1867, the *Carthage Republican* printed on its first page a column
entitled "Do Farmer's Wives Pay?"[94] The ladies' correspondent to the *Country
Gentleman,* from which the piece was reprinted, acknowledged that while a

farmer could estimate the value of his lands, stock, crop and labor, he could not assign a value to the labor performed by his wife.[95] She asked: What value would a farmer place on a dinner that he eats in twenty minutes that took her all morning to cook? What value would he place on eating from dishes that had been washed, dried, and put away after the last meal? How much was it worth to him to put on a clean, ironed shirt and darned socks, which "don't look much like the ones he pulled off last week, and threw down with the wash!" To fully appreciate the worth of farmer's wife, one had to decide how much she contributed by taking daily care of the milk and making butter. And what was her value in taking care of the children? Granted she had half interest in their welfare, but "is it really worth nothing to sooth, amuse, teach, feed and spank his half, to make and make over, and mend the clothes for his half?"

The final salvo of the ladies' correspondent aimed at the heart of the issue, the farm wife's financial dependence on the farmer. If her labor was fully appreciated, then when she asked for a little money for a book or "something not strictly necessary," should he not supply her readily with what she asks? Why should she feel she is asking for "his hardly earned means" instead of the surplus she is rightfully due? She worked much too hard to be considered still a beggar. She should be dependent on her husband's generosity only if the value of her labor did not equal her expenses, which would be difficult to prove given all the labor she expended in housekeeping, butter-making, and child rearing. According to the ladies' correspondent, he should loosen his purse strings and give her money when she asked for it.[96] The female reader of the paper in western Illinois could appreciate that the farmer's wife worked hard for the farm and would no longer settle for complete financial dependence.

Divorce: Coming Apart at the Seams

Higher rates of divorce signal the unwillingness of rural women to deliver what was demanded of them in physical toil and self-deprivation. It also was a sign of the economic stresses that farmers experienced as they took on more debt in a market-driven farm economy. They may have responded to those economic pressures by drinking or asserting their power in the home by physically abusing family members.[97] In short, the changes in gender ideologies and the hazards of the market made this a time when gender rights and duties were renegotiated to challenge the power of rural patriarchy.[98]

The sources which reveal the private workings of the farm family household must be used with caution, because they are biased toward what constituted the acceptable grounds for divorce. Furthermore, they represented atypical behavior that exceeded the bounds of propriety. Court records include bills of divorce by complainants and depositions of witnesses who observed the most intimate details of private life. Witnesses were as varied as an 11-year-old daughter who came home for lunch to find her mother in bed with her lover, "a quilt thrown over their feet," to a man who watched his friend "committing the act of adultery" with a prostitute in a river town.[99] Nevertheless, they open a window into the nature of family relationships.

Consistent with nationwide trends, rates of divorce rose steadily in Hancock County during the nineteenth century, from 1.5 for every 100 marriages in 1831 to 4 for every 100 in 1880.[100] The overwhelming majority of divorce proceedings were initiated by women, who sued for divorce in 70 percent of the cases. In the postbellum period, the law limited the complaint of divorce to desertion, physical abuse, drunkenness, or infidelity. The major causes incident to divorce in a sample of one-fourth of the divorce cases in the county show that the most common cause was desertion (65 percent), followed by charges of adultery (29 percent), abuse (24 percent), and intemperance (8 percent) (Table 6.6). Many divorces resulted from a combination of these circumstances. It was rare to find a divorce case in which neither party had deserted.[101]

Women who sought divorce in the first five years of marriage (when half of all divorces occurred) cited homesickness, lack of knowledge about the partner, or simple incompatibility. These cases suggest an initial period of adjustment in a marriage, since some of these cases did not result in divorce.[102] At least some women, realizing they had made a mistake in marrying (either in their choice of husband or in their locale), headed for the safety of home at the earliest opportunity. Before the birth of children complicated the family situation, women could get out of an intolerable marriage simply by leaving.[103]

The conflicts in the following two divorce cases show how the economic unit of the family farm was composed of separate persons, each of whom possessed separate interests, often at odds with each other. Because private gender rights were embedded in public practices, contestations over gender rights reveal the limits to patriarchal authority amid the external tensions that market engagement imposed on those most vulnerable to financial risk. The strategies women used to deal with family violence—appealing to local authorities or relying on the goodwill of neighbors—reveal the links between the domestic domain and the public arena. Family violence and divorce expose the process by which the patriarchal prerogatives of the lineal farm family were giving way to the emerging companionate ideal of the early twentieth century.[104]

The case of Mary Aldrich of Fountain Green demonstrates the role of drunkenness and physical abuse in the decision to divorce and the limited options open to a farm wife. In 1881 when she filed for divorce, Mary was 47 years old, and her husband, George, was about 50. Mary chose Manier & Miller, the most prominent lawyers in Carthage, to represent her. In the statement she gave to her solicitors, Mary cataloged a train of abuses that took place over seven years. The couple had married in LaHarpe on June 1, 1858, and were the parents of seven children ranging in age from 7 to 21. During the time of her marriage, Mary claimed to have been a "faithful, chaste and affectionate wife."[105]

But George, "wholly disregarding his marriage vows and obligations," was guilty of "extreme and repeated cruelty" toward her. The most recent incident, and the one that caused her to leave him, took place on August 17, 1881, at their house.

> George H. Aldrich struck your oratrix a violent blow with his fist, that She run and left their house to avoid further blows from the said George H. Aldrich that he followed her, and caught her by the hair of her head, and jerked her down upon the ground, and commenced kicking her and otherwise abusing her, until one of their children interfered and thus prevented him from further injuring your oratrix.[106]

Rescued by one of her children, Mary went back to their house and prepared supper for her husband and their children, even though she had been beaten. At 11 P.M., George came to her room, "with a club and again struck her a violent blow upon her head with said club, and threatened to kill her." Mary left the house to avoid his blows, and George locked her out. She stated that she had not lived with him since. Perhaps she stayed with the same neighbors who had harbored her for two days in June after a similar beating. She further stated that when he beat her, and many other times, he had directed toward her and the children "the most obscene, profane and opprobrious language rendering her life miserable."[107]

Mary blamed his shocking behavior on the use of alcohol, which began a few years after they were married. For the last several years he had been habitually drunk, which prevented him from attending to his business. When he was drunk, he was "very quarrelsome and ill-treats his family." His behavior made her condition "intolerable, and her life burdensome," so she was "compelled to withdraw from his house." Mary also made clear that because of his drinking habits, George was not a fit parent and should not be granted custody of the children.[108]

Mary Aldrich's bill for divorce included a request for alimony. George was "abundantly able to supply all the necessities and wants" of Mary and the children. She thought his real estate holdings were worth $6,400. She also noted that he owned a large amount of personal property worth at least $1,500: horses, cattle, hogs, grain, wagons, buggy, household furniture, and farm implements. Her work had contributed to their wealth; in 1880 she produced 200 pounds of butter and kept 60 chickens. She argued that she rightfully deserved to share in a portion of this wealth, since she was "poor and without means to support her[self], and her children, and to prosecute this suit." It must have been humiliating for her to be dependent on friends and relatives for daily subsistence. The children lacked sufficient clothing and the "comforts of life suitable to her and their condition in life." Mary asked for a restraining order to prevent George from selling his property to avoid paying alimony. She wanted property or payments that would allow her to support the minor children.[109]

Her attorneys had taken a substantial case that had all the elements necessary to result in a successful outcome. It featured a wealthy and prominent member of the county community who was extremely abusive toward his wife. Neighbors and children witnessed the beatings and could corroborate Mary's allegations. On the twentieth of August an order was written to summon George to appear at the October 1881 term of Circuit Court. But on September tenth, Mary wrote a note to her attorneys instructing them to "pleas dismis the suit I Commensed against George H Aldrich."[110]

We can only speculate about the reasons Mary changed her mind. Perhaps it was the fear of public attention attendant to a trial, or maybe she was cowed by threats from George. More likely Mary's suit frightened George into reform. By filing suit for divorce, Mary may have used the liberalized provisions of divorce law to her own advantage, pressuring George into good behavior by pursuing public action. After all, she had a lot to lose by carrying through on her threat to divorce him—status, wealth, security. She clearly had no means of support beyond alimony, and that may have been difficult to obtain. We cannot know how the two settled their differences, but we can appreciate the constraints on Mary's choices that trapped her in an abusive marriage for the remainder of her life.[111]

We can see that in rural society, even though farm homesteads may have been relatively isolated, patterns of sociability with kin and neighbors could serve as insurance against incidents of abuse. To ameliorate their disadvantaged position in terms of economic capital, women such as Mary Aldrich used their social capital to construct networks that served as a safety net. They constructed social bonds to protect themselves against undue patriarchal authority and appealed to civil authority to protect their own interests. Both strategies weakened rural patriarchy, limiting the power of husbands over their wives.[112]

A second case demonstrates how market tensions and changing gender roles lessened the power of the patriarch by weakening his hold on land ownership. A rural patriarch's authority was grounded in land-holding; when that was at risk, so was his power. In February 1874, Celestia Slattery filed a bill of divorce on the grounds of extreme and repeated cruelty. The depositions collected by her attorneys and those hired by her estranged husband, Trevor Slattery, contain complex and contradictory testimony. Celestia was then living with her parents, and the couple's two daughters (ages 2 and 4) were in the care of his parents.[113]

According to Celestia, about two years after they had married (in 1868) her husband became "extremely abusive and cruel," apparently without provocation. Her lawyer chose to lead his deposition with an incident in which she alleged having been whipped by her husband. As she recalled, "While your oratrix was sitting in a carriage of the said husband and trying to control back and manage a pair of mules under the directions of said Trevor E. Slattery, he became angry and struck your oratrix a heavy blow with a whip used by him leaving his marks over the back and shoulders thereby bruising your oratrix and causing her much pain." He continued whipping her at home on her back and legs, causing her "much pain and suffering and leaving marks . . . which were visible for weeks." The lawyer knew that the whipping was out of bounds and would immediately arouse the sympathies of the judge.

Celestia's whipping was one in a string of violent events she claimed to have suffered at the hands of her husband. The event that convinced her to leave him in January 1874 (a month before she filed her suit) also involved a whipping, which she alleged resulted in a miscarriage of her pregnancy. She charged that during the time of her confinement and labor he failed to "render her the proper and necessary care and attention," and when she cried out in pain, he responded with "not sympathy nor pity—only cussing and abuse." As soon as she was able, Celestia removed herself to the home of her father, leaving her daughters behind.

Celestia's complaint of divorce reveals a pattern of abuse that occurred when she failed to meet her husband's expectation while she was helping on "his" farm. (Throughout the deposition, the property is referred to as his: *his* residence, *his* carriage, *his* barnyard.) He whipped her when she could not control the team of mules, he hit her with the axe handle when she was helping him repair the gate, he whipped her when she could not swiftly drive the cattle into the yard while he was busy pressing hay. Celestia argued in her deposition that she was unfairly asked to do more than was normally expected of a woman, even being made to get out of bed at night alone to tend the horses! As a woman on the farm, she had her rights and duties, and his requests were trespassing on those rights and expectations. His demands of her crossed the lines of what was customary and expected of a woman. Consonant with her duties of motherhood, instead of his cursing and neglect, she had the right to receive medical care and sympathy when she underwent a miscarriage.

This is not, then, just a story of patriarchal authority, a husband abusing his wife. As we turn to the husband's story, we can better see that it is a contest over the place of men and women in a gendered culture. Celestia's estranged husband, Trevor Slattery, denied the accusations of abuse as "wholly untrue." He did acknowledge that his estranged wife had suffered a miscarriage but denied having beat her. Instead, he accused her of bringing it on herself by not taking proper care of her health. He stated that she "had for many nights just previous to this miscarriage . . . been to dancing parties at different places and frequently danced nearly all night against the protestations of this defendant, and did many other things such as running and jumping & lifting heavy things which were imprudent for a pregnant woman to do." In his view, she was not fulfilling her duties to reproduce, to responsibly carry and bear his children who would be an economic asset to the farm. Furthermore, he stated that this was not the first miscarriage, but was the fifth, and that "all of which were of male infants and that each of said miscarriages happened at about the same stage of pregnancy, and that she has never had a male infant born alive." Trevor Slattery made a point of noting the sex of the babies; clearly he was deeply and bitterly disappointed that she had failed in her duties as a farm wife to provide male heirs who would grow to help him on the farm and perhaps inherit it one day. He clearly felt he had the right to expect her to bear children, especially male children to whom he could bequeath the family land.

It is in the dispute over custody, over who had the resources to raise and educate their children, that we glimpse the effects of market risk on rural families. Both Celestia and Trevor pleaded for custody of the children. She wanted him to pay her support, but he said he simply did not have the money. As Trevor explained his financial standing, he was a man in trouble. He did own land, but after a down payment of $1,000, he still owed another two or three thousand dollars. In the Depression of 1873, land values had declined to the point that he could not sell the land at cash sale for more than enough to pay off the balance. The amount of his personal property had also declined precipitously. Most of the value of his property had been invested in young livestock, which he had been planning to fatten for market. However, he claimed that in order to pay the lawyers their $400 fee, he had to sell off his stock early in the spring "at a great sacrifice." If he had to sell his land, he would be reduced to nothing more than a farm hand, "dependent upon his personal labor." His climb up the agricultural ladder toward independent property ownership would become a swift descent to the ranks of the common laborer. Caught in the jaws of the market, he was overextended and vulnerable to the financial disaster of the divorce. It is even likely that his straitened financial circumstances had led him to expect her to help him in tasks that ordinarily one would expect of a hired hand. He was losing his land, the basis of his authority in the farm family and his standing in the public community. Despite Trevor Slattery's impassioned plea, the judge granted the divorce, awarded Celestia Slattery the custody of their children, and ordered him to pay support.

We will never know which of the parties to the divorce was telling the truth. What the case does reveal is the impact of changing notions of class and gender which challenged bedrock lineal family values which tied men to land and women to men to bear children and keep land in the family. Increased access to manufactured goods elevated standards of living for many, which in general diminished the drudgery of farm women's work. Rising rates of tenancy and the use of wage labor threatened the farm family's traditional reliance on their own labor and independent land ownership. Thus, the primacy of market agriculture eroded a measure of the farmer's autonomy. Saddled with debt and beset by risks, some farmers resorted to wife-beating to vent their frustrations.

Equally important to the transformation of the farm family were changing gender ideologies, notably bourgeois notions of domesticity with its intolerance of abusive behavior. Rising expectations for women and the idea of romantic love in the companionate family ideal may have led some to feel their marriages were no longer to be tolerated. Liberalization of divorce laws offered a remedy for those who felt their gender rights were being irretrievably harmed. The intensification of agrarian capitalism exerted pressures on rural people, women and men differently, that were manifested in domestic violence. For women the great transformations raised expectations; men experienced the transformation as increased risk which weakened their hold on land and command of labor. The crisis within the household was mirrored by the community crisis symbolized by the Grange protest; both would threaten not only the family farm but also the Fountain Green community of which it was a part.

7

"Ours is no slouch of a village"
Unmaking Fountain Green

On a hot Friday night in August 1880, Thomas Duff murdered Alvin Salisbury on the steps of the Fountain Green Presbyterian Church. The men were attending a Republican rally for presidential candidate James A. Garfield, featuring favorite son Major Robert W. McClaughry, warden of the state prison at Joliet. The church was so full that the torchlight parade crowded at the doors of the church. Salisbury had recently turned Republican, and when questioned by a leading Democrat about the change in his loyalties, Salisbury replied with an insult: "Show me a democrat and I will show you a drunkard, or show me a drunkard and I will show you a democrat." Duff spoke up to defend his father, saying, "We are both republicans, but my father is a democrat and he is no drunkard and you know it." Salisbury, described in the paper as a "tall, bony, and muscular" man in his mid-forties, ordered Duff to stay out of the argument. The short and stocky Duff retorted he would say what he pleased. Salisbury then handed his lamp to a bystander and turned to strike Duff. Duff dodged the blow and stabbed Salisbury in the chest and upper arm. Salisbury stepped back, and Duff plunged the blade of the knife into his forehead.[1]

Salisbury staggered into the church for a doctor, while Duff fled the scene on horseback. After identifying Duff as his assailant, Salisbury fell unconscious. Both Dr. Ferris and a doctor from Carthage were called in to assist in the case, but Salisbury remained unconscious and died late the following evening. After an all-night search, a posse found Duff, who was immediately jailed, found guilty at a trial which drew large local crowds, and sentenced to the penitentiary. Farmer Salisbury left a widow and four children. Although Salisbury was a member of the Majorville Methodist Church, so many wanted to attend his funeral that it was held at the larger Fountain Green Presbyterian Church, the site of his murder. The large crowd made a funeral procession to Webster, where he was buried.[2]

Further probing into the motives for the murder reveals a long-standing feud between the two families. Residents of the township remembered a late-night "shooting match" between the two in 1873, for which Salisbury took Duff to circuit court. Despite the fact that Duff's shots grazed the scalps of Salisbury and his sister, Duff was acquitted, perhaps because Salisbury also emptied his revolver.[3] Duff was probably still smarting from his appearance at the circuit court in 1873, still angry that Salisbury had pressed charges and brought him to trial. The feud between Salisbury and Duff is characteristic of family feuds, in which small incidents can build up over a long period of time into resentments that culminate in violence. Although both men rented the land they farmed, neither man was a transient; their families had been among the area's earliest settlers. To make things worse, both men were known for having a bad temper, and jealousy may have been part of the trouble.[4]

The murder was more than an altercation between two men; it reveals the currents that roiled beneath the surface in the small farming community near century's end. If we take Duff at his word, he murdered Salisbury to defend the reputation of his father, and by extension, other Democrats. Salisbury's insult, that Democrats were drunkards, deeply offended Duff, prompting him to draw his knife. It may seem to us a harmless remark, but Salisbury's equation of Democrats and drunkards insinuated that Democrats such as Duff's father were unmanly because they could not control their drinking. The virtue of self-control had become a hallmark of the newer ideals of masculinity promoted by middle-class Republicans such as Salisbury. The insult, and Duff's violent re-action, is one sign of the contestation over the bourgeois ideal that self-control was essential to character. Salisbury was not simply insulting Duff's Kentucky-born father, he was challenging a set of traditional values represented by the Democratic party, supported most strongly by the southern-born and their descendants. The confrontation between Salisbury and Duff was thus more than merely personal; it is symbolic of the acceptance of middle-class values by some rural people and rejection of such values by the traditionalists who defended their masculine prerogatives. It also speaks to the cultural divisions between the political cultures of the Democrats and Republicans, differences associated with class.[5]

As the murder intimates, communities such as Fountain Green became more susceptible to urban middle-class ways, eroding the distinctive nature of the local farm culture. While the turn toward middle-class mainstream values was undoubtedly part of the corporatization of America, the adoption of new values was also stimulated by the realization of the shortcomings of rural life.[6] The small towns of rural communities suffered as their commercial prospects dimmed and Main Street shops began to close one by one. In hopes of holding on to those who were drawn away by multiplying links to the metropolis and the lure of opportunity in the West, local boosters sought to revitalize society by molding churches, schools, and clubs to middle-class ideals. The reformers cultivated a bourgeois consciousness characterized by gendered notions of genteel behavior which was resisted by those who clung to habits of rural sociability by which men controlled public space and women stayed home.

Thus, in communities long riven by a consciousness of difference between northerners and southerners, distinctions began to be made on the basis of class toward the end of the century; such distinctions were sometimes linked to political identities. At the same time that class tensions came to the fore, the agrarian dreams of the past were being replaced by the vision of an industrial future. The nation was undergoing an ideological shift that made farming as a way of life appear anachronistic, even outmoded. In the closing decades of the century, the farm families of Fountain Green Township began to cope with the ironic consequences of the world they had made. Those consequences, and what they meant for the future of Fountain Green Township, became clear as the last of the old settlers died. It was the end of an era for rural community in Fountain Green and throughout the Midwest.

Unmaking Fountain Green

In August 1880, journalist Noble L. Prentiss of Kansas returned to visit his cousins in Fountain Green after an absence of fifteen years. As he looked around, he commented that the town had not changed much in ten years and had not grown in size for the past twenty years. Prentiss blamed the sleepiness of the town upon its lack of railroad. Waxing philosophical, he mused, "The railroads make and unmake towns in this age; and what they unmake seems to be more than they make. . . . If you would take things as you find them and leave them as they are, you must have no railroad." Prentiss, who had seen a great deal of the West, concluded, "Fountain Green has no railroad, and so the names of fifty years ago remain today."[7]

Prentiss was partly right about Fountain Green staying the same. Many of the families who had settled the township put down roots that survived the great washing in and out of migratory tides. Dominated by the Scots-Irish Presbyterians from Pennsylvania and New York, the group took control of local government and other social institutions. Like the Norwegiau of Trempeleau County, Wisconsin, or the Germans of Stearns County, Minnesota, by the 1870s a particular ethnic group was associated with Fountain Green, even though the group was native-born.[8] Prentiss's observations reinforce what historians have learned about settled rural communities: out-migration makes them stable and homogeneous.[9]

However, the relative permanence of this core group of town residents and farm families lent the illusion of continuity while the population was heading into an inexorable decline. Between 1870 and 1900, Fountain Green township lost about one-third of its population, falling from 1,500 to about 1,000 inhabitants. Half of that loss occurred in the decade of the 1870s. The population decline in Fountain Green township was part of a larger depopulation of the settled farm lands of western Illinois. Hancock County population decreased 12 percent, from about 36,000 to 32,000 in the same thirty years. The number of foreign-born in the county dropped 35 percent in the period 1870–1900, from 12 to 8.5 percent of the total county population. Lowered rates of fertility and reduced rates of immigration meant the population was not replenished by those who stayed.[10]

Such out-migration was typical of the rural Midwest in the United States in the nineteenth century. The population curve initially moved rapidly upward with the frontier boom of settlement, leveled off as immigration ceased, then declined as the land filled with settlers and their children. Barring any change in the use of land that would support more people, the population would continue to decline as changes in farming practices lowered demands for labor. As the population declined, country towns also began to shrink, further reducing local opportunity. Rural people migrated to larger towns or cities for employment or to western frontiers for land.

Although the changes in farming freed many farm children from family obligations, on some family farms in Fountain Green, it seemed as if the changes reduced opportunities for farm children on the family farm homestead. Many of Fountain Green's young men had to go west for land to carry out their ambitions. Although some went as bachelors, most left Fountain Green after they had married and tried to get a farm in the township.[11] The number of persons in their thirties dropped 58 percent in the 1870s, from 185 to 108.[12] The smaller size of this group was a factor contributing to the shrinking number of children, since there were fewer households with adults in the prime years for producing children. The population of the township was aging; the average age of household heads increased from 41.6 years in 1860 to 45.5 years in 1880.[13]

The West was a logical choice for landless farmers' sons because of the abundance of cheap land. The liberal land policies of the Homestead Law and the opening of Kansas and Nebraska coincided with the return of the Civil War veterans. They were persuaded by letters in the paper, local agents who sold railroad lands, and, perhaps most important, friends and relatives who migrated and encouraged them to follow. Even the folks at home saw the West as a place of opportunity for the farm boys of Illinois. Susan Geddes, writing to her son Thomas at school in Iowa, marveled: "What a grate outlet there is going to be for young men in the new Territories it is astonishing to read how fast the western world is filling up & a good chance for young men to make their mark in the world."[14]

James M. Foy's migration to the West is a good example. His recollections, made when he later applied for a pension, vividly convey the winds of fate that blew some away from Fountain Green. Foy married a local farmer's daughter after his return from the war, and the couple had several children. After a few years working his forty-acre farm, he decided that "farming was an impossible occupation." He mortgaged his property to buy a flouring mill, but "the business wrecked my health and the borrowed capital served the purpose of wiping me off the financial map during the panic of 1873." He took his family west to Kansas in 1883 to have another try at farming. He wrote, "Open air life on the western plains partialy restored my health and when riding machinery for farm use became available I drifted back to successful farming." He managed for a while, but in about 1900, "advancing age and severe cold weather drove me to cover and induced neumonia that so near finished it all that I have not since braved a northern winter. Six years ago this compeled the abandonment of my interest in farming and the proceeds have now shrunk to insignificance."[15] His health broken, his wife dead, and children gone, Foy retreated to Florida to live with a friend, who, at his request, wrapped the old soldier in the flag for his burial in 1926.[16]

Foy was one of Fountain Green's forty-nine Civil War veterans who filed for a pension. Eighteen stayed in Fountain Green and three more went to other towns within the county. However, like Foy, well over half the veterans left western Illinois. Most migrated to the midwestern states of Iowa, Missouri, and Kansas, with a few scattered in Illinois. Several found their way to Oklahoma, and at least one ended up in California.[17]

The migrants tended to cluster together in colonies in Kansas and Oklahoma, arriving there in staged migrations. The most striking example is the clustering of veterans around Reno County, Kansas, where six of the eight veterans who moved to Kansas settled. Most migration decisions were permanent. Only two veterans returned to Fountain Green after a sojourn out west.[18]

Young farmers were drawn westward by letters from Civil War soldiers who had gone west to claim their homestead or to buy railroad land. The letters appealed to those without land—renters and mechanics—thus tapping the hallowed agrarian yearning for independent land-ownership. Descriptions of Kansas and Nebraska sounded much like the guidebooks to the prairies of Illinois that so appealed to their fathers and grandfathers who had left Kentucky or Pennsylvania in the 1830s. A young man who left the county for central Kansas wrote in February 1873 that once the prairie was broken, the soil was "rich, deep and black and very productive," with corn yields reaching twenty to thirty bushels an acre. They were no farther than eighteen miles from the nearest railroads. Water was abundant, and rainfall was adequate. He summed it up with this statement: "So it seems there is no very serious difficulty while there is plenty of good land yet to be settled, where poor men can soon become independent."[19] Like their fathers and grandfathers, Fountain Green's emigrants pursued cheap, fertile land located near transport routes so they could be independent.

Like their grandparents who had migrated from the East to Illinois in the 1830s, those who moved west in the closing decades of the century also moved to maintain farming as a way of life. The cheap government lands of the West gave them the opportunity to start over and to provide a chance for their children. Going west was a conservative choice, a choice to preserve the life they had lived while land was still available. Their migration meant that they would, in a certain sense, repeat the process of settlement that had founded Fountain Green earlier in the century. Their movement westward transplanted the mid-western farm family culture in new environments, where practices would be altered but values would persist.

Those who left for larger towns or cities sought a different way of life. In the city they would trade the independence of farming for dependence on a salary or a wage. In exchange, they were offered middle-class standards of living and the excitement of a vibrant environment. The records of the Fountain Green Presbyterian Church show that while some members left for Iowa, Kansas, Colorado, and California, others moved to towns and cities in Illinois. Charles Chamberlin, whose mother opened a millinery shop in Fountain Green after her husband died in the Civil War, left for Burlington, Iowa, in January 1871. In January 1875 Miss Maggie Kious transferred her membership to the Fifth Presbyterian Church of Chicago; her parents and sister moved to Kansas a few years later.[20]

Like Maggie and Charles, unmarried farmers' daughters and the children of the townspeople were better candidates for urban migration than the farmer-veterans. Only a few of the veterans who left Fountain Green sought opportunity in the region's cities. Benjamin Wood went to Keokuk, Iowa, to be municipal superintendent of wood boats, then to Alexandria, Missouri, where he was lumberyard foreman for the railroad. The veterans from Fountain Green went to nearby Keokuk, Iowa, Galesburg and Joliet in Illinois, or Hannibal, Missouri.[21]

The outward migration did not mean a lasting separation, like it had for the generation who settled Fountain Green. Train travel made visiting relatives back in Illinois more feasible, whether one had gone to the city or to Kansas. The mobility provided by trains meant that family ties were maintained across long distances even after people moved away from the township. Indeed, family members of many who had gone west to settle found their way back to Fountain Green with some regularity. For example, in the spring of 1879, young Alexander Walker and his wife visited from Rock Island, Illinois, a newlywed couple returned from Missouri, and a bachelor returned to town to look for a wife to take back to Kansas.[22] Well-to-do women of Fountain Green traveled by train to visit family members throughout the United States.[23]

By the end of the century, the shortage of land and local opportunity meant that only a select group of children, and even fewer grandchildren, of Fountain

Green Township's settlers could stay. Opportunity on the western frontier beckoned, offering land to sustain farming as a way of life. It was a timeworn strategy to maintain an agrarian existence. Some farm children opted out of country life altogether, lured by nearby cities and waged work. The departure of the descendants of the original settlers who came to Illinois for its abundant land was just one of the ironic consequences of market agriculture in Fountain Green. Carrying farm values throughout the nation was another irony, because by so doing the hallmarks of family farm culture would persist long after farming ceased to be a way of life for the nation's majority.

A Little City Style

The departure of so many of its sons and daughters dramatically transformed the small towns which had been the commercial anchors and social centers of rural community in Fountain Green Township. The depopulation was a sign of larger trends which eroded the supremacy of the local centers of commerce. The railroad was the most obvious culprit, but equally important was the pressure of long-distance trade mechanisms to replace local credit with cash-based exchange. The village leaders valiantly attempted to recoup their losses by making the town more attractive, building new churches, and promoting the town's virtues in the local press. They even built a mill to boost local productivity. Far from being complacent about their fate, those who had a stake in the community tried to save a sinking ship.

As Prentiss had proclaimed, in this era, the railroad was key to growth. After repeated tries in the 1850s, one last effort to bring a railroad to Fountain Green in 1870 failed completely. LaHarpe got the road, and Fountain Green was consigned to an insular position that severely limited its growth. Villages such as Fountain Green and Webster lost population to places such as LaHarpe and Carthage (where there were rail depots) and regional entrepôts such as Macomb, Galesburg, and Keokuk. In 1875 one local booster wrote to the newspaper that he was having trouble finding news because "our village does not find much to get excited over. We need a little city style—'our city'—you know, like LaHarpe, with a railroad and a 'nowspaper' to give us dignity and items."[24]

The extension of the Topeka, Peoria, & Wabash Railroad (TP&W) to LaHarpe in 1868 stimulated the town's expansion. In the spring of 1867, LaHarpe contained about 1,600 residents, who were served by a panoply of dry goods, drug, clothing, and grocery stores. A steam flour mill and two steam sawmills processed the grain and timber farmers brought in to town. When the TP&W railroad reached LaHarpe in the summer of 1868, a bank and thirty new homes had been built, and town fathers were arranging for a town newspaper.

Stock shipped out daily from the local yards to put LaHarpe "in the front ranks of the stock shipping points on the TP&W."[25]

In contrast, by 1880 many of Fountain Green's craftsmen had left, victims of the increased availability of manufactured consumer goods as well as the decline of neighborhood traffic (see Table 7.1). The shoemaker, tinner, chair maker, and harness maker of 1860 were joined by a cooper, dressmaker, and boot maker by 1870. However, by 1880 only two shoemakers practiced in Fountain Green Township. Seven carpenters and three brick makers made a living there in 1870, but ten years later there were only two carpenters and two masons. Because goods no longer had to be hauled to the river ports, demand for wagons declined, and the number of wagonmakers halved from six in 1860 to only three by 1880. The number of blacksmiths, who shod horses and made hand tools, fell from nine in 1870 to only four in 1880.[26]

The retail community suffered the most from the competition of larger rail towns. The seven merchants in 1860 were supplemented by two peddlers, but only four merchants made a living in the township in 1880. Small country stores could not hope to maintain the inventory necessary to provide the selection available in larger town stores that advertised in local papers. In Carthage, John Culkin dealt in boys' and men's clothing, while at Pruett & Buckner one could buy boots, shoes, and gaiters.[27] Stores also carried sewing machines and a large variety of yard goods and trimming for women's apparel.[28] A farm family could travel to Carthage to buy carpets, curtains, or oilcloth. In Burlington or Keokuk they could purchase a piano for the parlor, come home with a new suit, and have a good time on the outing.[29]

Shopping in larger towns was powered by a new thirst for consumer goods, in part a result of the rise of domesticity in the countryside. Farmers and their wives made their homes more comfortable with carpets, curtains, clocks, and reading material. Alongside an advertisement in the *Carthage Republican* for Kirby's American Harvester in 1866, Younker & Brothers of Keokuk, Iowa advertised a wide variety of carpets. In 1873, Lange and Van Metre of Burlington, Iowa, advertised the Excelsior Piano for $325. Chicago companies also advertised in the local newspaper, complete with a picture of the Wm. Knabe & Co's pianoforte.[30] The piano was the consummate symbol of middle-class respectability; by 1878 there were over 200 pianos and nearly 600 melodeons in the homes of Hancock County.[31]

The acquisition of certain consumer goods, such as washing machines, eased daily tasks, while the purchase of ready-made clothing or parlor curtains were class markers which conveyed a yearning for a more genteel style of life.[32] By purchasing fancy ribbons, gloves, corsets, and hosiery, rural women were consuming urban class identities which disguised their rural character. Although women were critical to the spread of rural consumerism, they were by no means the sole source of desire for the trappings of bourgeois identity. The county paper featured full-sized pictures of men and boys advertising the latest fashions, and the local gossip reported that "several of our citizens have been to Keokuk the past week, and from all appearances found new suits cheap." Such bold and pervasive advertising was a sign of the competitive commercial community of the 1870s, in which merchants fought for the dollars of farmers.[33]

Peddlers and the availability of mail order also cut into the business of local retailers. Peddlers found it easier to sell their goods during the day when the men were not at home. The paper accused them of watching the house until the men left: "When they find the coast is clear of the masculine element, then they sail in on the defenseless women with an impudence little short of downright ruffianism."[34] By marketing directly to farm women in their homes, peddlers appealed to women's desire for consumer goods without the interference of a penny-pinching husband.

A compelling factor in the movement of trade to larger centers was the phasing out of the credit system. Connected tightly to a national market that demanded rapid payment of debt, rural storekeepers were forced to conform to the financial practices of the large urban centers. Once specie was widely available in the community, merchants were quick to move from a credit to a cash business. This eliminated the expense of pursuing debts through local courts and business losses when debtors skipped town. The editor of the county paper in Carthage supported the new standards of trade, noting that "in country places it seems difficult, as yet, to get full settlements of accounts oftener than once a year." The regular settling of accounts would benefit the consumer because the savings would be passed along in lower prices, in contrast to the "old fogy plan of long credits."[35] The webs of credit which bound members of the rural community to each other in the early days were replaced by an impersonal cash nexus, so farmers felt less loyalty to shop at local stores.

The elimination of local credit was one sign of the maturation of rural capitalism as the countryside became enmeshed within a national market structure. As early as the summer of 1866, stores featured the phrase "cash only" in their newspaper advertisements.[36] Advertisers in the county paper defensively declared in 1870: "We pay cash for goods and we cannot do a credit business. We hope our friends will not insist upon it. Quick sales, small Profits, Ready Cash is our motto."[37] Now that farmers were paid cash for their crops three and four times a year, merchants expected them to be ready to put greenbacks on the counter.[38] In Fountain Green it was said that grocer Uncle Tommy Campbell "sells cheap for cash, and growls no little when it has to be set down [in the daybook]."[39] With the elimination of store credit, farmers had little incentive to trade in town when they could get goods cheaper at Keokuk, Iowa, whose merchants advertised extensively in the county's two newspapers.[40]

Fountain Green merchant Charles C. Tyler was able to retain a loyal base of customers through shrewd marketing practices. Although Tyler continued to offer credit to his customers, his cash sales steadily increased.[41] The store he built in 1864 became a landmark; going to "the Arcade" reproduced the city shopping excursion in the rural village. Tyler's store was well stocked, and he was known around town as a courteous and fair dealer. Shoppers at the Arcade could combine the excitement of the city with the security of the country store. With an eye for fashion, Tyler decorated the windows of his store and laid in an extra stock of goods in the centennial year of 1876. A local promoter complimented him as "a man of excellent taste."[42] Country shoppers at the Arcade who wanted an outing in Fountain Green could stay overnight at Alexander McConnell's hotel. Women could find a bonnet to match their purchase at the town's millinery business, run by a succession of widows and young unmarried women.[43]

It was clear to the local elite that their prosperity was being threatened by the decline of the farm villages. While in the 1850s the obvious solution was to attract a railroad, twenty years later towns were clamoring for factories to bring them prosperity.[44] The leaders of Fountain Green followed this strategy when they invested in a flour mill in an attempt to strengthen business prospects. The anchors of the community—Major John G. Fonda, storekeeper C. C. Tyler, Dr. Ferris, and Justice of the Peace Kendrick Leach—founded the Fountain Green Milling Company in February 1870, managed by miller John Frank. The stockholders were among the richest men in the township: storekeeper John Everett, Major R. W. McClaughry of Joliet (heir to the fortune of Matthew McClaughry), premier farmer and stock raiser Andrew Bullock, and wealthy farmer Alexander W. McConnell. They each bought a share of the $10,000 capital; miller Frank owned two shares and controlling interest.[45]

The mill did a brisk business, drawing in customers from as far as Colchester, Blandinsville, and Macomb in McDonough County to the east. Farm families brought in grain and paid for the grinding by toll. The mill ran day and night five days a week and was known for its fine quality. The local newspaper correspondent tried to drum up business for the mills in May 1880 when he reported that miller John Frank had recently installed $300 worth of new machinery and that a "scientific miller" cleaned and sharpened the burrs so he could make "as good flour as can be made in the state."[46] By the end of the century, however, the mill could no longer compete with the larger mills, and farmers were buying flour from stores instead of grinding their own at the local mill.[47]

Ordinary citizens were less forthcoming with funds to improve the prospects of the towns. Fannie Leach complained of being cooped up in the house in March 1865, all because "the Fountain Green people think they *can't* afford side walks." The spring rains made the roads a quagmire, leaving her the choice "to wade through the mud, or stay at home."[48] Mud was all right for farmers in their boots, but not for fashionable young ladies in their long skirts and dainty shoes. When the question of sidewalks arose in 1867, the opposition was vo-ciferous. Susan Geddes wrote to her son Thomas about the lively town meeting:

> Had a quite exciting time in the Green one evening about sidewalks & debating about another month school everybody was interested & everyone wanted the floor. Mull had a drum & Mr. Barr was loud. The foursome of the Ministers could hardly keep the peace. Leach called some one a d----d fool. Rob said it was as good as a play.[49]

Townspeople were divided in their opinions about being taxed to improve the municipality. In the civic exchange of rural democracy, decisions were openly debated, policed by religious leaders. Women such as Mrs. Geddes may have been present, but the major characters in the drama were men, the legal voters of the community. Perhaps if the women whose skirts dragged in the muddy streets had been able to vote, the motion to build sidewalks would have carried. The failure of the sidewalk initiative meant many farmers no longer identified with the interests of the farm villages such as Fountain Green, a place which once had been the center of trade and commerce for the wider farm com-munity.

Evangelical Religion

Like the elites who remodeled stores and built a factory, churches also employed new techniques to retain their congregants. The decreasing popula-tion remodeled the social practice of religion for all the local churches, who borrowed methods from urban evangelists to maintain their vitality. While an evangelism had flourished in the American backcountry in the early nineteenth century, the new evangelism was an outgrowth of religious phenomena in Chi-cago and other large midwestern cities. Religion had long played an important role in the perpetuation of bonds of kinship and community in rural Fountain Green; now the forms of religious sociability introduced new habits of worship and association.

The Fountain Green Presbyterian Church suffered noticeably from the de-population of the postwar era. In 1867, the church numbered 150 members, including old families from Pennsylvania and New York, and newer German immigrants such as the Schwedeses and Sweigerts.[50] Membership declined in the next decade, and by 1878 only 107 were regular communicants. The same trends that diminished the size of the general population—lower fertility and out-migration of members—also affected the community churches. Fewer children were baptized into membership as time went on: thirty-nine in the 1850s, eighteen in the 1860s, and only eleven in the 1880s. Even fewer attended Sunday School and weekly prayer meetings, and benevolent contributions declined. County historian Thomas Gregg lamented in 1880 that the additions to church membership had not made up for the losses. In language reminiscent of reports of the decline of the Path Valley, Pennsylvania, church in the 1830s, Gregg wrote that "this church has stood in the relation of a feeder to many newer congregations in the localities beyond the Mississippi."[51] Again the West claimed the people from home.

Improved roads contributed to religious mobility within the county. Those who left for Carthage may not have been moving from their homes, but they may have chosen to attend a more fashionable and vibrant church than the old Fountain Green one led by an aging Rev. Walker. With so many of the original Pennsylvanian founders of the church in their old age, the church may have become too sedate for those accustomed to more fashionable sermons and songs and a more convivial social group. Or perhaps they did not want the financial responsibility of maintaining the church at a cost of $600 a year.[52]

The Presbyterian elders hoped a new building would improve their fortunes. Before the downward slide of population was evident, the Fountain Green Presbyterians constructed an imposing new church building in 1872 that was sixty-five feet long and forty feet wide and had a steeple reaching ninety feet into the sky. Town promoters were proud of its size and appearance. Cyrus Geddes, son of church elder Thomas Geddes, boasted in 1872, "It has stained glass windows of handsome design, and its interior finish and decoration would be creditable to a city church of much greater pretensions."[53] Its beautiful new building, as nice as any in the city, became home to not only worship services but also to community activities such as school pageants and political rallies.

The decreasing population meant that smaller churches closed their doors. In 1870, the first defectors to the United Presbyterian Church (founded in 1858) began to return to their original church, perhaps in response to the national reunification of Presbyterian churches.[54] By then the Fountain Green Church did not have a permanent minister but was served by a circuit clergyman. In a final irony, Mrs. McClaughry, whose husband had built the United Presbyterian Church, returned to the original Presbyterian church in June 1880.[55] The religious community was becoming less diverse, just as the commercial community had; both trends were attributable to the shrinking population.

The other churches in the township, while similarly active in attracting congregants in the post-war years, were not so tightly linked to an ethnic identity. As the towns became increasingly marginalized in the region's commercial network, the churches had to struggle to sustain themselves. To rise to that challenge, they adopted an evangelical approach that had worked very well in the region's cities.[56] The evangelistic efforts meant that in the 1870s religion took on an increasingly social character that contrasted with the solemn piety of mid-century religion. Newspapers reported a continual round of outdoor camp meetings conducted by area ministers and traveling preachers.[57] The families of the township attended Sunday school picnics together, eating their basket dinners while they listened to outdoor sermons. Young people partook of the excitement of the meetings and converted in entire groups. Young women were especially responsive to the evangelical movement conducted by visiting preachers from outside the county. The open nature of the meetings fostered a public display of spirituality not typical of the township. Part of a regional religious awakening, rural people who felt uneasy about the social dislocations of prosperity and out-migration sought security in the institutional safety of a church.

The Methodist church was the most active in promoting this new style of religion. They moved into the old Presbyterian church in the autumn of 1872 and rapidly gained converts through the medium of the protracted meeting. Such meetings would extend for weeks at a time, drawing in people from the farms and villages to be a part of the event. In February 1873, their success attracted the notice of the county correspondent: "They did not even have a class organized when they commenced their meeting four weeks ago, but they have now taken in about 50 members, and there are converts who expect to join the other churches."[58]

The protracted meetings likewise revitalized the Fountain Green Presbyterian Church, whose young people, especially women, confessed the faith in groups. Twelve young people were admitted on examination in March 1868, among them Walkers, Campbells, Witherows, and Millers. Another group of sixteen young people joined in December 1875; all but one were women.[59] The following March, seventeen young people joined in a group. Seeking official admittance to the church connected the young people to the larger community as adults, not as children, and it was a step in recognizing Fountain Green as their home.[60]

Women continued to play a role in promoting religious commitment in the domestic sphere. While young Thomas Geddes was away, his mother, Susan, advised him to "look to the proper source for direction in all your movements. It is quite a critical period in life when we first we set out on our own Look without any experience & very little money." She quoted the Bible, suggesting that "if you commit your ways to him he will direct you safe your path through the world so far has been very pleasant and prosperous & if you do your duty you may safely trust him for the rest." After all, she concluded, "It is the storms & adverse gales that makes the skillful mariners."[61] While certainly not all sons who wandered west remained church-goers, mothers such as Susan Geddes admonished their sons to remember the habits of home.

The survival of the Presbyterians and the success of the Methodists stand in stark contrast to the virtual disappearance of the Catholic presence in the township. The few Catholics still in the township attended church either at Tennessee in McDonough County or in LaHarpe. The churches they attended were far different from the ones they had founded when the township was settled. The influx of Irish Catholics who stayed in the area after laboring on the railroads meant that few in the parish were native-born. Ivo Hardy's son William married the daughter of an Irishman who came to America in 1859 to labor on the railroad. When Eliza Yager, a farmer's daughter, was married in LaHarpe in 1880, the ceremony was performed by an Irish priest.[62] The decay and abandonment of St. Simon's in the 1850s meant that the Catholic origins of the township's founders faded into obscurity. The only reminder of their presence was the Catholic cemetery, which achieved notoriety as the place where President Lincoln's relatives were buried.[63]

Evangelism allowed religion to remain a central social force in the township; however, the revivals altered religious practice. Denominational piety gave way to an ecumenical conviviality where sexes mixed in amusements at picnics and revivals in the wooded groves around the villages. Although it no longer defined an ethnic identity as strongly as it had in the community's early years, the Presbyterian church remained the flagship of the community—home to funerals, school programs, and Republican rallies. No longer the ethnic enclave on the frontier, the church came to represent a broader middle-class agrarian culture.

Changing Identities: From Ethnicity to Class

Half a century after the founding of the community, the regional divisions that were initially important in shaping the community's character had fused into a distinctive local farm culture. It was a culture stamped with a particular ethnic identity as a core group of families from Pennsylvania and New York dominated the religious, educational, and civic institutions of the township. William Spangler, who wrote from California to Fountain Green in 1873, closed his letter to Thomas M. Geddes with this injunction, "Give my kind regards to all at Geddesburg."[64] Spangler's use of Geddesburg as a nickname for Fountain Green betrayed the Pennsylvania character of the small Illinois town. The differences of region of origin that had divided Fountain Green lost their saliency over time. As the ethnic culture of those from the middle states, particularly the Pennsylvanian Scots-Irish clans, became dominant, what had once been distinctive became typical of local culture. In the process, distinctions of ethnicity gave way to distinctions of class, but not without a fight.[65]

Fountain Green had become the preserve of families from Pennsylvania. Three groups of settlers had settled the township, but only the Pennsylvanian stream had been strengthened by continued chain migration. Although the original settlers from the mid-Atlantic states were aging, continued immigration allowed them to retain their numerical dominance in the township. Forty percent of the household heads in 1870 were from the middle states, and in 1880, their Illinois-born progeny made up 35 percent of the household heads in the township (see Tables 7.2 and 7.3). They proved themselves remarkably capable of taking advantage of the agrarian marketplace and in handing family land down to their children. Their prosperity and their endogamous patterns of marriage tied them tightly to the land and to each other in massive kin networks. They dominated the local government, built the largest church, and supplied the schoolteachers who taught their values to the township's children.

The original clans of southern-born families persisted on the land, but they did not have the numerical strength or perhaps the inclination to exercise control of the local institutions in the way those from Pennsylvania did. The proportion of households headed by the southern-born declined from one-fourth in 1850 to about one-tenth of the township's population in 1880, but their children accounted for one-third of the Illinois-born. The southern-born and their children who remained in the township congregated around Webster. Their presence makes the political and social dominance of the northern-born even more striking. Bruised in the local struggle at the time of the Civil War, their identity was submerged by the prominence of the northern victory in the war and political control by northerners at home.

Like the southern contingent, the number of those born in the North (New England and New York) similarly declined, to half of their original strength (Tables 7.2 and 7.3). More cosmopolitan, the children of the town's elite Yankees moved out of Fountain Green when it began to be perceived as a backwater. College educated and well traveled, they could see that opportunity lay elsewhere. For example, Dr. Charles Ferris, son of community stalwart Dr. Leonard T. Ferris, closed his medical practice and moved to Carthage in 1894.[66] The village tradesmen shuttered their shops and headed to other towns to make a living. Yankee farm families parceled out their land, but it was not enough for all their progeny, some of whom migrated West to stay in farming.

A growing group in the population of the township were the Germans, who were buying farms from the native-born who sought opportunity elsewhere. Hancock County had been a destination for German immigrants since the middle of the century; they constituted about 60 percent of the total foreign-born in the county into the early twentieth century.[67] Their infiltration did not go unnoticed. In 1879, the local correspondent to the paper reported the purchase of a farm by Bavarian-born Lewis Schwerer, "our old German friend." Schwerer paid $2,500 for a farm which had been sold a few years previously for $8,000. Since then, another forty acres had been cleared. The farm was valuable—100 of the 150 acres were cleared, and it boasted an orchard and a good house. The country correspondent approved the transaction as "the best bargain that has been obtained in real estate in this section for a long time."[68] The prudent immigrant was able to escape tenancy by purchasing a choice piece of land for a relatively low price.

His was an extremely productive farm, thanks to family labor and the assistance of a hired hand. The 240-acre farm consisted of eighty-five acres of corn, which fed the seventy-five hogs and twenty-six cattle Schwerer raised. His wife must have been involved in the yearly production of the 500 pounds of butter from the milk of ten cows. Schwerer's older children were daughters, who may have helped with the dairying and perhaps worked in the fields. Schwerer paid 21-year-old Swiss-born John Solent to help him on his farm in 1880. Solent lived with the family but may have been paid in shares, because Schwerer claimed to have paid only twenty dollars for two weeks of labor in 1879.[69] Schwerer's brother Jacob and his family joined him in Fountain Green, and several other German immigrant families lived in the immediate neighborhood.[70]

Schwerer's purchase provided a legacy for future generations of his family, who were still farming in the township in the 1950s. The German families were successful because of their continued reliance upon family land and labor to compete in the marketplace. Their habit of passing land to their children before death enabled them to stay on the land far longer than many of the native-born who saw the homestead as an asset to be liquidated to provide a portable inheritance for their children.[71] The German Methodist church they had founded in the 1860s helped them sustain a sense of community, allowing them to worship in their native language and persist in many of their native customs.[72] In many ways, their family structure and farm operation mimicked the tight family-centered pattern of the early native-born settlers in Fountain Green. As many of the native-born families proved unable to accommodate their children on farms, or left farming altogether, the German-born and their children stood ready to take over their operations.

Class distinctions in Fountain Green society rested in part on changes in the distribution of wealth in the farming community. While there had always been social distinctions in the community and a hierarchy of status, even if they were based only on the size of one's farm, the range of difference between poor and rich steadily widened as wealth became more concentrated at the top. The top quintile of farmers in the township held 31 percent of the total value of farms in 1860; in 1880 they held 46 percent of the total value of farms in Fountain Green Township. In 1870, Pennsylvania farmers such as Alexander and Samuel Walker were among the wealthiest, owning $15,000 and $19,000, respectively. Old Tennessee settler Hickerson Wright likewise had achieved great wealth totaling $19,600 in 1870.[73] Townspeople had also amassed greater quantities of capital by 1870, such as retired farmer Matthew McClaughry, who was worth $23,000, or miller John Curry, who owned property totaling $18,000. [74]

The wealth of the community's best was evident at the twenty-fifth wedding anniversary of Dr. and Mrs. Leonard T. Ferris in 1875, which was reported in detail in the county newspaper. Son Charles and daughter Lelia organized the grand event, which was attended by those prominent in wider regional social networks of county society. Many of them were formerly of Fountain Green, such as Ferris's brothers, banker Hiram G. Ferris and Judge John M. Ferris, of Carthage.[75] The guests from Fountain Green included representatives of "all the old families of the township, "whose rank was due not only to their wealth, but also to their years in township government or church leadership.

Symbols of wealth and standing, the "elegant and costly" gifts brought by the guests were publicly displayed on a center table in the entry hall to the Ferris home: a silver tea set worth $180 and other items of silver, including napkin rings, forks and knives, nine goblets, a platter, and a watch case. After gazing at the display of fine silver gifts, guests were served dinner from three long tables in the "ample dining room." The county correspondent noted: "It is needless to say that the tables were loaded with every substantial and delicacy the country and season could afford, and was elegantly prepared and admirably served." The signal event of the evening was the presentation by Charles Ferris to his parents of an ebony cane with silver fittings, engraved with their names and the date of their marriage. The gifts and food were not only tokens of appreciation and hospitality but also a display of wealth and taste. The upper ranks of local society, most of whom were descended from early Yankee or Pennsylvanian settlers, moved within a wider social circle in the region, and they were attuned to the value systems of the provincial elites.[76]

The elites of Fountain Green also controlled the political apparatus of township government. They routinely elected Republican supervisors by comfortable majorities, most of whom were Pennsylvanians or some relation to the Scots-Irish clans. While the county voted for the Democratic presidential candidate through the end of the century, Fountain Green voters favored Republicans, awarding them 62 percent in 1872. The political history of Fountain Green suggests not a Republican hegemony but contested victory by Democrats who drew in part on a strong tradition of agrarian independence. This tension is most visible in places such as Hancock County in the midsection of the Midwest, where the legacy of settlement cultures pulled people both ways, unlike southern Illinois, which tended to be Democratic, and unlike the northern part of the state which tended to be Republican. While certainly the loyalty of Lincoln's soldiers was powerful in determining party affiliation, ethnic and regional cultural identities were likewise critical in creating a Republican Midwest and its cultural agenda.[77]

The widening distance between rich and poor, high and low, meant a larger group of those occupying the middle. The middle class consisted of the mass of farmers, owner-operators at the top and young tenants at the bottom. Because they farmed on a smaller scale than the elites, they could not as handsomely reap the benefits of the market-driven economy. The value of the holdings of the average farmer remained fairly constant at around $3,000 from 1860 to 1880.[78] Tenants produced corn for the elite stock raisers and breeders while they raised hogs and fed cattle on a small scale. The lower middle class was comprised of the renters, mostly the sons of reputable farmers waiting for land.

The middling group of township society was descended from an array of founding families, including those from the South, unlike the Yankee-dominated elite group. Several of the core group of families in Fountain Green were new German immigrants. Their families were larger than the elite families, and their children tended to stay in the township. They led the community by filling the lesser township offices or by serving occasionally as justice of the peace.

The middling group of Fountain Green Township was constructed of interlocking networks of kin and neighbor who retained many traditional forms of rural sociability. The interdependent nature of the community was clear in November 1873, when the house of the Glass family caught on fire while they were asleep in bed. All that remained after the fire was the bedding they wrapped around themselves as they fled the flames. Neighbors rallied to alleviate their plight. Within three days, Glass and his neighbors had cut enough timber for a small house. Kendrick Leach charged him nothing to saw the lumber at his mill. Within the week, the two-story house was ready to be plastered and finished. Not only did the neighbors help rebuild the house, but merchants in the country towns donated supplies and labor.[79]

Three years later, when the house of Nathaniel Midcap's family burned down with all its contents, friends canvassed the neighborhood with subscription papers to raise donations for the family. The country reporter boasted: "We are charitable people here and I haven't the least doubt these friends are, at least, twenty five dollars better off now than they were before this misfortune. The citizens of Fountain Green are better pay than any 'insurance company,' and a great deal more honest."[80] In a catastrophe the farm families of Fountain Green depended on the community, and the act of helping engendered a sense of communal pride and belonging. Indeed, the reporter argued, they were so self-sufficient that they did not need to buy insurance, the modern corporate solution to personal disasters. Through assistance in times of crisis and everyday exchange of labor, the core farm families in Fountain Green provided a central gravity that held the community together.

At the very bottom of rural society were the perennial renters and farm laborers who formed a rural proletariat, wage laborers whose youth and independence put them beyond the traditional bounds of rural society girded by family, church, and school. A portion of the young men had always worked as farm laborers, either for their fathers or for other farmers, but near the end of the century much of the farm labor force was supplied by men who were not native to the community. At least two-thirds of the farm laborers in 1880 were young men who were not living with families or relatives, in contrast to a decade earlier when all but eight of the farm laborers were living with families or relatives. In 1880, twenty-two were between the ages of 15 and 30; only eight were older than 30 years.[81]

The economic foundations of class difference were strengthened by a growing sense of rural inferiority. Rural self-improvement efforts grew out of the awareness that farm children were leaving the county in droves. Country people were well aware of how their own environments lacked the comforts and refinement of city life. In 1874, "Ruralist" from Warsaw wrote to the newspaper about "why so many of our sons and daughters have such a distaste of rural life, and sigh for the excitement and bustle and glitter of the city." He thought it was because farmers had worked their children too hard on the farm. Farm families had become "the most abject slaves, laboring fourteen hours per day beneath the burning rays of the sun."[82] Child labor, long an important part of the family farm economy, was threatened by the newer ideals of a playful, leisured childhood.

According to "Ruralist," children left because of the run-down farm environment. A typical farmyard was "enclosed with a rickety fence overgrown with weeds, and in the yard may be found a collection of dilapidated implements, plows, planters, reapers, wagons, and hay racks, while the grass is utilized by a numerous family of pigs." The result of the farmer's stinginess was that his children rejected him and his way of life. The well-furnished farm home with a beautiful yard provided the right setting for the training of farm children, who would become "the honored, earnest men and cultured women, who are to shape and control the affairs of the nation." In a house equipped with books, flowers, and the comforts of middle-class life, "the children are contented and happy and have no desire for the unnatural excitement of city life." If farmers wanted to keep their children close by, they would have to give themselves and their children greater opportunities for "social enjoyment and intellectual culture, and to make our homes beautiful and our calling attractive and honorable." If they did that, farm sons and daughters would not reject the rural life in favor of the wealth and fame of the city.[83]

To create a "higher social life for the rural classes," county leaders established a college in Carthage in 1875.[84] The editor of the newspaper represented the county leaders when he argued: "It would increase the value of all property. It would refine society. It would bring in numbers of the very best class of settlers. Elegant and tasteful houses would spring up, and it would do more for the real advancement of this town than many railroads." Besides, he added, "Our sons and daughters must be educated, and why not here?"[85] Refinement, elegance, taste—the college was thought to bring all that the best citizens of the county desired for themselves and for their children.

Business and religious leaders met to consider funding; they aspired to the status of Galesburg, which with its college was able to lure two railroads to its doors.[86] Among the organizers were Major Robert W. McClaughry and Hiram G. Ferris, men who were raised in Fountain Green and used their college education as a springboard out of the tiny farm town.[87] Eventually, the German Lutherans in Warsaw agreed to provide support for the local college.[88] The establishment of the college was a recognition that many farm families wanted their children to have more of an education than was offered in the common schools. Although the value of a college education for farmer's daughters remained controversial (critics felt that women used it as an escape to shirk their duties as farmwives), the establishment of the college acknowledged that farmer's sons could choose not to be farmers.[89]

The opening of Carthage College in 1875 meant that the children of the wealthy families in Fountain Green could keep their children nearby for their education.[90] They absorbed new values of educational attainment and broadened their social contacts beyond the rural hamlet. When they were home on weekends, the women students enlivened the local literary society by reading essays and recitations.[91] Often their friends from around the county joined them for a respite in the countryside of Fountain Green. The local newspaper correspondent admitted that the town was "dull" when they were gone away to school.[92]

The college-trained were cultural missionaries who tirelessly promoted a genteel middle-class culture. Children of prosperous farmers and townspeople, they returned with a more cosmopolitan outlook and a wider circle of friends. For many young women, college provided the training to return to the township to teach school. Nearly all the township's eight teachers were women, most of Yankee origin.[93] The dominance of those of Yankee stock among schoolteachers meant that their values were being inculcated in a younger generation. They socialized farm children to a set of entrepreneurial values as they simultaneously made the school a focal point of community activity. The end-of-the-year school program in the spring was a major community event managed by the female schoolteachers. Proud parents crowded the schoolroom or, for larger groups, the Presbyterian church to see their children perform their recitations and locutions, the result of self-discipline and expert coaching in habits of genteel speech.[94]

College students led the effort to improve the quality of rural social life by importing exclusive organizations to promote their middle-class ideals. Their meetings were attuned to political party platforms, and they argued about such subjects as the need for tariffs. The most stalwart members were sons and daughters of wealthy farmers originally from New England and Pennsylvania who favored the Republican agenda. Young women attended the debates but rarely took part. Instead, they were involved in the entertainments, such as an evening in April 1879 "consisting of declamations, dialogues, essays, tableaux," and music. The local correspondent to the paper, ever the promoter of life in the country, quipped that the existence of a literary society showed that "ours is no 'slouch' of a village."[95]

Because the Literary Society was exclusive in its membership, it became a target for those who lampooned their pretensions at gentility. The society had to abandon the schoolhouse as a meeting place in 1875 because their meetings were disturbed by "rowdies." They arranged to rent the United Presbyterian Church, where "they could exclude all such unprincipled persons, and if necessary, enforce the municipal laws of our land," meaning liquor laws.[96] One way to limit who came was to levy an admission fee of fifteen cents. The proceeds were to go toward the improvement of the town's sidewalks, "which certainly need it."[97] The college-educated young people went to great lengths to improve the social life, as they defined it, in Fountain Green. Club members imported notions of class and respectability, notions which set them apart from the plain farmers and the young carousers. Their behavior was resisted by the rowdies, who eventually were excluded by moving the meetings to an institution that was the symbol of middle-class Republican respectability.

Young people were not the only ones swayed by the newer forms of social organization. More mature men established a chapter of the A.O.U.W. (Ancient Order of United Workmen) in 1879.[98] The founding of the Workman's Lodge was among the signs that marked the transformation of a rural community based on neighborliness to a translocal society depended upon national organizations to meet social needs. A major attraction of the A.O.U.W was the life insurance benefit it offered to its dues-paying members: $2,000 for the widow of the deceased.[99] The popularity of the fraternity is evidence of the desire for the protection of life insurance in the farming community. While neighbors could help rebuild a house that burned down, widows could no longer subsist on charity or pauper's benefits paid by the county.

Except for partisan political clubs and the Farmers' Clubs of the Grange era, the A.O.U.W. was the first formal association organized by the citizens of the township. Some of the men had been active in Masonry, but the lodges were in Carthage and LaHarpe. While young men had joined together in the Literary Society, and farmers in the Grange, the lodge welcomed older men of any occupation. The lodge also organized the members' female companions, who accompanied them to social activities.[100] The officers of the middle-class organization represented a broad cross-section of the community. Wealthy farmer John H. Parker, originally from Virginia, was chosen as Master Workman. Among the other officers was James H. Walker, a farmer only 32 years old from Pennsylvania, who had inherited part of his farm, worth $5,000. The three other farmers who were officers rented their land. The lowest office was held by H. M. Shilling, a shoemaker from Pennsylvania, who was married with two small children.[101]

Like the Literary Society which was pestered by the "rowdies," the A.O.U.W. also met resistance by the carousers of the community. After the club spent months refurbishing a defunct store into an acceptable meeting place, they held a masked sociable, which was spoiled by some "half-drunk" people of "low breeding" who tried to remove people's masks.[102] The formation of the A.O.U.W. accentuated the distinctions between those who were cultured and those of "low breeding." The payment of dues gave them the privilege of excluding the undesirable elements of the community from their activities. While the A.O.U.W. fraternity mixed farmers and townspeople, owners and renters, it excluded those who did not meet class-based standards of manhood. The order made distinctions between those who drank and caroused and those who discussed ideas and enjoyed such novelties as wearing masks at a dance. Thus the fraternity organized the rural citizens in ways they had not been grouped before. The establishment of the A.O.U.W. conspicuously displayed the acceptance of middle-class demeanor and its gendered meanings in the rural township.[103]

The new middle class not only formed social organizations for themselves, they also attempted to impose their cultural norms upon the entire community by targeting the rowdy elements of society. Just when a youthful underclass was wriggling free from the confining bonds of family and church by asserting their masculine prerogative by drinking and fighting, the village bourgeoisie clamped down on their disorderly behavior. Prominent among the constellation of bourgeois values which spread to the countryside were altered notions of gender which reflected a growing sensitization to violence and an intolerance for disorder.[104]

Civil authorities joined in the campaign to civilize the countryside. A rise in the number of charges of assault accounted for most of the increase in the rate of violent crime in the postwar period.[105] Charges for attempted murder also climbed sharply in this decade. While some of the increase may have been caused by an increase in the number of assaults, the increase may also have resulted from increased prosecution, indicating a growing tendency on the part of victims to appeal to state authority, perhaps because of a decreasing tolerance for disorder. For example, charges of riot, or disorderly conduct, were the most volatile, peaking with the Civil War period draft resistance, then sharply rising again in the 1870s. The sudden rise in charges of disorderly conduct may better reflect increased policing and prosecution than an actual increase in the incidence of crime, sign of a growing intolerance for disorder in rural society.

As seen by the increased prosecution of rural men on charges of assault, the pressure to civilize the rowdies created tensions in rural society; those who were unwilling to change resisted stubbornly. Trapped at the bottom of the agricultural ladder, with declining prospects of ever owning a farm, the rowdiness of farm laborers was a form of resistance to the status quo. Propertyless and adrift in local society, they fiercely defended their sense of self-importance through contests of masculinity.[106] Assaults often resulted from drinking rituals of male sociability that at times led to accidental murder. A fight which began at a village tavern ended with Gleason punching Mathews to the ground. Mathews rose and "fired at him three times with a Colt's revolver, but failed to hit." Mathews was arrested on a charge of assault with intent to kill and was placed under $1,000 bond.[107] Horse races were also a hazardous scene of male sociability, where liquor flowed and gambling enlivened the competition. At a horse race outside the Webster country store, the paper reported that there was "iron rods, rowdyism, rye, rot gut, and razors."[108] Horse races provided excitement for the young farm laborers who had no families to monitor their behavior.

The saloons provided a haven for those who clung to habits of male sociability—drinking, gaming, and hunting. These habits had long been tolerated, and even local reporters played down the disturbances:

> The boys of our town on last Saturday evening had a little fuss. Three or four of them . . . took a glass or two more than they were able to bear, and which made them quarrelsome. A knife was drawn by one party and a pistol by the other. They were forced to put them up before any harm was done.[109]

To hold one's liquor, to win a fight, were desirable qualities of character for these men. So vital were virility and honor to rural men that inflammatory behavior occurred not only in saloons but also at community gatherings such as Christmas parties or neighborhood singing schools. In 1879, two young men at a Christmas party at a rural schoolhouse got into a fistfight; as the victor prepared to leave, the man on the ground, "somewhat under the influence of liquor," drew his revolver and shot his opponent in the heart. He died instantly and his killer fled.[110]

Rural men were sensitive to slights which called into question their own sense of dignity and male prerogative. Defense of one's manhood or defense of the reputation of a family member frequently provided the grounds for a fight which could lead to accidental murder. Robert McGinley attempted to avenge an insult upon his sister by calling the offending man out of doors at a singing school two weeks later. The men exchanged words, and McGinley wounded the man with a slingshot. The man stabbed McGinley with a knife in the eye and in the neck, severing the jugular vein and causing McGinley's death.[111] Violence which might have been tolerated in frontier days shocked and offended those who aspired to a more civilized countryside.

The saloons in Webster provided a haven for those who resisted the new middle-class codes of cosmopolitan behavior. Habits of southern male sociality—drinking, gaming, and hunting—had long been tolerated in Webster's southern-dominated community. In March 1875, thirteen men in the township were indicted for gaming and fined $10 each. Three of them were Wrights, from

Kentucky. A month later, Frederick Barnett, originally from Vermont, was indicted for keeping a gaming house and fined $100. His patrons were not only young farm laborers but also farmers and shopkeepers around Webster.[112] Clearly these were not young transients; they were the center of the local commercial community. Most of those charged were of southern descent, older men who set the patterns that the younger men would follow.

The new middle class, most prominently women, waged war on the drinking and gambling in the pages of the county newspaper and in mass temperance meetings. Their successful campaign to restrict the sale of alcohol through local legislation was an attempt to regulate the growing unruliness of the farm laborers in the township. The anti-drinking campaign was part of the effort to elevate the standards of rural sociability to better conform to ideals of middle-class manliness: respectability, moral restraint, and prosperity. As "May Bell," the "Country News" correspondent from Webster lamented:

> Oh! What a sad sight to see young men of respectable connections, with fine talents and bright prospects for the future, thus creating an appetite for poison, which all experience proves they will soon lose the moral power to restrain and the indulgence of which, will eventually lead them into the downward path of degradation, poverty and shame.[113]

By the late 1870s, local women such as "May Bell" were thoroughly involved in the temperance effort, which challenged the male prerogatives of rural patriarchy. They held offices in the Good Templars organization and organized a county Woman's Christian Temperance Union.[114] Temperance advocates sponsored performances of "Ten Nights in a Bar-Room," visited prominent offenders, and staged demonstrations at saloons.[115] They also imposed the new ideals of gendered behavior on the rowdies through local legislation against drinking. When a saloonkeeper accidentally killed a drunk patron in 1874, the limits of community tolerance were reached. Saloons were closed during the next horse race, and the following year local voters elected an anti-licensing board to restrict the sale of liquor.[116] However, enforcement of liquor laws was uneven, which gave female temperance advocates cause to complain that if men would not enforce the law, women would.[117]

As the people of Fountain Green Township were exchanging their agricultural produce for manufactured goods from the city they were also consuming urban ideals. The adoption of urban notions of gender and class created new axes of solidarity in the community as regional identities were discarded for class identities associated with political identities. The village bourgeoisie adopted the cultural agenda of the Republican Party, and women's temperance agitation imposed ideals of middle-class domesticity on a rowdy masculine sub-culture which violently resisted reform as it clung to traditional forms of rural sociability. Higher education, which farmers began to see as desirable for their children, heightened the sense of disparity between city and country. Ironically, the adoption of urban ideology may only have served to accelerate the unmaking of Fountain Green. The nation itself was undergoing an ideological shift which made farming as a way of life appear anachronistic and outmoded. The industrial age had taken hold.

Primeval Settlers

As the century drew to a close, the last of the pioneer settlers faded into history. Noble Prentiss observed that "one generation has passed away since the primeval settler came, and another generation casts a long shadow in the setting sun."[118] In 1875, a reporter from Fountain Green took note of the old people who had come to vote in the April township elections. Eight of the old men who cast their ballots were over 80 years of age, among them Hickerson Wright from Tennessee and Ivo Hardy, a Catholic from Kentucky. Daniel Prentiss, who came to the county in the 1830s from Vermont, was still holding onto his farmland at age 76.[119] Stooped with age, the old settlers still took seriously the right to vote, a right they had defended more than once.

There were other signs that those who had spent their lives in the community they built were aging. Dr. Ferris fell out of his buggy when he could not control his frisky young horse, who startled at a loose paper in the road. His son, Charles L. Ferris, patched him up and took over the medical calls while the old man contemplated his mortality. The next year Charles brought a bride from the "best society" of Warsaw to Fountain Green, where he was said to have a "lucrative" practice.[120] Rev. Walker of the Presbyterian church retired in April 1876. He was replaced by a traveling minister.[121]

Then the death of the pioneers in twos or threes sent the entire community into mourning. Matthew McClaughry, 76 years old, attended the Old Settlers Reunion in August 1879 in fine form, along with five other old men from the township. Within a few days he had succumbed to kidney disease, despite the ministrations of young Dr. Ferris.[122] Old Rachel Glass, who had come from Pennsylvania in 1833 to raise seven children and four grandchildren in Illinois, died the same week.[123]

The grim reaper took a bounteous harvest in those closing years of the decade. Col. Miller, who had been the commander of a militia in Pennsylvania, died at Webster in August 1879. The 81-year-old man, his legs partially paralyzed, had spent the last summers of his life reading a Bible under a tree in front of his house, chatting with people who happened by.[124] When old Kentucky settler James Yager, a founder of the old Catholic St. Simon Church, died in 1880, his funeral was held at the Catholic church in LaHarpe.[125] James Welch of

Webster "dropped dead while dressing" early one morning in April 1876. He was 84.[126]

Grandma Lucy Alton, who came from western New York with her husband in 1836, attracted a great deal of notice in the way she died. Barely able to hear or see in her ninety-second year, she simply stopped eating on April 3, 1880. She lived another thirty-five days, with weekly reports in the newspaper on her intentions to leave this world. At her death on May 8, she left behind a remnant of her immense progeny of 159 descendants. Five of her eleven children and twenty-six of her grandchildren had preceded her to the grave.[127] Martha McConnell Walker's husband, Alexander, passed away on Christmas 1879.[128] Col. Thomas Geddes and his wife, Susan Walker Geddes, died within a few weeks of each other in January 1892.[129]

As the century drew to a close, the people of Fountain Green dealt with the ironic consequences of their success in agrarian capitalism. Foremost among them was the inability to settle all the descendants of the pioneers on land in the township. Some chased their agrarian dreams westward, while others forsook farming as a way of life for the attractive urban scene. Those who stayed behind promoted the ideals of the middle class, remodeling local communal institutions, citifying the countryside, and constructing class identities which enforced gendered notions of behavior. The attempts of the village bourgeoisie to reform rural traditionalists met with only limited success, resulting in an agrarian society which, underneath its patina of gentility, retained a crude earthiness. Ultimately, the dominant Scots-Irish Presbyterian culture was transformed into the archetypal midwestern culture—middle-class, Republican, Protestant, respectable. That the midwestern set of values became American was due in part to the migration of farm people to the West and to the nation's towns and cities. Even as their former way of life became obsolete, the children who chose not to stay in the country carried agrarian values which would be reified into a national myth.

One such farm girl was Jennie Hopkins, daughter of Martin and Fidelia Beebe Hopkins, early settlers from Connecticut. Born in 1859, she was adopted by the Hopkinses and raised on their large farm. She taught school in Fountain Green, attended two years at Carthage College, then struck out for the West to write for a newspaper in Denver. In Colorado she met Louis Seibold, also a journalist, and the couple married and made their careers in New York City, where she wrote a play and worked on the staff of *Harper's*. In 1884 she published a collection of her writings, including several stories drawn from her reminiscences of Fountain Green.[130]

Much of Hopkins's writing is highly sentimentalized, almost maudlin, but the stories about the farm ring true in their detailed portrait of the life Hopkins once led. In contrast to the bitterness of Hamlin Garland, Hopkins presents a romanticized image of rural life. The story "June Roses" is filled with inviting imagery as the narrator, a city woman, visits her cousins in the country. The farmhouse is not luxurious; Hopkins described it as "a long, low rambling red house, with faded green shutters and small high windows," the walk edged with flowerbeds. The household is orderly and tidy, and "she actually devours her supper of snowy, home-made bread, served with the sweetest butter and honey," and falls asleep "amid the billowy softness of the old four-poster and is far away upon the wings of those sweet dreams known only to healthy, happy girl-hood."[131]

Hopkins lyrically describes her day in the country, entertaining her readers with pastoral scenes of hearty meals and pleasant farm people working together. The city visitor arrives for breakfast overdressed in a white dress: "She praises the country ham and eggs, ecstasizes over the rich cream as it is generously lavished upon her coffee; and in short, so takes the whole table by storm, that the young farmers, stalwart good-looking fellows too, glance slyly at her as they pass on the way across the wide porch to the scene of their daily labor." She is taken on a tour of the house by the housewife, who has lived in the home since her marriage forty years before. The visitor "is particularly amused by the great piles of rag carpeting which the house-wife has stored away in the garret, against a time of need and with the multitudinous gayly-colored calico bed quilts which every cupboard and closet in the house is literally pressed down and running over." Not only is the housewife an accomplished needlewoman, she and her daughters also make butter. They carry a rocking chair to the dairy for their guest "and let her sit there in the cool, stone building, while they fashion the golden butter she loves so well." In the evening, their "own strong willing hands" harness trusted Old Dobbin and they take their visitor for a drive about the country.[132]

Hopkins's idealized version of farm and country life portrayed a haven of cleanliness, order, beauty, and harmony. Her inviting imagery of handsome farmers, billowy beds, golden butter, and gaily colored quilts suggests stability, a sense of tradition, of a family working productively together. They impart a bittersweet feeling for a pastoral childhood, a longing for a place where the author no longer wants to live but somehow cannot part with, its memories lingering in her mind. The stories of Hopkins, who rejected country life for the excitement and sophistication of the city, show the agrarian myth in the making.

Conclusion

To celebrate the 100th anniversary of the founding of Hancock County, in 1925 the residents of Fountain Green assembled in the Woodman's Hall to view a collection of historical relics that had been passed down from family to family. Each object of importance so carefully saved was a key that unlocked memories of past events.

The most interest was aroused by tokens of war, which elicited memories of events of obvious gravity to the participants. Frank Walker of Webster showed off the flintlock revolver and sword used by his grandfather, Francis McConnell, veteran of the War of 1812, one of the first to claim title to the Military Tract. Walker also displayed a deed for land in the Military Tract signed by President Martin Van Buren's secretary. Arthur Geddes brought the sword worn by his grandfather, Col. Thomas Geddes, in the Mormon war. Descendants of the old settlers brought more peaceful relics of Mormon times—a picture of the Mormon temple in Nauvoo and a deed signed by Joseph Smith for land in Macedonia. The picture of the huge banner of Abraham Lincoln, awarded to the Wide Awake Club of Fountain Green at a political rally in 1860, symbolized the Republican and northern dominance of the township during the Civil War. The bayonet brought by another was a stark reminder of the mortal combat in battle, shadowed by the conflict at home.

Others displayed farm tools that were vestiges of primitive agriculture—an old grain cradle made without nails and a cleaver used to butcher hogs in 1836. The men who would soon replace their horse-drawn reapers with tractors must have scoffed at the notion that anyone could farm with a wooden pitchfork or the reap hook brought from New York in 1837. Tools made of wood, iron, steel, and then machinery pulled by horses had changed the way the farmers went about their work. An old rifle and powder horn brought back memories of pioneers hunting for turkeys for the stewpot or shooting birds for sport at Christmas, both male rituals.

Women brought treasured reminders of their foremothers: flax hatchels used to separate the fine linen fibers from the rough tow, a wooden bread bowl in which the farm wife turned flour ground from grain raised in the field into the family's daily bread, an old potato masher which transformed dirty vegetables into fluffy white wisps, and a wooden mortar used to make rusks for the Sunday evening meal. Someone had carried a sturdy wooden rocking chair to the meeting which a mother had made sure to bring to Illinois in 1830. One could no more raise babies in Illinois without a rocker than harvest grain without a reap hook.

Also on display were relics of town institutions. The people in Woodman's hall hefted the great key to the Presbyterian church that was built in the 1870s. They turned the pages of the 1837 daybook that lay on the counter in Stephen Tyler's general store and saw that families paid with produce, not money, for their goods. They might have imagined the conviviality of the general store, where women fingered calico and men gathered around the stove to read newspapers and talk of distant scenes. Someone brought a silver sugar bowl purchased by Mary Jane Leach at the store in 1856, a symbol of the refinement of domestic life available to those who prospered at farming. Dr. Ferris's saddlebags, still loaded with medicine, were a reminder of another community institution, evidence of the cycle of birth and death that connected the past with the present.

The antiques that drew so much attention in 1925 were tools that farm families used to carry out the tasks of their lives—tools used to farm, to feed families, to bring up babies, to wage war, to have a good time. In one sense of the word "relics," they were objects preserved in veneration of the primeval settlers who founded the farming community. The handing down of objects from one generation to another kept alive the stories and memories of an earlier time. To see a wooden pitchfork or flax hatchels reminded the settler's progeny of the ruggedness of everyday life in the nineteenth century. The swords and bayonet were proof of the struggles to preserve the way of life they believed in. The key to the Presbyterian church and the daybooks of Tyler's general store were evidence of the importance of institutions, whether religious or commercial, that drew the community together.

The antiques on display in 1925 were relics in another sense. This alternate meaning of relics refers to them as a trace of some outmoded practice, custom, or belief. The agricultural economy of the township had undergone massive changes in the first century of its existence. The farm families shifted from production of wheat to a diversified mix of grains and livestock. Machinery replaced hand tools, manufactured goods replaced domestic products, and railroad cars replaced bulky farm wagons in getting produce to market. Old ways of farming were made obsolete by the integration of the farm economy into the national marketplace as agrarian capitalism developed.

Agrarian capitalism developed out of adaptations farm families made to maintain their values. Adjustments occurred in four critical areas of farming as a way of life: family labor, independent ownership of land, social relations, and politics. First, agrarian capitalism diminished a traditional dependence on family labor. Families became smaller in size, and the work roles of children were trimmed to fit new ideas of childhood and adolescence. Mechanized implements and hired hands eased the labor of the farmer while it increased his expenditures. Women turned away from domestic production to household management and the nurture of children.

Second, independent land ownership became more of an ideal than a reality by the close of the community's first fifty years. Farm families were originally lured to Illinois by cheap government land that would enable them to earn a competence and settle their sons around them. But by 1880, there was not room for all the sons who wanted to stay, nor was it attractive to farmer's daughters who, like Theodore Dreiser's Sister Carrie, longed for the excitement of city life.[1] Many migrated west for cheaper land where they could preserve farming as the way of life they had known, while others pursued careers in the towns and cities of the region. Patriarchal control of land was reduced by increasing rates of tenancy and children's lack of desire to stay on the farm. Renting land became an acceptable way of life for many in the farm community who preferred farming to other occupations.

Third, changing notions of gender and class altered rural social relations in public and private. Rural society at mid-century consisted of a web of obligations; people were linked by kin ties, churches, political affiliations, and voluntary associations. Churches reinforced an ethnic identity through religious association, resulting in a place increasingly dominated by the Scots-Irish. Later in the century, more egalitarian gender ideals wore away at rural patriarchy, weakening the foundations of the family farm culture. The emergence of a permanent class of tenants and wage laborers resulted in the creation of more rigid class boundaries, and village elites adopted middle-class ideals. Their attempt to establish class-based codes of gendered behavior provoked a violent resistance by those who defended male prerogative in agrarian society.

Finally, changes occurred in the political realm. True, farm people still relied on grassroots government to resolve differences and carry out common goals: building roads, financing local railroads and town sidewalks, building and administering schools, and settling petty debts or domestic disputes in the justice of the peace court. When that governmental structure failed to carry out the communal will, as happened during the Mormon conflict, shadow governments were set up to maintain communal ideals. However, as the Civil War approached, partisan identities connected rural people more tightly to the national polity. Democratic hegemony was threatened by the new Republican Party, which not only made electoral inroads but whose adherents attempted to impose on the rest of the populace their cultural ideals, which ran counter to agrarian values of independence and aversion to government interference as a threat to personal liberty. Nevertheless, families depended on the federal government for land in the Military Tract, for roads and railroads on which to ship produce, and for homestead land out west.

The history of Fountain Green teaches us that the midwestern way of life was a product of cultural patterns transported to a new environment. Regional cultural identities mattered: the peculiar character of midwestern community was created from the meshing of cultures from the southern, northern, and mid-Atlantic regions. The relative strength of those population streams, the sequence of their settlement, and the isolation of rural community were important determinants of the community that would form. A characteristic process of midwestern rural community was localization, in which a key group dominated local institutions and determined the course of commercial and political development. Fountain Green acquired a distinctive identity in the region as Republican, Pennsylvanian, and Presbyterian. The generalization that southerners settled the Midwest and Yankees took it over overlooks the role those from the middle states played in the localization process. It also glosses over the peculiarities of place and time crucial to the creation and development of local community in the Midwest.

The history of Fountain Green suggests promising areas for future research. The history of capitalism in the countryside can challenge current understandings of the transformations that took place during the nineteenth century. By showing that industrial capitalism was dependent upon capitalism in the countryside, we challenge the notion that all change radiated from urban core to periphery. The construction of class and gender identities took a different path in the countryside, delayed and largely unrecognized. Nevertheless, such identities became articulated within rural society and challenged the patriarchal nature of family farming and the social rituals of the rural neighborhood. The mechanism by which those identities developed, and their distinctiveness in a rural setting, deserve further attention.

We must pursue an analysis of gender to lay bare the causal relationships between individual farm households and the massive shifts in the larger economy and society. Gender tensions within the household reduced domestic production and increased consumption of manufactured goods such as clothing. Changing notions of masculinity surely played a part in the exodus of farmer sons from the patriarchal estate. We need to move beyond a model of monolithic and unchanging patriarchy to understand the intersections of gender and class for women and men on the farm.

Because the unfolding of agrarian capitalism took place within a cultural framework, it is worth considering more carefully the components of local culture and how they affected approaches to the market. The recognition of a localization process requires that historians examine the process by which a group came to dominate community and commerce and the consequences of that dominance for rural capitalism. By conceding that economic development was shaped by cultural values, we shift the engines of change from structures to people. This diversity of interactions with the market tempers the structuralist market imperative that has characterized both the history of the commercialization of agriculture and the social history of rural capitalism. People are not the victims or objects of larger structural changes, but their actions, repeated and magnified, set those changes in motion.

We need to examine local political culture in rural areas, not only for signs of agrarian protest but also for a commitment to grassroots democracy. That belief in local democracy is among the more potent legacies of rural life for twentieth-century political culture. Reliance on government to solve problems may have fueled the rise of the modern state, which has assumed control of areas previously thought to be in the private domain. That trust in government has resulted in today's agricultural economy, which is highly dependent on government regulation and subsidies. As politicians transfer power from the national to the state governments, and as social critics call for a renewal of a civil society so vital to modern democracy, the past of places such as Fountain Green is instructive.

Class remains almost untilled ground for research in rural society. We cannot assume that the mechanisms of class formation or the construction of categories of class were identical for urban and rural areas. Again, the relative isolation of rural areas must be taken into account as a factor in accommodating to or resisting the spread of notions of bourgeois behavior. We might also consider what the shift from agrarian ideology to bourgeois capitalism cost the farming community. This cost was not only felt in how they saw themselves, but in how they were seen by the rest of the nation.

We must move beyond the boundaries of the urban/rural dichotomy to consider the significance of the countryside to the country as a whole. To integrate the rural experience into the history of the United States, to see city and countryside as connected by flows of people, commodities, and ideas, is to see it whole. The histories of city and countryside were not two separate tracks to the present; the countryside and cities developed with and because of each other. By neglecting the countryside, rural values of independence, hard work, piety, and patriotism that farm people brought to America's cities remain mere nostalgia. Only by separating the myth from the reality of rural life (insofar as we are able to reconstruct that reality) can we explain the lasting power of agrarian ideology in an age of agricultural crisis.

The ironies of the Jeffersonian vision of independent farmers are plainly visible more than 150 years after the community's founding. Today, Webster and Fountain Green are regarded as "the sticks" by people in Carthage, the county seat. Heartened by the success of their sesquicentennial celebration on the town square in 1989, the people of Webster hold an annual pork roast and parade of old cars the first Saturday in August. Their sesquicentennial celebration was a selective remembrance of the past; they rejected the Mormon church's proposal to erect a historical marker where Macedonia began on Ute Perkins's land. Across the road from the town park, a modern pig house emits a foul odor which pollutes the air. David Leach's brick farmhouse is the only remnant of the nineteenth century's prosperity.

Little is left of the town of Fountain Green. The grand homes of Matthew McClaughry and Dr. Ferris burned down long ago. Small frame houses and trailer homes provide modern comforts at a price farm people can afford. The Leach home, built during the Civil War, is slowly decomposing—bricks fall out of the facade, shutters sag, wallpaper peels off the walls. The name McConnell dominates the telephone directory, thanks to the intermarriage of their ancestors from Pennsylvania. The Fountain Green Presbyterian Church still stands proudly at the south edge of town, served now by a visiting minister. Women still gather in the basement every week to talk while they quilt.

The ruins of the towns stand in contrast to the verdant farms that surround them. The land—cleared and fenced, drained and plowed—still provides a living for the farm families who listen to the crop reports on their radios early each morning. Cattle and hogs stand around the muddy ponds on the slopes of hilly farms. Farmers gather in their overalls late every afternoon to talk about prices and the weather. Crooked Creek still runs.

APPENDIX 1
Tables

TABLE 1.1

Fountain Green Settlers by Region of Origin, 1825–1840

Southerners (not Catholic)	Kentucky Catholics	New York and New England	Pennsylvania
Brewer	Berry	Alton	Duffy
Cox	Branham	Beebe	Geddes
Day	Cambron	Ferris	Glass
Dill	Gittings	Hobart	Huston
Duff	Hardy	Hopkins	McConnell, A.
Duncan	Jones	Leal	McConnell, F.
Parker	Kelley	McClaughry	Miller
Perkins	Lincoln	Mull	Spangler
Renshaw	Mudd	Ostrander	Walker
Roberts	Riley	Prentiss	Witherow
Saylors	Shipley	Tyler	Yetter
Williams	Yeager	White	---

Sources: U.S. Land Office Records, Quincy District, Illinois State Archives, Springfield, Illinois; Thomas Gregg, *History of Hancock County* (Chicago: Charles C. Chapman, 1880); Charles J. Scofield, ed., *History of Hancock County* (Chicago: Munsell Publishing Co., 1921); George C. Tyler, "Centennial History," *Carthage Republican,* 22 April 1925.

TABLE 1.2

Farm Productivity by Region of Birth, Fountain Green Township, 1850 (Average per farm)

Regions	All	South	North	Middle	Midwest/West	Foreign
Number	128	39	39	41	9	12
Age of Head**	42.1	42.3	42.7	42.6	27.2	48.4
Household Size	6.3	6.7	5.7	6.9	5.4	6
Property* ($)	946	901	1,011	1,196	237	551
Acres Improved**	55.5	58.3	53.8	68.3	44.3	42.2
Farm Value* ($)	1,018	1,039	969	1,355	477	738
Implement Value**	91	84.4	83.3	118	65.6	72
Corn (bu.)	530	562	443	639	428	408
Wheat (bu.)**	138	129	121	184	93	99
Corn/Wheat	5.2	5.6	5.0	4.3	8.1	5.1
Stock Value ($)	291	342	260	331	205	228
Swine**	26	30.4	20.8	33.1	22.8	14.7
Cattle	7.8	9.2	7.8	9	6.7	6.8
Cows	3.8	4.3	3.6	4.2	4.9	4.6

*F-statistic for differences by region significant at 90% level.
**F-statistic for differences by region significant at 95% level.

Source: U.S. Census of Agriculture, Manuscript Schedules for Illinois, 1850. Illinois State Archives, Springfield, Illinois (hereafter Agricultural Schedules for Illinois, 1850). U.S. Census of Population, Manuscript Schedules for Illinois, 1850. Washington, D.C.: National Archives, microfilm (hereafter Census of Population, 1850).

TABLE 3.1

Leading Farm Indicators, Fountain Green Township, 1850, 1860

Indicator	1850	1860
Number of Farms	140	121
Acres per Farm	151	148
Improved Acres	57	76
Farm Value	$1,050	$3,188
Land Value (Farm Value/Improved Acres)	$18.42	$41.95

Source: Agricultural Schedules for Illinois, 1850 and 1860.

TABLE 3.2

Selected Products per Farm, Fountain Green Township, 1850–1870

Product	1850	1860	1870
Wheat (bu.)	138	70	148
Corn (bu.)	529	641	593
Corn/Wheat	5.2	13.2	5.7
Swine	27	16	22
Cattle	8.0	7.7	6.3
N =	140	121	168

Source: Agricultural Schedules for Illinois, 1850–1870.

TABLE 3.3

Farm Productivity by Region of Birth, Fountain Green Township, 1860 (Average per farm)

Regions	All	South	North	Middle	Midwest/ West	Foreign
Number	121	24	41	43	8	5
Age**	45.7	46	46.6	47.5	29.1	47.6
Household Size	4.8	5.1	4.6	4.9	3.5	6.4
Real Estate ($)	3,005	2,575	2,843	3,507	2,363	3,400
Acres Improved	75.7	69.4	68.7	86.3	69.4	84
Farm Value ($)	3,188	2,783	3,126	3,560	2,675	3,260
Implement Value ($)	108	90	107	120	94	114
Corn (bu.)	640	577	555	796	488	560
Wheat (bu.)**	70.3	53.4	42.2	112.7	20.6	96
Corn/Wheat	13.2	12.3	14.6	11.6	15.7	8.6
Stock Value ($)	685	933	580	656	550	820
Swine	15.9	15.9	14.4	18.1	15.8	11.4
Cattle	7.7	5.4	7.8	8.1	10.9	9.8
Cows	4.1	3.4	3.9	4.5	4.8	5.6
Butter (lbs.)	219	190	230	231	161	260

*F-statistic for differences by region significant at 90% level.
**F-statistic for differences by region significant at 95% level.
Source: Agricultural Schedules for Illinois, 1860; Census of Population, 1860.

TABLE 3.4

Butter Production by Region of Birth, Fountain Green Township, 1850 to 1880 (Average per farm)

Year	All	South	North	Middle	Midwest	Foreign	Foreign (non-English)
1850	146	163	135	150	119	126	---
1860	219	190	230	231	161	260	---
1870	169	163	130	188	205	90	161
1880	153	107	155	154	160	150	157

Source: Agricultural Schedules for Illinois, 1850–1880; Census of Population, 1850–1880.

TABLE 3.5

Eggs And Butter Brought in to Trade at C. C. Tyler's Store, 15 March to 15 April, 1856 to 1880

Period	Eggs (in dozens)	Butter (in pounds)
1856–59	42.5	22.5
1861–65	47.5	9.5
1866–70	34.8	2.8
1871–75	117.4	28.8
1876–80	24.2	6.6

Source: C. C. Tyler Store Records, Fountain Green, Illinois. Illinois State Historical Library, Springfield, Illinois.

TABLE 3.6

Age of Mothers at Birth of First Child, Fountain Green Township, 1850–1880 (For husband-wife household)

Age Cohort	1850	1860	1870	1880
Women 20–29	20.1	19	20	20.7
Women 30–39	21.8	25.4	21	22.5
Women 20–39	21	22.6	20.6	21.2

Source: Census of Population, 1850–1880.

TABLE 3.7

**Marital Fertility, Fountain Green Township, 1850–1880
(Number of children per married woman)**

Age Cohort	1850	1860	1870	1880
Married women 20–39	3.4	3.2	3.3	2.8
N =	99	125	110	107
Married women 20–49	3.6	3.7	3.7	3.2
N =	139	159	160	148

Source: Census of Population, 1850–1880.

TABLE 3.8

Size of Farm Households, Fountain Green Township, 1850 to 1880

Indicator	1850	1860	1870	1880
Persons in Household	5.92	5.34	5.19	4.93
Child/Woman Ratio*	1,567	1,344	1,195	1,130
Age of Head	42.1	45.5	44.7	41.9

*Number of children under ten per 1,000 women ages 15–44.
Source: Agricultural Schedules for Illinois, 1850–1880; Census of Population, 1850–1880.

TABLE 3.9

Male Farm Labor Supply in Fountain Green Township, 1850–1860

Occupational Title in Census	1850		1860	
Sons: "farmer"	38		64	
Sons: "farm laborer"	23		12	
Total sons		61		76
Non-sons: "farmer"	4		11	
Non-sons: "farm laborer"	9		15	
Total non-sons		13		26
Total		74		102

Source: Census of Population, 1850 and 1860.

TABLE 3.10

Farm Families Persisting from 1860–1880, Fountain Green Township

Category	1860	To 1870	To 1880
Number of farmers	121	---	---
Farmers persisting	---	54 (45%)	27 (22%)
Son or widow persisting	---	15 (12%)	33 (27%)
Other family persisting	---	5 (4%)	3 (3%)
Total persisting	---	74 (61%)	63 (52%)

Source: Agricultural Schedules for Illinois, 1860–1880; Census of Population, 1860–1880.

TABLE 3.11

Rates of Persistence, Farmers versus All Household Heads, Fountain Green Township, 1850–1880 (percent)

Household Type	1850 to 1860	1860 to 1870	1870 to 1880
Farm households	29	44	41
N =	140	122	169
All household heads	27	37	36
N =	227	248	260

Source: Agricultural Schedules for Illinois, 1860–1880; Census of Population, 1860–1880.

TABLE 3.12

Type of Will, Four Rural Townships, 1843–1894

Type of Will	Before 1859	1860–1869	1870–1879	1880–1894	All Years
Impartible				1	1
Partible	7	9	10	10	36
Preferential	10	8	14	14	46
All to spouse	2	5	4	9	20
N =	19	22	28	34	103

Source: Will Books 1, A, B, C, D and Will Record [n.d.]. Hancock County, Clerk of the County Courts, Hancock County Courthouse, Carthage, Illinois.

TABLE 4.1

Nativity of Household Heads by Region, Fountain Green Township, 1850–1860 (percent)

Region	1850	1860
North	30	30
Middle	32	39
South	25	17
Midwest and West	3	7
Other	9	4
Missing	0	2
N =	228	248

Key to regions:

North: Connecticut, Maine, Massachusetts, New Hampshire, New York, Rhode Island, Vermont

Middle: Delaware, New Jersey, Pennsylvania, Ohio, Virginia

South: Alabama, Arkansas, Georgia, Kentucky, Maryland, Mississippi, North Carolina, South Carolina, Tennessee

Midwest and West: Illinois, Indiana, Iowa, Kansas, Missouri

Other: Canada, England, France, Germany, Ireland, Poland, Scotland, Switzerland

Source: Patricia Jewell Ballowe, et al., transcribers. *The 1850 Census of Illinois, Hancock County* (Richland, Wash.: Locust Grove Press, 1977); Tri-County Genealogy Society, transcribers. *1860 Handcock [Hancock] County, Illinois Census* (Augusta, Ill.: Tri-County Genealogy Society, ca. 1983).

TABLE 5.1

Visible Partisans in Fountain Green Township, 1860

	Democrats	Republicans
Average Age (Years)	37.7	45.6
Average Wealth	$3,413	$6,483
Occupation		
Farmer	21	20
Craftsman	7	2
Professional/Merchant++	7	
Laborer	2	
Nativity		
North	27 (79%)	17 (71%)
South	7 (21%)	3 (12%)
Illinois		3
Canada		1
N =	43	25

++ Merchant (4), doctor (1), clerk (1), minister (1).

Note: Information not known for all characteristics. Age known for 34 Democrats, 13 Republicans; wealth known for 24 Democrats, 12 Republicans.

Source: Database constructed from newspaper reports of township elections, political clubs, appointment of party delegates, and entries in county histories and biographical compendiums (especially Thomas Gregg, *History of Hancock County*; *Portrait and Biographical Record of Hancock, McDonough and Henderson Counties, Illinois* [1894; reprint, Owensboro, Ky.: McDowell Publications, 1982]; *Republicans of Illinois: A Portrait and Chronological Record of Members of the Republican Party* [Chicago and New York: Lewis Publishing Co., 1905]; and Charles J. Scofield, ed., *History of Hancock County* [Chicago: Munsell Publishing Co., 1921]).

TABLE 5.2

Election Returns, Fountain Green Township and Hancock County, 1852–1876

Election Year	Candidates	Fountain Green	Percent	Hancock County	Percent
1856	Buchanan D	1??*	53%	2011	49%
	Fremont R	59	---	1120	---
	Fillmore Am	70	---	998	---
1860	Lincoln R	170	53%	2674	---
	Douglas D	152	---	3063	52%
	Breckinridge D	---	---	31	---
	Bell Union	---	---	121	---
1864	Lincoln R	133	54%	2654	---
	McClellan D	112		2929	52%
1868	Grant R	182	55%	3596	---
	Seymour D	146	---	3687	51%
1872	Grant R	174	62%	3141	---
	Greeley D	106	---	3328	51%
1876	Hayes R	NA	NA	3496	---
	Tilden D			4207	55%

*Figure missing.

Source: Thomas Gregg, *History of Hancock County,* 453–463; *Carthage Republican,* 11 November 1856; 8 and 15 November 1860; 10 and 24 November 1864; 14 November 1872; *Warsaw Express,* 19 November 1860; *Daily Warsaw City Bulletin,* 19 November 1860.

TABLE 5.3

Civil War Soldiers Enlisted in Fountain Green, by Regiment

Regiment	Number	Percent
118th Infantry Co. A	60	43
2nd Cavalry Co. G	25	18
12th Cavalry Co. G	8	6
51st Infantry Co. K	7	5
64th Infantry Co. D	7	5
14th Infantry Co. C	7	5
Other*	20	14
Missing data	6	4
Total	140	100

*Six of the twenty were the only men from Fountain Green in their companies.

Source: Brig. Gen. J. N. Reece, comp. and rev. *Report of the Adjutant General of the State of Illinois,* vols. 1–8 (Springfield, Ill.: Phillips Bros., 1900–1902), 1: 447–450, 613–615; 2: 13–16, 75–77; 3: 233–236, 471–474, 581–584; 4: 326–328; 612–613; 5: 155–157; 6: 293–295; 7: 268–269, 302–304, 506–509; 8: 352–355.

TABLE 6.1

Livestock Production, Fountain Green Township, 1850–1880

Animal	1850	1860	1870	1880
Swine (total)	3736	1935	3792	5292
Swine (per farm)	27	16	22	28
Cattle (total)	1132	932	1125	907
Cattle (per farm)	8.0	7.7	6.3	7.2
N =	140	121	168	189

Source: Agricultural Schedules for Illinois, 1850–1880. Averages mask the specialization of some farmers in the breeding and raising of cattle.

TABLE 6.2

Shift from Wheat to Corn, 1860–1880

Grain (in bushels)	1870	1880
Wheat	148	162
Corn	593	991
Corn/Wheat	5.7	9.5
N =	168	189

Source: Agricultural Schedules for Illinois, 1860–1880.

TABLE 6.3

Rise in Price of Land Sold, Fountain Green Township, 1851–1885

Years	N	Average Price (dollars)	Average Size (acres)	Average Value (dollars/acre)
1851–55	87	526.33	75.65	8.01
1856–60	61	649.51	87.77	9.88
1861–65	55	1202.13	98.47	37.56
1866–70	66	1233.00	70.59	31.57
1871–75	67	1119.74	56.55	24.71
1876–80	32	899.52	77.90	19.41
1881–85	29	1903.97	109.39	35.55

Source: Sample of deed transactions of persisting families in Fountain Green Township. Deed Records, Hancock County, Illinois, Office of the County Recorder, Hancock County Courthouse, Carthage, Illinois.

TABLE 6.4

Leading Farm Indicators, Fountain Green Township, 1860–1880

Indicator	1860	1870	1880
Acres per Farm	148	104	130
Improved Acres	75.7	71	77
Farm Value	$3,188	$3,879	$3,106
N =	121	168	189

Source: Agricultural Schedules for Illinois, 1860–1880.

TABLE 6.5

**Leading Farm Indicators, Fountain Green Township,
Owners versus Tenants, 1880 (Average per farm)**

Indicator	All Farmers	Owner/ Operator	Rent on Shares	Cash Renters
Improved acres	77	88.4	65.5	106.3
Unimproved acres	52.6	34.8	86.5	62.1
Implement value	106.90	113.7	110	111
Farm value	3106	3564	2348	6472
Wages	53.17	69.17	33.57	63.78
Corn/Wheat Ratio (bu.)	9.5	8.3	12.0	10.2
Livestock Value	472	609	317	480
Cattle Sold	4.1	5.6	2.6	2.2
N =	191	106	67	9

Source: Agricultural Schedules for Illinois, 1880.

TABLE 6.6

Grounds for Divorce, Hancock County, 1855–1884 (percent)

Years	Number of Cases	Adultery	Abuse	Drink
1855–59	17	21	29	24
1860–64	9	33	11	---
1865–69	25	36	16	4
1870–74	24	38	29	---
1875–79	6	83	33	---
1880–84	15	25	40	13
N =	96	33	26	7

Source: Hancock County Chancery Court Files, Clerk of Circuit Court, Hancock County Courthouse, Carthage, Illinois.

TABLE 7.1

Occupations of Household Heads, Fountain Green Township, 1860–1880

Occupation	1860	1870	1880
Farmers and farm laborers*	172	186	192
Retail	8	12	10
Crafts and trades	24	32	14
Milling	3	3	1
Professionals	4	8	6
Laborers	22	3	8
Women (housekeepers, keeping house, wash woman)	1	14	22
No occupation listed	7	10	4
Total	241	268	257

*Includes 11 retired farmers in 1870.
Source: Census of Population, 1860–1880.

TABLE 7.2

Birthplace of Heads of Households by Region, Fountain Green Township, 1850–1880

Region	1850	1860	1870	1880
North	69 (30%)	74 (30%)	62 (24%)	41 (6%)
Middle	72 (32%)	97 (39%)	99 (38%)	73 (28%)
South	58 (25%)	43 (17%)	35 (13%)	28 (11%)
Midwest and West	8 (3%)	18 (7%)	47 (18%)	96 (37%)
Other	21 (9%)	11 (4%)	17 (7%)	10 (4%)
Missing	0	5 (2%)	0	9 (4%)
Total Heads	228	248	261	257
Total Population	1,347	1,410	1,450	1,243

Key to regions (for the rationale behind the regional categories, see Chapter 3):

North: Connecticut, Maine, Massachusetts, New Hampshire, New York, Rhode Island, Vermont

Middle: Delaware, New Jersey, Pennsylvania, Ohio, Virginia, Washington, D.C.

South: Alabama, Arkansas, Georgia, Kentucky, Maryland, Mississippi, North Carolina, South Carolina, Tennessee, West Virginia

Midwest and West: California, Illinois, Indiana, Iowa, Kansas, Missouri, Wisconsin

Other: Belgium, Canada, China, England, France, Germany, Ireland, Luxembourg, Poland, Scotland, Switzerland

Source: Census of Population, 1850–1880.

TABLE 7.3

Parentage of Illinois-Born Farmers, Fountain Green Township, 1880 (percent)

Region of Birth	Father	Mother
North	21	22
Middle	35	30
South	32	36
Midwest and West	8	9
Foreign-born	4	3
N =	75	76

Source: Agricultural Schedules for Illinois, 1880; Census of Population, 1880.

APPENDIX 2
A Sample of Wills

Wills for all known decedents of Fountain Green to 1894 (who were identified in the manuscript population censuses, 1850–1880) were collected for analysis. This resulted in a sample of forty-eight wills. In order to enlarge the sample of wills beyond what was provided by the decedents of Fountain Green, household heads with the occupational title of farmer or farm laborer in three adjacent rural townships (Hancock, Pilot Grove, and LaHarpe) were culled from the 1860 census and matched against the indexes for the will records. The sample added 55 additional wills to the Fountain Green sample of 48, for a total of 103 wills.[1] The 103 wills represent about 10 percent of all wills made in Hancock County from 1849 to 1884.[2]

The testacy rate is difficult to determine, since death records were not uniformly kept by the county until state law required it in 1913. In lieu of death records, I counted the number of male decedents over the age of 30 who died between 1849 and 1895 who were buried in the cemeteries in Fountain Green.[3] Obviously this number of deceased includes men who did not make wills and excludes women (who were almost always widows). Using this method, the testacy rate is 28 percent, which means that better than one in four males left a will.

Of the 103 wills, 83 percent were made by men. Due to the nature of the sampling procedure, the rate of will-making by women was slightly higher in Fountain Green, where women wrote one-fourth of the wills, than in the other three townships.[4] The types of will provisions did not measurably change over the half-century surveyed, nor did they vary appreciably by status of will-maker (Tables 1 and 2). The proportion of wills which stipulated impartible, preferential, partible, or all to spouse remained nearly identical. The proportions also remained fairly constant for subsets of will-makers in the sample.

Notes

1. The breakdown by township is as follows: Fountain Green (48), LaHarpe (19), Hancock (15), Pilot Grove (15), Carthage (2), unknown (4).

2. The indices to the wills list a total of 919 names, thus the sample of 103 over-represents farmers and rural decedents in the county. Will Book 1 (1849–1876) contained 270 wills, Will Book A (1866–1880) 251 wills, Will Book B (1880–1888) 249 wills, Will Book C (1850–n.d.) 56 wills, and Will Book D (1888–1891) 93 wills.

3. Records for Fountain Green, McConnell, Webster, Majorville, and Spangler Cemeteries, James and Doris Lawton, comp., Hancock County Historical Society, Carthage, Illinois. The records are in good order and when compared to the headstones have proved to be complete and reliable.

4. For the entire sample, 86 of the wills were written by men and 17 by women. For the Fountain Green sample, 37 of the will-makers (77 percent) were male, and 11 (23 percent) were female. This is probably due to the collection process; the widows of Fountain Green were more easily identified than widows in other townships.

TABLE 1

Inheritance Strategies, Four Rural Townships, 1849–1891 (percent)

Type of Will	Before 1865	1865 and After	Total
Impartible	---	1	1
Partible	35	35	36
Preferential	45	44	46
All to spouse	19	20	20
N	31	72	103

Source: Sample of wills from Fountain Green, Hancock, Pilot Grove, and LaHarpe, all in Hancock County, Illinois.

TABLE 2

Inheritance Strategy by Status of Will-Maker, Four Rural Townships, 1849–1891

Will-Maker Cohort	Impartible	Partible	Preferential	All to spouse
All will-makers				
N = 103	1	36 (35%)	46 (45%)	20 (19%)
Men only				
N = 86	0	29 (34%)	40 (47%)	17 (20%)
Fountain Green				
N = 48	0	19 (40%)	18 (38%)	11 (23%)

Source: Sample of wills from Fountain Green, Hancock, Pilot Grove, and LaHarpe, all in Hancock County, Illinois.

NOTES

Introduction

1. "Nonmetro Population Continues Post-1990 Rebound and Rural-Urban Migration Patterns Shift," *Rural Conditions and Trends* 6 (Spring 1995): 6–13; and U.S. Census Bureau, *Residents of Farms and Rural Areas: 1991* (Washington, D.C.: Government Printing Office, 1993). See also B. F. Stanton, "Changes in Farm Size and Structure in American Agriculture in the Twentieth Century," in *Size, Structure, and the Changing Face of American Agriculture,* edited by Arne Hallam (Boulder, Colo.: Westview Press, 1993), 42–70. The problems of rural America regularly surface in the national and regional press; see for example, Jon Margolis, "The Reopening of the Frontier," *New York Times Magazine,* 15 October 1995, 51–57. The scholarly approach to the decline of rural life is discussed in Patrick M. Mooney, *My Own Boss? Class, Rationality and the Family Farm* (Boulder, Colo.: Westview Press, 1988); Gary Comstock, *Is There a Moral Obligation to Save the Family Farm?* (Ames: Iowa State University Press, 1987); and Peggy F. Barlett, *American Dreams, Rural Realities: Family Farms in Crisis* (Chapel Hill: University of North Carolina Press, 1993).

2. Allen W. Palmer, "Country Magazines: Margins of American Culture," *Magazine Forum* 5 (1995): 29–37; Russ Rymer, "Back to the Future: Disney Reinvents the Company Town," *Harper's Magazine,* October 1996, 65; "New Disney Vision Making the Future a Thing of the Past," *New York Times,* 23 February 1997, Y18; Eric Pooley, "The Great Escape," *Time Magazine,* 8 December 1997, 52ff. See also Robert Goldman and David R. Dickens, "The Selling of Rural America," *Rural Sociology* 48 (1983): 585–606.

3. Abraham Lincoln, *Speeches and Letters,* edited by Peter J. Parish (London: J. M. Dent, 1993), 226.

4. Andrew R. L. Cayton and Peter S. Onuf, *The Midwest and the Nation: Rethinking the History of an American Region* (Bloomington: Indiana University Press, 1990), 84. Because the notion of region is a mental construct, it must be understood that the meaning of what we call the Midwest has changed greatly over time. Illinois was situated in what was known at its founding in 1818 as the Old Northwest, but today we refer to that region as the Midwest, a constellation of states in its most expansive definition ranging from Ohio to Kansas. For the changing definitions of the Middle West, see James R. Shortridge, *The Middle West: Its Meaning in American Culture* (Lawrence: University Press of Kansas, 1989). Theoretical consideration of the meaning of region is addressed in Katherine G. Morrissey, *Mental Territories: Mapping the Inland Empire* (Ithaca, N.Y. Cornell University Press, 1997), introduction; and it is thoroughly discussed in Edward L. Ayers, Patricia Nelson Limerick, Stephen Nissenbaum, and Peter S. Onuf, *All Over the Map: Rethinking American Regions* (Baltimore, Md.: Johns Hopkins University Press, 1996).

5. Thomas Jefferson, *Notes on the State of Virginia,* edited by William Peden (New York: W.W. Norton & Co., 1982), 164–165.

6. *Compendium of the Tenth Census* (1880) (Washington, D.C.: Government Printing Office, 1883), 654–658. Total population for this area rose from under 1 million (792,719) in 1830 to over 13 million (13,612,056) by 1880.

7. Alan Trachtenberg, *The Incorporation of America: Culture and Society in the Gilded Age* (New York: Hill and Wang, 1982); and Robert H. Wiebe, *The Search for Order, 1877–1920* (New York: Hill and Wang, 1967). For the rural version of these events, see

Hal S. Barron, *Mixed Harvest: The Second Great Transformation in the Rural North, 1870–1930* (Chapel Hill: University of North Carolina, 1997).

8. Nichole Etcheson, *The Emerging Midwest: Upland Southerners and the Political Culture of the Old Northwest, 1787–1861* (Bloomington: Indiana University Press, 1996).

9. George Rogers Taylor, *The Transportation Revolution, 1815–1860* (1951; reprint, New York: Harper Torchbooks, 1968); Charles Sellers, *The Market Revolution: Jacksonian America, 1815–1846* (New York: Oxford University Press, 1991); Harry L. Watson, *Liberty and Power: The Politics of Jacksonian America* (New York: Hill and Wang, 1990); Carol Sheriff, *The Artificial River: The Erie Canal and the Paradox of Progress, 1817–1862* (New York: Hill and Wang, 1996).

10. Richard Lyle Power, *Planting Corn Belt Culture: The Impress of the Upland Southerner and Yankee in the Old Northwest* (Westport, Conn.: Greenwood Press, 1953); John C. Hudson, *Making the Corn Belt: A Geographical History of Middle-Western Agriculture* (Bloomington: Indiana University Press, 1994); Susan E. Gray, *The Yankee West: Community Life on the Michigan Frontier* (Chapel Hill: University of North Carolina, 1996); John Mack Faragher, *Sugar Creek: Life on the Illinois Prairie* (New Haven, Conn.: Yale University Press, 1986). For rural radicalism see Catherine McNicoll Stock, *Rural Radicals: From Bacon's Rebellion to the Oklahoma City Bombing* (New York: Penguin Books, 1997).

11. Allan G. Bogue, *From Prairie to Cornbelt: Farming on the Illinois and Iowa Prairies in the Nineteenth Century* (1963; reprint, Ames: Iowa State University Press, 1994); Jeremy Atack and Fred Bateman, *To Their Own Soil: Agriculture in the Antebellum North* (Ames: Iowa State University Press, 1987); Mary Neth, *Preserving the Family Farm: Women, Community, and the Foundations of Agribusiness in the Midwest, 1900–1940* (Baltimore, Md.: Johns Hopkins University Press, 1995); Jane Adams, *The Transformation of Rural Life: Southern Illinois, 1890–1990* (Chapel Hill: University of North Carolina Press, 1994).

12. The timing of the emergence of rural history is due in large part to the debate over the transition to capitalism in early America. A useful summary of that debate, though now dated, is Allan Kulikoff, "The Transition to Capitalism in Rural America," *William and Mary Quarterly,* 3rd ser., 46 (January 1989): 120–144. The sharp polarities of the early stages of the debate have shaded into greater appreciation of the contradictions of capitalism in the countryside; see Christopher Clark, *The Roots of Rural Capitalism: Western Massachusetts, 1780–1860* (Ithaca, N.Y. Cornell University Press, 1990). For a recent summary of the transition literature, I recommend Paul A. Gilje, "The Rise of Capitalism in the Early Republic," 159–191, and Christopher Clark, "Rural America and the Transition to Capitalism," 223–236 in *Journal of the Early Republic* 16 (Summer 1996). A readable synthesis of the scholarship is provided by David B. Danbom, *Born in the Country: A History of Rural America* (Baltimore, Md.: Johns Hopkins University Press, 1995). Regarding gender, see Nancy Grey Osterud, "Gender and the Transition to Capitalism in Rural America," *Agricultural History* 67 (Spring 1993): 15–29.

13. Jon Gjerde's *The Minds of the West: Ethnocultural Evolution in the Rural Middle West, 1830–1917* (Chapel Hill: University of North Carolina Press, 1997) is a masterful synthesis of the formation of ethnic cultures in the Upper Midwest. See also Sonya Salamon, *Prairie Patrimony: Family, Farming, and Community in the Midwest* (Chapel Hill: University of North Carolina Press, 1992); and Kathleen Neils Conzen, "Immigrants in Nineteenth-Century Agricultural History," in *Agriculture and National Development,* edited by Lou Ferleger (Ames: Iowa State University Press, 1990), 303–342.

14. The term "Sucker" was applied by Missourians to emigrants from the South who could not afford to own slaves in the lead mines of Galena. Like the sprouts on the tobacco plants that had to be removed because they diverted nourishment from the main stem, the southerners were seen as a "burthen upon the people of wealth" (Thomas Ford, *A History of Illinois from Its Commencement as a State in 1818 to 1847* [Chicago: S. C. Griggs & Co., 1859; reprinted in 2 vols., Milo Milton Quaife, ed., Chicago: Lakeside Press, R. R. Donnelley & Sons, 1945], 1:86–87). For the upland southerners, see Etcheson, *The Emerging Midwest;* for the term Yankee, see Gray, *Yankee West,* introduction. For the middle group, see Kenneth J. Winkle, *The Politics of Community: Migration and Politics in Antebellum Ohio* (New York: Cambridge University Press, 1988); and Daniel J. Elazar, *Cities of the Prairie: The Metropolitan Frontier and American Politics* (New York: Basic Books, 1970).

1. Collected Springs

1. Lester E. Foote, ed., *Foote's 1940 Fountain Green Almanac and Historical Sketch* (Carthage: The Carthage Republican, 1940), 2.

2. Information about the Perkins family from records in possession of Eugene Perkins, Provo, Utah; see also Lucina Call Perkins and Elizabeth Belcher Bartholomew, "History of the Perkins Family, 1720–1930," Library, Historical Department, Church of Jesus Christ of Latter-day Saints, Salt Lake City, Utah (hereafter LDS Archives). For Ute's military service, see Pension Claim R.8118, filed in Carthage, Illinois, 1 December 1834, copy supplied by Eugene Perkins, Provo, Utah. Regarding the Illinois Military Tract, see Theodore L. Carlson, *The Illinois Military Tract: A Study of Land Occupation, Utilization, and Tenure,* Illinois Studies in the Social Sciences 32, no. 2 (Urbana: University of Illinois Press, 1951).

3. D. W. Meinig, *The Shaping of America: A Geographical Perspective on 500 Years of History,* vol. 2, *Continental America, 1800–1867* (New Haven, Conn.: Yale University Press, 1993), 264–284; Hudson, *Making the Corn Belt;* and Hudson, "North American Origins of Middlewestern Frontier Populations," *Annals of the Association of American Geographers* 78, no. 3 (1988): 395–413. An abbreviated version of the settlement story is sketched in Susan Sessions Rugh, "Creating a Farm Community: Fountain Green Township, 1825–1840," *Western Illinois Regional Studies* 13 (Fall 1990): 5–20. The use of the term "Yankee" to mean northerner would not become common until mid-century; for ease of understanding I occasionally use it here to label settlers from New England and New York.

4. For a broad-brushed picture of these changes, see Sellers, *Market Revolution;* Clarence Danhoff, *Change in Agriculture: The Northern States, 1820–1870* (Cambridge, Mass.: Harvard University Press, 1969); Taylor, *The Transportation Revolution;* Ray Allen Billington and Martin Ridge, *Westward Expansion: A History of the American Frontier* (New York: Macmillan, 1982).

5. Cayton and Onuf, *The Midwest and the Nation,* chapter 1.

6. Carlson, *The Illinois Military Tract,* 6. Fountain Green township was not officially named until 1851, when the township form of government was authorized by the state. But the township as a geographical unit of land started with the creation of the Illinois Military Tract.

7. Helen Hornbeck Tanner, ed., *Atlas of Great Lakes Indian History* (Norman: University of Oklahoma Press, 1987); Solon Justus Buck, *Illinois in 1818,* 2nd ed. rev.

(Chicago: A. C. McClurg & Co., 1918), 17–21, 240; Herbert Spencer Salisbury, "Old Trails of Hancock County," *Journal of the Illinois State Historical Society* 9 (1916): 177–183; Anthony F. C. Wallace, "Prelude to Disaster: The Course of Indian-White Relations Which Led to the Black Hawk War of 1832," in *The Black Hawk War, 1831–1832,* vol. XXXV, Collections of the Illinois State Historical Library (Springfield, Ill.: Illinois State Historical Library, 1970), 1–51.

8. Board of Supervisors, *History of Hancock County, Illinois* (Carthage, Ill.: Board of Supervisors, Hancock County, 1968), 85.

9. U.S. General Land Office Records, Quincy District, Illinois State Archives, Springfield, Illinois; Carlson, *The Illinois Military Tract,* 4–5, 7; Paul W. Gates and Robert Swenson, *History of Public Land Law Development* (Washington, D.C.: Public Land Law Review Commission, U.S. Government Printing Office, 1968), 263. Because not all the acreage was under cultivation (some was used for pasturage and woodlot), the typical farm in the West totaled eighty acres. Danhoff, *Change in Agriculture,* 137.

10. This seems to have also been true of Fountain Green township, since none of the warrant-holders are listed in the 1830 census. U.S. Census of Population, Manuscript Schedules for Illinois, 1830. Washington, D.C.: National Archives, microfilm (hereafter referred to as Census of Population, 1830). Warrants sold for as little as $10 or $15, and the patents were $25. Carlson, *The Illinois Military Tract,* 50–53, 59; Gates and Swenson, *History of Public Land Law Development,* 263ff. For a local case of timber plundering, see *Statement of the Situation Character and Value of the Lands in the State of Illinois, Owned by the Heirs at Law of William James, Deceased, Made by an Agent of the Said Estate, in the Year 1840* (Albany, N.Y.: Vance and Wendell, Atlas Office, 1841), 20.

11. Robert P. Swierenga has argued that the tax lien system provided affordable capital for frontier development by allowing the farmer to defer his tax burden. See *Pioneers and Profits: Land Speculation on the Iowa Frontier* (Ames: Iowa State University Press, 1968).

12. A list of such lands offered for auction in Hancock County in 1836 shows that of the original forty warrants issued, twenty-six were tax delinquent (*Carthagenian Extra* [Carthage, Illinois], 20 December 1836). Adding to the confusion over patent and tax titles was the fact that non-bounty land in the upper Military Tract was not available for entry at the Quincy Land Office until 1835, although the Quincy Land Office opened in 1831. Carlson, *The Illinois Military Tract,* 41. Excluding school lands, 239 parcels in Fountain Green Township were purchased in Quincy for the period 1835–1856. All but fourteen of this number were sold in the first three years government land was subject to entry, as follows: 96 parcels in 1835, 103 in 1836, and 26 in 1837. U.S. General Land Office Records, Quincy District, Illinois State Archives, Springfield, Illinois. For sales in the Military Tract as a whole, see Carlson, *The Illinois Military Tract,* 41ff.

13. John M. Peck, *A Gazetteer of Illinois* (Jacksonville, Ill.: R. Goudy, 1834); Peck, *New Guide for Emigrants to the West* (Boston: Gould, Kendall & Lincoln, 1837), 110.

14. A. D. Jones, *Illinois and the West, with a Township Map, Containing the Latest Surveys and Improvements* (Boston: Weeks, Jordan and Co., and Philadelphia: W. Marshall and Co., 1838), 204; Nicholas Biddle Van Zandt, *A Full Description of the Soil, Water, Timber and Prairies of Each Lot, or Quarter Section of the Military Lands between the Mississippi and Illinois Rivers* (Washington City: P. Force, 1818), 116–117, 127.

15. Carlson, *The Illinois Military Tract,* 11–17, 28–29; Bogue, *From Prairie to Corn Belt,* 148–150. Much has been made of the tendency of settlers to avoid the prairie; see Siyoung Park, "Perception of Land Quality and the Settlement of Northern Pike County,

1821–1826," *Western Illinois Regional Studies* 3 (Spring 1980): 5–21; and Douglas R. McManis, *The Initial Evaluation and Utilization of the Illinois Prairies, 1815–1840* (Chicago: University of Chicago, Department of Geography, Research Paper No. 94, 1964).

16. Carlson, *The Illinois Military Tract*, 28.

17. In settling along the damp bottoms of wooded streams, settlers unknowingly subjected themselves to fevers and ague, which afflicted them for a seasoning period of up to a year. Carlson, *The Illinois Military Tract*, 28–32.

18. Crooked Creek divided the township into soil regions of varying fertility. The upper two-thirds of the township is composed of forested soil of thick loess deposited during the glacial age. An irregular band across the bottom is composed of a more fertile prairie soil. A finger of river bottom land reaches from the east in a northwesterly direction. See J. B. Fehrenbacher et al., *Soils of Illinois*, Bulletin 778, University of Illinois at Urbana-Champaign College of Agriculture (Agricultural Experiment Station in Cooperation with the Soil Conservation Service, U.S. Department of Agriculture, 1984).

19. Van Zandt, *A Full Description of the Soil, Water, Timber and Prairies*, 57.

20. Ibid., 117.

21. Carlson, *The Illinois Military Tract*, 10, 15.

22. Daniel Vickers, "Competency and Competition: Economic Culture in Early America," *William and Mary Quarterly*, 3rd ser., 47 (January 1990): 3–29; also Vickers, *Farmers and Fishermen: Two Centuries of Work in Essex County, Massachusetts, 1630–1850* (Chapel Hill: University of North Carolina Press, 1994).

23. Jones, *Illinois and the West*, 145.

24. Ibid., 249.

25. Carlson, *The Illinois Military Tract*, 11, 26, 41; Office of the Secretary of State, Illinois, *Counties of Illinois* (Springfield, Ill.: Secretary of State, 1987).

26. Census of Population, 1830. For a typical frontier population, see Robert R. Dykstra, *The Cattle Towns* (Lincoln: University of Nebraska Press, 1983), 247–248.

27. Office of the County Clerk, Hancock County, Illinois, Commissioners' Records (microfilm, Salt Lake City, Utah, Genealogical Society of Utah, 1974) (hereafter HCCR), 40.

28. Peck, *A Gazetteer of Illinois*, 204.

29. *Counties of Illinois*, 62.

30. Carlson, *The Illinois Military Tract*, 38–39, 67; *Counties of Illinois*, 44.

31. HCCR, 2 March 1830, 16 and 6 September 1837. Cited in Thomas Gregg, *History of Hancock County* (Chicago: Charles C. Chapman, 1880), 234.

32. Family records of Eugene Perkins; Perkins and Bartholomew, "History of the Perkins Family"; S. J. Clarke, *History of McDonough County, Illinois* (Springfield, Ill.: D. W. Lush, 1878), 18. For the patterns of agriculture and trade in Tennessee, see Lewis Cecil Gray, *History of Agriculture in the Southern United States to 1860*, 2 vols. (Washington, D.C.: Carnegie Institution, 1933), 1:442–444; Steven V. Ash, *Middle Tennessee Society Transformed, 1860–1870: War and Peace in the Upper South* (Baton Rouge: Louisiana State University Press, 1988), 19–20; Thomas Perkins Abernethy, *From Frontier to Plantation in Tennessee: A Study in Frontier Democracy* (Chapel Hill: University of North Carolina Press, 1932), 199–201; and Anita Shafer Goodstein, *Nashville, 1780–1860: From Frontier to City* (Gainesville: University of Florida Press, 1989), 29–43.

33. Jo White Linn, *Abstracts of the Deeds of Rowan Co., N.C., 1735–1785*, vols. 1–10

(Salisbury, N.C.: J. W. Linn, 1983), 53; Perkins and Bartholomew, "History of the Perkins Family," 2; Ronald Vern Jackson and G. R. Teeples, eds., *Complete Index to Tennessee 1820 Census* (Salt Lake City: Accelerated Indexing Systems, 1974), 20, 369, 383; William C. Steward, comp., *1800 Census of Pendleton District, S.C.* (Washington, D.C.: National Genealogical Society, 1963); and Betty Willie, comp., *Pendleton District, S.C. Deeds, 1790–1806* (Easley, S.C.: Southern Historical Press, 1982).

34. U.S. General Land Office Records, Quincy District, Illinois State Archives, Springfield, Illinois.

35. Southern families could choose between the river route down the Ohio River at the southern border of Illinois and up the Mississippi River to Fort Edwards in Hancock County or the overland route to Jacksonville and Rushville before turning westward to the Military Tract. For the forces behind the migration, see "Panic of 1819," in *Encyclopedia of Southern History*, edited by David C. Roller and Robert W. Twyman (Baton Rouge: Louisiana State University Press, 1979), 952–953; Arthur Clinton Bogguess, *The Settlement of Illinois, 1778–1830*, vol. 5 (Chicago: Chicago Historical Society Collection, 1908), 166; William Vipond Pooley, *The Settlement of Illinois 1830–1850* (Bulletin of the University of Wisconsin, No. 220, Madison, 1908); and J. H. Young, "The Tourist's Pocket Map of the State of Illinois" (Philadelphia: S. Augustus Mitchell, 1835), Map Collection, Regenstein Library, University of Chicago. Despite their distaste for slavery, many early settlers from the South in Illinois practiced a de facto slavery sanctioned by state law. Paul Finkelman, "Evading the Ordinance: The Persistence of Bondage in Indiana and Illinois," *Journal of the Early Republic* 9 (Spring 1989): 21–51.

36. Orval W. Baylor, *Early Times in Washington County, Kentucky* (Cynthiana, Ky.: The Hobson Press, 1942), 61, 68; Richard D. Mudd, *The Mudd Family of the United States* (Ann Arbor, Mich.: Edwards Bros., 1951), 694–695, 1042–1043, 1063.

37. Benjamin J. Webb, *The Centenary of Catholicity in Kentucky* (1884; reprint, Utica, Ky.: McDowell Publications, 1987), 82–83; Willard Rouse Jillison, *Pioneer Kentucky* (Frankfort, Ky.: State Journal Co., 1934), 133; Thomas D. Clark, *Agrarian Kentucky*, The Kentucky Bicentennial Bookshelf (Lexington: University Press of Kentucky, 1977), 14, 50–51; see also Baylor, *Early Times in Washington County*, 68. Local agricultural habits and women's production of flax are discussed in Ellen Eslinger, *Citizens of Zion: The Social Origins of Camp Meeting Revivalism* (Knoxville: University of Tennessee Press, 1999), 34.

38. Mudd, *The Mudd Family of the United States*, 694–695, 1042–1043, 1063; Census of Population, 1830; Gregg, *History of Hancock County*, 909; Thomas W. Spalding, "The Maryland Catholic Diaspora," *U.S. Catholic Historian* 8 (1989): 163, 165, 167. Mordecai's son Abraham Lincoln has often been confused with his famous cousin, who was the son of Mordecai's brother Thomas. Thomas and his brother Josiah also left Kentucky about the time Mordecai migrated to Illinois. Josiah settled in Indiana; Thomas brought his family to Sangamon County. William E. Barton, *The Lincolns in Their Old Kentucky Home* (Berea, Ky.: Berea College Press, 1923), 16.

39. Gregg, *History of Hancock County*, 820–821; Board of Supervisors, *History of Hancock County, Illinois*, 301; Clarke, *History of McDonough County*, 24; Erma Griffin Clayton, "History of Anna Warren Perkins," 1; Perkins Family Records; Mudd, *The Mudd Family of the United States*, 695.

40. For the white yeoman farmer's economy and culture, see Gray, *History of Agriculture*, 440–445, 451–457, 488–490; and Ash, *Middle Tennessee Society Transformed*, 32–25, 14–22. Regarding the backwoods pattern of dispersed settlement, see David

Hackett Fischer, *Albion's Seed: Four British Folkways in America* (New York: Oxford University Press, 1989), 760. For the transplantation of a southern backwoods culture to south-central Illinois, see John Mack Faragher, *Sugar Creek*. A local account is in Board of Supervisors, *History of Hancock County, Illinois*, 13–16.

41. Clarence Beebe, *A Monograph of the Descent of the Family of Beebe* (New York: [C. Beebe], 1904), 9, 13–16, 33, 46, 63; Franklin Ellis, *History of Cattaraugus County, New York* (Philadelphia: L. H. Everts, 1879), 80, 422, 425–430.

42. Board of Supervisors, *History of Hancock County, Illinois*, 301.

43. Beebe bought the patent for $1,000 from Ira Weaver of Pike, Allegheny County (just east of Cattaraugus County). Panhollow had earned his 320-acre bounty for service in Sweet's Company, Connecticut 37th Company of Infantry. Hancock County, Illinois, Office of the Recorder of Deeds, Registry of Deeds. Hancock County Courthouse, Carthage, Illinois, Book 1:37; Book 5:446 (hereafter Hancock County Deeds).

44. Gregg, *History of Hancock County*, 707–710.

45. Hancock County Deeds, 1:18.

46. Thomas J. Schlereth, "The New England Presence on the Midwest Landscape," *Old Northwest* 9, no. 2 (1983): 125–142.

47. Gregg, *History of Hancock County*, 820; Peck, *Gazetteer of Illinois*, 205; Board of Supervisors, *History of Hancock County, Illinois*, 302.

48. Daniel I. Rupp, *History and Topography of Dauphin, Cumberland, Franklin, Bedford, Adams, and Perry Counties* (Philadelphia: Joseph M. Wilson, 1852), 452; Thomas F. Gordon, *A Gazetteer of the State of Pennsylvania* (Philadelphia: T. Belknap, 1832), 174; Kenneth E. Koons, "Families and Farms in the Lower-Cumberland Valley of Southcentral Pennsylvania, 1850–1880" (Ph.D. diss., Carnegie-Mellon University, 1986). For the family story see Allen Geddes, "History of the Geddes Family," 4–5, in possession of Jean Geddes Lynn, Peoria, Illinois (hereafter Geddes Family Records).

49. Family record, Geddes Family Bible, Geddes Family Records; Will of Paul Geddis [variant spelling], November 1832, Franklin County [Pennsylvania] Will Book D:247, microfilm copy, Genealogical Society of Utah, Salt Lake City, Utah; Hancock County Deeds, B:513. For the history of Path Valley and Scots-Irish migration, see Rupp, *History and Topography*; Gordon, *A Gazetteer of the State of Pennsylvania*, 312; *History of Franklin County, Pennsylvania* (Chicago: Warner, Beers & Co., 1887), 183–184, 604–606; I. H. McCauley, *Historical Sketch of Franklin County, Pennsylvania* (Chambersburg, Pa.: D. F. Pursel, 1878), 129; and E. Estyn Evans, "The Scotch-Irish: Their Cultural Adaptation and Heritage in the American Old West," in *Essays in Scotch-Irish History*, edited by E. R. R. Green (London: Routledge & Kegan Paul, 1969), 69–86.

50. Martha McConnell, Fountain Green, to Martha Walker, Path Valley, Pa., [ca. November 1840], *Hancock County Historical Society Newsletter* 1, no. 15 (May 1972): 5–7.

51. Ibid.

52. The predominance of the New York group on the map is deceptive because it displays ownership of land, not population. The unshaded squares denote lack of knowledge of the origins of the settlers, not unclaimed land. It is doubtful, however, that the addition of more information would completely counteract the initial clustering patterns displayed here.

53. U.S. General Land Office Records, Quincy District, Illinois State Archives, Springfield, Illinois.

54. For the stages of economic development in the Midwest, see Cayton and Onuf, *The Midwest and the Nation*, 35ff.

55. Martha McConnell Walker, Fountain Green, to Martha Walker, Path Valley, 18 June 1844, *Hancock County Historical Society Newsletter* 1, no. 16 (August 1972): 5–7.

56. Ibid.

57. Gjerde, *Minds of the West,* 171–174.

58. Martha McConnell Walker to Martha Walker, 18 June 1844.

59. Regarding rural patriarchy, see especially Deborah Fink, *Agrarian Women: Wives and Mothers in Rural Nebraska* (Chapel Hill: University of North Carolina Press, 1992); and Nancy Grey Osterud, *Bonds of Community: The Lives of Farm Women in Nineteenth-Century New York* (Ithaca, N.Y. Cornell University Press, 1991). For a contemporary sociological model of the "agrifamily system," see John W. Bennett, Seena B. Kohl, and Geraldine Binion, *Of Time and the Enterprise: North American Family Farm Management in a Context of Resource Marginality* (Minneapolis: University of Minnesota Press, 1982), 113–114.

60. *Alton Telegraph,* 22 March 1837.

61. Board of Supervisors, *History of Hancock County, Illinois,* 15.

62. *Warsaw Signal,* 9 July 1842.

63. Timothy R. Mahoney, *River Towns in the Great West: The Structure of Provincial Urbanization in the American Midwest, 1820–1870* (New York: Cambridge University Press, 1990), 205, 236.

64. John Roberts, Probate Record, Box 6; David Alton, Probate Record, Box 17. Both in Hancock County, Illinois, Clerk of the County Courts, Probate Records, Hancock County Courthouse, Carthage, Illinois (hereafter Hancock County Probate Records).

65. Carlson, *The Illinois Military Tract,* 137; Bogue, *From Prairie to Cornbelt,* 104–105.

66. *Warsaw Signal,* 25 June 1845 and 22 October 1845.

67. For the imprint of settlement culture, see Wilbur Zelinsky, *The Cultural Geography of the United States* (Englewood Cliffs, N.J.: Prentice Hall, 1973), 13. I define culture broadly as an evolving set of beliefs, values, and patterns of behavior that constitute a way of life. Regarding mid-Atlantic farmers, see James T. Lemon, *The Best Poor Man's Country: A Geographical Study of Early Southeastern Pennsylvania* (Baltimore, Md.: Johns Hopkins University Press, 1972); and Joan Jensen, *Loosening the Bonds: Mid-Atlantic Farm Women, 1750–1850* (New Haven, Conn.: Yale University Press, 1986).

68. Immigrants tended to adopt the predominant American pattern, although some ethnic communities created a niche for themselves in the market through distinctive production patterns. See Conzen, "Immigrants in Nineteenth-Century Agricultural History," 316–317; and Brian Q. Cannon, "Immigrants in American Agriculture," *Agricultural History* 65 (Winter 1991): 17–35. Bogue argues that while native-born farmers may have emphasized a different segment of farm production in a new environment, they did not have to learn to grow new crops or raise different species of livestock (*From Prairie to Cornbelt,* 238). For evidence that those from the north farmed differently from those from the south, see Power, *Planting Corn Belt Culture*; and Hudson, *Making the Corn Belt.*

69. Value of farms measured by averages of improved acreage, farm value, and implement value. The group of southern-born were third to the northern-born only in terms of total property, which included personal property.

70. The fact that they ranked higher in real estate than in farm size (because of ownership of a shop in town) confirms the success of the dual-income strategy practiced by the northern-born. U.S. Census of Population, Manuscript Schedules for Illinois, 1850

(7th Federal Census), Washington, D.C.: National Archives, microfilm (hereafter Census of Population, 1850); Illinois, Office of Secretary of State, Agricultural Schedules for Illinois, 1850 (7th Federal Census), Illinois State Archives, Springfield, Illinois (hereafter Agricultural Schedules for Illinois, 1850).

71. Martha McConnell to Martha Walker, ca. November 1840.

72. Ibid.

73. Ibid.

74. Robert McConnell, New Orleans, to Joanna Brewer, Fountain Green, 12 March 1848, Geddes Family Records.

75. Mahoney, *River Towns in the Great West;* William Cronon, *Nature's Metropolis: Chicago and the Great West* (New York: W.W. Norton, 1991); Cayton and Onuf, *The Midwest and the Nation.*

76. Mahoney, *River Towns in the Great West,* 140–150, 179–180.

77. *Warsaw Message,* 15 July 1843; Gregg, *History of Hancock County,* 637; Mahoney, *River Towns in the Great West,* 205, 236.

78. *Warsaw Signal,* 22 September 1841.

79. Mahoney, *River Towns in the Great West,* 205, 236; sample of prices from *Warsaw Signal,* 1841–1848.

80. Bogue, *From Prairie to Cornbelt,* 104–105, 123.

81. Mahoney, *River Towns in the Great West,* 112, 230–233; *Warsaw Signal,* 4 August 1841.

82. Foote, *Foote's 1940 Fountain Green Almanac,* 17; Salisbury, "Old Trails of Hancock County," 180; Charles J. Scofield, ed., *History of Hancock County* (Chicago: Munsell Publishing Co., 1921), 1327.

83. Martha McConnell to Martha Walker, ca. November 1840.

84. Faragher, *Sugar Creek,* 118.

85. This analysis was based on a survey of transactions the 20th day of each month of 1838, Daybook A (17 January 1838–23 August 1840), C. C. Tyler Store Records, Illinois State Historical Library, Springfield, Illinois (hereafter CCTSR).

86. CCTSR, Daybook A, 19 March, 29 April, and 22 May 1838.

87. CCTSR, Daybook A, 18 and 22 January 1838.

88. By the 1840s, upland southerners had overcome any earlier reservations about political parties as "tools of interests." Etcheson, *The Emerging Midwest,* 51.

89. Ibid., 62–66.

90. Ibid., 57–61.

91. Theodore Calvin Pease, *The Frontier State, 1818–1848,* vol. 2 (Urbana: University of Illinois Press, 1987).

92. HCCR (June 1830), 20; Gregg, *History of Hancock County,* 233–234. For local residents on juries see HCCR (March 1831), 38; (March 1833), 87; (March 1836), 202.

93. HCCR (September 1833), 100; (December 1833), 111; (December 1835), 181; and (March 1836), 200.

94. The state turned the collection of taxes over to the county in 1833. Carlson, *The Illinois Military Tract,* 43 n15, 95.

95. HCCR (December 1830), 37; (March 1833), 81.

96. Ibid., 34.

97. Ibid., 37, 60.

98. Ibid., 26–27.

99. Ibid., 80.

100. Gregg, *History of Hancock County,* 879; Board of Supervisors, *History of Hancock County, Illinois,* 310.

101. Jones, *Illinois and the West,* 156.

102. Ibid., 157.

103. Ebenezer S. Welch, Monmouth, Illinois, to Milton Welch, Monmouth, Maine, 19 September 1841, typed letter, Ebenezer S. Welch Collection, Archives and Manuscripts Department, Chicago Historical Society, Chicago.

104. Lincoln Family Papers, Illinois State Historical Library Archives, Springfield, Illinois; *Gregg's Dollar Monthly and Old Settlers Memorial* [Hamilton, Illinois] 1 (July 1873): 1.

105. Father John St. Cyr, Fountain Green, 6 August 1838, to the Archdiocese of St. Louis, 1838 (cited in a letter to the author from Sister Teresa Maria Eagan CSJ, Associate Archivist, The Catholic Center, Archdiocese of St. Louis, 20 February 1991); "Those Catholic Lincolns of Fountain Green," *The Catholic Post* [Peoria], 1 May 1977; and Alice Krauser et al., *A History of St. Paul Church, 1857–1986* (Macomb, Ill., n.p., 1986), 93–100; and Clarke, *History of McDonough County,* 573.

106. Vertical File, "Catholics," Illinois State Historical Library, Springfield, Illinois; Thomas Cleary, "The Organization of the Catholic Church in Central Illinois," *Mid-America,* new ser., 6 (1935): 105–124, and "A Note on the Catholic Church Organization in Central Illinois," *Mid-America,* new ser., 6 (1935): 185–190. For the Kentucky churches see Webb, *Centenary of Catholicity in Kentucky,* 56, 70, 72.

107. Jones, *Illinois and the West,* 120; Martha McConnell to Martha Walker, ca. November 1840.

108. *History of Franklin County* (1887), 606–607; Rev. Alfred Nevin, *Churches of the Valley, or, an Historical Sketch of the Old Presbyterian Congregations of Cumberland and Franklin Counties, in Pennsylvania* (Philadelphia: Joseph M. Wilson, 1852), 226.

109. One such certificate reads:

> The bearer Thomas Geddes & Susan R. his wife have been known to me from their infancy, have supported a good character, have been full members of the church for a number of years and now intending to remove to the west, are at their own request, dismissed as members in good & full standing. Amos A. McGinley, Pastor, Path Valley Presbyterian Church, 19 March 1837.

Geddes Family Records.

110. Register of Baptisms, Fountain Green Presbyterian Church (hereafter FGPC Session Records), 202–209. In possession of Don Bainter, LaHarpe, Illinois (copy in my possession).

2. Conflict in the Countryside

1. Most of what we know about the expulsion of the Mormons in 1846 has focused on their city of Nauvoo on the Mississippi River; no one has focused on the unrest in the rural areas surrounding Nauvoo. The best source on the history of Nauvoo remains Robert Bruce Flanders, *Nauvoo: Kingdom on the Mississippi* (Urbana: University of Illinois Press, 1965). The most authoritative history of the Mormon conflicts in the Midwest is Marvin S. Hill, *Quest for Refuge: The Mormon Flight from American Pluralism* (Salt Lake City: Signature Press, 1989). Also valuable are Kenneth H. Winn, *Exiles in a Land of Liberty: Mormons in America, 1830–1846* (Chapel Hill: University of North Carolina Press, 1989); and Annette P. Hampshire, *Mormonism in Conflict: The Nauvoo*

Years, Studies in Religion and Society, vol. 11 (New York and Toronto: Edwin Mellen Press, 1985). Recent anthologies include John E. Hallwas and Roger D. Launius, eds., *Cultures in Conflict: A Documentary History of the Mormon War in Illinois* (Logan: Utah State University Press, 1995); and Launius and Hallwas, *Kingdom on the Mississippi Revisited: Nauvoo in Mormon History* (Urbana: University of Illinois Press, 1996). An eyewitness account is supplied in Ford, *A History of Illinois.*

2. Sellers, *Market Revolution;* Watson, *Liberty and Power.*

3. For the threat of polygamy to the civil order, see Nancy F. Cott, "Giving Character to our Whole Civil Polity: Marriage and the Public Order in the Late Nineteenth Century," in *U.S. History as Women's History: New Feminist Essays,* edited by Linda K. Kerber, Alice Kessler-Harris, and Kathryn Kish Sklar (Chapel Hill: University of North Carolina Press, 1995), 107–121.

4. Hill, *Quest for Refuge* 17; K. Laurence Moore, *Religious Outsiders and the Making of Americans* (New York: Oxford University Press, 1986), 39–41; Klaus J. Hansen, *Mormonism and the American Experience* (Chicago: University of Chicago Press, 1981). Historians of Mormonism's communal approach to economic enterprise argue that Joseph Smith reacted to the market revolution by organizing "a structured haven in a society that seemed about to disintegrate from the excesses of individualism and pluralism." Leonard J. Arrington, Feramorz Y. Fox, and Dean L. May, *Building the City of God: Community and Cooperation among the Mormons,* 2nd ed. (1976; reprint, Urbana: University of Illinois Press, 1992), 2. While Mormon doctrine is outside the scope of this study, an alternative explanation for Mormonism's early appeal has stressed doctrinal affinity between two ideological traditions: folk magic and European hermeticism of the Radical Reformation. See D. Michael Quinn, *Early Mormonism and the Magic World View* (Salt Lake City: Signature Books, 1987); and John L. Brooke, *The Refiner's Fire: The Making of Mormon Cosmology, 1644–1844* (New York: Cambridge University Press, 1994). For a theological analysis of Mormonism in the context of American religious history, see Jan Shipps, *Mormonism: The Story of a New Religious Tradition* (Urbana: University of Illinois Press, 1985). The literature on the Second Great Awakening is too large to cite here; for the Mormons in that context see Nathan O. Hatch, *The Democratization of American Christianity* (New Haven, Conn.: Yale University Press, 1989), 113ff.

5. Lawrence M. Yorgason, "Preview on a Study of the Social and Geographical Origins of Early Mormon Converts, 1830–1845," *Brigham Young University Studies* 10 (1970): 279; Hill, *Quest for Refuge,* 16–17.

6. Frank Esshom, *Pioneers and Prominent Men of Utah* (Salt Lake City: Utah Pioneers, 1913), 970.

7. Benjamin Franklin Johnson, *My Life's Review* (Independence, Mo.: Zion's Printing and Publishing, 1947), 8.

8. Ibid., 9; Joel Hills Johnson, "Excerpts from a Journal or Sketch of the Life of Joel Hills Johnson," David Martin Collection of Nauvooiana, Western Illinois University Archives, Macomb, Illinois, 1.

9. Johnson, "Excerpts from a Journal," 1.

10. "Life of Joel H. Johnson," Utah Humanities Research Foundation Papers, University of Utah Library, Salt Lake City, Utah, 1.

11. Joseph Smith, Jr., *History of The Church of Jesus Christ of Latter-day Saints,* Introduction by B. H. Roberts, 2nd ed., 7 vols. (Salt Lake City: Deseret Book, 1971), 1:6. The history of Joseph Smith has been subject to wildly varying interpretations. The

most reliable account of his early years is Richard L. Bushman, *Joseph Smith and the Beginnings of Mormonism* (Urbana and Chicago: University of Illinois Press, 1984).

12. Bushman, *Joseph Smith and the Beginnings of Mormonism*, 143–144; *History of the Church of Jesus Christ*, 1:75–78.

13. Ibid., 179–188; *History of the Church of Jesus Christ*, 1:145–146.

14. Johnson, "Excerpts from a Journal," 1.

15. Leonard J. Arrington and Davis Bitton, *The Mormon Experience: A History of the Latter-day Saints* (New York: Alfred A. Knopf, 1979), 21.

16. Johnson, "Excerpts from a Journal," 1.

17. Hill, *Quest for Refuge*, Chapter 5.

18. Stephen C. LeSueur, *The 1838 Mormon War in Missouri* (Columbia: University of Missouri Press, 1987), 25.

19. Scholars disagree over whether or not Joseph Smith supported Danite activity. Hill argues that Smith was aware of the Danite activity in Missouri and secretly condoned their actions in order to punish dissenters from the church and retaliate against actions taken against Mormons. A turning point in the acceptance of such illegal activity was on July 4, 1838, when Mormon leader Sidney Rigdon licensed retaliatory action in a public speech vowing that Mormons would not submit to depredations. The Missourians interpreted the speech to mean that Mormons felt they were above the law. *Quest for Refuge*, 75–79, 95–98. The relevant point is that there were those in the church who justified their stealing with a religious motive and believed that their actions were secretly sanctioned by Smith (even if he publicly spoke out against them). Klaus Hansen contends that the Danites were the precursor to the political government of the church by the Council of Fifty in Nauvoo. *Quest for Empire* (East Lansing: Michigan State University Press, 1967), 57–58, 153–154.

20. "Life of Joel H. Johnson," 2.

21. Johnson, "Excerpts from a Journal," 6.

22. Reuben Perkins may have stayed in Missouri because he owned two slaves. Reuben's family united with the Hancock County Perkinses in 1848 at Council Bluffs, Iowa, before going on together to Utah (Perkins Family History, copy supplied by Eugene Perkins, Provo, Utah). Ephraim Perkins did not go West with the Mormons; he farmed and raised a family in Pilot Grove Township just west of Fountain Green. Patricia Jewell Ballowe et al., transcribers, *The 1850 Census of Illinois, Hancock County* (Richland, Wash.: Locust Grove Press, 1977).

23. "Life of Joel H. Johnson," 2.

24. *History of the Church of Jesus Christ*, 3:378.

25. *Times and Seasons* (Nauvoo) 1 (March 1840): 77. For local ecclesiastical organization, see Macedonia Branch Minute Book, 1839–1850, 15, 23, and 31 July 1840, pp. 8–10 (hereafter referred to as MBMB), LDS Archives.

26. There were twenty-four persons with the surname Perkins and nineteen persons with the surname Johnson. Together these two families made up 10 percent of the branch population. If one includes in-laws to the Johnsons and the Perkinses, the total belonging to these two families rises significantly.

27. MBMB, 15 July 1840, 9; *History of the Church of Jesus Christ*, 5:477.

28. MBMB, 15 November 1840, 14. On 16 November, tax title to an additional quarter section of land was purchased from Dr. John Charles of Carthage. *History of the Church of Jesus Christ*, 5:477.

29. *Times and Seasons* 2 (15 November 1840): 222–223; Hancock County Plat Book, 45–46.

30. MBMB, 65–71 [no date]. The primary source of information about the inhabitants of Macedonia is a list of branch members dating from before the spring of 1842. There are 426 persons on the list, 208 men and 218 women. The list probably includes only members of record, that is, baptized members over the age of eight. So with additional small children the branch numbered at least 500 and possibly near 600 people, as some accounts claim. An early settler estimated the town numbered about eighty families. The dating of the list is uncertain, but it includes the name of Francis Beckstead, who died in April 1842. Hancock County, Illinois, Clerk of the County Courts, Will Book A (1833–1843), 382. Hancock County Courthouse, Carthage, Illinois (hereafter Will Book). Small children were omitted from the list, but a rough guess suggests that at least an additional seventy-five children were in the community. Genealogical records of Perkins family supplied by Eugene H. Perkins, copies in my possession. British immigrant Robert Crookston estimated that Macedonia's Saints numbered eighty families. Robert Crookston, "Autobiography of Robert Crookston Senior," LDS Archives. A later county history gives the figure of 600 Mormons in Macedonia. Scofield, *History of Hancock County*, 1077.

31. *Hamilton Representative*, 17 July 1858; U.S. Census of Population, Manuscript Schedules for Illinois, 1840 (6th Federal Census), Illinois State Archives, Springfield, Illinois (hereafter Social Statistic Schedules for Illinois, 1840).

32. *Laws of the State of Illinois, 13th General Assembly*, 1842–1843 (Springfield, Ill.: State Printer, 1843), 304–307; and *Journal of the Senate*, 16 February 1843, 369, 450, 454–455. The origin of the name Macedonia is uncertain, but Macedon, New York, was partitioned from Palmyra, Joseph Smith's home, in 1823. See John H. French, *Historical and Statistical Gazetteer of New York State* (Syracuse, N.Y.: R. P. Smith, 1860), 692.

33. City Council, Macedonia, Illinois, Minutes, Joseph Ellis Johnson Papers, Special Collections, Marriott Library, University of Utah, Salt Lake City, Utah.

34. MBMB, 13 March 1843; HC 5:302.

35. Flanders, *Nauvoo: Kingdom on the Mississippi*, 139; *Nauvoo Neighbor*, 20 September 1843.

36. Joel Johnson was a miller, his brother Benjamin owned a store, and Briton Thomas Callister was a tailor. The above description of Macedonia in 1843 mentions "numerous mills" and "mechanics."

37. Only a handful of Mormon names can be located in the county deed records. Among them are John Quayle and Mathias Cowley, who jointly owned a parcel on Section 31; Franklin Taylor, who owned land on Section 30; and the aforementioned Miller, Perkins, and Wightman parcels of land. Hancock County Deeds, K:170; O:456. This analysis does not include town records.

38. CCTSR, Ledger B (1843–1845), 25–28, 53, 274; and Daybook B (1838–1840), 259.

39. Will Book A, 382.

40. Thomas and Betsy Carico, who may have come to the area with the initial Catholic migration, were baptized into the new church. The Yeager family name is associated both with the early Catholic migration and the Mormons at Macedonia. See Macedonia Branch List.

41. William Miller and William Wightman, who were selling land in the area as early

as the mid-1830s, were converts. Many of the branch members have surnames common to the area: Duff, Eaton, McConnell, Saylors, Shipley, Walker, White, and Yager. U.S. General Land Office Records, Quincy District, Illinois State Archives, Springfield, Illinois; Census of Population, 1840.

42. For example, the daughter of Mormons Lucinda and Frasier Eaton from New York was married to early non-Mormon settler Jary White. White and his brothers were active in the Mormon War, so in this case family ties did not lead to an avoidance of hostilities. Gregg, *History of Hancock County,* 838.

43. Martha McConnell to Martha Walker, ca. November 1840; Ballowe et al., *1850 Census of Illinois, Hancock County,* 130.

44. Martha McConnell to Martha Walker, 1844.

45. Ibid.

46. Peck, *A Gazetteer of Illinois,* 184.

47. Carlson, *Illinois Military Tract,* 79 for 1830 figure; Census of Population, 1840, for the 1840 totals.

48. Carlson, *Illinois Military Tract,* 79; State of Illinois, *Reports Made to the Senate and House of Representatives,* 1844–1845 (Springfield, Ill.: State Printer, 1845), 66, 68.

49. Gregg, *History of Hancock County,* 638. The 1845 figure is cited in Thomas Gregg's newspaper (*Hamilton Representative,* 17 July 1858). For the most definitive statement on the numbers of Mormons in Nauvoo based on church censuses, see Susan Easton Black, "How Large Was the Population of Nauvoo?" *Brigham Young University Studies* 35, no. 2 (1995): 91–94.

50. Donald Q. Cannon, "Spokes on the Wheel: Early Latter-day Saint Settlements in Hancock County, Illinois," *Ensign* 16 (February 1985): 62–68.

51. This summary is derived from Flanders, *Nauvoo: Kingdom on the Mississippi.* Hill found little evidence that the products of Nauvoo were sold to citizens outside the city. Hill, *Quest for Refuge,* 250 n16.

52. *Warsaw Signal,* 22 September 1841. It was well known that the title to the "half-breed tract" was spurious. Flanders, *Nauvoo: Kingdom on the Mississippi,* 28–35.

53. James L. Kimball, Jr., "The Nauvoo Charter: A Reinterpretation," *Journal of the Illinois State Historical Society* 64 (1971): 66–78.

54. Flanders, *Nauvoo: Kingdom on the Mississippi,* 97–99, 109–113. See also Glen M. Leonard, "Picturing the Nauvoo Legion," *Brigham Young University Studies* 35, no. 2 (1995): 95–135. Richard L. Saunders ("Officers and Arms: The 1843 General Return of the Nauvoo Legion's Second Cohort," *Brigham Young University Studies* 35, no. 2 [1995]: 138–151) suggests the Legion numbered as many as 3,000 men, a huge force by frontier standards.

55. Flanders, *Nauvoo: Kingdom on the Mississippi,* 97–99.

56. Ibid., 230.

57. Hill, *Quest for Refuge,* 129; Hampshire, *Mormonism in Conflict,* 123–124.

58. The gender ratio in the Mormon population differed from the county as a whole. The county's population was 47 percent female, that of Macedonia 52 percent (MBMB; and Census of Population for Illinois, 1840).

59. *Warsaw Signal,* 9 and 23 July 1842; Gregg, *History of Hancock County,* 284–287. For the Johnson case, see Johnson, *My Life's Review,* 90–93.

60. For the machinations to conceal polygamy, see Todd Compton, *In Sacred Loneliness: The Plural Wives of Joseph Smith* (Salt Lake City: Signature Books, 1996); and

Fawn McKay Brodie, *No Man Knows My History: The Life of Joseph Smith, the Mormon Prophet,* 2nd ed. (New York: Vintage Books, 1995). However, Thomas Gregg recalled that the accusations were "widely read and commented on." Gregg, *Prophet of Palmyra* (New York: John B. Alden, 1890), 225. The most detailed portrait of Joseph Smith's practice of polygamy can be found in Linda King Newell and Valeen Tippetts Avery, *Mormon Enigma: Emma Hale Smith—Prophet's Wife, "Elect Lady," Polygamy's Foe, 1804–1879* (New York: Doubleday & Co., 1984).

61. *Warsaw Signal,* 9 June 1841. A trenchant analysis of the politics of this period can be found in Flanders, *Nauvoo: Kingdom on the Mississippi,* 212ff.

62. *Warsaw Signal,* 6 August 1842.

63. Milton Kimball to Milton Badger, 15 August 1845, American Home Missionary Society Letters (Illinois), Amistad Research Center, New Orleans, Louisiana (hereafter cited as AHMS).

64. Milton Kimball to Milton Badger, 7 November 1845, AHMS.

65. William M. King, Plymouth, Illinois to Corresponding Secretary, American Home Missionary Society, 31 May 1842, AHMS.

66. HCCR, 16 October 1833, 102.

67. HCCR, September 1844, 141, 153–154. For example, George Miller was awarded $500 to view a road from Nauvoo to Appanoose. HCCR, September 1845, 357.

68. HCCR, September 1843 to March 1846.

69. Milton Kimball to Milton Badger, 15 August 1845, AHMS.

70. *Warsaw Signal,* 14 June 1844. Fountain Green was not among them, but nearby LaHarpe and Carthage were. Probably Fountain Green was thought to be too close to the large Mormon population in Macedonia.

71. HC 6:483; *Warsaw Signal,* 19 June 1844.

72. Johnson, *My Life's Review,* 98; Crookston, "Autobiography of Robert Crookston Senior," 8–9. The wet weather probably played a part in the hysteria of the summer. Crops were failing, bridges were out, and roads were under water. As Bathsheba W. Smith of Nauvoo wrote on 15 June 1844: "The roads have been so bad, the bridges are most all washed away that it is all most inpossable [*sic*] to go or come from Messedonia [Macedonia] here." *Women's Voices: An Untold History of the Latter-day Saints, 1830–1900,* edited by Kenneth W. Godfrey, Audrey M. Godfrey, and Jill Mulvay Derr (Salt Lake City: Deseret Book, 1982), 129. Wesley Williams of Carthage wrote to his son in Kentucky about mills being damaged and bridges swept away by floods. The prospects of a corn crop were "gloomy," but he hoped the wheat crop would survive. "We had last night one of the most gloomy storms I ever witnessed. There was all night a continuous stream of electricity and continual roaring of thunder. Scarcily a single moment of cessation attended with heavy falls of rain mixed with hail." Wesley Williams to John W. Williams, Carthage, 5 June 1844, typescript copy, Archives, Western Illinois University, Macomb, Illinois.

73. HC 6:485, 574–575.

74. Martha McConnell Walker to Martha Walker, 18 June 1844.

75. Ibid.

76. *Warsaw Signal,* 12 June 1844; Dallin H. Oaks, "The Suppression of the Nauvoo Expositor," *Utah Law Review* 9 (1965): 862–903; Dallin H. Oaks and Marvin S. Hill, *Carthage Conspiracy: The Trial of the Accused Assassins of Joseph Smith* (Urbana: University of Illinois Press, 1976), 17; Flanders, *Nauvoo: Kingdom on the Mississippi,* 308.

77. Eudocia Baldwin Marsh, "Mormons in Hancock County: A Reminiscence," edited by Douglas L. Wilson and Rodney O. Davis, *Journal of the Illinois State Historical Society* 64 (Spring 1971): 46.

78. Ford, "Message of the Governor of Illinois in Relation to the Disturbances in Hancock County," 78. Thomas Gregg reported Geddes as saying, "While the Smiths were in jail, I went to the jail in company with Governor Ford, and there we conversed with them for some time, the burden of Smith's talk being that they were only acting in self-defense, and only wanted to be let alone. After leaving the jail, and while returning from it, the Governor and I had still further conversation about the subject matter. After some time the Governor exclaimed, 'O, it's all nonsense; you will have to drive these Mormons out yet!' I then said, 'If we undertake that, Governor, when the proper time comes, will you interfere?' 'No, I will not,' said he; then, after a pause, adding, 'until you are through.'" Gregg, *History of Hancock County,* 372. This statement by Geddes is as close as the historical record comes to revealing the motives of Governor Ford. Flanders (*Nauvoo: Kingdom on the Mississippi,* 109) and George R. Gayler ("Governor Ford and the Death of Joseph and Hyrum Smith," *Journal of the Illinois State Historical Society* 50 [1957]: 391–411) argue that Ford did not foresee the danger to the Smiths.

79. Orville F. Berry, "The Mormon Settlement in Illinois," *Transactions of the Illinois State Historical Society* 11 (1906): 88–102, quote from 99.

80. A reliable account of the murder can be found in Oaks and Hill, *Carthage Conspiracy,* Chapter 2.

81. Marsh, "Mormons in Hancock County," 53.

82. Crookston, "Autobiography of Robert Crookston Senior."

83. Martha McConnell Walker to Martha Walker, 18 June 1844.

84. Ibid.

85. Ibid.

86. *Warsaw Signal Extra,* 7 August 1844.

87. "The Carthage trial was a classic case of jury nullification, displacing the written law against murder with the higher law of community approval." Oaks and Hill, *Carthage Conspiracy,* 213.

88. Ibid., 107, 111.

89. Ute Perkins, Sr., Will, Probate Record C (1844–1845), 20–21, Hancock County Probate Records. The will was probated on 19 April 1844.

90. Matthew McClaughry of Fountain Green, originally from New York, was Sharp's local agent for selling a thirty-three-page pamphlet, *Trial of the Murderers of Joseph Smith.* The residents of Fountain Green could easily obtain the Anti-Mormon view of the events of the spring. *Warsaw Signal,* 30 July 1845.

91. Benjamin A. Gallop, Carthage, to William S. Dodge, 17 September 1844, LDS Archives.

92. Theodore Calvin Pease, *The Frontier State, 1818–1848* (Springfield, Ill.: Centennial Commission, 1918; reprint, Urbana: University of Illinois Press, 1987).

93. Milton Kimball to Milton Badger, 10 February 1845, AHMS.

94. Ibid.

95. Kimball wrote on 24 July 1844: "Most of the land intended to be cultivated this season was deluged with a succession of great rains for more than two months and now is waste." Milton Kimball to Milton Badger, 24 July 1844, AHMS. The poor harvest as a result of the summer floods extended broadly throughout the Military Tract (Carlson,

The Illinois Military Tract, 94). Gov. Ford's report to the Senate mentioned that the agricultural conditions were affected by the weather (*Reports Made to the Senate and House of Representatives, 1844–1845*, 74).

96. *Warsaw Signal*, 10 February 1845.

97. *Warsaw Signal*, 22 September 1844. Their situation was not helped by the non-Mormon ban on renting farms to Mormons, resolved at a meeting at St. Mary's. *Warsaw Signal*, 1 November 1844.

98. Because of the Mormons at Macedonia, the Fountain Green township vote was fairly evenly split between Mormons and old citizens, but old citizens commanded the majority in the rest of the county. *Warsaw Signal*, 21 August 1844; Gregg, *History of Hancock County*, 450; Oaks and Hill, *Carthage Conspiracy*, 46.

99. HCCR, 235–254, 285, 309, 315–316.

100. *Warsaw Signal*, 30 October, 17 November, 20 November, 18 December, and 25 December 1844.

101. In late December the *Signal* reported that Nelson Maynard near Fountain Green had a yoke of "fine work cattle" stolen from his stable. *Warsaw Signal*, 25 December 1844. This is the only clue to thefts in the neighborhood of Macedonia and Fountain Green in the newspaper reports.

102. All the reports are from *Warsaw Signal*, 22 January 1845. The axe incident occurred in 1840; in 1838 an axe sold at Tyler's Fountain Green store for $1.75. CCTSR, Daybook A, 18 January 1838.

103. Early settler John Lionberger remembered that Nauvoo citizens were good customers for farm produce. "We made lots of flour and hauled it to Nauvoo where we found a ready market at fair prices. There were no mills of consequence nearer than Warsaw." (Board of Supervisors, *History of Hancock County, Illinois* 15).

104. *Warsaw Signal*, 25 December 1844.

105. Thomas Holt, St. Mary's, Illinois, to George Carver, Panther Creek, North Carolina, 19 September 1844, Ms. 126, LDS Archives.

106. Milton Kimball to Milton Badger, 10 February 1845, AHMS.

107. Benjamin A. Gallop, Carthage, to William S. Dodge, 17 September 1844, LDS Archives.

108. Kenneth W. Godfrey, in "Crime and Punishment in Mormon Nauvoo, 1839–1846," *Brigham Young University Studies* 32 (Winter and Spring 1991): 195–227, acknowledges the great number of accusations of crime, but largely dismisses them as the work of those outside Nauvoo.

109. Chrisman pled "innocence and persecution" to no avail. *Warsaw Signal*, 11 June 1845.

110. Salisbury, "Old Trails of Hancock County," 182; HCCR, March 1844, 84–85, 127.

111. William M. King, Plymouth, Illinois, to Corresponding Secretary, American Home Missionary Society, 25 February 1842, AHMS.

112. Affidavit of Justus Morse, LDS Archives.

113. MBMB, 4 and 12 November 1841, 20–23; *Times and Seasons* 3 (1 December 1841), 616.

114. *Times and Seasons* 3 (1 December 1841), 616–618.

115. *Warsaw Signal*, 8 and 15 January 1845.

116. *Warsaw Signal*, 15 January 1845.

117. "To the Democrats of the State of Illinois," *Warsaw Signal*, 14 May 1845. Four

Fountain Green signers were from Tennessee, two were from North Carolina, and one each was from Georgia, Virginia, Pennsylvania, and Ireland. Ballowe et al., *1850 Census of Illinois, Hancock County.*

118. HC 6:8.

119. *Warsaw Signal,* 14 May 1845. Information about the location of the signers is from Collector's Books, 1851–1880, County Clerk, Hancock County, Record Series 2.21, Illinois Regional Archive Depository System, Western Illinois University, Macomb, Illinois.

120. *Warsaw Signal,* 13 August 1845.

121. Gregg, *Prophet of Palmyra,* 327–328; *Warsaw Signal,* 3 September 1845. George Edmunds, an old settler, later recalled, "I have never had a doubt that these matters were instigated for the purpose of forcing the Mormon population to consent to leave this county and go west." Berry, "Mormon Settlement in Illinois," 97.

122. Thomas Callister, "Autobiographical Notes," LDS Archives.

123. Ibid.

124. "Journal History of the Church," 16–17 September 1845, LDS Archives.

125. Hill, *Quest for Refuge,* 175.

126. *Warsaw Signal,* 17 September 1845.

127. Callister, "Autobiographical Notes." There is no one by the name of Arnold McCleary in the census. He was probably referring to prominent Fountain Green citizen Matthew McClaughry.

128. "Journal History of the Church," 22 September 1834, 1–2. What Perkins called a "mob" could have been the local militia carrying out their customary fall encampment exercises.

129. Hill, *Quest for Refuge,* 177.

130. Ford estimated 150–175 houses were burned (*Reports Made to the Senate and House of Representatives,* 1844, 1–2); Flanders estimated 200. *Nauvoo: Kingdom on the Mississippi,* 328.

131. *Warsaw Signal—Extra,* 24 September 1845, Mormon Broadside Collection, Prints and Photographs Department, Chicago Historical Society, Chicago, Illinois.

132. Ibid.

133. "To the Anti-Mormon Citizens of Hancock and the Surrounding Counties," Camp Carthage, 4 October 1845, Mormon Broadsides Collection, Chicago Historical Society, Chicago, Illinois; see also Brigham Young to General John H. Hardin, 1 October 1845, John H. Hardin Collection, Chicago Historical Society, Chicago, Illinois. For the warning to Young, see Hill, *Quest for Refuge,* 176. Once the Mormons had agreed to leave, Mormon Edmund Durfee's murder on 15 November near Green Plains was anti-climactic; it was the subject of disapproval in local newspapers (*Warsaw Signal,* 19 November 1845).

134. MBMB, 5 April 1846, 50.

135. At Nauvoo they were asking "exorbitant prices" (*Warsaw Signal,* 19 November 1845). Land deed records for the town of Webster show that Thomas Geddes, Leonard T. Ferris, Hickerson Wright, and J. Callihan bought town lots directly from the departing Mormons. Others—such as Jabez Beebe, Matthew McClaughry, Robert McConnell, and James McElvain—waited to acquire the land at tax sales from the sheriff. Deed Record, Town of Webster, Hancock County Clerk's Office, Carthage, Illinois.

136. They spent three months slogging through muddy Iowa, wintered at Council Bluffs, Nebraska, and reached the Salt Lake Valley the following summer. See Wallace

Stegner, *The Gathering of Zion: The Story of the Mormon Trail* (1964; reprint, Lincoln: University of Nebraska Press, 1992).

137. Former missionaries Cowley and Quayle sold their farm in Section 31 the same day for $240. Hancock County Deeds, O:451, 458; R:465.

138. *Hancock Eagle* (Nauvoo), 17 April 1846.

139. Gregg, *History of Hancock County,* 836–839; Gregg, *Prophet of Palmyra,* 872; State of Illinois, *Reports made to the Senate and House of Representatives of the State of Illinois, 1846–47* (Springfield, Ill.: State Printer, 1847), 10.

140. Actually, a group of "leading ladies of Nauvoo" presented the governor with two petticoats: one made of black silk and the other fringed in red (*Warsaw Signal,* 14 and 21 November 1846). A handbill reported that the more respectable women presented the Governor with a flag. "Insult to the Governor! Proceedings of the officers and men belonging to the volunteers at Nauvoo" [n.d.], Mormon Broadsides Collection, Chicago Historical Society, Chicago, Illinois.

141. *Warsaw Signal,* 16 January 1847.

142. MBMB, 50ff. (The record was kept until April 1850.)

143. Fountain Green Ward Manuscript History, Historical Department, LDS Church; and Johnson, *My Life's Review,* 220.

3. "To keep the family together"

1. Hancock County Deeds, M:457–458; S:460–461; O:443–445.

2. The view of the farmer as yeoman is best represented by James Henretta, "Families and Farms: Mentalité in Pre-Industrial America," *William and Mary Quarterly,* 3rd ser., 35 (1978): 3–32. For the view of the farmer as market-oriented, see Winifred Rothenberg, "The Market and Massachusetts Farmers, 1750–1855," *Journal of Economic History* 41, no. 2 (June 1981): 283–314. A more complete explanation of the polarities between "market" and "social" historians can be found in Allan Kulikoff, "The Transition to Capitalism in Rural America," *William and Mary Quarterly,* 3rd ser., 46 (January 1989): 120–144. The range of views on this topic by historians has grown; see Christopher Clark, *The Roots of Rural Capitalism: Western Massachusetts, 1780–1860* (Ithaca, N.Y. Cornell University Press, 1990). The term "yeoman" has been applied to different groups, but common to all is a strong attachment to independent family land ownership. See Kulikoff, "Transition to Capitalism"; Stephanie McCurry, *Masters of Small Worlds: Yeoman Households, Gender Relations, and the Political Culture of the Antebellum South Carolina Low Country* (New York: Oxford University Press, 1995); and Salamon, *Prairie Patrimony.*

3. For example, farmers from New England in Michigan altered the meaning of patrimony. Gray, *The Yankee West.*

4. U.S. Bureau of the Census, *Agriculture of the United States in 1860* (8th Census) (Washington, D.C.: Government Printing Office, 1864), 30.

5. U.S. Bureau of the Census, *Statistics of the Population of the United States, 9th Census* (1870), vol. 1 (Washington, D.C.: Government Printing Office, 1872), 23 (hereafter *Statistics of the Population* [1870]). For the foreign-born element of the population, see U.S. Bureau of the Census, *Seventh Census of the United States* (1850) (Washington, D.C.: Government Printing Office, 1853), xcvii; U.S. Bureau of the Census, *Population of the United States in 1860* (8th Census) (Washington, D.C.: Government Printing Office, 1864), 102; U.S. Bureau of the Census, *Report of the Population of the*

United States in 1890 (11th Census) (Washington, D.C.: Government Printing Office, 1892), Pt. I, 408. In 1850, 9 percent of the county's population of 14,633 was foreign born; that proportion rose to 19 percent by 1860 (3,768 foreign born of a total population of 19,061).

6. *Carthage Republican,* 8 September 1859.

7. It is difficult to know if the number of farms in the township increased in this period, because the 1850 census did not observe township boundaries. It is clear that there were fewer than 140 farms in Fountain Green township in 1850 and that the number of farms in 1860 was 121 (see Table 3.1). Efforts to define the limits of the Fountain Green township population by backward linkage through both the population and agricultural censuses of the 1850s have been unsuccessful because there is no apparent pattern of data collection for the 1850 census. (For example, clusters of households in the township are found in at least five scattered locations throughout the manuscript schedules of the Hancock County Census of Population.) The census of agriculture similarly fails to follow township boundaries. Because the 1850 sample used in this study is inclusive rather than exclusive, it is larger than the number for the 1860 census.

8. The amount of improved acreage in the township rose from 7,944 to 9,165 between 1850 and 1860, a much smaller percentage increase (15 percent) than the 165 percent increase for the county as a whole (from 80,163 to 212,336 acres). This suggests that farmers in 1850 were already making good use of the township's land and that the township was well populated in comparison to other townships in the county that had not yet undergone substantial improvement. Township figures from Agricultural Schedules for Illinois, 1850; county figures from U.S. Bureau of the Census, *Agriculture of the United States in 1860,* 8th Census (Washington, D.C.: Government Printing Office, 1864), 30.

9. Agricultural Schedules for Illinois, 1850; Illinois, Office of Secretary of State, Agricultural Schedules for Illinois, 1860 (8th Federal Census), Illinois State Archives, Springfield, Illinois (hereafter Agricultural Schedules for Illinois, 1860).

10. Ibid.

11. James Walker, Probate Record, Boxes 61–62, Hancock County Probate Records; and James Walker, Inventory and Sale Record, D:269, Inventory and Sale Records, Hancock County, Illinois, Clerk of the County Courts, Hancock County Courthouse, Carthage, Illinois.

12. *Carthage Republican,* 24 April 1855.

13. *Carthage Republican,* 30 April 1857.

14. *Carthage Republican,* 3 February, 17 February, 3 March, and 2 June 1859.

15. *Warsaw Express,* 1 June and 13 July 1854.

16. *Carthage Republican,* 5 July 1860.

17. *Agriculture of the United States in 1860,* 31. In Fountain Green Township, farms produced an average of 529 bushels of corn and 138 bushels of wheat in 1849, for a ratio of 5:2 (Agricultural Schedules for Illinois, 1850 and 1860). Local estimates placed the wheat crop at ⅚ of its expected size, averaging about 20 bushels per acre. Social Statistic Schedules for Illinois, 1860.

18. A plausible explanation is that the 1850 figure reflects an early enthusiasm for hogs, which weakened in the rush to wheat in the 1850s, shown in the low figure of sixteen hogs per farm. The number of hogs per farm climbed again in the 1860s and the 1870s, signaling a steady increase in tandem with corn production. The average produc-

tion per Illinois farm in the Bateman-Foust sample was 5.5 cattle and 14.1 hogs in 1860. Jeremy Atack and Fred Bateman, *To Their Own Soil: Agriculture in the Antebellum North*, Henry A. Wallace Series on Agricultural History and Rural Studies (Ames: Iowa State University Press, 1987), 112.

19. The amount of cattle shipped on the Chicago, Burlington, and Quincy Railroad rose from 9 million pounds in 1856 to 45 million in 1858, a 500 percent increase in less than two years (Carlson, *The Illinois Military Tract,* 130–131). The newspapers carried market prices for local towns, regional entrepôts such as Quincy and Keokuk, and larger cities such as St. Louis, Chicago, and New York (*Daily Warsaw City Bulletin,* 19 October 1860).

20. "The Farmer" column made its debut on page three of the *Carthage Republican,* 12 May 1855. It included advice that would interest the farmer and his family on such topics as the education of farmers' daughters, growing wool, gardening, and raising poultry.

21. Illinois State Agricultural Society, *Transactions of the Illinois State Agricultural Society* II (n.p., 1856–1857): 225. For the history of agricultural fairs, see Leslie Mina Prosterman, *Ordinary Life, Festival Days: Aesthetics in the Midwestern County Fair* (Washington, D.C.: Smithsonian Institution Press, 1995).

22. *Carthage Republican,* 5 October 1860.

23. *Carthage Republican,* 18 November 1858.

24. Farmers could buy implements at steep annual interest rates of 19 percent (Atack and Bateman, *To Their Own Soil,* 198). For the chattel loans see Justice of the Peace Docket, 1850–1865, Fountain Green, Illinois, Illinois State Historical Library, Springfield, Illinois. This volume is not paginated, and the mortgages are not numbered. There were two justices in the township, so presumably one could roughly double the number of mortgages to find the total for the township. There was one mortgage each in 1851, 1852, and 1855, but a dozen in the two-year period 1858 and 1859. From 1858 to 1862 there were four mortgages per year, except in 1859, when this amount doubled to eight. Mortgage-taking followed a seasonal pattern; there was an average of three mortgages per month from August through January, six in February, and one in the spring months (Justice of the Peace Docket, 1850–1865). Only two of the thirty-two mortgages were between persons of the same surname, presumably members of the same family. This may indicate that family members did not formally record their loans with the justice of the peace and instead relied on their word for security.

25. The number of farms growing sorghum in the township doubled from twenty-four in 1850 (17 percent of farms) to fifty-four in 1860 (47 percent of farms), while those producing honey declined in the same period (Agricultural Schedules for Illinois, 1850 and 1860).

26. Agricultural Schedules for Illinois, 1860; CCTSR 6:621.

27. Samuel Jacob Wallace, "The Prairie Fruit Garden," *Transactions of the Illinois State Agricultural Society* 3 (1857–1858): 512–517.

28. Most were apple orchards, but a few farms also had peach trees. The size of the orchards generally ranged from 30 to 50 trees, but a few farms grew as many as 150 trees in their orchards. The size of the orchards indicates production for market, certainly beyond what a family would need in their diet. Illinois, Office of Secretary of State, Agricultural Schedules for Illinois, 1880 (10th Federal Census), Illinois State Archives, Springfield, Illinois (hereafter Agricultural Schedules for Illinois, 1880).

29. CCTSR 3:303.

30. *Carthage Republican,* 15 November 1860.

31. *Carthage Republican,* 27 October 1859.

32. The regional divisions are as follows: North (Connecticut, Maine, Massachusetts, New Hampshire, New York, Rhode Island, Vermont); Middle (Delaware, New Jersey, Pennsylvania, Ohio, Virginia); South (Alabama, Arkansas, Georgia, Kentucky, Maryland, Mississippi, North Carolina, South Carolina, Tennessee); Foreign Born (Canada, England, France, Germany, Ireland, Poland, Scotland, Switzerland). Two methods were used to define these regions. First, migration patterns were reconstructed using family and county histories. For example, Maryland (although adjacent to Delaware) has been placed in the South region because most of the parents of the Catholic farmers from Kentucky were originally from Maryland. Second, the 1880 census was analyzed for parental birthplaces. For example, Ohio-born farmers were grouped with their parents' birthplaces (usually Delaware and Virginia), and New York–born farmers were grouped with their parents' birthplaces (usually New England).

33. In 1850, four farmers in Fountain Green Township had been born in Ireland, two in Scotland, and one in England. All but one of the Irish farmers had moved away by 1860, but in that year the ranks of the immigrant farmers were strengthened by four farmers born in Canada (sons of a Scot) and three born in Germany (Agricultural Schedules for Illinois, 1850 and 1860; Census of Population, 1850; Social Statistic Schedules for Illinois, 1860).

34. In both 1849 and 1859 the mid-Atlantic group owned on average over $30 more in farm implements than any other group, although the value of implements in 1859 was only slightly more than the value in 1849. Census of Population, 1850 and 1860; Illinois, Office of Secretary of State, Census of Population, 1870 (9th Federal Census), Illinois State Archives, Springfield, Illinois (hereafter Census of Population, 1870); Agricultural Schedules for Illinois, 1850, 1860; Illinois, Office of Secretary of State, Agricultural Schedules for Illinois, 1870 (9th Federal Census), Illinois State Archives, Springfield, Illinois (hereafter Agricultural Schedules for Illinois, 1870).

35. The stock value was high among southerners because a few farmers owned many horses. Calvin Simmons owned fifteen, Eliza Dill owned ten, two more farms owned six each, one owned seven, and two owned five (Agricultural Schedules for Illinois, 1850 and 1860).

36. The corn belt was created by the transplantation of agricultural patterns from the South to the Midwest by the southern-born. Hudson, *Making the Corn Belt.*

37. In fact, in 1860 they cultivated only 35 percent of what they had grown in wheat ten years earlier. In contrast, those born in the mid-Atlantic region grew 61 percent of what they had previously grown. Agricultural Schedules for Illinois, 1850 and 1860.

38. Agricultural Schedules for Illinois 1850 and 1860; Census of Population for Illinois, 1850 and 1860.

39. Because my regional analysis uses the variable of the place of birth of the farmer and not of the farmer's wife, it does not truly capture regionality for wives of farmers who may have come from a different region than their husbands. Thus, the lack of cultural patterns in butter production may be due more to my methodology than to the actual data.

40. Jeanne Boydston, *Home and Work: Housework, Wages, and the Ideology of Labor in the Early Republic* (New York: Oxford University Press, 1990).

41. *The Hamilton Representative,* 22 May 1858.

42. When a Carthage family's food-storage shed burned down, the loss was estimated at $200. Gone were the winter's supply of flour and meat, a large quantity of sorghum, preserved fruits, honey, and butter. *Carthage Republican,* 23 January 1862.

43. "Farm and Household—How to Do Up Shirt Bosoms," *Carthage Republican,* 18 March 1874.

44. It was notable that women were in the field helping replant corn after bad weather destroyed the first crop. *Carthage Republican,* 11 June 1875.

45. See the pastoral scenes in Jennie Hopkins, *Juanita and Other Sketches* (Denver: The Zalinger Press, 1884), written by a farmer's daughter who was reared in Fountain Green township, especially 203–208.

46. In 1850 only a half-dozen farm households cultivated flax; among them was the family of Francis McConnell, which produced 100 pounds of the fiber during the year. By 1860 the cultivation of flax was discontinued completely. Agricultural Schedules for Illinois, 1850 and 1860.

47. CCTSR 4:234 (8 August 1853).

48. On 1 October 1853, two women each purchased a set of "Knitting pins" for five cents apiece (CCTSR 4:289.) In his autobiographical novel set in the mid-1870s, Hamlin Garland refers to wearing knitted wool scarves made by mothers, sisters, or girlfriends of the farm boys. *Son of the Middle Border* (New York: Macmillan, 1923), 162.

49. The farms in the township (which had an average of 3.8 cows in 1850 and 4.1 cows in 1860) produced an average of 146 pounds of butter in 1850, which increased to 219 pounds in 1860 (Agricultural Schedules for Illinois, 1850 and 1860). Following the methodology of Joan Jensen, I used 150 pounds for home consumption per household (25 pounds per person in a household of six persons) as the threshold for market production. The amount of butter consumed per person ranged from 15 to 25 pounds in the nineteenth century. During the early national period, butter production could furnish most of the commodities the family could not produce themselves. Joan Jensen, *Loosening the Bonds: Mid-Atlantic Farm Women, 1750–1850* (New Haven, Conn.: Yale University Press, 1986), 81–83. The production of poultry and eggs was thought of until the middle of the twentieth century as a woman's task; the proceeds were used at her discretion. See Deborah Fink, *Open Country Iowa: Rural Women, Tradition and Change* (Albany: State University of New York Press), 158–159.

50. A longitudinal survey was conducted by sampling the C. C. Tyler daybooks from 16 March to 15 April for every available year on record. The results (averaged by five-year period) may show a decline because of competition from another collection point. A spot-check of the store records shows that even well-to-do farmers received store credits for eggs. See Table 3.5.

51. The drop in fertility rates in Fountain Green is consistent with findings for other areas. Yasakuchi Yasuba, *Birth Rates of the White Population in the United States, 1800–1860: An Economic Study,* Johns Hopkins University Studies in Historical and Political Science, Series 79, No. 2 [1961] (Baltimore, Md.: Johns Hopkins Press, 1962), 49, 61. Atack and Bateman calculated a child/woman ratio of 1,110 in the East and 1,519 in the West (Atack and Bateman, *To Their Own Soil,* 49).

52. Hancock County Cemetery Records, comp. Doris Lawton and James Lawton, Hancock County Historical Society, Carthage, Illinois; Census of Population, 1860, 1870, and 1880. Information about childhood illnesses was noted by the 1880 census marshall for Fountain Green, young Dr. Charles Ferris. In June 1880, three children had

the mumps, six had whooping cough, and one had pneumonia. Their ages ranged from ten months to ten years. The incidence of whooping cough clustered in families and neighborhoods, evidence of its contagious nature. Only one adult was ill; Charles Duff, twenty-four, had the mumps. U.S. Census of Population, Manuscript for Illinois, 1880 (10th Federal Census), Washington, D.C.: National Archives, microfilm (hereafter Census of Population, 1880).

53. *Biographical Review of Hancock County, Illinois* (Cleveland, Ohio: Bell and Howell, 1967, facs. of Chicago: Hobart Publishing Co., 1907), 246–249.

54. Civil War Pension File, Marcus Alton, Veterans Administration, Record Group 15, Civil War Pension Records, National Archives and Records Administration, Washington, D.C. (hereafter Civil War Pension File).

55. Judith Walzer Leavitt, *Brought to Bed: Childbearing in America, 1750–1950* (New York: Oxford University Press, 1986), 154ff; Richard W. Wertz and Dorothy C. Wertz, *Lying-In: A History of Childbirth in America* (New York: Schocken Books, 1979), 47, 125.

56. *Carthage Republican*, 21 September 1871 (see also *Carthage Republican*, 25 July 1872; *Carthage Republican*, 20 May 1874; and *Carthage Gazette*, 28 June 1866 for similar incidents). The status of children within the farm family has been largely overlooked. A revelatory exception is Liahna Babener, "Bitter Nostalgia: Recollections of Childhood on the Midwestern Frontier," in *Small Worlds: Children and Adolescents in America, 1850–1950*, edited by Elliott West and Paula Petrick (Lawrence: University Press of Kansas, 1992), 301–320.

57. Up to 200 people searched until evening in the woods of Crooked Creek east of Carthage, where a lost child was found two or three miles from his original location (*Carthage Republican*, 5 July 1866).

58. *Carthage Gazette*, 31 January 1867.

59. See Richard A. Easterlin, "Factors in the Decline of Farm Family Fertility in the United States: Some Preliminary Research Results," *Journal of American History* 63 (1976): 600–614; Easterlin, "Population Change and Farm Settlement in the Northern United States," *Journal of Economic History* 36 (1976): 45–75; and Richard A. Easterlin, George Alter, and Gretchen A. Condran, "Farms and Farm Families in Old and New Areas: The Northern States in 1860," in *Family and Population in Nineteenth-Century America*, edited by Tamara K. Hareven and Maris A. Vinovskis (Princeton, N.J.: Princeton University Press, 1978), 22–84.

60. Atack and Bateman, *To Their Own Soil*, 11.

61. At the other extreme was the household of townsperson Dr. Leonard T. Ferris, whose wife must have been taking in boarders. In addition to Dr. Ferris, his wife, their three children, his parents, and his aunt, the household accommodated a German tailor, two merchants, the school teacher, a tinner, and a farmer. All household profiles drawn from the Census of Population for Illinois, 1860.

62. Census of Population for Illinois, 1850 and 1860. Because the census did not request information about the relationship of household members to the head, these relationships have been inferred and should be regarded as estimates only. Overall, nearly all the households (97 percent) had a nuclear family at the core. The taxonomy is borrowed from Koons, "Families and Farms in the Lower-Cumberland Valley," 190. Caution must be used in typing households because the structure of farm households changed with the stages of that household. For example, a household consisting only of a married couple could be a newly married couple or a mature couple whose children had left home.

63. Boys usually turned over all or part of their earnings to their father until they were twenty-one years of age. David E. Schob, *Hired Hands and Plowboys: Farm Labor in the Midwest, 1815–60* (Urbana: University of Illinois Press, 1975), 175.

64. *Carthage Republican,* 12 August 1858.

65. *Carthage Republican,* 25 April 1867. The age of the boy was not stated.

66. *Carthage Republican,* 26 October 1865 and 11 May 1871.

67. Garland, *A Son of the Middle Border,* 86.

68. William Spangler, California, to Thomas M. Geddes, Fountain Green, 25 January 1873, in Geddes Family Records.

69. Scofield, *History of Hancock County,* 1238.

70. When farm households are compared to the general population, we see that household heads who were farmers were twice as likely to persist as non-farmers were. For every decade, farmers were more likely to survive than household heads who were not farmers. Compare to the rates of persistence for Chelsea, Vermont, where 32.1 of the household heads persisted from 1840 to 1860, and 34.3 persisted from 1860 to 1880. The persistence rate for farm operators for the period 1860 to 1880 was 39 percent. Hal S. Barron, *Those Who Stayed Behind: Rural Society in Nineteenth-Century New England* (New York: Cambridge University Press, 1984), 79. For the community of Sugar Creek in Illinois, Faragher found that 36.8 percent of 1840 households persisted to 1850; this percentage fell to 31.7 percent in the following decade (Faragher, *Sugar Creek,* 239).

71. The twenty-seven farmers who persisted from 1860 to 1880 were augmented by another sixty-two farmers in 1880 who were sons of 1860 farmers. These figures do not correlate exactly with Table 3.11 because seven sons were already on the land in 1860. The 50 percent persistence rate is calculated by adding 62 sons, 3 other families, and 29 persisters for a total of 94 out of 189 (49.7 percent). Some of those heirs rented and did not own the family land. The strength of the paternal tie was clear by 1880. Half of the farm operators in 1880 were either persisters from 1860 or were direct descendants of those who farmed in 1860. Census of Population for Illinois, 1860, 1870, and 1880; Agricultural Schedules for Illinois, 1860, 1870, and 1880.

72. Census of Population, 1850, 1860, 1870, and 1880; Agricultural Schedules for Illinois, 1880.

73. The firstborn was the most likely to be settled; of sixty-four farmers' sons in the 1880 census, twenty-eight were oldest sons. The birth order of the sons as a factor in acquiring land is not conclusive; it would be necessary to do a study of birth order in the context of the number of sons in the family. The birth order is: firstborn (28), second (15), third (10), fourth (4), fifth (3), sixth through eighth (4). This is not to argue that the firstborn were the most likely to inherit land; it may be that they were simply the first to acquire land because they were older.

74. Nearly all farmers owned the farms they operated. In 1850, 31 of 153 farmers owned no land, creating a tenancy rate of 20 percent. By 1860, only three farmers owned no land whatsoever, and if we arbitrarily set $1,000 as a threshold for a viable farm, in 1860, just 14 of 127 farmers fell below that benchmark, for a tenancy rate of 11 percent. A tenant was one who was listed as a farmer in the agricultural census but who did not own real estate (listed in the census of population). This method of finding "farmers without farms" follows standard practice (Bogue, *From Prairie to Cornbelt,* 64). In 1860, half of the farmers without farms were under thirty years of age. Only one-fourth were over forty years of age. In 1860, over half of them were sons waiting for land from a

father or sons with younger brothers who were more likely to receive the home farm (Agricultural Schedules for Illinois, 1850 and 1860; Census of Population, 1850 and 1860). Tenancy for the post–Civil War period is treated in Chapter 6. The most persuasive evidence for the agricultural ladder can be found in Donald L. Winters, *Farmers without Farms: Agricultural Tenancy in Nineteenth-Century Iowa* (Westport, Conn.: Greenwood Press, 1978).

75. Because of the voluminous nature of these data, and because no title company has maintained records for the county, two comparative samples were obtained from the county deed records: persisters (those who stayed) and transients (those who moved). The sample of deeds was gathered by extracting information for a pre-selected group of thirty families who persisted in the township for at least three censuses, thereby ensuring that they owned land in the township for at least twenty years. The sample of persisters is not random; it is biased toward those who stayed a long time on the land. The total number of surnames exceeded 200.

The sample of transients consisted of families who were shown as landholders on an 1859 plat map but who were not listed on the next plat map in 1874. The sample of transients was augmented by studying the deed transfers of farmers who did not survive from one decadal census to the next. The sample of deeds of those who persisted numbered 547; of transients, 368, for a total of 915 deeds. Because the index to deed records is by location of land and not by family name, the sample should not be regarded as reflecting the total land holdings of any one family. The method of sampling excluded information about land held outside the township. The cadastral maps are "Map of Hancock County, Illinois" ([Buffalo]: Holmes and Arnold, Publishers, 1859); and Alfred Theodore Andreas, *An Illustrated Historical Atlas of Hancock County, Illinois* (Chicago: A. T. Andreas, 1874), 30. Regarding the sample of those classified as transients, twenty-six farms did not survive from 1860 to 1870; I traced the land records of eleven (42 percent) of these transients. Forty-eight farms did not survive in the decade of the 1870s; of these, I traced twenty-four (51 percent).

76. Hancock County Deeds, S:475; X:107; 51:287; 52:365–366; 60:364; 61:573–576; and 78:478; Mortgages and Bonds, 2:011, 6:408, 7:125, 9:557, 8:516, and 9:154, Hancock County, Illinois, Office of the County Recorder, Hancock County Courthouse, Carthage, Illinois, Records of Mortgage and Bonds (hereafter Hancock County Mortgage and Bond Records); Census of Population, 1860; Agricultural Schedules for Illinois, 1860.

77. Fifteen percent (139) were between persons of the same surname, and 5 percent (41), were between those known to be related by marriage. Obviously, this is a minimum measure of those related.

78. Hancock County Deeds, K:205; X:442; 32:622; 40:167; 72:406; and 109:140; and Will of Alexander Walker, 1880, Will Book A, 218.

79. The listing "retired farmer" for ten men in the 1870 census illustrates this phenomenon. (The designation "retired" was not used in other censuses.) Those designated as retired were sixty-four years or older, and they owned from twenty to 480 acres of land.

80. Gregg, *History of Hancock County,* 832–833.

81. Journal of David Leach, Hancock County Historical Society, Carthage, Illinois.

82. Agricultural Schedules for Illinois, 1870 and 1880; Census of Population, 1870 and 1880; Ivo Hardy, 1872, Will Book A, 193. For the stem family see Michel Verdon, "The Stem Family: Toward a General Theory," in *The American Family in Social-*

Historical Perspective, edited by Michael Gordon, 3rd ed. (New York: St. Martin's Press, 1983), 24–37; and Lutz K. Berkner, "Inheritance, Land Tenure and Peasant Structure: A German Regional Comparison," in *Family and Inheritance: Rural Society in Western Europe, 1200–1800,* edited by Jack Goody, Joan Thirsk, and E. P. Thompson (Cambridge: Cambridge University Press, 1976), 71–95.

83. In Illinois, married women gained the right to hold property independently in 1861. See Eugene L. Gross, ed., *Statutes of Illinois: An Analytical Digest of All the General Laws of the State, 1818–1869* (Springfield, Ill.: E. L. & W. L. Gross, 1872), 439. See also Marylynn Salmon, *Women and the Law of Property in Early America* (Chapel Hill: University of North Carolina Press, 1986), 140–145.

84. *Letitia Yager, Catharine Yager & George W. Yager, who sue by Catherine Yager their Guardian;* and *Mary Jane Yager, Isaac H.G. Yager, Isaac Y. Vance, & Martha Vance his wife, Alfred Benson & Hetty E. Benson his wife versus Urijah H. Yager,* Hancock County, Complete Chancery Book A, p. 47 (19 October 1846), microfilm, Genealogical Society of Utah. The Yager story is complicated by the fact that the parties to the suit were Mormons (MBMB, 65–71). It is possible that the court suit was an effort to divest the family of lands in the township for the best price in the climate of the Mormon exodus from the county.

85. Toby Ditz, *Property and Kinship: Inheritance in Early Connecticut, 1750–1820* (Princeton, N.J.: Princeton University Press, 1986).

86. Ibid., 61–62.

87. Martin Yetter, 1873, Will Book 1:486.

88. Samuel Spangler, 1853, Will Book 1:530.

89. William M. Hamrick, 1873, Will Book 1:463.

90. Alonzo Barnes, 1860, Will Book 1:273.

91. Thomas Massie, 1858, Will Book 1:223.

92. Martin Yetter, 1873, Will Book 1:486.

93. Benjamin Crabill, 1894, Will Book D:318.

94. Anthony Duff, 1881, Will Book B:71.

95. Carole Shammas, Marylynn Salmon, and Michel Dahlin, *Inheritance in America: From Colonial Times to the Present* (New Brunswick, N.J.: Rutgers University Press, 1987), 64–67.

96. John Brewer, 1853, Will Book 1:83.

97. These were all men except widow Nancy E. Stearnes, who left her estate in trust with the income to be paid to her only daughter (Nancy E. Stearnes, 1882, Will Book B:36). She made it clear that under no condition was the principal to be used.

98. State of Illinois, *Laws of the State of Illinois, 1846–47* (Springfield, Ill.: State Printer, 1847), 168.

99. In 1871, Mary Mathewson left her eighty acres of land in Section 14 to her married daughter, whom she expected to pay her debts (Mary Mathewson, 1871, Will Book C:71).

100. Lucinda Hadley, 1859, Will Book 1:249.

101. Emmeline Wright, 1882, Will Book B:48.

102. Catherine Yetter, 1879, Will Book D:247.

103. William Hamrick, 1873, Will Book 1:463; Francis Shutwell, 1876, Will Book B:95.

104. Philip Ebert, Will Book B:196.

105. John Day, 1852, Will Book 1:66.

106. Samuel Fortney, 1859, Will Book 1:248.

4. "A greater pleasure in living"

1. *Carthage Republican,* 18 May 1912.

2. Ibid.

3. Ibid.

4. Ibid.

5. For the market challenge to rural sociability, see especially Henretta, "Families and Farms"; and Faragher, *Sugar Creek.* However, the shift from a close-knit community to an impersonal, differentiated society may better characterize urban places. See Barron, *Those Who Stayed Behind.* Social commentators today refer back to small-town community as a model for civil community in a democracy. See Jean Bethke Elshtain, *Democracy on Trial* (New York: Basic Books, 1995); and Gerald Gamm and Robert D. Putnam, "The Growth of Voluntary Associations in America, 1840–1940," *Journal of Interdisciplinary History* 29 (Spring 1999): 511–557.

6. For cities, see Cronon, *Nature's Metropolis;* Cayton and Onuf, *The Midwest and the Nation;* Mahoney, *River Towns in the Great West;* and Mahoney, *Provincial Lives.* Small towns in the Midwest are broadly explored by Lewis Atherton, *Main Street on the Middle Border* (Bloomington: Indiana University Press, 1954). For two case studies, see Don Harrison Doyle, *The Social Order of a Frontier Community: Jacksonville, Illinois, 1825–1870* (1978; reprint, Urbana: University of Illinois Press, 1983); and Richard O. Davies, *Main Street Blues: The Decline of Small-Town America* (Columbus: Ohio State University Press, 1998).

7. Cayton and Onuf, *The Midwest and the Nation,* chapter 5 passim.

8. *Statistics of the Population* (1870), 24, 112; Ballowe et al., *1850 Census of Illinois, Hancock County;* and Tri-County Genealogical Society, transcribers, *The 1860 Handcock [Hancock] County, Illinois Census* (Augusta, Ill.: Tri-County Genealogical Society, [ca. 1983]), hereafter *1860 Census.* For the definition of regions, see Chapter 3, note 32.

9. *Statistics of the Population* (1870), 24, 112; *Illinois State Gazetteer and Business Directory for the Years 1864–65* (Chicago: J. C. W. Bailey, 1864), 370, 597.

10. *Map of Hancock County, Illinois* (Buffalo: Holmes and Arnold, Publishers, 1859), Illinois State Historical Society Library, Springfield, Illinois; *Carthage Republican,* 12 July 1855; Illinois, Office of Secretary of State, State Census, 1855. Illinois State Archives, Springfield, Illinois.

11. Clark, *Roots of Rural Capitalism,* Chapter 6.

12. Andreas, *Illustrated Historical Atlas of Hancock County,* 36; and C. C. Tyler, "Hancock County History," *Carthage Republican,* 18 May 1912. For the suicide, see *Carthage Republican,* 29 May 1856. Francina Ferris Tyler succumbed on 8 August 1859 at the age of 40 (Hancock County Cemetery Records). Because Tyler and his wife were childless, Tyler's parents sued his widow for two-thirds of the estate. Her death in 1859 left them with the store and dwelling on the Fountain Green lot. See Hancock County, Clerk of Circuit Court, Chancery Court Files, Box 185, Case 94, Hancock County Courthouse, Carthage, Illinois (hereafter Hancock County Chancery Court Files); and *Illinois Supreme Court Reports* 19 (1857–1858) (Chicago: Callaghan & Co., 1871): 151–155.

13. Illinois, vol. 84, p. 240, R. G. Dun & Co. Collection, Baker Library, Harvard Business School, Cambridge, Mass.

14. Illinois, vol. 84, p. 240, 325, R. G. Dun & Co. Collection; Gregg, *History of Hancock County,* 837–838.

15. CCTSR vol. 4:332, 373; vol. 3:162.

16. CCTSR vol. 3:41, 142, 331, 415.

17. CCTSR, vol. 3:12, 25, 302, 333, 373.

18. *Carthage Republican,* 23 April 1857.

19. CCTSR vol. 3:12; 8:411.

20. "Business Statement," following index, vol. 20, CCTSR.

21. Salisbury, "Reminiscences," 6; L. T. Ferris to W. W. Green, 30 October 1848, Noah Green Papers, Iowa State Historical Society, Iowa City, Iowa.

22. *Montague's Illinois and Missouri State Directory for 1854–55* (St. Louis: Wm. L. Montague, Publisher, 1854), 23, 59, 105, 131, 143, 147, 154, 178, 198, 215, 240, 250, 256, 268.

23. Illinois, vol. 84, p. 258, R. G. Dun & Co. Collection.

24. Illinois, vol. 84, pp. 278–279, R. G. Dun & Co. Collection. For the biographical information, see Board of Supervisors, *History of Hancock County, Illinois,* 304; and Gregg, *History of Hancock County,* 831–832.

25. *Carthage Republican,* 23 April 1857.

26. Illinois, vol. 85, pp. 258, 295, 389, R. G. Dun & Co. Collection.

27. FGPC Session Record.

28. Robert P. Swierenga, "The Little White Church: Religion in Rural America," *Agricultural History* 71 (Fall 1997): 415–441; Gray, *The Yankee West,* chapter 5.

29. Session records show that during the 1850s thirty-eight new members moved into the congregation, sixteen joined by examination, and thirty-nine joined by baptism. The numbers were reduced by twelve departures and at least two deaths, for a total gain of sixty-five for the decade. See FGPC Session Records. For a history of the itinerant clergy who preceded Walker, see Presbyterian Church in the U.S.A., *Minutes of the General Assembly* (Philadelphia: Presbyterian Board of Publication, 1846–1852), vol. XI (1846): 307; vol. XII (1848): 120; vol. XII (1849): 336; vol. XII (1850): 550; vol. XIII (1851): 102; vol. XIII (1852): 297.

30. Ballowe et al., *1850 Census of Illinois, Hancock County; 1860 Census.*

31. Gregg, *History of Hancock County,* 821; Board of Supervisors, *History of Hancock County, Illinois,* 306; Interview with Ida Jackson, Fountain Green, Illinois, June 1991.

32. FGPC Session Record, 8; Gregg, *History of Hancock County,* 838; *1860 Census.*

33. FGPC Session Record, 17–18, 21; *Minutes of the General Assembly,* 1855–1862.

34. FGPC Session Record, 10, 16–17, 19; *Minutes of the General Assembly* (1846), XI:229; *Carthage Republican,* 8 June 1851.

35. FGPC Session Record, 6 March and 29 June 1867; 9 January 1877.

36. FGPC Session Record.

37. Mary P. Ryan, *Cradle of the Middle Class: The Family in Oneida County, New York, 1790–1865* (New York: Cambridge University Press, 1981); Barbara Welter, "The Cult of True Womanhood," *American Quarterly* 18 (1966): 151–174.

38. *Carthage Republican,* 23 April, 8 October, and 15 October 1857; 14 July 1859.

39. Eliza McClaughry had come from the Dutch Reformed Church of New York City and Mrs. Mull from the Associated Reformed Church of Hobart, New York (FGPC Session Record, May 13, 1854; August 19, 1856).

40. The various reform branches of Presbyterianism joined in 1858 to become the United Presbyterian Church. Sydney E. Ahlstrom, *A Religious History of the American People* (New Haven, Conn.: Yale University Press, 1972), 278.

41. In 1857, their numbers dropped from seventy-seven to fifty-five members (FGPC Session Records, 9, 22, 25).

42. A longitudinal analysis of infant baptism makes the Pennsylvanian character of the congregation even more clear; of ninety-six infants baptized, most were born to parents of immediate Pennsylvanian ancestry (FGPC Session Records, Record of Baptisms, 202–209).

43. Of twelve persons who asked for certificates of dismissal, six moved out of town and six joined other churches in Fountain Green or nearby LaHarpe (FGPC Session Records, 9, 22, 25).

44. Clarke, *History of McDonough County*, 573.

45. In a public lecture, local journalist and historian Thomas Gregg delivered a lecture which "severely handled" Know Nothingism, answered by an opposing view. Gregg thought the Know Nothings "were more dangerous and illiberal than the Catholics." The same evening, there was a military ball well attended by "numerous specimens of Young America" (*Warsaw Express*, 28 December 1854).

46. Social Statistic Schedules for Illinois, 1860; Andreas, *Illustrated Historical Atlas of Hancock County*, 49; *Webster Sesquicentennial History* (Webster, Ill.: n.p., 1989), 8; Gregg, *History of Hancock County*, 710.

47. Historical Sites Committee, *Historic Sites and Structures of Hancock Co., Illinois* (Carthage, Ill.: Hancock County Bicentennial Commission, 1979), 323; *Carthage Republican*, 7 July 1886; Fay Day, comp., "Souvenir and Historical Sketch of the Majorville Church" (Hancock County Historical Society, n.d.); Board of Supervisors, *History of Hancock County, Illinois*, 306.

48. Glenn E. Altschuler and Stuart M. Blumin, "Limits of Political Engagement in Antebellum America: A New Look at the Golden Age of Participatory Democracy," *Journal of American History* 84 (December 1997): 855–885, a rejoinder to William E. Gienapp, "'Politics Seems to Enter into Everything': Political Culture in the North, 1840–1860," in *Essays on American Antebellum Politics, 1840–1860*, edited by Stephen E. Maizlish and John J. Kushma, 15–69 (College Station: Texas A&M University Press, 1982). Of particular interest to the rural historian is the assertion of Altschuler and Blumin that rural voters were so absorbed in the routines of daily life that they were in a state of "disengaged belief" and displayed a "vernacular liberalism." Glenn C. Altschuler and Stuart M. Blumin, "'Where Is the Real America?' Politics and Popular Consciousness in the Antebellum Era, "*American Quarterly* 49, no. 2 (1997): 225–267, especially 230. The data for Fountain Green suggest otherwise.

49. Kenneth J. Winkle, "The Representative Man of the Unsophisticated People: Participatory Democracy and the Rise of Abraham Lincoln," paper presented at meeting of Organization of American Historians, Toronto, April 1999; see also Winkle, "The Voters of Lincoln's Springfield: Migration and Political Participation in an Antebellum City," *Journal of Social History* 25 (Spring 1992): 595–611. For the power of early settlers who persisted to imprint a political identity, see Winkle, *The Politics of Community: Migration and Politics in Antebellum Ohio* (New York: Cambridge University Press, 1988), 147–164. For the role of the "visible partisans" in community politics, see Paul Bourke and Donald DeBats, *Washington County: Politics and Community in Antebellum America* (Baltimore, Md.: Johns Hopkins University Press, 1995), 149–150.

50. Ballowe et al., *1850 Census of Illinois, Hancock County*.

51. In 1850, all were farmers except merchant Stephen H. Tyler, Jr., who ranked sixth

in amount of property owned. In 1860, all were farmers except Presbyterian minister Thomas M. Walker and two merchants. Of the fifty-three who owned more than $4,000 in real estate, those who were not farmers were blacksmith Frederick Albright, hotel-keeper Alexander Walker, and physician Leonard T. Ferris. In 1860, the elite were on average about seven years older than the average household head in the township. The median amount of property owned was $400 in 1850 and $1,900 a decade later. The top quartile of wealth holders owned more than $1,000 in 1850 and $4,000 by 1860. Those in the top 5 percent owned over $3,000 in 1850, and $8,000 in 1860 (Ballowe et al., *The 1850 Census of Illinois, Hancock County*; Tri-County Genealogical Society, *The 1860 Handcock [Hancock] County, Illinois Census*).

52. Foote, *Foote's 1940 Fountain Green Almanac,* 23.

53. Gregg, *History of Hancock County,* 471; *General Laws of the State of Illinois, Seventeenth General Assembly* (1851) (Springfield, Ill.: Lanphier & Walker, Printers, 1851), 35–49.

54. The supervisors were (with terms of office, party affiliation, and birthplace): Stephen H. Tyler (1850–1853, Democrat, Connecticut); James M. Renshaw (1853–1856, Whig, Georgia); Martin Hopkins (1856–1859, Republican, Connecticut); James Campbell (1859–1861, Republican, Pennsylvania); Daniel Prentiss (1861–1863, 1867–1868, Republican, Vermont); Robert McConnell (1863–1864, Democrat, Pennsylvania); Thomas Geddes (1864–1866, 1869–1870, Republican, Pennsylvania); T. McGinley Campbell (1866–1867, Republican, Pennsylvania); John G. Fonda (1870–1871, Republican, New York); A.W. McConnell (1871–1873, 1880, Republican, Pennsylvania); John H. Bullock (1873–1874, 1876–1878, Republican, Canada); Samuel Walker (1875–1876, Republican, Pennsylvania); and Andrew R. Simmons (1878–1880, Republican, Tennessee). Birthplace from *1850 Census; 1860 Census;* Census of Population, 1870 and 1880. Party affiliations from Gregg, *History of Hancock County,* 706, 826, 828, 829, 832, 835, 836, 840; *Portrait and Biographical Record of Hancock, McDonough and Henderson Counties, Illinois* (Chicago: Lake City Publishing Co., 1894; reprinted 1982, 384–385); Scofield, *History of Hancock County,* 1199–1200. See also *Carthage Republican,* 8 September 1859, 3 April 1862, 17 September 1863 and 16 April 1875; *Carthage Gazette,* 14 August 1878; *Warsaw Express,* 14 September 1854.

55. In August 1854, the County Maine Law Alliance held its quarterly meeting in Fountain Green (*Warsaw Express,* 1 June and 20 July 1854). In October 1854, Thomas Geddes was selected as a delegate to the Senatorial Convention by "The Friends of a Prohibitory Law" at a Carthage meeting. Geddes, James N. Renshaw, and three other men were selected to prepare an address to the voters to be published in the county paper (*Warsaw Express,* 12 October 1854); for the vote on prohibition, see *Carthage Republican,* 14 June 1855.

56. *Carthage Republican,* 9 April 1857. The average value is calculated by excluding Matthew McClaughry, whose wealth totaled $18,000. The Whigs were Leonard T. Ferris, Martin Hopkins, Thomas Geddes, Kendrick Leach, and Daniel Prentiss. Democrats were James W. Roberts and probably Matthew McClaughry (his son was an active Democrat). The commitment of Parker and Campbell are unknown. Political affiliation from the *Carthage Republican,* 22 July 1858; *Warsaw Express,* 14 September 1854. Geddes and Campbell were from Pennsylvania, Leach and William Parker from New York, Daniel Prentiss from Vermont, and Martin Hopkins from Connecticut (Census of Population, 1860).

57. *Carthage Republican,* 12 May 1858.

58. *Carthage Republican,* 7 and 23 June 1859.

59. Gregg, *History of Hancock County,* 832, 835, 879. Justice James Renshaw, born in Georgia, was forty-six in 1850 and the prosperous owner of a 300-acre farm worth $4,000 (*1850 Census*). Kendrick Leach arrived from New York in 1852, a veteran of the Mexican War. He bought Jabez Beebe's farm after Beebe moved to Webster and built the township's most imposing home in 1863. His land was worth $4,000 in 1860 (Gregg, *History of Hancock County,* 832–835; *1860 Census*).

60. Justice of the Peace Docket, Fountain Green, Illinois, 1850–1865, Illinois State Historical Library, Springfield, Illinois. Regarding the jurisdiction of the peace courts, see N. H. Purple, ed., *Statutes of the State of Illinois,* 2nd ed., Part I (Chicago: Keen & Lee, Booksellers, 1857), 659ff.

61. Justice of the Peace Docket, Fountain Green. The docket is not paginated; it has two sequentially numbered sets of cases and some are not numbered. Unfortunately, the Tyler store ledgers are missing from this time period, so a more precise picture of debt is not available.

62. *People vs. Elijah R. Williams,* Case 76 (30 May 1853), Justice of the Peace Docket.

63. The justice did not assess court costs to the plaintiff, which was the normal procedure if the defendant was found not guilty. See *State of Illinois vs. James Harris,* Case 77 (23 July 1853), Justice of the Peace Docket.

64. However, James Harris and family were present when the Illinois state census was taken in 1855 (1855 Census, State of Illinois; and Census of Population, 1860).

65. *State of Illinois vs. Elijah Cox,* 22 June 1863, Justice of the Peace Docket; Census of Population, 1860.

66. *State of Illinois vs. Caleb Thompson,* Case 37 (3 November 1853), Justice of the Peace Docket.

67. *Warsaw Express and Journal,* 20 September 1855, reprinted from the *Republican.*

68. L. T. Ferris to W. W. Green, 30 October 1848.

69. Illinois General Assembly, "Report of the State Superintendent of Public Instruction," in *Reports Made to the Nineteenth General Assembly of the State of Illinois Convened January 1, 1855* (Springfield, Ill.; State Printers, 1856): 65–119.

70. Wayne E. Fuller, *The Old Country School: The Story of Rural Education in the Middle West* (Chicago: University of Chicago Press, 1982); Cayton and Onuf, *The Midwest and the Nation,* 59ff.; for Illinois, see Etcheson, *The Emerging Midwest,* 78ff; and Robert Gehlmann Bone, "Education in Illinois before 1857," *Journal of the Illinois State Historical Society* 50 (Summer 1959): 119–140.

71. Board of Supervisors, *History of Hancock County, Illinois,* 307–308.

72. In 1860 the inhabitants of the township paid $346 of the $1,161 needed to support the local schools (Social Statistic Schedules for Illinois, 1860).

73. "Election Notice," paper found in CCTSR, Ledger 10:282.

74. There were 135 male teachers and 118 female teachers in 157 public and 18 private schools in the county (*Carthage Republican,* 29 November 1860). Regarding pay disparities, see Allen Geddes, "Early Fountain Green Schools," copy of typescript in Geddes Family Records. Geddes's knowledge was based on the account book of the McGuffy School he found in his attic and the accounts his grandfather kept while he was a township school trustee from 1845 to 1860.

75. Geddes, "Fountain Green Schools."

76. Because the press of farm work delayed boys' schooling, it was not uncommon for

young men of age twenty or twenty-one to be attending school. However, most of them left school in their middle teen years. In Fountain Green, the gender disparity was usually only a few percentage points. Countywide, boys were more likely than girls to attend school, and they composed 54 percent of the student body (Census of Population, 1860). By 1880, only 15 percent of the 300 local children did not attend school (*1860 Census;* Census of Population, 1870 and 1880).

77. William M. Walker, Monmouth, to Thomas M. Geddes, Fountain Green, October 25, 1869, Geddes Family Records. Robert McClaughry, the Geddes offspring, and the Ferris brothers all attended regional colleges at Galesburg and Macomb (Gregg, *History of Hancock County,* 706–707, 728–729).

78. Board of Supervisors, *History of Hancock County, Illinois,* 111.

79. Scofield, *History of Hancock County,* 1139; "Hon. O. F. Berry" and "Hiram G. Ferris," *Biographical Review of Hancock County, Illinois,* 53–55, 730–733; Gregg, *History of Hancock County,* 706–707.

80. William Walker to Thomas Geddes, October 25, 1869.

81. Thomas Geddes used his position as trustee of schools to good advantage: his son Walker taught in 1857, and nephews and nieces William Walker, Martha Walker, Sarah Ann McConnell, James Campbell, and Rozela Campbell all served terms as teachers (Geddes, "Fountain Green Schools").

82. *Carthage Republican,* 10 January 1859.

83. John Williston Cook, *Educational History of Illinois* (Chicago: Henry O. Shepard Co., 1912), 169; William L. Gross, ed., *Statutes of Illinois, 1818–1873,* vol. 3 (Springfield, Ill.: William L. Gross, 1873), 122.

5. "Awful calamities now upon us"

1. C. C. Tyler, "Reminiscences of Fountain Green, Ill.," *Journal of the Illinois State Historical Society* 8, no. 1 (1915): 55–64. Before it was moved to the Old State Capitol Building, the trophy hung near Lincoln's tomb.

2. Altschuler and Blumin, "'Where Is the Real America?,'" 230.

3. For a recent review of the literature, see Phillip Shaw Paludan, "What Did the Winners Win? The Social and Economic History of the North during the Civil War," in *Writing the Civil War: The Quest to Understand,* edited by James M. McPherson and William J. Cooper (Columbia: University of South Carolina Press, 1998), 174–200. For war resistance, see Iver Bernstein, *The New York City Draft Riots: Their Significance for American Society and Politics in the Age of the Civil War* (New York: Oxford University Press, 1990); Eugene C. Murdock, *One Million Men: The Civil War Draft in the North* (Madison: State Historical Society of Wisconsin, 1971). For the Midwest, see Michael Fellman, *Inside War: The Guerrilla Conflict in Missouri during the American Civil War* (New York: Oxford University Press, 1989); Frank L. Klement, *The Copperheads in the Middle West* (Chicago: University of Chicago Press, 1960); and Klement, *Dark Lanterns: Secret Political Societies, Conspiracies, and Treason Trials in the Civil War* (Baton Rouge: Louisiana State University Press, 1984). The struggles in Illinois are discussed in Robert D. Sampson, "'Pretty damned warm times': The 1864 Charleston Riot and 'the inalienable right of revolution,'" *Illinois Historical Journal* 89 (Summer 1996): 99–116; Aretas A. Dayton, "The Raising of Union Forces in Illinois during the Civil War," *Journal of the Illinois State Historical Society* 34 (1941): 401–438; Robert E. Sterling, "Civil War Draft Resistance in Illinois," *Journal of the Illinois State Historical Society* 64 (1971): 244–266;

and Frank L. Klement, Copperhead Secret Societies in Illinois in the Civil War," *Journal of the Illinois State Historical Society* 48 (1955): 152–180. For a general history of the military campaigns of Illinois units, see Victor Hicken, *Illinois in the Civil War* (1966; reprint, Urbana: University of Illinois Press, 1991).

4. James M. McPherson, *For Cause and Comrades: Why Men Fought in the Civil War* (New York: Oxford University Press, 1997), 180, 182. For the importance of studying rural community, see Barron, *Those Who Stayed Behind*, introduction. Notable community studies of the Civil War era include Michael H. Frisch, *Town into City: Springfield, Massachusetts and the Meaning of Community, 1840–80*; Ash, *Middle Tennessee Society Transformed*; Emily J. Harris, "Sons and Soldiers: Deerfield, Massachusetts and the Civil War," *Civil War History* 30 (1984): 157–171; and Thomas R. Kemp, "Community and War: The Civil War Experience of Two New Hampshire Towns," in Maris A. Vinovskis, *Toward a Social History of the American Civil War: Exploratory Essays* (New York: Cambridge University Press, 1990), 31–77.

5. For the connection between the soldier and his home community, see Reid Mitchell, *The Vacant Chair: The Northern Soldier Leaves Home* (New York: Oxford University Press, 1993); and Mitchell, "Soldiering, Manhood, and Coming of Age: A Northern Volunteer," in *Divided Houses: Gender and the Civil War*, edited by Catherine Clinton and Nina Silber (New York: Oxford University Press, 1992), 43–54.

6. For the implications of the Union victory for the Midwest, see Cayton and Onuf, *The Midwest and the Nation*. For the post-bellum Republican dominance in the Midwest, see Richard J. Jensen, *The Winning of the Midwest* (Chicago: University of Chicago Press, 1971); and Paul Kleppner, *The Cross of Culture: A Social Analysis of Midwestern Politics, 1850–1900* (New York: Free Press, 1970). Richard Franklin Bensel (*Yankee Leviathan: The Origins of Central State Authority in America, 1859–1877* [New York: Cambridge University Press, 1990]) suggests the national implications of Republican and northern dominance.

7. For a recent study of Illinois politics in this period, see Kenneth J. Winkle, "The Second Party System in Lincoln's Springfield," *Civil War History* 414, no. 4 (December 1998): 267–284. Stephen L. Hansen (*The Making of the Third Party System: Voters and Parties in Illinois, 1850–1876* [Ann Arbor: UMI Research Press, 1980]) argues that in 1860 Democrats carried all southerners, those born in Illinois to southern-born parents, the Irish, one-third of the Germans, and 33 percent of voters from the mid-Atlantic states (p. 138).

8. Gregg, *History of Hancock County*, 453; William E. Gienapp, *The Origins of the Republican Party, 1852–1856* (New York: Oxford University Press, 1987), 414.

9. *Carthage Republican*, 11 November 1856.

10. *Carthage Republican*, 19 July 1860. For Republican anti-Catholicism, see Joel Silbey, *A Respectable Minority: The Democratic Party in the Civil War Era, 1860–1868* (New York: W. W. Norton, 1977), 173. Perhaps the influx of Irish Catholic railroad laborers in Tennessee township provoked a nativist reaction in Fountain Green. The number of foreign-born in McDonough County rose from 206 in 1850 to 1,213 in 1860. By 1870, when such statistics were first collected, 420 Irish were counted in McDonough County. *Compendium of the Seventh Census* (1850) (Washington, D.C.: Government Printing Office, 1854), 219; *Compendium of the Eighth Census* (1860) (Washington, D.C: Government Printing Office, 1864), 102; *Compendium of the Ninth Census* (1870) (Washington, D.C.: Government Printing Office, 1872), 1:408; *Compendium of the Tenth Census* (1880) (Washington, D.C.: Government Printing Office, 1883), 1:500.

Hancock County was home to 484 Irish in 1880 (*Compendium of the Tenth Census* [1880] 1:504).

11. Foote, *Foote's 1940 Fountain Green Almanac,* 13; see also Allen Geddes, "A Night They Remembered," Geddes Family Records.

12. Gienapp, *Origins of the Republican Party,* 429–430; Jean H. Baker, *Affairs of Party: The Political Culture of Northern Democrats in the Mid-Nineteenth Century* (Ithaca, N.Y.: Cornell University Press, 1983), 320.

13. Gregg, *History of Hancock County,* 391, 395. For the history of the *Carthage Republican,* see E. A. Snively, "James M. Davidson," *Journal of the Illinois State Historical Society* 8 (1915): 184–194.

14. For the Democratic party, see Silbey, *A Respectable Minority;* Baker, *Affairs of Party;* and Bruce Collins, "The Ideology of the Ante-bellum Northern Democrats," *American Studies* 11, no. 1 (1977): 103–121. For a thorough treatment of sectionalism in Midwestern party politics, see Etcheson, *The Emerging Midwest.*

15. *Carthage Republican,* 4 October 1860.

16. *Daily Warsaw City Bulletin,* 1 November 1860. For Republican free soil ideology, see Eric Foner, *Free Soil, Free Labor, Free Men: The Ideology of the Republican Party before the Civil War* (1970; reprint, New York: Oxford University Press, 1995).

17. *Daily Warsaw City Bulletin,* 5, 6 November 1860.

18. Silbey, *A Respectable Minority,* 163–165.

19. For the term *visible partisans,* see Paul Bourke and Donald DeBats, *Washington County: Politics and Community in Antebellum America* (Baltimore, Md.: Johns Hopkins University Press, 1995), 14. Information for visible partisans obtained from news accounts of township meetings, county histories, and regional biographies.

20. *Carthage Republican,* 11 October 1860.

21. The rally is reported in *Carthage Republican,* 11 October 1860. For a description of the uniforms, see *Carthage Republican,* 23 August 1860. The colors of red, white, and blue were emblematic of the symbols shared by both parties, reinforcing a national as well as a partisan loyalty. Baker, *Affairs of Party,* 202–203.

22. *Carthage Republican,* 11 October 1860.

23. *Daily Warsaw Bulletin,* 10 October 1860; regarding Wide-Awakes, see David Herbert Donald, *Lincoln* (New York: Simon & Schuster, 1995), 254–255; and Arthur Charles Cole, *The Era of the Civil War, 1848–1870,* vol. 3 of *The Centennial History of Illinois,* edited by Clarence Walworth Alvord (Springfield, Ill.: Illinois Centennial Commission, 1919), 197–198.

24. *Daily Warsaw City Bulletin,* 12 October 1860; *Gate City* (Keokuk, Iowa), 9 and 11 October 1860. Transparencies were signs painted on translucent material that was lit from behind.

25. *Gate City* (Keokuk, Iowa), 11 October 1860; and Tyler, "Reminiscences of Fountain Green."

26. *Gate City,* 11 October 1860.

27. *Gate City,* 9 October 1860.

28. *Daily Warsaw City Bulletin,* 9 November 1860; Gregg, *History of Hancock County,* 454.

29. *Carthage Republican,* 8 and 15 November 1860; *Warsaw Express,* 19 November 1860.

30. *Carthage Republican,* 27 December 1860.

31. *Carthage Republican,* 18 April 1861.

32. Baker argues that national Democratic party leaders were supportive of the war effort (*Affairs of Party*, 226–338); but Michael Holt argues that they may have been less valiant at the local level ("An Elusive Synthesis: Northern Politics during the Civil War," in *Writing the Civil War*, edited by MacPherson and Cooper, 112–134). There is no question that Democratic party leaders in Illinois dragged their feet in organizing a militia and declaring their support for the war. Cole, *Era of the Civil War*, 297–299.

33. Cole, *Era of the Civil War*, 298–299.

34. The editor of the *Carthage Republican* was G. M. Childs, whose extreme anti-war rhetoric led to his replacement by Robert W. McClaughry in 1861, who supported the Union cause. When McClaughry enlisted in August 1862, J. M. Davidson of Fulton County purchased the paper. After the war it again became a Democratic sheet. Snively, "James M. Davidson," 184–194; *Carthage Republican*, 8 October 1863.

35. Earl J. Hess, *Liberty, Virtue, and Progress: Northerners and Their War for the Union* (New York: Fordham University Press, 1988), 92–93; Bernstein, *The New York City Draft Riots*, 11; Baker, *Affairs of Party*, 156.

36. *Carthage Republican*, 26 February and 5 March 1863. The Spartan Band (S.B.) was a short-lived organization of Republicans which originated in Chicago in early 1863. The Union League, organized to promote Republican candidates for office, was extremely successful in Illinois. It led all other states in the number of members (140,000) and number of local councils (1,088) by December 1863. The Union League helped Lincoln win the presidential election of 1864. Klement, *Dark Lanterns*, 49–53, 57, 62–63.

37. *Carthage Republican*, 17 March 1864.

38. Baker downplays the Knights of the Golden Circle as a product of "the over-heated imaginations of army commanders and midwestern Republicans." *Affairs of Party*, 340.

39. Geddes, "A Night They Remembered" and "The Home Guard during the Civil War," Geddes Family Records.

40. James Woodruff to James B. Fry, 30 June 1863, Records of the Provost Marshall General's Bureau, 4th District Illinois, Letters Sent, Record Group 110, National Archives and Records Administration. For the trial of the offenders see *United States vs. James Peter Cherry et al.*, 8th Circuit Court of Illinois, January 1864, Circuit Court Records, vol. 4:557–558, 579, 605, Hancock County Courthouse, Carthage, Illinois. Among those who posted bail for the offenders was Democratic Sheriff Melgar Couchman.

41. Scofield, *History of Hancock County*, 766–771. The local Republicans were enraged by the murder, and after the war ended the returning soldiers celebrated him as a martyr. Ritter's body was removed from the pauper's grave to which the Democratic sheriff had consigned him and in November 1865 was re-interred in the city's best cemetery with full military honors attended by a large crowd (*Carthage Gazette*, 13 and 20 July 1865).

42. Geddes, "The Home Guard during the Civil War"; corroborated by Mr. and Mrs. John F. Wright, "History of the Hickerson Wright Family," typescript in possession of John Wright, Carthage, Illinois, 36.

43. Both the *Carthage Republican* and the *Hancock New Era* blamed the raid on bushwhackers, probably from Missouri (*Carthage Republican*, 20 October 1864; *Hancock New Era*, 20 October 1864). See also Bob Sterling, "Discouragement, Weariness, and War Politics: Desertions from Illinois Regiments during the Civil War," *Illinois Historical Journal* 82 (Winter 1989): 239–262.

44. *New Era* (Warsaw), 3 November 1864; "The Simmons Family in Hancock County," *Hancock County Historical Society Newsletter* 7 (February 1991): 3. The story is repeated with variations in most subsequent local histories. The band entered from McDonough County, but they were said to have crossed from Missouri.

45. *Hancock New Era*, 27 October 1864; *Carthage Republican,* 27 October 1864.

46. Tyler, "Centennial History," *Carthage Republican,* 22 April 1925; *Carthage Republican,* 27 October 1866.

47. Critics charged that the draft bounty proposal had been approved without a full quorum of supervisors. By 1 December 1864, $80,000 of the bounty payments had been issued and county Republicans had engineered a resolution calling for accountability by the Democratic county treasurer in disbursing the funds (*Hancock New Era,* 24 November and 1 December 1864). For a useful comparison, see Stephen J. Buck, "'A contest in which blood must flow like water': Du Page County and the Civil War," *Illinois Historical Journal* 87 (Spring 1994): 2–20.

48. McDonough County spent a total of $161,576, Adams County spent $80,111, and Henderson County spent $28,441. *Report of the Adjutant General of the State of Illinois,* revised by Brig. Gen. J. N. Reece (Springfield, Ill.: Phillips Bros., State Printers, 1900), 1:203–209. At a board of supervisors meeting on October 13, $120,000 was approved, $400 for each soldier who volunteered, was drafted, or furnished a substitute. The funds were to be distributed at the township level (*Carthage Republican,* 27 October 1864).

49. Fannie M. Leach, Fountain Green, to Friend, 8 March 1865, Kendrick Leach Collection.

50. *Carthage Republican,* 8 August 1865. The well-to-do may have been protesting the downward redistribution of wealth. Robin Einhorn, *Property Rules: Political Economy in Chicago, 1833–1872* (Chicago: University of Chicago Press, 1991), 202.

51. The twenty-eight men of Company C of Montebello Township sent a letter dated November 6 which pleaded with the township officials (who had appropriated $5,000 to pay volunteers to fill the draft quota) to extend the bounty provision retroactively to them (*Hancock New Era,* 1 December 1864).

52. Those who refused to pay applied to the courts for an injunction against the seizure, which was refused by the local court but was on its way to the state Supreme Court when the state legislature repealed the bounty law on 23 February 1867 and ordered tax collector Jacob S. Ross to return the money. Transcript of the repeal order signed by F. Corwin, Speaker of the House of Representatives and Wm. Bross, Speaker of the Senate, forwarded by clerk R. J. Oglesby, 13 February 1867, Kendrick N. Leach Collection.

53. The average value of farm implements per farm in Fountain Green rose from $106 in 1859 to nearly $200 in 1869 (Agricultural Schedules for Illinois, 1860 and 1870). The value of implements was affected by high rates of inflation. U.S. Department of Commerce, *Historical Statistics of the United States, Colonial Times to 1970* (Washington, D.C.: U.S. Government Printing Office, 1975), Part I, Series E, 52–63, 186, 201. Soldiers earned about one-third less than they would have earned at home (Einhorn, *Property Rules,* 197).

54. The number of live hogs shipped on the Chicago, Burlington, and Quincy Railroad climbed from 35 million in 1859 to 166 million in 1864, and shipments of cattle on the railroad increased from 105 million in 1862 to 136 million by 1866. Carlson, *The Illinois Military Tract,* 126–128, 131–133. The total number of swine in Fountain Green Township almost doubled in the 1860s—from 1,968 to 3,792 hogs—

and the total number of cattle on Fountain Green farms rose from 955 in 1859 to 1,125 in 1869 (Agricultural Schedules for Illinois, 1860 and 1870). See also Russell Howard Anderson, "Agriculture in Illinois during the Civil War Period, 1850–1870," Ph.D. diss., University of Illinois, 1929; and Paul W. Gates, *Agriculture and the Civil War* (New York: Alfred A. Knopf, 1965).

55. Output in Fountain Green township rose from 1,726 pounds of wool in 1855 to 5,885 pounds in 1865. Illinois State Census, Hancock County, 1855 and 1865, State Archives, Springfield, Illinois. After a lackluster performance on the market in the 1850s, the price wool commanded shot up during the war. Carlson, *The Illinois Military Tract*, 133–135; *Journal of the Illinois State Agricultural Society* 1, no. 10 (October 1862): 30.

56. *Carthage Republican*, 7 July 1864.

57. *Carthage Republican*, 10 July 1862.

58. Defined as over 200 pounds per farm; see Chapter 3 for a more complete analysis of the production of butter. The editor accused the dairies of supplying foreign markets rather than the home market (*Carthage Republican*, 25 August 1864).

59. *Transactions of the Illinois State Agricultural Society*, vol. 5 (1861–1864) (Springfield, Ill.: Baker & Phillips, Printers, 1865), 331–333.

60. *Prairie Farmer* 35 (10 June 1865): 466.

61. *Transactions of the Illinois State Agricultural Society* 5:254, 256.

62. Ibid., 5:584.

63. *Carthage Republican*, 11 August 1864. Carthage women also became involved in the Sanitary Commission, collecting supplies for soldiers. The women who neglected to come were urged to remember "that it is *men* their husbands and brothers—who are making the *sacrifices* and braving hell for the sake of wives and sisters at home" (*Carthage Republican*, 25 September 1862). Farm women probably did not have time for these charitable pursuits.

64. *Carthage Gazette*, 16 August 1866.

65. Andreas, *Illustrated Historical Atlas of Hancock County*, 67.

66. A recent review of the field argues that historians generally agree on the importance of a sense of duty to soldiers; see Reid Mitchell, "'Not the General but the Soldier,'" in *Writing the Civil War*, edited by MacPherson and Cooper, 81–95. MacPherson makes the point emphatically in *For Cause and Comrades*.

67. Company D of the Sixteenth was organized out of Warsaw and Hamilton, predominantly Republican towns in Hancock County. *Report of the Adjutant General*, 1:459, 632; 2:14–15; 6:315.

68. *Report of the Adjutant General*, 6:318. The threat of the draft was a potent force in stimulating enlistment in Illinois. Cole, *Era of the Civil War*, 275. See also James M. McPherson, *Battle Cry of Freedom*, 491.

69. Civil War Pension File, Thomas J. Campbell.

70. Daybook B, CCTSR.

71. Mitchell, *Vacant Chair*, 154; Gerald Linderman, *Embattled Courage: The Experience of Combat in the American Civil War* (New York: Free Press, 1987), 36.

72. The average term of service was twenty months; the shortest term was twenty-seven days and the longest was over four years. Most (63) were discharged in 1865 when the war ended. There was no occupation listed for 18 of the 60, but most of these were sons of farmers. It is not surprising that one-third of those who served were born in Illinois, because their average age in 1860 was 23.5 years (Civil War Pension Files and *1860 Census*). Twenty-five men (53 percent) served less than one year (*Report of the*

Adjutant General, see listing in Table 5.3). For the linkage between manliness and civic duty, see Mitchell, "Soldiering, Manhood, and Coming of Age"; and for manliness and courage, see Linderman, *Embattled Courage,* 26.

73. Of the 140 soldiers, 85 (about 60 percent) served in the 118th Regiment (60 in infantry, 25 in cavalry). See *Report of the Adjutant General,* 1:447–450, 613–615; 2:13–16, 75–77; 3:233–236, 471–474, 581–584; 4:326–428, 612–613; 5:155–157; 6:293–295; 7:268–269, 302–304, 506–509; 8:352–355.

74. Twenty-eight men enlisted in 1861, sixty-four in 1862, and just two in 1863. (See Table 5.3 for a complete listing of service units.) Enlistment patterns and lists of officers from *Report of the Adjutant General,* 1:447–450, 613–615; 2:13–16, 75–77; 3:233–236, 471–474, 581–584; 4:326–328, 612–613; 5:155–157; 6:293–295; 7:268–269, 302–304, 506–509; 8:352–355. Ages and proportion of men in service were calculated from the 1860 federal census. The number of men from Fountain Green means the number of those who enlisted at either the Fountain Green or the Webster post office, so it includes men who lived outside the township and enlisted within it. Similarly, it excludes men who lived in the township but enlisted outside of it. Of the 140 men from the township, 120 listed Fountain Green as home and 15 listed Webster. The proportion of enlistees to the male population is comparable to that for Newburyport, Massachusetts, where 45 percent of the white male population aged 13–43 enlisted. Maris A. Vinovskis, "Have Social Historians Lost the Civil War?" in *Toward a Social History of the American Civil War,* 1–30.

75. See ibid., 16. Using the 1860 age figures, twenty-two men were less than 20 years old, another twenty-five were between the ages of 20 and 29, and just thirteen were over the age of 30. Further proof of the youth of the cohort is that thirteen of the sixty were attending school when the 1860 census was taken.

76. Gregg, *History of Hancock County,* 729, 829; *Report of the Adjutant General,* 4:293. Fonda briefly served as commander of Camp Butler; see William S. Peterson, "A History of Camp Butler, 1861–1866," *Illinois Historical Journal* 82 (Spring 1989): 74–92. An early settler of Hancock County, Fonda was a veteran of the Mexican War, a civil engineer and county surveyor, and was married to Mary McConnell of Fountain Green Township. He enlisted early in the Second Illinois Cavalry, where he was appointed lieutenant and was later appointed major of the 12th Illinois Cavalry, in command of Camp Butler. In October 1862, he was made colonel of the 118th. After his war service, he settled on a farm near his wife's family in Fountain Green. Gregg, *History of Hancock County,* 829.

77. Walker was given a leave of absence by the Presbyterian Church's ruling elders on 9 November 1862 (FGPC Session Records, 33).

78. *Report of the Adjutant General,* 1:168.

79. Expressed in percentages, 22 percent died (85 percent of them from disease), 7 percent were discharged due to disability, and 54 percent were mustered out with no record of disease or disability. Of the nine pension claims made because of the death of a soldier, the cause of death due to illness included dysentery (4), typhoid (2), malaria (1), pneumonia (1), and unspecified (1). Of the soldiers who survived, thirty-five filed for pensions as invalids, indicating that the war experience may have left many of them permanently diseased or disabled. Data from Civil War Pension Files and *Report of the Adjutant General* (see Table 5.3). Of the group of 140 soldiers, pension claims were filed for forty-eight of them. Thirty-five soldiers filed invalid claims for themselves, and another eight were filed by a widow or bereaved parent. If one adds the number of invalid pension claims to the number of deaths from disease during wartime (twenty-

three), the total is fifty-eight, or 41 percent of the group of 140 (Civil War Pension Files; *Report of the Adjutant General*). The rate of death of Fountain Green soldiers was 191 per 10,000 in population, higher than the national rate of 182 deaths per 10,000. Like the national figure for the North, about 8 percent of males aged 13–43 died in the war. The Fountain Green death rate (from wounds or disease) of 22 percent was higher than the national average of 17 percent and the 13 percent for the Newburyport, Massachusetts, cohort. Vinovskis, "Have Social Historians Lost the Civil War?" 18.

80. *Report of the Adjutant General,* 6:293; Civil War Pension File, Thomas Wilson Campbell.

81. John Wilson Campbell was promoted to the rank of captain to fill the vacancy (*Report of the Adjutant General,* 6:292–318). Major McClaughry praised the men in his address at the reunion of the 118th (*Carthage Gazette,* 8 October 1873).

82. Civil War Pension File, John Wilson Campbell.

83. *Carthage Republican,* 18 December 1863 (dated 12 November 1863, Vermillion Bayou, Louisiana); *Carthage Republican,* 17 March 1864; see also *Report of the Adjutant General,* 6:316.

84. Mitchell, "Soldiering, Manhood, and Coming of Age," 49.

85. *Hancock New Era,* 6 April 1865; 21 July 1864.

86. *Hancock New Era,* 12 January 1865.

87. Ibid.

88. *Carthage Republican,* 10 and 24 November 1864; *Hancock New Era,* 1 December 1864. The vote must be interpreted carefully, because Illinois was one of the few major states that did not provide for absentee balloting of soldiers (McPherson, *Battle Cry,* 804), and the Democrats did not campaign among soldiers (Baker, *Affairs of Party,* 291).

89. *Carthage Republican,* 10 and 24 November 1864.

90. *Carthage Republican,* 6 April 1865.

91. *Carthage Republican,* 20 April 1865.

92. Laura A. Geddes, Normal, Ill., to Susan R. Geddes, Fountain Green, 7 May 1865, Geddes Family Records.

93. Sheet music for two military marches (No. 205a "Kriegers Eizug" and No. 205b "Defilier-March," published by John F. Stratton, New York) were found in the pages of the daybooks of Tyler's store for 9 June 1865 (CCTSR 8:113–114).

94. *Carthage Republican,* 13 July 1865.

95. Ibid. J. W. may have been John Wright, listed in the 1860 census as a farmer, 24, married with two children and no land. His reference to Maryland leads one to suspect that J. W. may have been a Catholic, which Wright was not.

96. *Carthage Gazette,* 11 October 1866 and 14 March 1867.

97. *Carthage Republican,* 10 August 1865; *Hancock New Era,* 6 April 1865; *Report of the Adjutant General* 6:318; Scofield, *History of Hancock County,* 955.

98. *Hancock New Era,* 8 September, 13 October, and 3 November 1864; *Warsaw Weekly Public Record,* 9 November 1865.

99. Gregg, *History of Hancock County,* 457–458.

100. *Carthage Republican,* 14 November 1872; *Carthage Gazette,* 12 November 1868.

101. *Report of the Adjutant General,* 6:318; Scofield, *History of Hancock County,* 955.

102. *Carthage Republican,* 23 October 1865.

103. Ibid.

104. *Carthage Gazette,* 10 January 1867.

105. Kendrick Leach to David Leach, 27 July 1864, David Leach Journal, Hancock County Historical Society.

106. Civil War Pension File, Alexander Walker Geddes.

107. Laura A. Geddes to Susan R. Geddes, 7 May 1865.

108. When Rev. Walker returned in October 1863 from army duty, he heard reports that Mrs. Eveline McConnell and Miss Eveline Geddes were guilty of "immoral conduct." They were notified not to take communion until the rumors could be investigated. It was not until March 1864 that the session took their case under consideration, but action was postponed until May, when "final action was taken." The supporting documents that would tell us the specifics of the charges and the disciplinary action taken are missing, so the best we can do is speculate. McConnell may have been instrumental in arranging the affairs of Eveline and the father of her child. One presumes we can rule out the possibility of rape, since Geddes was charged with immoral conduct. McConnell seemed to be a member in good standing. She and her husband Alexander had brought their baby Anna to be baptized the year before in October 1862. See FGPC Session Record 34 (23 October 1863): 35–36 (14 March 1864; 21 May 1864); see also Register of Baptisms, FGPC, 202–209.

109. Civil War Pension Files, Hiram Chamberlin, Richard Brandon.

110. George Lathrop's mother filed a claim in 1868 when her husband, a veteran who had lost a leg in the War of 1812 and was "not in his right mind," deserted her (Civil War Pension Files, Marion Conkey, George Lathrop).

111. *Cyrus Fuller vs. Clarinda Fuller,* Hancock County Chancery Court Files, Box 138, Case 1032 (January 1865).

112. Civil War Pension Files for James J. Foy, William Yetter, John P. Day, James C. Robinson, and Thomas A. Bullock.

6. "A market at his door"

1. *Carthage Gazette,* 31 December 1879.

2. William Spangler, California, to Thomas M. Geddes, Fountain Green, 25 January 1873, Geddes Family Collection. Spangler later moved to North Dakota to farm. *Biographical Review of Hancock County,* 726.

3. William Spangler to Thomas Geddes, 25 January 1873.

4. Social relations in farm families are conditioned by gender roles of work. Neth, *Preserving the Family Farm.*

5. Linda Gordon defines patriarchy as a family structure in which the father holds authority over the other family members in an economic system in which the family is the unit of production. Linda Gordon, *Heroes of Their Own Lives: The Politics and History of Family Violence: Boston, 1880–1960* (New York: Penguin Books, 1988), vi.

6. The irony of agrarian ideology is its valuation of independence while requiring the dependency of women (Fink, *Agrarian Women*). The Turnerian frontier thesis likewise overlooked the role of women in the settlement of the West; see Susan Armitage and Elizabeth Jameson, eds., *The Women's West* (Norman: University of Oklahoma Press, 1987).

7. *Carthage Republican,* 27 September 1866.

8. *Carthage Republican,* 3 June 1869 and 18 November 1874.

9. *Carthage Republican,* 16 July 1875.

10. Stock-raising changed from a way to market corn to a business that was sensitive to corn prices, rail rates, drought, and disease. Carlson, *The Illinois Military Tract,* 130–131. The census is not a completely reliable indicator of the extent of a farmer's herd. For example, G. H. Dorothy reported a herd of only seventeen, but he had purchased and sold sixty-eight head of cattle that year. Eleven farms owned more than twenty head of cattle at the time the census was taken; the highest were A. R. Bullock's herd of fifty-three and Solomon Dill's herd of fifty-eight. Agricultural Schedules for Illinois, 1880. Few stayed with raising sheep as the demand dropped for wool in the post-war era. The price paid for wool slid from $3.77 in 1866 to $1.65 in 1870 (Anderson, 269–270).

11. *Carthage Republican,* 6 October 1875.

12. *Carthage Gazette,* 7 February and 21 February 1880.

13. *Carthage Gazette,* 2 June 1875. The weekly columns of local news always mentioned the names of those who were shipping livestock that week; names gleaned from reports in the *Carthage Republican* and the *Carthage Gazette,* 1874 and 1875.

14. *Carthage Gazette,* 10 December 1879.

15. *Carthage Gazette,* 25 December 1880.

16. *Carthage Republican,* 11 April 1866, 11 July 1867, 9 July 1868, and 15 July 1869.

17. *Carthage Gazette,* 30 July 1879. Regarding mechanization of farming in the Midwest, see Bogue, *From Prairie to Corn Belt,* Chapter 8; and Atack and Bateman, *To Their Own Soil,* Chapter 11.

18. In just one month in 1872, Fountain Green farmers brought in 112 dozen eggs to C. C. Tyler's Arcade (15 March to 15 April). They also brought in twenty-four pounds of butter, for which they were paid thirteen cents per pound. The eggs (which sold for twelve-and-a-half cents a dozen) were produced by twelve families, some of whom brought in more than one batch of eggs during the month; the batches ranged from two to sixteen dozen (CCTSR Daybook E, 16 March to 16 April 1872).

19. Agricultural Schedules for Illinois, 1880. The fact that data regarding poultry and egg production were not collected until 1880 reflects a bias against recognizing women's production on the farm.

20. On 15 April 1872 the daybook shows a purchase of $10.69 by Solomon Dill, which included thirty-five yards of calico, 1¾ yds. gingham, thread, buttons, a set of cups, a can of molasses, and two pairs plow shoes (CCTSR Daybook E: 26).

21. CCTSR, Journal/Daybook I: 303 (9 October 1885) notes a credit of $109.91 cash from the creamery in Carthage for milk collected.

22. Some historians have theorized that the withdrawal of women from productive farm work resulted in a loss of social status. The reduction of women's production directly for market may have masked their economic contribution to the farm enterprise in the form of housework and reproduction. Regarding the defeminization of agricultural work, see Sally McMurry, *Transforming Rural Life: Dairying Families and Agricultural Change, 1820–1885* (Baltimore, Md.: Johns Hopkins University Press, 1995); and Bengt Ankarloo, "Agriculture and Women's Work: Directions for Change in the West, 1700–1900," *Journal of Family History* 4 (Summer 1979): 111–120. Whether or not women's work became devalued is a matter of wide-ranging opinion; see Osterud, "Gender and the Transition to Capitalism." In contrast to John Mack Faragher's argument that women were excluded from economic exchange in frontier society, and thereby assumed a second-rate status within that society, Fountain Green women were more involved at the sites of exchange during the frontier period, when their products

served as a medium of exchange. John Mack Faragher, *Women and Men on the Overland Trail* (New Haven, Conn.: Yale University Press, 1979), 112, 115. The disparity may be explained by regional habits of commerce. That is, southern women may have been more removed from commerce than Yankee women.

23. Women were involved in making quilts (certainly a form of textile production), but quilts were fabricated for home use, not for sale. At the county agricultural fairs, women were awarded prizes for jeans, linen, flannel, linsey, and wool, along with patchwork and worsted quilts, woven and knitted counterpanes, wool blankets, and knitted socks (*Carthage Republican*, 14 July 1870).

24. *Carthage Gazette*, 15 October 1866.

25. *Daily Warsaw City Bulletin*, 8 December 1860; *Warsaw Weekly Public Record*, 12 August 1865.

26. State of Illinois, *Reports to the General Assembly, Illinois (29th Session)*, vol. 1 (Springfield, Ill.: State Printers, 1873), 275–279; and State of Illinois, *Reports to the General Assembly, Illinois (31st Session)* (1879) 2:101–105.

27. *Carthage Republican*, 28 October 1874; CCTSR Daybook E:21.

28. *Carthage Republican*, 17 October 1872; CCTSR Daybook B:21 (6 November 1866). See also Susan Geddes to Thomas M. Geddes, autograph letter, 10 February 1869, in Geddes Family Records.

29. *Carthage Republican*, 15 February 1872. Refrigerators were advertised by a Carthage store in 1873 (*Carthage Republican*, 4 June 1873).

30. *Carthage Gazette*, 15 October 1866. For the price of a reaper, see Atack and Bateman, *To Their Own Soil*, 196.

31. Social Statistic Schedules for Illinois, 1860, 1870, and 1880.

32. *Carthage Republican*, 3 March 1870.

33. Questions regarding tenancy were first asked in the 1880 agricultural census. Using the value of $1,000 as a threshold for a viable farm as a way to measure tenancy, the tenancy rate in 1860 was 11 percent. Only three farmers in 1860 owned no land whatsoever (2 percent) (Agricultural Schedules for Illinois, 1860, 1870, and 1880; Census of Population, 1860 and 1870). The tenancy rate for Hancock County as a whole was lower, at 32 percent in 1880. *Compendium of the Tenth Census* (1880), 3:44–45.

34. Bogue, *From Prairie to Cornbelt*, 62.

35. *Carthage Gazette*, 31 March 1875.

36. Danhoff, *Change in Agriculture*, 92. A small group of renters paid cash, not produce, to the owner. In 1880 nine rented for cash and sixty-seven rented for shares in Fountain Green Township (Agricultural Census, 1880).

37. Agricultural Schedules for Illinois, 1880.

38. Ibid.

39. Agricultural Schedules for Illinois, 1860, 1870, and 1880; Social Statistic Schedules for Illinois, 1860, 1870, and 1880.

40. Scofield, *History of Hancock County*, 1272.

41. Census of Population, 1860, 1870, and 1880; Agricultural Schedules for Illinois, 1860, 1870, and 1880.

42. Census of Population, 1870.

43. Miller had purchased the land in 1840, 1848, and 1853. See Hancock County Deeds, O:51; 72:324; 36:221. For the transactions with the Miller sons, see Hancock County Deeds, 103:36, 41; 98:375; 54:270; and Hancock County Mortgages, Book 32:34.

Age and marital status from the Census of Population, 1870. Miller died in December 1878 (*Carthage Gazette,* 1 January 1879).

44. Evaluation of mortgage-taking practices is from a sample of deed records. For a study of farm mortgages for a later period in the Midwest, see Allan G. Bogue, *Money at Interest: The Farm Mortgage on the Middle Border* (1955; reprint, Lincoln: University of Nebraska Press, 1969).

45. William Smith, 1873, Will Book 1:472; Samuel White, 1855, Will Book 1:468. Both in Hancock County, Clerk of the County Courts, Will Books.

46. Agricultural Schedules for Illinois, 1870 and 1880; Census of Population, 1870 and 1880.

47. The trend in school attendance is clearly upward for this period. See Chapter 4 above.

48. In addition to the 30 young men in 1880, another handful of older men without family ties were working in the township. A case in point is 38-year-old David Bennett of Tennessee, who was widowed or divorced before he drifted into the township. Several other drifters such as Bennett worked on farms in the township (Census of Population, 1880).

49. Agricultural Schedules for Illinois, 1880.

50. Agricultural Schedules for Illinois, 1880; Census of Population, 1880.

51. *Carthage Republican,* 15 August 1872.

52. Historians using a Marxist framework have seen such protests, from Shays's Rebellion to the Populist movement of the 1890s, as a form of class rebellion by an agrarian proletariat against capitalist power. See Alan Kulikoff, *The Agrarian Origins of American Capitalism* (Charlottesville: University Press of Virginia, 1992); and Steven Hahn, *The Roots of Southern Populism: Yeoman Farmers and the Transformation of the Georgia Upcountry, 1850–1890* (New York: Oxford University Press, 1983). My argument that the Grange protest was not a wholesale rejection of agrarian capitalism but rather a selective strike against what farmers perceived as abusive middlemen has been influenced by Scott G. McNall, *The Road to Rebellion: Class Formation and Kansas Populism, 1865–1900* (Chicago: University of Chicago Press, 1988). The continuities of rural radicalism are explored in Stock, *Rural Radicals.*

53. For the movement in Illinois, see Solon Justus Buck, *The Granger Movement: A Study of Agricultural Organization and Its Political, Economic and Social Manifestations, 1870–1880* (Cambridge, Mass.: Harvard University Press, 1913).

54. For historical interpretations of the broader Grange movement I have relied on D. Sven Nordin, *Rich Harvest: A History of the Grange, 1867–1900* (Jackson: University Press of Mississippi, 1974); Donald B. Marti, *Women of the Grange: Mutuality and Sisterhood in Rural America, 1866–1920,* Contributions in Women's Studies, No. 124 (New York: Greenwood Press, 1991); and Thomas A. Woods, *Knights of the Plow: Oliver H. Kelley and the Origins of the Grange in Republican Ideology* (Ames: Iowa State University Press, 1991).

55. Buck, *The Granger Movement,* 48, 54; Carlson, *The Illinois Military Tract,* 168.

56. Carlson, *The Illinois Military Tract,* 162–164.

57. The Interstate Commerce Act of 1887 finally curbed the railroad abuses. Ibid., 170–171.

58. *Carthage Gazette,* 19 February 1873.

59. *Carthage Republican,* 11 June and 18 June 1873.

60. *Carthage Gazette,* 4 June 1873.

61. *Carthage Gazette,* 4 March 1872. The Farmer's Club was organized on 15 March 1872.

62. Fonda's farm was worth $10,000 in 1870. He was also involved in the agricultural market; he paid $600 in wages that year and owned farm implements worth $500. Leach's standing confirms the pattern of elite participation. Leach, also middle-aged, owned a 200-acre farm worth $10,000. He owned implements worth $300 and paid $500 in wages. Agricultural Schedules for Illinois, 1870; Census of Population, 1870.

63. *Carthage Republican,* 22 October 1873.

64. *Carthage Gazette,* 10 December 1873.

65. *Carthage Gazette,* 7 January 1874.

66. *Carthage Gazette,* 10 October 1872.

67. The Grange was led by elite farmers in Union County and Champaign County, Illinois. See Jane Adams, "1870s Agrarian Activism in Southern Illinois: Mediator between Two Eras," *Social Science History* 16 (Fall 1992): 365–400; and Roy V. Scott, "Grangerism in Champaign County, Illinois, 1873–1877," *Mid-America* 43 (July 1961): 139–163.

68. *Carthage Republican,* 6 August 1873; *Carthage Gazette,* 6 August 1873.

69. *Carthage Gazette,* 10 December 1873.

70. Quote from *Carthage Gazette,* 3 September 1873; see also *Carthage Republican,* 3 September 1873. The Republican *Gazette* estimated the crowd at 2,000; the Democrat *Carthage Republican* at 5,000.

71. Ibid. Among the Democrats was *Republican* editor J. M. Davidson.

72. *Carthage Gazette,* 24 September 1873.

73. The People's ticket earned a majority only in the five townships that traditionally voted for Republican presidential candidates (*Carthage Gazette,* 5 November 1873).

74. *Carthage Republican,* 12 February 1875.

75. *Carthage Republican,* 1 July 1874.

76. *Carthage Republican,* 18 November 1875.

77. Sally McMurry, *Families and Farmhouses in Nineteenth-Century America: Vernacular Design and Social Change* (New York: Oxford University Press, 1988), 5, 88, 116–118. McMurry takes care to point out that farmhouses were not mere imitations of those in the city, but that the plan of the farmhouse was influenced by its setting, 5–6. Linda K. Kerber cautions that the bourgeois notions of domesticity were an ideal and not a reality; see Kerber, "Separate Spheres, Female Worlds, Woman's Place: The Rhetoric of Women's History," *Journal of American History* 75 (June 1988): 9–39.

78. *Carthage Republican,* 11 April 1872; Eugene L. Gross and William L. Gross, eds., *Statutes of Illinois, 1818–1872,* vol. 2 (Springfield, Ill.: E. L. & W. L. Gross, 1872), 428. The law was the product of the Illinois Supreme Court decision denying Myra Bradwell a license to practice law; see Gwen Hoerr McNamee, ed., *Bar None: 125 Years of Women Lawyers in Illinois* (Chicago: Chicago Bar Association Alliance for Women, 1998). I thank Barbara Young Welke for this insight.

79. *Carthage Republican,* 17 February 1870; William L. Gross, ed., *Statutes of Illinois, 1818–1873,* vol. 3 (Springfield, Ill.: William L. Gross, 1873), 122.

80. *Carthage Gazette,* 2 May 1867; the editor was citing an editorial from the *Chicago Republican,* which argued that allowing women to vote would purify the process of politics and help the cause against all kinds of immorality.

81. Prior to that time a woman's rights to property rested on laws passed in 1845, which stipulated that at marriage she gave up her rights under coverture. Gross and Gross, *Statutes of Illinois 1818–1872*, 439–440.

82. In Illinois this broadening of a woman's rights to property included her right to wages she earned, which prior to that time accrued to her husband. Gross and Gross, *Statutes of Illinois 1818–1872*, 439. However, money farm women earned from production of poultry, eggs, and butter remained within the husband's purview because such activities took place within the household. See Amy Dru Stanley, *From Bondage to Contract: Wage Labor, Marriage, and the Market in the Age of Slave Emancipation* (New York: Cambridge University Press, 1998), 213.

83. W. H. Underwood, *Statutes of Illinois Construed* (St. Louis, Mo.: W. J. Gilbert, 1878), 507–514. Although the women's rights movement was agitating for reform of property laws, creditors also urged their enactment to better define "the legal relationship between the married couple and the commercial world." Norma Basch, *In the Eyes of the Law: Women, Marriage, and Property in Nineteenth-Century New York* (Ithaca: Cornell University Press, 1982), 114, 161.

84. Gross, *Statutes of Illinois, 1818–1873*, 50–52.

85. Basil Wright, 1865, Will Book 1:363.

86. Of the thirteen transactions, six deeds were executed between 1839 to 1863 and seven in the period 1871 to 1876. Hancock County Deeds sample. The nature of the sample is explained in Chapter 3, note 75.

87. Hancock County Deeds, 90:364; Andreas, *Illustrated Historical Atlas of Hancock County*, 34.

88. For example, Eveline Geddes, unmarried daughter of Thomas, sold a 120-acre parcel of land to cousin Samuel Walker in February 1873, which he mortgaged for $1,000. Hancock County Mortgages, Book 26:97; Hancock County Mortgages, Releases Book B:114; Andreas, *Illustrated Historical Atlas of Hancock County*, 34. Widow Elizabeth Cox financed George W. McElvain's purchase of sixty acres in December 1852 (Hancock County Mortgage Book 5:281).

89. Tax records show an increasing number of women as landowners. In 1860, seven women owned a total of 316 acres of land. That doubled within the decade to fourteen women who owned nearly 800 acres of land. Collector's Books, 1871, County Clerk, Record Series 2.21, Illinois Regional Archives Depository System, Western Illinois University, Macomb, Illinois.

90. *Carthage Republican*, 17 March 1870.

91. *Warsaw Signal*, 28 July 1841.

92. *Carthage Republican*, 16 February 1871, reprinted from the *American Agriculturist*.

93. *LaHarper*, 12 November 1875.

94. *Carthage Republican*, 7 February 1867.

95. Ibid.

96. Ibid.

97. Today unemployment is a significant risk factor that can contribute to spousal abuse. See Richard J. Gelles and Claire Pedrick Cornell, *Intimate Violence in Families*, 2nd ed. (Newberry Parks, Calif.: Sage, 1990).

98. Steve J. Stern, *The Secret History of Gender: Women, Men, and Power in Late Colonial Mexico* (Chapel Hill: University of North Carolina Press, 1995).

99. The daughter reported, "I did not stay to see further but went away." See *Andrew J. Clampit vs. Hannah Adaline Clampit,* March 1880, Box 215, Case 2168; *Mary Wright vs. George W. Wright,* March 1881, Box 218, Case 2207. Both in Hancock County Chancery Court Files.

100. To study divorce in Hancock County, a sample of 96 cases was culled from the chancery court records, which represents about one-fourth of the total divorce cases filed. Because the cases are not filed by date, the sample was not evenly spread over time, making time-based analysis difficult. The chronological breakdown is as follows: 1855–1864 (26), 1865–1874 (49), 1875–1884 (21). The rates of divorce in Hancock County are not inconsistent with rising national rates of divorce. See Glenda Riley, *Divorce: An American Tradition* (New York: Oxford University Press, 1991), 79. See also Robert Griswold, *Family and Divorce in California, 1850–1890* (Albany: State University of New York Press, 1982), 1.

101. Obviously the complaint for divorce was tailored to meet the provisions of divorce law. The conditions for which divorce was granted in Illinois included adultery, desertion for two years, habitual drunkenness for two years, attempted poisoning, extreme and repeated cruelty, or commitment of a felony. The provisions for extreme and repeated cruelty were not satisfied by "austerity of temper . . . rudeness of language, a want of civil attentions, occasional sallies of passion"; the complainant must have been in "personal danger" or "bodily harm." The behavior did not need to last a full two years to be grounds for divorce. See Underwood, *Statutes of Illinois Construed,* 503. The provisions are substantially the same as the provisions made in 1845. In 1867–1871, 13 percent of divorces in the United States were secured on grounds of cruelty. The proportions of women filing for divorce are roughly the same in Hancock County (70 percent) and the nation (67 percent). Elizabeth Pleck, *Domestic Tyranny: The Making of Social Policy against Family Violence from Colonial Times to the Present* (New York: Oxford University Press, 1987), 56.

102. The divorces that occurred in the first years of a marriage were often due to insufficient familiarity of the marriage partners. This may have occurred because of high geographical mobility; the partners had not been in the community long enough to know their prospective spouses. The extreme of this situation occurred when a man discovered that his wife was already pregnant by someone other than himself (*John Peyron vs. Jane M. Peyron,* June 1869, Box 195, Case 1397, Hancock County Chancery Court Files).

103. Only 3.4 percent of the divorces occurred within the first year of marriage; an additional 4 percent occurred during the second year. The third year was pivotal. One-fourth of all divorces occurred before the end of the third year (an additional 16 percent), and 35 percent occurred before the end of the fourth year. The probable reason for the rise in the number of divorces in the third year is that complainants waited a year after desertion to file for divorce. Few simple desertions occurred later in the marriage.

104. Elizabeth Pleck has defined family violence flexibly as "sexual coercion or threats or the use of intentional physical force with the aim of causing injury." *Domestic Tyranny,* 4.

105. *Mary Aldrich vs. George Aldrich,* October 1881, Box 219, Case 2270, Hancock County Chancery Court Files.

106. Ibid.

107. Ibid.

108. Ibid. Women and their attorneys capitalized on the fact that society abhorred intemperance more than wife-beating by connecting the two behaviors. Pleck, *Domestic Tyranny*, 50–52.

109. *Aldrich vs. Aldrich.* The 1880 Agricultural Schedules for Illinois show George as the owner of a 160-acre farm valued at $4,000, with stock worth $500. The farm produced 1,500 bushels of corn and 20 bushels of wheat.

110. *Aldrich vs. Aldrich.*

111. Mary and George share a tombstone in the Fountain Green Cemetery (Fountain Green Cemetery Records, Hancock County Historical Society). She died in 1905, and he died in 1913.

112. However, neighbors could consciously look the other way. See Patricia L. Bryan, "Stories in Fiction and Fact: Susan Glaspell's 'A Jury of Her Peers' and the 1901 Murder Trial of Margaret Hossack," *Stanford Law Review* 49 (1997): 1293–1364.

113. *Celestia Slattery vs. Trevior E. Slattery,* February 1874, Box 1765, Case 204, Hancock County Chancery Court Files.

7. "Ours is no slouch of a village"

1. *Carthage Gazette,* 28 August 1880.

2. *Carthage Gazette,* 28 August and 4 September 1880.

3. The shooting match occurred late on a Sunday evening as Alvin's brother Frederick Salisbury and a married sister were returning from a visit to their mother, who lived on the other side of Duff's property. Joshua Duff and his three grown sons (Thomas, William, and James) started shooting at Salisbury when their dogs began to bark. Salisbury returned fire, emptying his revolver, then the Duffs fired back. Once the guns were empty, the incident ended. Salisbury brought them to court before Judge John M. Ferris in Carthage. Joshua and his son Thomas were required to post bail of $800 each (*Carthage Republican,* 11 June 1873). For their acquittal, see *Carthage Gazette,* 4 September 1880.

4. Altina L. Waller, *Feud: Hatfields, McCoys and Social Change in Appalachia, 1860–1900* (Chapel Hill: University of North Carolina Press, 1988). Duff may have been jealous of Salisbury's success; Salisbury's was a much better farm and he was a wealthier farmer. Nearly all of Salisbury's 80-acre farm was cleared land, worth $2,000; just over half of Duff's 80-acre farm was cleared. Salisbury owned farm implements worth $200; Duff valued his implements at only $50. Salisbury's stock was worth $570; Duff owned only $455 in stock. Duff's produce was worth only a third of what Salisbury produced. Salisbury owned and sold cattle; Duff raised just hogs and chickens. His yields of corn and wheat were lower than those of Salisbury. Manuscript Agricultural Schedules for Illinois, 1880.

5. For the adoption of middle-class values, see Stuart M. Blumin, *The Emergence of the Middle Class: Social Experience in the America City, 1760–1900* (New York: Cambridge University Press, 1989); Karen Halttunen, *Confidence Men and Painted Women: A Study of Middle-Class Culture in America, 1830–1870* (New Haven, Conn.: Yale University Press, 1982); and Kenneth Cmiel, *Democratic Eloquence: The Fight over Popular Speech in Nineteenth-Century America* (New York: William Morrow & Co., 1990). For a developing masculine ethic of self-mastery, see E. Anthony Rotundo, *American Manhood: Transformations in Masculinity from the Revolution to the Modern Era* (New York:

Basic Books, 1993); Gail Bederman, *Manliness and Civilization: A Cultural History of Gender and Race in the United States, 1880–1917* (Chicago: University of Chicago Press, 1995); and David Peterson Del Mar, *What Trouble I Have Seen: A History of Violence against Wives* (Cambridge, Mass.: Harvard University Press, 1996). By gender I mean the construction of the social category of men and women, defined not only by anatomical difference but also by a constellation of meanings attached to gender identity. For the cultural process of constructing gender categories, see Bederman, *Manliness and Civilization,* 6–7. For the linkage between class and politics through cultural definition see Cayton and Onuf, *The Midwest and the Nation,* 90, 112–113. For the cultural meanings of politics in relation to masculine independence, see Etcheson, *The Emerging Midwest,* Chapter 3. The underpinnings of later class development in the Midwest is explored in Mahoney, *Provincial Lives.*

6. Trachtenberg, *Incorporation of America.*

7. Tyler, "Reminiscences of Fountain Green," 59–60. Tyler included the article written by Prentiss, dated August 10, 1880, newspaper unknown. For a biographical sketch of Prentiss's life, see Frank W. Blackmar, ed., *Kansas: A Cyclopedia of State History,* vol. 2 (Chicago: Standard Publishing Co., 1912), 498–499.

8. Jane Marie Pederson, *Between Memory and Reality: Family and Community in Rural Wisconsin, 1870–1970* (Madison: University of Wisconsin Press, 1992); Kathleen Neils Conzen, "Peasant Pioneers: Generational Succession among German Farmers in Frontier Minnesota," in *The Countryside in the Age of Capitalist Transformation: Essays in the Social History of Rural America,* edited by Steven Hahn and Jonathan Prude, 259–292.

9. Barron, *Those Who Stayed Behind;* Osterud, *Bonds of Community;* Pederson, *Between Memory and Reality.* The dour farmer and his daughter in Grant Wood's painting *American Gothic* (1930) is the most popular visual image of settled midwestern rural life.

10. *Compendium of the Tenth Census* (1880), vol. 1, 145–147; vol. 6, part 1, 16; *Compendium of the Eleventh Census* (1890), vol. 1, part 1, 408. For township figures, see Census of Population, 1870 and 1880.

11. It was common for young men who had gone west to return for wives. In February 1873, J. H. Lee of Warsaw put a notice in the *Gazette:* "Wanted, a Wife—A young man in comfortable circumstances, intending to make his home in the far West, appeals to any respectable, agreeable, intelligent and healthy young lady to go with him," preferably between the ages of 22 and 28 (*Carthage Gazette,* 12 February 1873).

12. The number of men in their twenties increased slightly in those decades while the general population declined, signal perhaps of a generation in limbo waiting for land or trying to make up their mind about their options. However, by the time they reached their thirties, many had left. The changes in the population of men did not parallel those for women. While there were roughly the same number of males as females through the teen years, there were fewer males than females in their twenties in 1870 and 1880. This may indicate that women left home at a later age. There were fewer women than men in their thirties, probably due to the hazards of childbearing. As the population aged, there were fewer men than women. Women in their forties in 1880 outnumbered men, probably a result of Civil War mortality in that age cohort. Census of Population, 1870 and 1880.

13. Ibid.

14. Susan Rebecca Walker Geddes to Thomas M. Geddes, 10 February 1869, Geddes Family Records.

15. Civil War Pension File, Jonathan Foy, letter dated 22 September 1910, probably from Palatka, Florida, where he died on 10 February 1926. In 1872, Foy sold his interest in land that had been in the family since 1837. He had purchased 40 acres in 1860 through a mortgage which he paid off in 1862. He took on a larger mortgage in 1866 to his father, which he cleared a year later through sale of the land. For the transactions see Hancock County Deeds, L:4; 68:562; 78:49; and Hancock County Mortgage Book 16:494.

16. Civil War Pension File, Jonathan M. Foy. Foy died at the home of William M. Durfee, who wrote: "Mr Foy was loyal to his Flag and country till the last. His wish was for me to wrap his Flag around him and bury him like his comrades."

17. Information about migration paths was culled from the Records of the Veteran's Administration, Record Group 15, Civil War Pension Files, National Archives and Records Administration, Washington, D.C. Often the soldier himself was required to outline his movements since the war. For some veterans the migration path had to be inferred from the changing locations of post offices from which they sent their requests.

18. Although men from the county relocated in Colorado or California, the second daughter community was in Lawton, Oklahoma. When C. C. Tyler visited his son there in 1900, he reported that widow Brandon's son James was there, as was Silas Leach, the son of Kendrick Leach. He reported that they were "well pleased with the country" (*Carthage Republican,* 6 November 1901). Some moved west sequentially, such as Levi M. Brunson, who stayed in Fountain Green until 1876, then moved to Appanoose County, Iowa, until 1907, then to Mitchell County, Nebraska. Civil War Pension Files of Levi M. Brunson, Clement Day, Hezekiah Day, and Henry M. Fortney. Reno County was a natural destination for the Civil War veterans of Fountain Green and other midwestern states who left their homes after the war. In 1890 there were 1,035 Union veterans living in the county; 235 of them were from Illinois. See Sheridan Ploughe, *History of Reno County, Kansas* (Indianapolis: B. F. Bowen & Co., 1917), 269, 272, 276, 277, 297.

19. *Carthage Gazette,* 12 February 1873.

20. FGPC Session Records.

21. Civil War Pension File, Benjamin F. Wood.

22. *Carthage Gazette,* 30 July 1879, 19 February 1879, 10 July 1878.

23. *Carthage Republican,* 23 April 1879.

24. *Carthage Republican,* 25 March 1875.

25. *Carthage Republican,* 21 March 1867; *Carthage Republican,* 14 November 1867; *Carthage Gazette,* 11 July 1872.

26. The number of different occupational titles of household heads rose from twenty-two in 1860 to thirty-nine in 1870 but dropped back to twenty-three by 1880. Census of Population, 1860, 1870, and 1880.

27. *Carthage Republican,* 19 November 1873; *Carthage Gazette,* 13 March 1880.

28. *Carthage Republican,* 5 September 1872; *Carthage Gazette,* 14 April 1878.

29. *Carthage Gazette,* 23 December 1874.

30. *Carthage Republican,* 31 May 1866; 5 February 1873; *New Era* (Warsaw), 17 November 1864.

31. *Reports to the General Assembly, Illinois (29th Session)* (Springfield, Ill.: State Printers, 1873), 1:270–272; *Reports to the General Assembly, Illinois (31st Session)* (Springfield, Ill.: State Printers, 1879), 2:101–105.

32. For the intertwining relationship of capitalist striving and the desire for goods, see Richard L. Bushman, *The Refinement of America: Persons, Houses, Cities* (New York: Random House, 1993).

33. *Carthage Gazette,* 23 December 1874; *Carthage Republican,* 19 November 1873; *Carthage Gazette,* 26 August 1874; *Carthage Gazette,* 14 April 1878; *Carthage Gazette,* 13 March 1880; *Carthage Gazette,* 24 April 1878.

34. *Carthage Republican,* 24 May 1876.

35. *Carthage Republican,* 21 December 1871.

36. *Carthage Republican,* 26 July 1866.

37. *Carthage Republican,* 18 May 1871.

38. *Carthage Republican,* 18 June 1875.

39. *Carthage Gazette,* 14 July 1875.

40. *Carthage Gazette,* 1 October 1879; *Carthage Republican,* 26 August 1874.

41. Sample of the daybooks of C. C. Tyler.

42. *Carthage Republican,* 5 March 1876.

43. *Carthage Republican,* 26 May 1875.

44. *Carthage Republican,* 5 February 1873.

45. Illinois 84:379, 404, R. G. Dun & Co. Collection.

46. *Carthage Republican,* 8 May 1880.

47. The executors of Matthew McClaughry's estate noted in 1883 that they were unable to sell his shares of stock in the mill, then worth only $700 (Box 128, Hancock County Probate Records).

48. Fannie Leach to Dear Friend, 8 March 1865.

49. Susan Geddes to Thomas M. Geddes, Jr., 10 February 1869 (punctuation added).

50. FGPC Session Records.

51. Gregg, *History of Hancock County,* 822.

52. FGPC Session Records.

53. *Carthage Republican,* 4 March 1872. The Presbyterian Church Erection Fund loaned the trustees (William Spangler and Alexander Walker) of the local congregation $600 (Hancock County Deed Records, 91:82–84, 2 December 1872).

54. *Carthage Republican,* 3 June 1869; *Carthage Republican,* 21 April 1870; Martin E. Marty, *Pilgrims in Their Own Land: 500 Years of Religion in America* (New York: Penguin Books, 1987), 342.

55. Nevertheless, in September 1880 his son, Major Robert W. McClaughry, had the large brick church repainted and a new fence and hitching rack put around it (*Carthage Gazette,* 11 September 1880).

56. See William G. McLoughlin, *Revivals, Awakenings and Reform: An Essay in Religion and Social Change in America, 1607–1977* (Chicago: University of Chicago Press, 1978); and Darrel M. Robertson, *The Chicago Revival, 1876: Society and Revivalism in a Nineteenth-Century City* (Metuchen, N.J.: Scarecrow Press, 1989).

57. The *Gazette* reported revivals in Keokuk, Burlington, and Quincy, as well as local places such as Fountain Green and LaHarpe (*Carthage Gazette,* 5 March 1872). These regional cities may have been responding to revivals in Chicago.

58. *Carthage Republican,* 26 February 1873.

59. *Carthage Gazette,* 17 November 1875; and FGPC Session Records.

60. *Carthage Republican,* 22 February 1872.

61. Susan Geddes to Thomas M. Geddes, 10 February 1869.

62. Scofield, *History of Hancock County,* 1225; *Carthage Gazette,* 31 January 1880.

63. John E. Hallwas, "The Lincolns of Fountain Green," in *Western Illinois Heritage* (Macomb: Illinois Heritage Press, 1983).

64. William Spangler to Thomas M. Geddes, 25 January 1873.

65. Regarding class and rurality, I have found Cmiel, *Democratic Eloquence* and Halttunen, *Confidence Men and Painted Women* to be particularly helpful.

66. Scofield, *History of Hancock County,* 1199.

67. *Compendium of the Tenth Census* (1880), vol. I, 106, 504; *Compendium of the Eleventh Census* (1890), 115, 618, 624; *Compendium of the Twelfth Census* (1900), 745. By 1910, the German-born and those whose parents were German-born made up nearly 10 percent of the county's population. *Compendium of the Thirteenth Census* (1910), vol. II (Population), 490.

68. *Carthage Gazette,* 19 February 1879.

69. Agricultural Schedules for Illinois, 1880; Census of Population, 1880.

70. Census of Population, 1880.

71. Salamon, *Prairie Patrimony;* Gray, *Yankee West.*

72. *Historic Sites and Structures of Hancock County,* 323.

73. Agricultural Schedules for Illinois, 1850, 1860, 1870, and 1880.

74. Census of Population, 1870.

75. *Carthage Republican,* 28 May 1875.

76. Mahoney, *Provincial Elites.*

77. Kleppner, *Cross of Culture;* Jensen, *Winning of the Midwest.* For the politics of cultural definition see Cayton and Onuf, *The Midwest and the Nation,* 85.

78. Agricultural Schedules for Illinois, 1860, 1870, 1880, and 1880.

79. *Carthage Republican,* 26 November 1873.

80. *Carthage Republican,* 1 March 1876.

81. Agricultural Schedules for Illinois, 1870 and 1880; Census of Population, 1870 and 1880.

82. *Carthage Republican,* 8 April 1874.

83. Ibid.

84. The cornerstone was laid on 10 March 1871 and the first classes were held in 1875 (*Carthage Republican,* 18 May 1871).

85. *Carthage Republican,* 24 May 1866; see also *Carthage Republican,* 30 December 1869.

86. *Carthage Republican,* 24 May 1866.

87. *Carthage Republican,* 14 May 1868.

88. *Carthage Republican,* 30 December 1869.

89. For criticism of women's education, see Mrs. John R. Woods, "Education of Farmers' Daughters," *Transactions of the Illinois State Agricultural Society,* edited by John P. Reynolds, vol. 5 (1861–1864) (Springfield, Ill.: Barker & Phillips, 1865), 576–584. An example of a farmer's son whose career was launched by a college education was Orville F. Berry. He studied law in Carthage and later served in the state legislature. *Republicans of Illinois: A Portrait and Chronological Record of Members of the Republican Party* (Chicago: Lewis Publishing Co., 1905), 165.

90. Hiram G. and John M. Ferris, Robert W. McClaughry, and Laura and Thomas Geddes all went away to college. Gregg, *History of Hancock County,* 706–707, 728–729, 837–838; Geddes Family Records.

91. *Carthage Gazette,* 26 February 1873; *Carthage Republican,* 2 December 1874.

92. *Carthage Republican,* 2 December 1875, 15 September 1875, and 26 July 1876.

93. Among the teachers were Thomas Geddes's daughters Laura and Julia. Most of the teachers were daughters of farmers. Census of Population, 1870 and 1880.

94. *Carthage Republican,* 7 March 1872.

95. *Carthage Republican,* 7 May 1875; *Carthage Gazette,* 18 July 1875; *Carthage Gazette,* 2 April 1879; *Carthage Republican,* 4 February 1874.

96. *Carthage Republican,* 14 May 1875.

97. *Carthage Gazette,* 2 April 1879.

98. *Carthage Gazette,* 23 April 1879.

99. Alvin J. Schmidt, *Fraternal Organizations* (Westport, Conn.: Greenwood Press, 1980), 356–358.

100. Within a decade the women had likewise organized into adjunct organizations. The Royal Neighbors, sister lodge to the Modern Woodmen of America (which followed the A.O.U.W.), was organized in 1896. Scofield, *History of Hancock County,* 1431.

101. *Carthage Gazette,* 31 January 1880; Census of Population, 1870; Agricultural Schedules for Illinois, 1870.

102. *Carthage Gazette,* 19 June 1880.

103. This interpretation differs from the argument Mary Ann Clawson makes about masonry in *Constructing Brotherhood: Class, Gender and Fraternalism* (Princeton, N.J.: Princeton University Press, 1990). She argues that masonry constructed a horizontal sociability that leveled men of different ranks in society to an equal standing (p. 76). I argue here that while the ritual may indeed have leveled ranks and created solidarity within the lodge, the establishment of the lodge created a distinction between those within it and outsiders who were not accepted into membership. That distinction did not rest upon sectarian difference, but upon differences of class and standing in the community.

104. For aversion to violence, see Karen Halttunen, "Humanitarianism and the Pornography of Pain in Anglo-American Culture," *American Historical Review* 100 (April 1995): 303–334; and Thomas L. Haskell, "Capitalism and the Origins of Humanitarian Sensibility, Part I," *American Historical Review* 90 (1985): 339–361. Social historians have interpreted early-nineteenth-century temperance as a campaign by propertied classes to raise profits by controlling the habits of laborers; see John J. Rumbarger, *Profits, Power and Prohibition: Alcohol Reform and the Industrializing of America, 1800–1930* (Albany: State University of New York Press, 1989), 187–188. The later temperance movement can also be seen as a struggle between domesticity and recreation; see Ted Ownby, *Subduing Satan: Religion, Recreation, and Manhood in the Rural South, 1865–1920* (Chapel Hill: University of North Carolina Press, 1990).

105. Hancock County, Clerk of the County Court, Circuit Court Index, Record Group 4.2, Illinois Regional Archives System at Western Illinois University, Macomb, Illinois. Records after 1879 were not filmed, and the records themselves are in disarray in the vaults at the County Court House in Carthage, Illinois. I am grateful to Paul Ferguson, Research Assistant, Department of History, Western Illinois University, for his assistance in extracting this data. I recognize the limited utility of arrest records, but they are the most dependable source for violence in Hancock County.

106. In Columbus, Ohio, farm laborers were a major cause of social disruption in those most common crimes—fighting and stealing. Young and highly mobile, they were less subject to controls of family and community. See Eric Monkkonen, *The Dangerous Class: Crime and Poverty in Columbus, Ohio, 1860–1885* (Cambridge, Mass.: Harvard University Press, 1975).

107. *Carthage Republican,* 12 August 1874.

108. *Carthage Gazette,* 11 September 1878.

109. *Carthage Republican,* 19 August 1874.

110. *Carthage Gazette,* 1 January 1879.

111. *Carthage Republican,* 25 November 1874.

112. Hancock County Court, Record Group 4.2, Illinois Regional Archives System, Western Illinois University, Macomb, Illinois. Clerk of the Circuit Court Index, 1869–1879, 110–120. The men included storekeeper John M. Cox, blacksmith Lewis Van Dine (55), day laborer Uriah Champlin (37), farmer Harvey Thompson, carpenter Frederick Barnett (41), Hickerson's son Seneca Wright (43, moneybroker), John Wright (farm laborer), and Skellet Wright. Most of the men were descended from southern-born settlers (Census of Population, 1870 and 1880). The county criminal court dockets show repeated prosecutions of men around Webster for infractions of the ordinances involving vice.

113. *Carthage Gazette,* 5 August 1874.

114. *Carthage Republican,* 28 August 1862; 5 July, 16 August, and 13 September 1866.

115. *Carthage Republican,* 26 January 1871; *Carthage Gazette,* 14 July 1875; *Carthage Gazette,* 11 September 1878.

116. *Carthage Gazette,* 16 September 1874 and 5 May 1875.

117. *Carthage Gazette,* 11 June 1879.

118. C. C. Tyler, "Reminiscences of Fountain Green."

119. *Carthage Gazette,* 14 April 1875.

120. *Carthage Gazette,* 25 September 1878 and 1 January 1879.

121. *Carthage Republican,* 8 March 1876.

122. *Carthage Gazette,* 13 August 1879.

123. *Carthage Gazette,* 27 August 1879.

124. *Carthage Gazette,* 3 September 1879.

125. *Carthage Gazette,* 30 October 1880.

126. *Carthage Republican,* 19 April 1876.

127. *Carthage Gazette,* 1, 12, and 15 May 1880.

128. *Carthage Gazette,* 31 December 1879.

129. Susan Geddes died on 13 January 1892; Thomas died a few weeks later on 31 January (Hancock County Cemetery Records).

130. Board of Supervisors, *History of Hancock County, Illinois,* 111; Hopkins, *Juanita and Other Sketches.*

131. Hopkins, *Juanita and Other Sketches,* 74–75.

132. Ibid., 75–78.

Conclusion

1. Theodore Dreiser, *Sister Carrie: A Novel* (New York: Harper, 1912).

BIBLIOGRAPHY

Primary Sources

Archival and Manuscript Collections

American Home Missionary Society Letters, Amistad Research Center, New Orleans, Louisiana.

"Catholics," Vertical File, Illinois State Historical Library, Springfield, Illinois.

Clerk of Circuit Court, Hancock County, Illinois, Circuit Court Index, 1857–1880, Record Series 4.2, Illinois Regional Archives Depository System, Western Illinois University, Macomb, Illinois.

County Clerk, Hancock County, Illinois, Collector's Books, 1851–1880, Record Series 2.21, Illinois Regional Archives Depository System, Western Illinois University, Macomb, Illinois.

R. G. Dun & Co. Collection, Baker Library, Harvard Business School, Cambridge, Massachusetts.

Fountain Green Presbyterian Church Session Records, in possession of Don Bainter, LaHarpe, Illinois.

Fountain Green Ward Manuscript History, Historical Department, Church of Jesus Christ of Latter-day Saints, Salt Lake City, Utah.

Geddes Family Records, in possession of Jean Geddes Lynn, Peoria, Illinois.

Fountain Green Township, Illinois, Justice of the Peace Docket [1850–1865], Illinois State Historical Library, Springfield, Illinois.

Fountain Green Township, Illinois, Justice of the Peace Docket [1865–1880], Kendrick N. Leach Collection, in possession of Randall Little, Fountain Green, Illinois.

Noah Green Papers, Iowa State Historical Society, Iowa City, Iowa.

Hancock County Cemetery Records, comp. Doris Lawton and James Lawton, Hancock County Historical Society, Carthage, Illinois.

Hancock County, Illinois, Clerk of Circuit Court. Hancock County Courthouse, Carthage, Illinois. Chancery Court Files.

———. Circuit Court Files.

Hancock County, Illinois, Clerk of the County Courts. Hancock County Courthouse, Carthage, Illinois. Inventory and Sale Records.

———. Probate Records.

———. Will Books 1, A, B, C, D.

Hancock County, Illinois, Office of the County Clerk. Hancock County Courthouse, Carthage, Illinois. Commissioners' Records.

———. Supervisors' Records.

Hancock County, Illinois, Office of the County Recorder. Hancock County Courthouse, Carthage, Illinois. Deed Records.

———. Records of Mortgage and Bonds.

Illinois, State of. Census of 1855, 1865. Illinois State Archives, Springfield, Illinois.

John J. Hardin Collection, Chicago Historical Society, Chicago, Illinois.

Joseph Ellis Johnson Papers, University of Utah Special Collections, Marriott Library, Salt Lake City, Utah.

Journal History of the Church, Archives, Church of Jesus Christ of Latter-day Saints, Salt Lake City, Utah.

David Leach Journal, Hancock County Historical Society, Carthage, Illinois.

Kendrick Leach Collection, in possession of Randy Little, Fountain Green, Illinois.

Lincoln Family Papers, Illinois State Historical Library Archives, Springfield, Illinois.

Macedonia [Branch] Minute Book, [1839–1850], Archives, Church of Jesus Christ of Latter-day Saints, Salt Lake City, Utah.

David Martin Collection of Nauvooiana, Western Illinois University Archives, Macomb, Illinois.

Miscellaneous Manuscripts, Archives, Church of Jesus Christ of Latter-day Saints, Salt Lake City, Utah.

Mormon Broadsides Collection, Chicago Historical Society, Chicago, Illinois.

Perkins Family Records, in possession of Eugene Perkins, Provo, Utah.

Perkins, Lucina Call, and Elizabeth Belcher Bartholomew. "History of the Perkins Family, 1720–1930," Library, Historical Department, Church of Jesus Christ of Latter-day Saints, Salt Lake City, Utah.

C. C. Tyler Store Records, 1838–1915, Illinois State Historical Library, Springfield, Illinois.

U.S. Bureau of the Census. Census of Agriculture, Manuscript Schedules for Illinois, 1850, 1860, 1870, 1880. Illinois State Archives, Springfield, Illinois.

———. Census of Population, Manuscript Schedules for Illinois, 1830, 1840, 1850, 1860, 1870, 1880. Washington, D.C.: National Archives, microfilm.

———. Industrial Schedules for Illinois, 1850, 1860, 1870, 1880. Illinois State Archives, Springfield, Illinois.

———. Social Statistics Schedules for Illinois, 1850, 1860. Illinois State Archives, Springfield, Illinois.

Ebenezer S. Welch Collection, Chicago Historical Society, Chicago, Illinois.

Wesley Williams Letters, Archives, Western Illinois University, Macomb, Illinois.

Wright Family Collection, in possession of John Wright, Carthage Illinois.

Published Primary Sources

Andreas, Alfred Theodore. *An Illustrated Historical Atlas of Hancock County, Illinois.* Chicago: A. T. Andreas, 1874.

Ballowe, Patricia Jewell, Violet Michaelis Jewell, and Carol Watkins Lundgren, transcribers. *The 1850 Census of Illinois, Hancock County.* Richland, Wash.: Locust Grove Press, 1977.

Barton, William E. *The Lincolns in Their Old Kentucky Home.* Berea, Ky.: Berea College Press, 1923.

Baylor, Orval W. *Early Times in Washington County, Kentucky.* Cynthiana, Ky.: Hobson Press, 1942.

Berry, Orville F. "The Mormon Settlement in Illinois." *Transactions of the Illinois State Historical Society* 11 (1906): 99.

Biographical Review of Hancock County, Illinois. Chicago: Hobart Publishing Co., 1907; reprint, Cleveland: Bell and Howell, 1967.

Beebe, Clarence. *A Monograph of the Descent of the Family of Beebe.* New York: [C. Beebe, 1904].

Blackmar, Frank W., ed. *Kansas: A Cyclopedia of State History.* Vol. 2. Chicago: Standard Publishing Co., 1912.

Board of Supervisors of Hancock County. *History of Hancock County, Illinois.* Illinois

Sesquicentennial Edition. Prepared by Robert M. Cochran, Mary H. Siegfried, Ida Blum, David L. Fulton, Harold T. Garvey, and Olen L. Smith. Carthage, Ill.: Journal Printing Co., 1968.

Clarke, S. J. *History of McDonough County, Illinois.* Springfield, Ill.: D.W. Lush, 1878.

Cook, John Williston. *Educational History of Illinois.* Chicago: Henry O. Shepard Co., 1912.

Day, Fay, comp. *Souvenir and Historical Sketch of the Majorville Church.* Hancock County Historical Society, Carthage, Illinois, n.d.

Ellis, Franklin. *History of Cattaraugus County, New York.* Philadelphia: L. H. Everts, 1879.

Esshom, Frank. *Pioneers and Prominent Men of Utah.* Salt Lake City: Utah Pioneers, 1913.

Fehrenbacher, J. B., et al. *Soils of Illinois.* Bulletin 778, University of Illinois at Urbana-Champaign, College of Agriculture, Agricultural Experiment Station in Cooperation with the Soil Conservation Service, U.S. Department of Agriculture, 1984.

Foote, Lester E., ed. *Foote's 1940 Fountain Green Almanac and Historical Sketch.* Carthage, Ill.: The Carthage Republican, 1940.

Ford, Thomas. *A History of Illinois From Its Commencement as a State in 1818 to 1847.* Chicago: S. C. Griggs & Co., 1859; reprinted in 2 vols., edited by Milo Milton Quaife, Chicago: Lakeside Press, R. R. Donnelley & Sons, 1945 and 1946.

French, John H. *Historical and Statistical Gazetteer of New York State.* Syracuse, N.Y.: R. P. Smith, 1860.

Garland, Hamlin. *Son of the Middle Border.* New York: Macmillan, 1923.

Gordon, Thomas F. *A Gazetteer of the State of Pennsylvania.* Philadelphia: T. Belknap, 1832.

Gregg, Thomas. *History of Hancock County.* Chicago: Charles C. Chapman, 1880.

———. *The Prophet of Palmyra.* New York: John B. Alden, 1890.

Gross, Eugene L., and William L. Gross, eds. *Statutes of Illinois: An Analytical Digest of All the General Laws of the State . . . 1818–1872.* Vol. 2. Springfield, Ill.: E. L. and W. L. Gross, 1872.

Gross, William L. *Statutes of Illinois: An Analytical Digest of All the General Laws of the State . . . 1818–1873.* Vol. 3. Springfield, Ill.: W. L. Gross, 1873.

Historical Sites Committee. *Historic Sites and Structures of Hancock Co., Illinois.* Carthage, Ill.: Hancock County Bicentennial Commission, 1979.

History of Adams County, Illinois. Chicago: Murray, Williamson and Phelps, 1875.

History of Delaware County, New York. New York: W. W. Munsell & Co., 1880.

History of Franklin County, Pennsylvania. Chicago: Warner, Beers & Co., 1887.

Hopkins, Jennie L. *Juanita and Other Sketches.* Denver: Zalinger Press, 1884.

Illinois, State of.

———. *Journal of the Senate.* Springfield, Ill.: State Printer, 1843.

———. *Laws of the State of Illinois, 13th General Assembly.* Springfield, Ill.: State Printer, 1843.

———. *Laws of the State of Illinois, 17th General Assembly.* Springfield, Ill.: State Printer, 1851.

———. *Laws of the State of Illinois, 1846–47.* Springfield, Ill.: State Printer, 1847.

———. *Reports Made to the Senate and House of Representatives of the State of Illinois, 1844–45.* Springfield, Ill.: State Printers, 1845.

———. *Reports Made to the Senate and House of Representatives of the State of Illinois, 1846–47.* Springfield, Ill.: State Printers, 1847.

———. *Reports Made to the Nineteenth General Assembly of the State of Illinois.* Springfield, Ill.: State Printers, 1856.

———. *Reports to the General Assembly, Illinois (29th Session).* Vol. 1. Springfield, Ill.: State Printers, 1873.

———. *Reports to the General Assembly, Illinois (31st Session).* Vol. 2. Springfield, Ill.: State Printers, 1879.

———. Office of the Secretary of State. *Counties of Illinois.* Springfield, Ill.: Secretary of State, 1987.

Illinois State Agricultural Society. *Transactions of the Illinois State Agricultural Society,* Vol. 5. Springfield, Ill.: Baker & Phillips, Printers, 1865.

Illinois State Gazetteer and Business Directory for the Years 1864–65. Chicago: J. C. W. Bailey, 1864.

Illinois Supreme Court Reports, Vol. 19. Chicago: Callaghan & Co., 1871.

[Jackson, Ida C]. *History of Fountain Green, Illinois, 1835–1985 Sesquicentennial.* n.p., 1985.

Jackson, Ronald Vern, and G. R. Teeples. *Complete Index to Tennessee 1820 Census.* Salt Lake City: Accelerated Indexing Systems, 1974.

Jefferson, Thomas. *Notes on the State of Virginia,* edited by William Peden. New York: W. W. Norton & Co., 1982.

Jillison, Willard Rouse. *Pioneer Kentucky.* Frankfort, Ky.: State Journal Co., 1934.

Johnson, Benjamin Franklin. *My Life's Review.* Independence, Mo.: Zion's Printing and Publishing, 1947.

Jones, A. D. *Illinois and the West, With a Township Map, Containing the Latest Surveys and Improvements.* Boston: Weeks, Jordan and Co., and Philadelphia: W. Marshall and Co., 1838.

Lincoln, Abraham. *Speeches and Letters,* edited by Peter J. Parish. London: J. M. Dent, 1993.

Linn, Jo White. *Abstracts of the Deeds of Rowan Co., N.C., 1735–1785, Vols. 1–10.* Salisbury, N.C.: J. W. Linn, 1983.

Krauser, Alice, Donald A. O'Harra, Elizabeth Rourke, and Mary Lou Torgerson. *A History of St. Paul Church, 1857–1986.* Macomb, Ill.: n.p., 1986.

Lewis, Sinclair. *Main Street.* New York: Harcourt, Brace & Rowe, 1920.

McCauley, I. H. *Historical Sketch of Franklin County, Pennsylvania.* Chambersburg, Pa.: D. F. Pursel, 1878.

Montague's Illinois and Missouri State Directory for 1854–55. St. Louis: Wm. L. Montague, Publisher, 1854.

Mudd, Richard D. *The Mudd Family of the United States.* Ann Arbor: Edwards Bros., 1951.

Nevin, Rev. Alfred. *Churches of the Valley, or, an Historical Sketch of the Old Presbyterian Congregations of Cumberland and Franklin Counties, in Pennsylvania.* Philadelphia: Joseph M. Wilson, 1852.

Peck, John M. *A Gazetteer of Illinois.* Jacksonville, Ill.: R. Goudy, 1834.

———. *New Guide for Emigrants to the West.* Boston: Gould, Kendall and Lincoln, 1837.

Portrait and Biographical Record of Hancock, McDonough and Henderson Counties, Illinois. Chicago: Lake City Publishing Co., 1894; rep. Owensboro, Ky.: McDowell Publications, 1982.

Ploughe, Sheridan. *History of Reno County, Kansas.* Indianapolis: B. F. Bowen & Co., 1917.

Presbyterian Church in the U.S.A. *Minutes of the General Assembly of the Presbyterian*

Church in the U.S.A, vols. XI, XII, XIII. Philadelphia: Presbyterian Board of Publication, 1846–1852.

Purple, N. H., ed. *Statutes of the State of Illinois,* 2nd ed., Parts I & II. Chicago: Keen & Lee, Booksellers, 1857.

Republicans of Illinois: A Portrait and Chronological Record of Members of the Republican Party. Chicago and New York: Lewis Publishing Co., 1905.

Reece, Brig. Gen. J. N., comp. and rev. *Report of the Adjutant General of the State of Illinois,* vols. 1–7. Springfield, Ill.: Phillips Bros., 1900–1902.

Rupp, I. Daniel. *History and Topography of Dauphin, Cumberland, Franklin, Bedford, Adams, and Perry Counties.* Philadelphia: Joseph M. Wilson, 1852.

Salisbury, Herbert Spencer. "Old Trails of Hancock County." *Journal of the Illinois State Historical Society* 9 (1916): 177–183.

Smith, Joseph, Jr. *History of the Church of Jesus Christ of Latter-day Saints,* edited by B. H. Roberts. 2nd ed., rev. 7 vols. Salt Lake City: Deseret Book, 1971.

Snively, E. A. "James M. Davidson." *Journal of the Illinois State Historical Society* 8 (1915): 184–194.

Statement of the Situation, Character and Value of the Lands in the State of Illinois, Owned by the Heirs at Law of William James, Deceased, Made by an Agent of the Said Estate, in the Year 1840. Albany, N.Y.: Vance and Wendell, Atlas Office, 1841.

Steward, William C., comp. *1800 Census of Pendleton District, S.C.* Washington, D.C.: National Genealogical Society, 1963.

Tri-County Genealogical Society, transcribers. *1860 Handcock [Hancock] County, Illinois Census.* Augusta, Ill.: Tri-County Genealogy Society, [ca. 1983].

Tyler, Charles C. "Reminiscences of Fountain Green, Illinois." *Journal of the Illinois State Historical Society* 8 (April 1915): 55–64.

Underwood, W. H. *Statutes of Illinois Construed.* St. Louis: W. J. Gilbert, 1878.

U.S. Bureau of the Census. *Agriculture of the United States in 1860,* 8th Census. Washington, D.C.: Government Printing Office, 1864.

———. *Compendium of the Seventh Census* (1850). Washington, D.C.: Government Printing Office, 1854.

———. *Compendium of the Eighth Census* (1860). Washington, D.C.: Government Printing Office, 1864.

———. *Compendium of the Ninth Census* (1870). Washington, D.C.: Government Printing Office, 1872.

———. *Compendium of the Tenth Census* (1880). Washington, D.C.: Government Printing Office, 1883.

———. *Compendium of the Eleventh Census* (1890). Washington, D.C.: Government Printing Office, 1892.

———. *Population of the United States in 1860,* 8th Census. Washington, D.C.: Government Printing Office, 1864.

———. *Report of the Population of the United States in 1890,* 11th Census. Washington, D.C.: Government Printing Office, 1897.

———. *Seventh Census of the United States,* 1850. Washington, D.C.: Government Printing Office, 1853.

———. *Statistics of the Population of the United States, 9th Census* (1870), vol. 1. Washington, D.C.: Government Printing Office, 1872.

U.S. Census Bureau. *Residents of Farm and Rural Areas: 1991.* Report P20-472 (Washington, D.C.: Government Printing Office, 1993).

U.S. Department of Agriculture, Economic Research Service. "Nonmetro Population

Continues Post-1990 Rebound." *Rural Conditions and Trends* 6 (Spring 1995): 6–13.

United States. General Land Office. Records, Quincy District. Record Group 49. Public Domain Sales Land Tract Record Listing. Illinois State Archives, Springfield, Illinois.

———. Records of the Provost Marshall. Record Group 110, National Archives and Records Administration, Washington, D.C.

———. Records of the Veterans Administration. Civil War Pension Records, Record Group 15, National Archives and Records Administration, Washington, D.C.

Van Zandt, Nicholas Biddle. *A Full Description of the Soil, Water, Timber and Prairies of Each Lot, or Quarter Section of the Military Lands between the Mississippi and Illinois Rivers.* Washington City: P. Force, 1818.

Wallace, Anthony. "Prelude to Disaster: The Course of Indian-White Relations which Led to the Black Hawk War of 1832." In *The Black Hawk War, 1831–1832.* Vol. 35, Collections of the Illinois State Historical Library, 1–51. Springfield: Illinois State Historical Library, 1970.

Wallace, Samuel Jacob. "The Prairie Fruit Garden." *Transactions of the Illinois State Agricultural Society* 3 (1857–1858): 512–517.

Webb, Benjamin J. *The Centenary of Catholicity in Kentucky.* Louisville, Ky.: Charles A. Rogers, 1884; reprint, Utica, Ky.: McDowell Publications, 1973.

Webster Sesquicentennial History. Webster, Ill.: n.p., 1989.

Willie, Betty, comp. *Pendleton District, S.C. Deeds, 1790–1806.* Easley, S.C.: Southern Historical Press, 1982.

Maps (By date of publication)

Map of the Bounty Lands in Illinois Territory, [ca. 1812–1818]. Map Collection, Regenstein Library, University of Chicago.

Geographical, Statistical, and Historical Map of Illinois. [182?]. Map Collection, Regenstein Library, University of Chicago.

J. H. Young. *The Tourist's Pocket Map of the State of Illinois.* Philadelphia: S. Augustus Mitchell, 1835.

John G. Fonda. *Sectional Map of Hancock County, Illinois.* St. Louis, Mo.: Egloffstein & Zwanziger, 1853. Illinois State Historical Society Library, Springfield, Illinois.

Great Western Railway Guide. Chicago: D. B. Cooke & Co., 1856.

Map of Hancock County, Illinois. Buffalo: Holmes and Arnold, Publishers, 1859. Illinois State Historical Society Library, Springfield, Illinois.

Miniature Railway Map of the Great West. Chicago: D. B. Cooke & Co., 1860.

Newspapers and Periodicals

Alton Telegraph
Carthage Gazette
Carthage Republican
Catholic Post (Peoria, Illinois)
Daily Warsaw City Bulletin
Gate City (Keokuk, Iowa)
Gregg's Dollar Monthly and Old Settlers Memorial (Hamilton, Illinois)
Hamilton Representative

Hancock County Historical Society Newsletter (Carthage, Illinois)
Hancock Eagle (Nauvoo, Illinois)
Hancock New Era (Warsaw, Illinois)
Nauvoo Neighbor (Nauvoo, Illinois)
Prairie Farmer (Chicago, Illinois)
Times and Seasons (Nauvoo, Illinois)
Warsaw Express
Warsaw Message
Warsaw Signal
Warsaw Weekly Public Record

Interviews

Jackson, Ida. Fountain Green, Illinois, June 1991.
Lynn, Jean Geddes. Peoria, Illinois, December 1991.

Secondary Sources

Abernethy, Thomas Perkins. *From Frontier to Plantation in Tennessee: A Study in Frontier Democracy.* Chapel Hill: University of North Carolina Press, 1932.
Adams, Jane. "1870s Agrarian Activism in Southern Illinois: Mediator between Two Eras." *Social Science History* 16 (Fall 1992): 365–400.
Ahlstrom, Sydney E. *A Religious History of the American People.* New Haven, Conn.: Yale University Press, 1972.
Altschuler, Glenn E., and Stuart M. Blumin. "Limits of Political Engagement in Antebellum America: A New Look at the Golden Age of Participatory Democracy." *Journal of American History* 84 (December 1997): 855–885.
———. "'Where Is the Real America?' Politics and Popular Consciousness in the Antebellum Era." *American Quarterly* 49, no. 2 (1997): 225–267.
Anderson, Russell Howard. "Agriculture in Illinois during the Civil War Period, 1850–1870." Ph.D. diss., University of Illinois, Urbana, Ill., 1929.
Ankarloo, Bengt. "Agriculture and Women's Work: Directions for Change in the West, 1700–1900." *Journal of Family History* 4 (Summer 1979): 111–120.
Appleby, Joyce. "Commercial Farming and the 'Agrarian Myth' in the Early Republic." *Journal of American History* 68 (1982): 833–849.
Armitage, Susan, and Elizabeth Jameson, eds. *The Women's West.* Norman: University of Oklahoma Press, 1987.
Arrington, Leonard J., and Davis Bitton. *The Mormon Experience: A History of the Latter-day Saints.* New York: Alfred A. Knopf, 1979.
Arrington, Leonard J., Feramorz Y. Fox, and Dean L. May. *Building the City of God: Community and Cooperation among the Mormons.* 2nd ed. Salt Lake City, 1976; reprint, Urbana: University of Illinois Press, 1992.
Ash, Stephen V. *Middle Tennessee Society Transformed, 1860–1870: War and Peace in the Upper South.* Baton Rouge: Louisiana State University Press, 1988.
Atack, Jeremy, and Fred Bateman. *To Their Own Soil: Agriculture in the Antebellum North.* Ames: Iowa State University Press, 1987.
Atherton, Lewis. *Main Street on the Middle Border.* Bloomington: Indiana University Press, 1954.
Ayers, Edward L., Patricia Nelson Limerick, Stephen Nissenbaum, and Peter S. Onuf.

All Over the Map: Rethinking American Regions. Baltimore, Md.: Johns Hopkins University Press, 1996.

Babener, Liahna. "Bitter Nostalgia: Recollections of Childhood on the Midwestern Frontier." In *Small Worlds: Children and Adolescents in America, 1850–1950,* edited by Elliott West and Paula Petrik, 301–320. Lawrence: University Press of Kansas, 1992.

Baker, Jean H. *Affairs of Party: The Political Culture of Northern Democrats in the Mid-Nineteenth Century.* Ithaca, N.Y.: Cornell University Press, 1983.

Barlett, Peggy F. *American Dreams, Rural Realities: Family Farms in Crisis.* Chapel Hill: University of North Carolina Press, 1993.

Barron, Hal S. *Mixed Harvest: The Second Great Transformation in the Rural North, 1870–1930.* Chapel Hill: University of North Carolina Press, 1997.

———. *Those Who Stayed Behind: Rural Society in Nineteenth-Century New England.* New York: Cambridge University Press, 1984.

Basch, Norma. *In the Eyes of the Law: Women, Marriage, and Property in Nineteenth-Century New York.* Ithaca, N.Y.: Cornell University Press, 1982.

Bederman, Gail. *Manliness and Civilization: A Cultural History of Gender and Race in the United States, 1880–1917.* Chicago: University of Chicago Press, 1995.

Bennett, John W., Seena B. Kohl, and Geraldine Binion. *Of Time and the Enterprise: North American Family Farm Management in a Context of Resource Marginality.* Minneapolis: University of Minnesota Press, 1982.

Bensel, Richard Franklin. *Yankee Leviathan: The Origins of Central State Authority in America, 1859–1877.* New York: Cambridge University Press, 1990.

Bergen, John V. "Maps and Their Makers in Early Illinois: The Burr Map and the Peck-Messinger Map." *Western Illinois Regional Studies* 10 (Spring 1987): 5–31.

Berkner, Lutz K. "Inheritance, Land Tenure and Peasant Structure: A German Regional Comparison." In *Family and Inheritance: Rural Society in Western Europe, 1200–1800,* edited by Jack Goody, Joan Thirsk, and E. P. Thompson, 71–95. Cambridge: Cambridge University Press, 1976.

Bernstein, Iver. *The New York City Draft Riots: Their Significance for American Society and Politics in the Age of the Civil War.* New York: Oxford University Press, 1990.

Billington, Ray Allen, and Martin Ridge. *Westward Expansion: A History of the American Frontier.* New York: Macmillan, 1982.

Black, Susan Easton. "How Large Was the Population of Nauvoo?" *Brigham Young University Studies* 35, no. 2 (1995): 91–94.

Blumin, Stuart M. *The Emergence of the Middle Class: Social Experience in the American City.* New York: Cambridge University Press, 1989.

Boggess, Arthur Clinton. *The Settlement of Illinois, 1778–1830.* Chicago: Chicago Historical Society Collection, 1908.

Bogue, Allan G. *From Prairie to Corn-Belt: Farming on the Illinois and Iowa Prairies in the Nineteenth Century.* Chicago: University of Chicago Press, 1963; reprint, Ames, Iowa: Iowa State University Press, 1994.

———. *Money at Interest: The Farm Mortgage on the Middle Border.* Ithaca, N.Y.: Cornell University Press, 1955; reprint, Lincoln: University of Nebraska Press, 1969.

Bone, Robert Gehlmann. "Education in Illinois before 1857." *Journal of the Illinois State Historical Society* 50 (Summer 1959): 119–140.

Bourke, Paul, and Donald DeBats. *Washington County: Politics and Community in Antebellum America.* Baltimore, Md.: Johns Hopkins University Press, 1995.

Boydston, Jeanne. *Home and Work: Housework, Wages, and the Ideology of Labor in the Early Republic*. New York: Oxford University Press, 1990.

Brodie, Fawn McKay. *No Man Knows My History: The Life of Joseph Smith, the Mormon Prophet*. 2nd ed. New York: Vintage Books, 1995.

Brooke, John L. *The Refiner's Fire: The Making of Mormon Cosmology, 1644–1844*. New York: Cambridge University Press, 1994.

Bryan, Patricia L. "Stories in Fiction and Fact: Susan Glaspell's 'A Jury of Her Peers' and the 1901 Murder Trial of Margaret Hossack." *Stanford Law Review* 49 (1997): 1293–1364.

Buck, Solon Justus. *The Granger Movement: A Study of Agricultural Organization and Its Political, Economic and Social Manifestations, 1870–1880*. Cambridge, Mass.: Harvard University Press, 1913.

———. *Illinois in 1818*. 2nd ed. Chicago: A. C. McClurg & Co., 1918.

Buck, Stephen J. "'A contest in which blood must flow like water': Du Page County and the Civil War." *Illinois Historical Journal* 87 (Spring 1994): 2–20.

Bushman, Richard L. *Joseph Smith and the Beginnings of Mormonism*. Urbana: University of Illinois Press, 1984.

———. *The Refinement of America: Persons, Houses, Cities*. New York: Alfred A. Knopf, 1992.

Cannon, Brian Q. "Immigrants in American Agriculture." *Agricultural History* 65 (Winter 1991): 17–35.

Cannon, Donald Q. "Spokes on the Wheel: Early Latter-day Saint Settlements in Hancock County, Illinois." *Ensign* (February 1985): 62–68.

Carlson, Theodore L. *The Illinois Military Tract: A Study of Land Occupation, Utilization, and Tenure*. Illinois Studies in the Social Sciences, vol. 32, no. 2. Urbana: University of Illinois Press, 1951.

Cayton, Andrew R., and Peter S. Onuf. *The Midwest and the Nation: Rethinking the History of an American Region*. Bloomington: Indiana University Press, 1990.

Clark, Christopher. *The Roots of Rural Capitalism: Western Massachusetts, 1780–1860*. Ithaca, N.Y.: Cornell University Press, 1990.

Clark, Christopher. "Rural America and the Transition to Capitalism." *Journal of the Early Republic* 16 (Summer 1996): 223–236.

Clark, Thomas D. *Agrarian Kentucky*. Lexington: University Press of Kentucky, 1977.

Clawson, Mary Ann. *Constructing Brotherhood: Class, Gender and Fraternalism*. Princeton, N.J.: Princeton University Press, 1990.

Cleary, Thomas. "The Organization of the Catholic Church in Central Illinois." *Mid-America*, new ser., 6 (1935): 105–124.

———. "A Note on the Catholic Church Organization in Central Illinois." *Mid-America*, new ser., 6 (1935): 185–190.

Clinton, Catherine, and Nina Silber, eds. *Divided Houses: Gender and the Civil War*. New York: Oxford University Press, 1992.

Cmiel, Kenneth. *Democratic Eloquence: The Fight over Popular Speech in Nineteenth-Century America*. New York: William Morrow & Co., 1990.

Cole, Arthur Charles. *The Era of the Civil War, 1848–1870*. Vol. 3. *The Centennial History of Illinois*, ed. Clarence Walworth Alvord. Springfield: Illinois Centennial Commission, 1919.

Collins, Bruce. "The Ideology of the Ante-bellum Northern Democrats." *American Studies* 11, no. 1 (1977): 103–121.

Compton, Todd. *In Sacred Loneliness: The Plural Wives of Joseph Smith.* Salt Lake City: Signature Books, 1996.

Comstock, Gary. *Is There a Moral Obligation to Save the Family Farm?* Ames: Iowa State University Press, 1987.

Conzen, Kathleen Neils. "Immigrants in Nineteenth-Century Agricultural History." In *Agriculture and National Development: Views on the Nineteenth Century,* edited by Lou Ferleger, 303–342. Ames: Iowa State University Press, 1990.

———. "Peasant Pioneers: Generational Succession among German Farmers in Frontier Minnesota." In *The Countryside in the Age of Capitalist Transformation: Essays in the Social History of Rural America,* edited by Steven Hahn and Jonathan Prude, 259–292. Chapel Hill: University of North Carolina Press, 1985.

Cott, Nancy F. "Giving Character to Our Whole Civil Polity: Marriage and the Public Order in the Late Nineteenth Century." In *U.S. History as Women's History: New Feminist Essays,* edited by Linda K. Kerber, Alice Kessler-Harris, and Kathryn Kish Sklar, 107–121. Chapel Hill: University of North Carolina Press, 1995.

Cronon, William. *Nature's Metropolis: Chicago and the Great West.* New York: W. W. Norton, 1991.

Danbom, David B. *Born in the Country: A History of Rural America.* Baltimore, Md.: Johns Hopkins University Press, 1995.

Danhoff, Clarence H. *Change in Agriculture: The Northern United States, 1820–1870.* Cambridge, Mass.: Harvard University Press, 1969.

Davies, Richard O. *Main Street Blues: The Decline of Small-Town America.* Columbus: Ohio State University Press, 1998.

Dayton, Aretas A. "The Raising of Union Forces in Illinois during the Civil War." *Journal of the Illinois State Historical Society* 34 (December 1941): 401–438.

Ditz, Toby L. *Property and Kinship: Inheritance in Early Connecticut, 1750–1820.* Princeton, N.J.: Princeton University Press, 1986.

Donald, David Herbert. *Lincoln.* New York: Simon and Schuster, 1995.

Doyle, Don Harrison. *The Social Order of a Frontier Community: Jacksonville, Illinois, 1825–1870.* 1978; reprint, Urbana: University of Illinois Press, 1983.

Dykstra, Robert R. *The Cattle Towns.* New York: Alfred A. Knopf, 1968; reprint, Lincoln: University of Nebraska Press, 1983.

Easterlin, Richard A. "Factors in the Decline of Farm Family Fertility in the United States: Some Preliminary Research Results." *Journal of American History* 63 (1976): 600–614.

———. "Population Change and Farm Settlement in the Northern United States." *Journal of Economic History* 63 (1976): 45–75.

Easterlin, Richard A., George Alter, and Gretchen A. Condran. "Farms and Farm Families in Old and New Areas: The Northern States in 1860." In *Family and Population in Nineteenth-Century America,* edited by Tamara K. Hareven and Maris A. Vinovskis, 22–84. Princeton, N.J.: Princeton University Press, 1978.

Einhorn, Robin. *Property Rules: Political Economy in Chicago, 1833–1872.* Chicago: University of Chicago Press, 1991.

Elazar, Daniel J. *Cities of the Prairie: The Metropolitan Frontier and American Politics.* New York: Basic Books, 1970.

Elshtain, Jean Bethke. *Democracy on Trial.* New York: Basic Books, 1995.

Eslinger, Ellen. *Citizens of Zion: The Social Origins of Camp Meeting Revivalism.* Knoxville: University of Tennessee Press, 1999.

Etcheson, Nicole. *The Emerging Midwest: Upland Southerners and the Political Culture of the Old Northwest, 1787–1861.* Bloomington: Indiana University Press, 1996.

Faragher, John Mack. *Sugar Creek: Life on the Illinois Prairie.* New Haven, Conn.: Yale University Press, 1986.

———. *Women and Men on the Overland Trail.* New Haven, Conn.: Yale University Press, 1979.

Fellman, Michael. *Inside War: The Guerrilla Conflict in Missouri during the American Civil War.* New York: Oxford University Press, 1989.

Ferleger, Lou, ed. *Agriculture and National Development.* Ames: Iowa State University Press, 1990.

Fink, Deborah. *Agrarian Women: Wives and Mothers in Rural Nebraska, 1880–1940.* Chapel Hill: University of North Carolina Press, 1992.

———. *Open Country, Iowa: Rural Women, Tradition and Change.* Albany: State University of New York Press, 1986.

Finkelman, Paul. "Evading the Ordinance: The Persistence of Bondage in Indiana and Illinois." *Journal of the Early Republic* 9 (Spring 1989): 21–51.

Fischer, David Hackett. *Albion's Seed: Four British Folkways in America.* New York: Oxford University Press, 1989.

Flanders, Robert Bruce. *Nauvoo: Kingdom on the Mississippi.* Urbana: University of Illinois Press, 1965.

Foner, Eric. *Free Soil, Free Labor, Free Men: The Ideology of the Republican Party before the Civil War.* 2nd ed. 1970; reprint, New York: Oxford University Press, 1995.

Frisch, Michael H. *Town into City: Springfield, Massachusetts and the Meaning of Community, 1840–80.* Cambridge, Mass.: Harvard University Press, 1972.

Fuller, Wayne E. *The Old Country School: The Story of Rural Education in the Middle West.* Chicago: University of Chicago Press, 1982.

Gamm, Gerald, and Robert D. Putnam. "The Growth of Voluntary Associations in America, 1840–1940." *Journal of Interdisciplinary History* 39 (Spring 1999): 511–557.

Gates, Paul W. *Agriculture and the Civil War.* New York: Alfred A. Knopf, 1965.

Gates, Paul W., and Robert Swenson. *History of Public Land Law Development.* Washington, D.C.: Government Printing Office, 1968.

Gayler, George R. "Governor Ford and the Death of Joseph and Hyrum Smith." *Journal of the State of Illinois Historical Society* 50 (1957): 391–411.

Gelles, Richard J., and Claire Pedrick Cornell. *Intimate Violence in Families.* 2nd ed. Newbury Park, Calif.: Sage, 1990.

Gienapp, William E. *The Origins of the Republican Party, 1852–1856.* New York: Oxford University Press, 1987.

———. "'Politics Seems to Enter into Everything': Political Culture in the North, 1840–1860." In *Essays on American Antebellum Politics, 1840–1860,* edited by Stephen E. Maizlish and John J. Kushma, 15–69. College Station: Texas A&M University Press, 1982.

Gilje, Paul A. "The Rise of Capitalism in the Early Republic." *Journal of the Early Republic* 16 (Summer 1996): 151–191.

Gjerde, Jon. *From Peasants to Farmers: The Migration from Balestrand, Norway, to the Upper Middle West.* New York: Cambridge University Press, 1985.

———. *The Minds of the West: Ethnocultural Evolution in the Rural Middle West, 1830–1917.* Chapel Hill: University of North Carolina Press, 1997.

268 | BIBLIOGRAPHY

Godfrey, Kenneth W. "Crime and Punishment in Mormon Nauvoo, 1839–1846." *Brigham Young University Studies* 32 (Winter and Spring 1991): 195–227.

Godfrey, Kenneth W., Audrey M. Godfrey, and Jill Mulvay Derr, eds. *Women's Voices: An Untold History of the Latter-day Saints, 1830–1900.* Salt Lake City: Deseret Book, 1982.

Goldman, Robert Goldman, and David R. Dickens. "The Selling of Rural America." *Rural Sociology* 48 (1983): 585–606.

Goodstein, Anita Shafer. *Nashville, 1780–1860: From Frontier to City.* Gainesville: University of Florida Press, 1989.

Gordon, Linda. *Heroes of Their Own Lives: The Politics and History of Family Violence: Boston, 1880–1960.* New York: Penguin Books, 1988.

Gray, Lewis Cecil. *History of Agriculture in the Southern United States to 1860.* 2 vols. Washington, D.C.: Carnegie Institution, 1933.

Gray, Susan E. Gray. *The Yankee West: Community Life on the Michigan Frontier.* Chapel Hill: University of North Carolina Press, 1996.

Green, E. R. R. *Essays in Scotch-Irish History.* London: Routledge & Kegan Paul, 1969.

Griswold, Robert. *Family and Divorce in California, 1850–1890.* Albany: State University of New York Press, 1982.

Hahn, Steven. *The Roots of Southern Populism: Yeoman Farmers and the Transformation of the Georgia Upcountry, 1850–1890.* New York: Oxford University Press, 1983.

Hahn, Steven, and Jonathan Prude. *The Countryside in the Age of Capitalist Transformation: Essays in the Social History of Rural America.* Chapel Hill: University of North Carolina Press, 1985.

Hallam, Arne, ed. *Size, Structure, and the Changing Face of American Agriculture.* Boulder, Colo.: Westview Press, 1993.

Hallwas, John E. *Western Illinois Heritage.* Macomb, Ill.: Illinois Heritage Press, 1983.

Hallwas, John E., and Roger D. Launius, eds. *Cultures in Conflict: A Documentary History of the Mormon War in Illinois.* Logan: Utah State University Press, 1995.

———. *Kingdom on the Mississippi Revisited: Nauvoo in Mormon History.* Urbana: University of Illinois Press, 1996.

Halttunen, Karen. *Confidence Men and Painted Women: A Study of Middle-Class Culture in America, 1830–1870.* New Haven, Conn.: Yale University Press, 1982.

———. "Humanitarianism and the Pornography of Pain in Anglo-American Culture." *American Historical Review* 100 (April 1995): 303–334.

Hampshire, Annette P. *Mormonism in Conflict: The Nauvoo Years.* New York: Edwin Mellen Press, 1985.

Hansen, Klaus J. *Mormonism and the American Experience.* Chicago: University of Chicago Press, 1981.

———. *Quest for Empire.* East Lansing: Michigan State University Press, 1967.

Hansen, Stephen L. *The Making of the Third Party System: Voters and Parties in Illinois, 1850–1876.* Ann Arbor: UMI Research Press, 1980.

Hareven, Tamara K., and Maris A. Vinovskis. *Family and Population in Nineteenth-Century America.* Princeton, N.J.: Princeton University Press, 1978.

Harris, Emily J. "Sons and Soldiers: Deerfield, Massachusetts and the Civil War." *Civil War History* 30 (1984): 157–171.

Haskell, Thomas L. "Capitalism and the Origins of Humanitarian Sensibility, Part I." *American Historical Review* 90 (1985): 339–361.

Hatch, Nathan O. *The Democratization of American Christianity.* New Haven, Conn.: Yale University Press, 1989.

Henretta, James. "Families and Farms: *Mentalité* in Pre-Industrial America." *William and Mary Quarterly,* 3rd ser., 35 (1978): 3–32.

Hess, Earl J. *Liberty, Virtue, and Progress: Northerners and Their War for the Union.* New York: Fordham University Press, 1988.

Hicken, Victor. *Illinois in the Civil War.* 2nd ed. 1966; reprint, Urbana: University of Illinois Press, 1991.

Hill, Marvin S. *Quest for Refuge: The Mormon Flight from American Pluralism.* Salt Lake City, Utah: Signature Books, 1989.

Hudson, John C. *Making the Corn Belt: A Geographical History of Middle-Western Agriculture.* Bloomington: Indiana University Press, 1994.

Hudson, John C. "North American Origins of Middlewestern Frontier Populations." *Annals of the Association of American Geographers* 78, no. 3 (1988): 395–413.

Jensen, Joan. *Loosening the Bonds: Mid-Atlantic Farm Women, 1750–1850.* New Haven, Conn.: Yale University Press, 1986.

Jensen, Richard J. *The Winning of the Midwest.* Chicago: University of Chicago Press, 1971.

Kemp, Thomas R. "Community and War: The Civil War Experience of Two New Hampshire Towns." In *Toward a Social History of the American Civil War: Exploratory Essays,* edited by Maris A. Vinovskis, 31–77. New York: Cambridge University Press, 1990.

Kerber, Linda K. "Separate Spheres, Female Worlds, Woman's Place: The Rhetoric of Women's History." *Journal of American History* 75 (June 1988): 9–39.

Kimball, James L., Jr. "The Nauvoo Charter: A Reinterpretation." *Journal of the Illinois State Historical Society* 64 (1971): 66–78.

Klement, Frank L. *The Copperheads in the Middle West.* Chicago: University of Chicago Press, 1960.

———. Klement, Frank L. "Copperhead Secret Societies in Illinois in the Civil War." *Journal of the Illinois State Historical Society* 48 (1955): 152–180.

———. *Dark Lanterns: Secret Political Societies, Conspiracies, and Treason Trials in the Civil War.* Baton Rouge: Louisiana State University Press, 1984.

Kleppner, Paul. *The Cross of Culture: A Social Analysis of Midwestern Politics, 1850–1900.* New York: Free Press, 1970.

Koons, Kenneth E. "Families and Farms in the Lower-Cumberland Valley of South-central Pennsylvania, 1850–1880." Ph.D. diss., Carnegie-Mellon University, 1986.

Kulikoff, Allan. *The Agrarian Origins of American Capitalism.* Charlottesville: University of Virginia Press, 1992.

———. "The Transition to Capitalism in Rural America." *William and Mary Quarterly,* 3rd ser., 46 (January 1989): 120–144.

Leavitt, Judith Walzer. *Brought to Bed: Childbearing in America, 1750–1950.* New York: Oxford University Press, 1986.

Lemon, James T. *The Best Poor Man's Country: A Geographical Study of Early Southeastern Pennsylvania.* Baltimore, Md.: Johns Hopkins University Press, 1972.

Leonard, Glen M. "Picturing the Nauvoo Legion." *Brigham Young University Studies* 35, no. 2 (1995): 95–135.

LeSeur, Stephen C. *The 1838 Mormon War in Missouri.* Columbia: University of Missouri Press, 1987.

Linderman, Gerald. *Embattled Courage: The Experience of Combat in the American Civil War.* New York: Free Press, 1987.

McCurry, Stephanie. *Masters of Small Worlds: Yeoman Households, Gender Relations, and the Political Culture of the Antebellum South Carolina Low Country.* New York: Oxford University Press, 1995.

McLoughlin, William G. *Revivals, Awakenings and Reform: An Essay in Religion and Social Change in America, 1607–1977.* Chicago: University of Chicago Press, 1978.

McManis, Douglas R. *The Initial Evaluation and Utilization of the Illinois Prairies, 1815–1840.* University of Chicago, Dept. of Geography, Research Paper no. 94, Chicago, Ill., 1964.

McMurry, Sally. *Families and Farmhouses in Nineteenth-Century America: Vernacular Design and Social Change.* New York: Oxford University Press, 1988.

———. *Transforming Rural Life: Dairying Families and Agricultural Change, 1820–1885.* Baltimore, Md.: Johns Hopkins University Press, 1995.

McNall, Scott G. *The Road to Rebellion: Class Formation and Kansas Populism, 1865–1900.* Chicago: University of Chicago Press, 1988.

McNamee, Gwen Hoerr, ed. *Bar None: 125 Years of Women Lawyers in Illinois.* Chicago: Chicago Bar Association Alliance for Women, 1998.

McPherson, James M. *The Battle Cry of Freedom: The Civil War Era.* New York: Ballantine Books, 1988.

———. *For Cause and Comrades: Why Men Fought in the Civil War.* New York: Oxford University Press, 1997.

McPherson, James M., and William J. Cooper, Jr. *Writing the Civil War: The Quest to Understand.* Columbia: University of South Carolina Press, 1998.

MacQuillen, D. Aidan. *Prevailing over Time: Ethnic Adjustment on the Kansas Prairies, 1875–1925.* Lincoln: University of Nebraska Press, 1990.

Mahoney, Timothy R. "Down in Davenport: The Social Response of Antebellum Elites to Regional Urbanization." *Annals of Iowa* 50 (Fall 1990): 593–622.

———. *Provincial Lives: Middle-class Experience in the Antebellum Middle West.* New York: Cambridge University Press, 1999.

———. *River Towns in the Great West: The Structure of Provincial Urbanization in the American Midwest, 1820–1870.* New York: Cambridge University Press, 1990.

Margolis, Jon. "The Reopening of the Frontier." *New York Times Magazine,* 15 October 1995: 51–57.

Marsh, Eudocia Baldwin. "Mormons in Hancock County: A Reminiscence," edited by Douglas L. Wilson and Rodney O. Davis. *Journal of the Illinois State Historical Society* 64 (Spring 1971): 46–65.

Marti, Donald B. *Women of the Grange: Mutuality and Sisterhood in Rural America, 1866–1920.* New York: Greenwood Press, 1991.

Marty, Martin E. *Pilgrims in Their Own Land: 500 Years of Religion in America.* New York: Penguin Books, 1987.

Meinig, D. W. *The Shaping of America: A Geographical Perspective on 500 Years of History.* Vol. 2. *Continental America, 1800–1867.* New Haven, Conn.: Yale University Press, 1993.

Mitchell, Reid. *The Vacant Chair: The Northern Soldier Leaves Home.* New York: Oxford University Press, 1993.

———. "Soldiering, Manhood, and Coming of Age: A Northern Volunteer." In *Divided Houses: Gender and the Civil War,* edited by Catherine Clinton and Nina Silber, 43–54. New York: Oxford University Press, 1992.

Monkkonen, Eric. *The Dangerous Class: Crime and Poverty in Columbus, Ohio, 1860–1885.* Cambridge, Mass.: Harvard University Press, 1975.

Mooney, Patrick M. *My Own Boss? Class, Rationality and the Family Farm.* Boulder: Westview Press, 1988.

Morrissey, Katherine G. *Mental Territories: Mapping the Inland Empire.* Ithaca, N.Y.: Cornell University Press, 1997.

Murdock, Eugene C. *One Million Men: The Civil War Draft in the North.* Madison: State Historical Society of Wisconsin, 1971.

Neth, Mary. *Preserving the Family Farm: Women, Community, and the Foundations of Agribusiness in the Midwest, 1900–1940.* Baltimore, Md.: Johns Hopkins University Press, 1995.

Newell, Linda King, and Valeen Tippetts Avery. *Mormon Enigma: Emma Hale Smith, Prophet's Wife, "Elect Lady," Polygamy's Foe, 1804–1879.* New York: Doubleday & Co., 1984.

Nordin, D. Sven. *Rich Harvest: A History of the Grange, 1867–1900.* Jackson: University Press of Mississippi, 1974.

Oaks, Dallin H., and Marvin S. Hill. *Carthage Conspiracy: The Trial of the Accused Assassins of Joseph Smith.* Urbana: University of Illinois Press, 1976.

Oaks, Dallin H. "The Suppression of the Nauvoo *Expositor.*" *Utah Law Review* 9 (1965): 862–903.

Osterud, Nancy Grey. *Bonds of Community: The Lives of Farm Women in Nineteenth-Century New York.* Ithaca, N.Y.: Cornell University Press, 1991.

———. "Gender and the Transition to Capitalism in Rural America." *Agricultural History* 67 (Spring 1993): 15–29.

Ownby, Ted. *Subduing Satan: Religion, Recreation, and Manhood in the Rural South, 1865–1920.* Chapel Hill: University of North Carolina Press, 1990.

Palmer, Allen W. "Country Magazines: Margins of American Culture." *Magazine Forum* 5 (1995): 29–37.

Paludan, Phillip Shaw. "What Did the Winners Win? The Social and Economic History of the North during the Civil War." In *Writing the Civil War: The Quest to Understand,* edited by James M. McPherson and William J. Cooper, Jr., 174–200. Columbia: University of South Carolina Press, 1998.

Park, Siyoung. "Perception of Land Quality and the Settlement of Northern Pike County, 1821–1826." *Western Illinois Regional Studies* 3 (Spring 1980): 5–21.

Pease, Theodore Calvin. *The Frontier State, 1818–1848.* Vol. 2. Urbana: University of Illinois Press, 1987.

Pederson, Jane Marie. *Between Memory and Reality: Family and Community in Rural Wisconsin, 1870–1970.* Madison: University of Wisconsin Press, 1992.

Peterson, William S. "A History of Camp Butler, 1861–1866." *Illinois Historical Journal* 82 (Spring 1989): 74–92.

Pleck, Elizabeth. *Domestic Tyranny: The Making of Social Policy against Family Violence from Colonial Times to the Present.* New York: Oxford University Press, 1987.

Pooley, Eric. "The Great Escape." *Time Magazine,* December 8, 1997, 52.

Pooley, William Vipond. *The Settlement of Illinois 1830–1850.* Bulletin of the University of Wisconsin, No. 220. Madison, 1908.

Power, Richard Lyle. *Planting Corn Belt Culture: The Impress of the Upland Southerner and Yankee in the Old Northwest.* Indianapolis: Indiana Historical Society, 1953.

Prosterman, Leslie Mina. *Ordinary Life, Festival Days: Aesthetics in the Midwestern County Fair.* Washington, D.C.: Smithsonian Institution Press, 1995.

Quinn, D. Michael. *Early Mormonism and the Magic World View.* Salt Lake City: Signature Books, 1987.

Raitz, Karl B. *The Kentucky Bluegrass: A Regional Profile and Guide.* Chapel Hill: University of North Carolina, Department of Geography, Studies in Geography No. 14, 1980.

Riley, Glenda. *Divorce: An American Tradition.* New York: Oxford University Press, 1991.

Robertson, Darrel M. *The Chicago Revival, 1876: Society and Revivalism in a Nineteenth-Century City.* Metuchen, N.J.: The Scarecrow Press, 1989.

Roller, David C., and Robert W. Twyman, eds. *Encyclopedia of Southern History.* Baton Rouge: Louisiana State University Press, 1979.

Rothenberg, Winifred. "The Market and Massachusetts Farmers, 1750–1855." *Journal of Economic History* 41 (1981): 283–314.

Rotundo, E. Anthony. *American Manhood: Transformations in Masculinity from the Revolution to the Modern Era.* New York: Basic Books, 1993.

Rugh, Susan Sessions. "Conflict in the Countryside: The Mormon Settlement at Macedonia, Illinois." *Brigham Young University Studies* 32 (Winter and Spring 1991): 149–174.

———. "Creating a Farm Community: Fountain Green Township, 1825–1840." *Western Illinois Regional Studies* 13 (Fall 1990): 5–20.

Rumbarger, John J. *Profits, Power and Prohibition: Alcohol Reform and the Industrializing of America, 1800–1930.* Binghamton: State University of New York Press, 1989.

Ryan, Mary P. *Cradle of the Middle Class: The Family in Oneida County, New York, 1790–1865.* New York: Cambridge University Press, 1981.

Rymer, Russ. "Back to the Future: Disney Reinvents the Company Town." *Harper's Magazine,* October 1996, 65.

———. "New Disney Vision Making the Future a Thing of the Past." *New York Times,* 23 February 1997, Y18.

Salamon, Sonya. *Prairie Patrimony: Family, Farming & Community in the Midwest.* Chapel Hill: University of North Carolina Press, 1992.

Salmon, Marylynn. *Women and the Law of Property in Early America.* Chapel Hill: University of North Carolina Press, 1986.

Sampson, Robert D. "'Pretty damned warm times': The 1864 Charleston Riot and 'the inalienable right of revolution.'" *Illinois Historical Journal* 89 (Summer 1996): 99–116.

Saunders, Richard L. "Officers and Arms: The 1843 General Return of the Nauvoo Legion's Second Cohort." *Brigham Young University Studies* 35, no. 2 (1995): 138–151.

Schlereth, Thomas J. "The New England Presence on the Midwest Landscape." *Old Northwest* 9, no. 2 (1983): 125–142.

Schmidt, Alvin J. *Fraternal Organizations.* Westport, Conn.: Greenwood Press, 1980.

Schob, David E. *Hired Hands and Plowboys: Farm Labor in the Midwest, 1815–60.* Urbana: University of Illinois Press, 1975.

Scofield, Charles J. *History of Hancock County.* Chicago: Munsell Publishing Co., 1921.

Scott, Roy V. "Grangerism in Champaign County, Illinois, 1873–1877." *Mid-America* 43 (July 1961): 139–163.

Sellers, Charles. *The Market Revolution: Jacksonian America, 1815–1846.* New York: Oxford University Press, 1991.

Shammas, Carole, Marylynn Salmon, and Michel Dahlin. *Inheritance in America: From Colonial Times to the Present.* New Brunswick, N.J.: Rutgers University Press, 1987.

Shipps, Jan. *Mormonism: The Story of a New Religious Tradition.* Urbana: University of Illinois Press, 1985.

Shortridge, James R. *The Middle West: Its Meaning in American Culture.* Lawrence: University Press of Kansas, 1989.

Silbey, Joel. *A Respectable Minority: The Democratic Party in the Civil War Era, 1860–1868.* New York: W. W. Norton, 1977.

Spalding, Thomas W. "The Maryland Catholic Diaspora." *U.S. Catholic Historian* 8 (1989): 163–172.

Stanley, Amy Dru. *From Bondage to Contract: Wage Labor, Marriage, and the Market in the Age of Slave Emancipation.* New York: Cambridge University Press, 1998.

Stegner, Wallace. *The Gathering of Zion: The Story of the Mormon Trail.* New York: McGraw-Hill, 1964; reprint, Lincoln: University of Nebraska Press, 1992.

Sterling, Robert E. "Civil War Draft Resistance in Illinois." *Journal of the Illinois State Historical Society* 64 (1971): 244–266.

———. "Discouragement, Weariness, and War Politics: Desertions from Illinois Regiments during the Civil War." *Illinois Historical Journal* 82 (Winter 1989): 239–262.

Stern, Steve J. *The Secret History of Gender: Women, Men, and Power in Late Colonial Mexico.* Chapel Hill: University of North Carolina Press, 1995.

Stock, Catherine McNicoll. *Rural Radicals: From Bacon's Rebellion to the Oklahoma City Bombing.* New York: Penguin Books, 1997.

Swierenga, Robert P. "The Little White Church: Religion in Rural America." *Agricultural History* 71, no. 4 (Fall 1997): 415–441.

———. *Pioneers and Profits: Land Speculation on the Iowa Frontier.* Ames: Iowa State University Press, 1968.

———. "The Settlement of the Old Northwest: Ethnic Pluralism in a Featureless Plain." *Journal of the Early Republic* 9 (Spring 1989): 73–105.

Tanner, Helen Hornbeck, ed. *Atlas of Great Lakes Indian History.* Norman: University of Oklahoma Press, 1987.

Taylor, George Rogers. *The Transportation Revolution, 1815–1860.* New York: Harper & Row, 1951; reprint, New York: Harper Torchbooks, 1968.

Trachtenberg, Alan. *The Incorporation of America: Culture and Society in the Gilded Age.* New York: Hill and Wang, 1982.

Verdon, Michel. "The Stem Family: Toward a General Theory." In *The American Family in Social-Historical Perspective,* edited by Michael Gordon, 24–37. New York: St. Martin's Press, 1983.

Vickers, Daniel. "Competency and Competition: Economic Culture in Early America." *William and Mary Quarterly,* 3rd ser., 47 (January 1990): 3–29.

———. *Farmers and Fishermen: Two Centuries of Work in Essex County, Massachusetts, 1630–1850.* Chapel Hill: University of North Carolina Press, 1994.

Vinovskis, Maris A., ed. *Toward a Social History of the American Civil War: Exploratory Essays.* New York: Cambridge University Press, 1990.

Watson, Harry L. *Liberty and Power: The Politics of Jacksonian America.* New York: Hill and Wang, 1990.

Waller, Altina L. *Feud: Hatfields, McCoys and Social Change in Appalachia, 1860–1900.* Chapel Hill: University of North Carolina Press, 1988.

Welter, Barbara. "The Cult of True Womanhood." *American Quarterly* 18 (1966): 151–174.

Wertz, Richard W., and Dorothy C. Wertz. *Lying-In: A History of Childbirth in America.* New York: Schocken Books, 1979.

West, Elliott, and Paula Petrik, eds. *Small Worlds: Children and Adolescents in America, 1850–1950.* Lawrence: University Press of Kansas, 1992.

Wiebe, Robert H. *The Search for Order, 1877–1920.* New York: Hill and Wang, 1967.

Winkle, Kenneth J. *The Politics of Community: Migration and Politics in Antebellum Ohio.* New York: Cambridge University Press, 1988.

Winkle, Kenneth J. "The Representative Man of the Unsophisticated People: Participatory Democracy and the Rise of Abraham Lincoln." Paper presented at meeting of Organization of American Historians, Toronto, April 1999.

———. "The Second Party System in Lincoln's Springfield." *Civil War History* 44 (December 1998): 267–284.

———. "The Voters of Lincoln's Springfield: Migration and Political Participation in an Antebellum City." *Journal of Social History* 25 (Spring 1992): 595–611.

Winn, Kenneth H. *Exiles in a Land of Liberty: Mormons in America, 1830–1846.* Chapel Hill: University of North Carolina Press, 1989.

Winters, Donald L. *Farmers without Farms: Agricultural Tenancy in Nineteenth-Century Iowa.* Westport, Conn.: Greenwood Press, 1978.

Woods, Thomas A. *Knights of the Plow: Oliver H. Kelley and the Origins of the Grange in Republican Ideology.* Ames: Iowa State University Press, 1991.

Yasuba, Yasakuchi. *Birth Rates of the White Population in the United States, 1800–1860: An Economic Study.* Baltimore, Md.: Johns Hopkins University Press, 1962.

Yorgason, Lawrence M. "Preview on a Study of the Social and Geographical Origins of Early Mormon Converts, 1830–1845." *Brigham Young University Studies* 10 (1970): 279.

Zelinsky, Wilbur. *The Cultural Geography of the United States.* Englewood Cliffs, N.J.: Prentice Hall, 1973.

INDEX

Page numbers of illustrations are *italicized*. Tables are indicated by an *italic t* following the page number.

SUSAN SESSIONS RUGH is Assistant Professor of History at
Brigham Young University.